ONEO

ENLIGHTENMENT OF ETERNAL LIFE THE ACCEPTANCE OF I, AND ONE WITH YOURSELF

CORNELIUS CHRISTOPHER

BALBOA.PRESS
A DIVISION OF HAY HOUSE

Balboa Press books may be ordered through booksellers or by contacting:

Balboa Press
A Division of Hay House
1663 Liberty Drive
Bloomington, IN 47403
www.balboapress.com.au
AU TFN: 1 800 844 925 (Toll Free inside Australia)
AU Local: 0283 107 086 (+61 2 8310 7086 from outside Australia)

Print information available on the last page.

ISBN: 978-1-5043-2089-4 (sc)
ISBN: 978-1-5043-2090-0 (e)

Balboa Press rev. date: 08/27/2020

CONTENTS

To K, my princess bride, best friend, wife and soul mate; I wouldn't even be here today if not for your unconditional love, kindness and support. And to my beautiful MUM, MJ, ZL, AF, EF, IRC, PBC, FB, P, C, C, and of course BB, and not forgetting HS.

I would also like thank RAL (12) for all her heart-based intentions, kind words, and amazing advice. In RAL I found a friend who walks into a room when everyone else leaves.

FOREWORD

I wrote this book for everyone who is suffering from mental illness, including their family and friends, as well as those who are unfortunately no longer with us. Mental illness doesn't just destroy your own life; it has the potential to destroy the lives of everyone you have ever touched.

ONEO is a self-reflective autobiography regarding how our behaviour and actions can affect others, enough for someone to consider taking their own life. Someone like me. By sharing my own journey of pain and inner transformation, I hope to inspire and connect with those seeking a deeper understanding of their own consciousness, and of how consciousness and reality are interconnected.

My own depression was like an invisible illness that slowly crept up on me throughout my entire life, going relatively unnoticed. I had no control over my thoughts or feelings, and after a while I didn't have the willpower to live or fight. I just wanted to be loved and to make friends, but every day was an endless struggle in a life of desolation and loneliness. My negative inner voice was constantly telling me I was worthless and useless, that I would never be good enough. I didn't want to die, but my inner voice convinced me into believing this was my only option to finally achieve inner peace.

This book is also about speaking up for millions who have been shamed into silence, even when they have done nothing wrong. Sometimes it's unbelievably raw, depicting scenes of abuse and molestation from my early childhood and all the way into adulthood. But what happened to me happens to millions of people around the world all the time; I was just fortunate to have an awakening which made me able tell my story. It's time for people to stop being ashamed for something that's not their fault, and it's time for everyone to understand the massive impact they can have on the lives of so many people with every unkind action.

The most recent World Health Organisation reports show that approximately 1 million people die from suicide each year. That's one death every forty seconds. In many places around the world we live our lives in constant fear, lacking self-love, self-acceptance, and respect for one another. Over two thousand people each day end up taking their lives in order to find peace. Countless others choose emotional suicide, living out their lives in apathy.

This book is part of my mission to be of service to humanity to change the way we treat one another and ourselves. To help those who have lost their way find their role and meaning in life; to receive strength and encouragement to heal themselves emotionally, mentally, physically and spiritually. To heal this world, one person at a time, starting from within.

1

MARCH 29TH 2019. TODAY I DIE
PART ONE

On the morning of Norman's stag-night, I just wasn't in the mood to entertain something fake, especially now that I knew that K and I were "filler-friends." I was hoping tonight would get cancelled.

I couldn't get over the fact that I had opened my heart to Norman, only to discover how he'd just been using us as his backdrop. He'd said we were his family, and all this time he'd been lying.

I wasn't in the right headspace to meditate, but I'd promised K that I would try one last time. This would be fifth time in my life; I'd given up on myself on all four previous attempts.

As I laid down on K's bed with my eyes closed, I tried to start my breathwork. But nothing was working. I began to get so frustrated with myself; I couldn't get Norman out of my head. I kept playing imaginative scenarios, over and over again, about what I would to say to him. I even had responses to his bullshit answers.

Like before, I gave up pretty much before I even started. Frustrated, I got up to go to the kitchen to make myself a cup of coffee and check my emails.

But I remembered I hated checking my emails. The thought of just opening them filled me with dread. I regularly half-closed my eyes while giving the new emails a quick scan, hoping that nothing terrifying was there.

I was so fucking disappointed with myself for giving up so quickly, I walked into the bathroom and stood directly in front of the mirror, hoping to confront myself. And even that I couldn't do! I didn't want to see my reflection staring back at me, with disappointment in my eyes for giving up.

"Fuck! What is wrong with me?! For fuck sakes, Cornelius, come on," I kept shouting at myself while banging and slapping my hands against my head and face.

"I want to die. I don't want to live anymore."

I slumped to the floor, leaning back against the vanity cabinet, crying into my hands. I was in so much pain. I curled up on the floor, wanting it to be all over.

After about fifteen minutes of crying until nothing was left in me, I managed to pull myself off the floor and walk back towards the kitchen. But the voice in my head continued giving me hateful messages. I desperately needed it to stop. As I walked past the refrigerator, my inner voice convinced me to smash my head against the refrigerator door until the pain and negative chatter stopped.

I stood there facing the door and holding onto the sides. I took a big deep breath, closed my eyes, and leaned my head back.

All of a sudden, I heard Zelda and Link simultaneously meowing loudly. I opened my eyes to find them sitting in front of the refrigerator.

I thought, *I can't do this, not in front of my little fur babies*, so I picked them both up and placed them into their "catio", something K had designed and built. It was their own secure, private, outdoor space. We lived on such a busy road where so many cats had been killed that we both decided Zelda and Link would be house cats. The thought of them being outside was terrifying to us.

Then I walked back to the refrigerator, placed both hands in the same spot, closed my eyes, leaned back, and...

Fuck me! They were both sitting in front of the fridge again, meowing simultaneously.

I looked down at them, and said, "You know what? Since you're not going to let me do this, what do you want from me?"

Zelda raced down the hallway and sat meowing outside K's bedroom.

I glanced towards her in disbelief, thinking, *What the fuck; you want me to meditate? Now I have seen it all.*

So I walked back towards K's room, laid back down on her bed, and started my breathing exercises. I was so impatient I just made them up on the spot.

During my breathing exercises, I slowly started to focus on what my last day on Earth would look like.

I would spend it with K, Zelda, and Link. I would wake up super early, make K breakfast in bed, followed by a long hot shower together, and then back to bed for some 'us' time. Afterwards, I would walk across the road to the supermarket and pick up our happy food.

Our happy food was a cooked roast chicken, coleslaw, carrot, kumara mash, soft white rolls, and chocolate eclairs. Afterwards, we'd bring the little ones in a secure cat dome and drive to our favourite location, which was a stunning secluded beach about two hours away, on the other side of Auckland. Once there, we'd play cards while listening to Calvin Harris, Rhianna, Miley Cyrus, and Taylor Swift. It was the simplest of days and over the last eight years, these days were the ones I cherished the most: just K, our beautiful babies, and me.

While I was focusing on my last day, I noticed that the chatter in my head wasn't as prominent, and I felt that I was meditating. I had no distractions or competing thoughts.

So, I started to focus on my funeral. What would that look like, what songs would K play?

I can't quite explain this surreal experience, but I would never be able to do it justice with words alone. I didn't just imagine my funeral; I was watching it as if I was there. I was watching my funeral from the balcony of the church.

I saw everyone who turned up to show their support. There weren't many people in attendance, but I watched some of the players from my Over 35 football team, past and present, turn up. I wasn't sure if they were here for me, or if they were here to support K. Although I did see K and she looked so heartbroken; she was in total shock that her husband was gone.

I started to cry, and I could feel the tears trickle down the side of my face.

In my present, observer state, which I will call the Now, I was very conscious of my surroundings, and I was starting to get cold. I grabbed the duvet and placed it on top of me to keep warm. I knew that Zelda and Link had joined me on the bed. I could feel them moving around, trying to snuggle next to me, but for some reason this didn't break whatever state I was in.

Still observing my funeral, I sat at the back of the church and watched as K stood up, fighting back the tears while she thanked everyone for showing up. MJ stood next to her daughter, holding her hand and comforting her while K made her speech.

"Eight years ago, I was feeling very lonely and sad. I wrote down ten attributes that I wanted in a person, and I asked the universe to guide me to this person, and they sent me my beautiful, amazing husband, Cornelius.

He was my everything; he was my everybody, my best friend, husband, and soul mate.

"These were my ten attributes, and this was my husband:

I asked for someone to love me - Including all my flaws; Cornelius never saw one flaw in me, even though they were there; he just saw me.

I asked for someone funny - Cornelius was one of the most hilarious, dry, humorous, sarcastic people you could ever meet.

Cornelius had such a surreal sense of humour, and there wasn't a day that went by without having full-on belly laughs; he always knew how to make me laugh, no matter how sad he was feeling.

I asked for someone kind - Cornelius was the kindest person you could ever meet; he always put himself second without fail, as long as you came first; he went out of his way all the time to help anyone who needed it.

I asked for someone sensitive - Cornelius always knew when I needed him, even without asking. When I wasn't feeling well, my husband was my warm blanket on those cold nights.

I asked for someone athletic - Cornelius lived for football; he would have been so happy to know that his football team are here wearing their shirts in support of their ex-manager and teammate. Cornelius loved Liverpool more than anything on this planet. My husband always joked that Liverpool only came second when it came to me. I never once believed him. Liverpool was his everything, and it breaks my heart that Cornelius never got the chance to see his beloved team lift the Premier League trophy."

Twenty-nine years I have been waiting for that moment.

"I asked for someone who could cook - Cornelius was a fantastic chef; he put his heart and soul into everything so that we could have something yummy to eat. He could never prepare for just the two of us, though. Cornelius always made something for about six people." K smiled at that sentence.

K was right; I had no idea how to cook for just two people.

"**I asked for someone who loves animals** - Cornelius was an amazing father to our first-born, Zelda, and his beautiful son Link.

I asked for someone who was family-orientated - Cornelius wanted to be a Dad more than anything, but sadly, he never got the chance to right the wrongs of his childhood. His love for his mum, Doris, was something so special. And his love for my mum was just something else. He was there for my mum when her two sons were not.

I asked for someone who was committed - Cornelius was committed to our marriage every day and provided for his family. Even when he took hit after hit, my husband got back up and provided, over and over again."

I did, I put everything I had into my marriage.

"**I asked for someone loyal** - Cornelius was so faithful even with my condition, when I know other people would have either strayed or left."

Which was so true. Countless times I was advised to have an affair.

"**I asked for someone ambitious** - If you looked up this word in the dictionary, my husband's name would be right there. Cornelius tried to make so many changes to better everyone's day-to-day life; sadly, they kept slamming the door on him, when I know he would have made a massive difference, especially in this city, never mind the world.

I asked for someone tall - I don't know anyone who stood taller than my husband. Cornelius was a giant even at 5'6". No matter how hard the cards of life dealt him, he found a way to get back on his feet and try again."

I listened so closely to K's eulogy; her words were so touching. It was bizarre to hear them read out aloud, and how she compared me to her list to the universe. It made me incredibly sad that I made her go through this ordeal. Reading her list was the toughest thing she has ever done; K has never told anyone about her wish list. All I wanted to do was to give her one last hug and tell her that I am coming home.

I was utterly zoned out; I wasn't sure how long I had been fixating on my funeral.

Well, if I saw my last full day on earth and my funeral, I might see how I die, still in this unique state.

I focused purely on that day.

I was lying in bed with K, but this time I was in my bedroom. I was wearing my beautiful baby blue wedding shirt, my grey, silver, and gold waistcoat, and my black jeans. I was wearing all my wedding rings, including the engagement wrist-cuff that K bought for me the day after she proposed to me on the bridge in Amsterdam. I was also wearing my mum's watch.

Lying on my chest was Chenzo, Pani, Coco, and Fosty bear. K and I called these our original babies. Chenzo was a little beanie pup; I have loved him for over 24 years. He came everywhere with me, including all of my adventures with Mum. Chenzo watched every Liverpool game with me, no matter what time or place, he was always there.

Pani was this beautiful, golden woolly bear who wore a black bow around his neck, but during the night somehow, he always managed to take it off. He loved being naked, and I bought him for K.

Coco is a small, ginger, cheeky beanie monkey. I went to buy petrol one day and saw her sitting alone on this shelf, where you pay for your petrol next to the chocolates. She looked so frigging cute, I walked out the main door towards my car, only to find myself walking back into the petrol station to rescue her and bring her back home.

Mum also had a beanie bear; he was Chenzo's brother, a small little brown bear with ears the size of Dumbo's. Mum had him for 23 years, and he always slept next to her. When I went to see Mum in the hospital just before she passed away, my sister had bought her a more significant, brand new white dog, and her little friend was left at home on the table like he was a piece of trash. So K and I decided to adopt him, and he became our Fosty bear.

Zelda and Link were also snuggling up to us, but they were not asleep; they just knew today was my last. K wasn't wearing anything apart from a pair of my boxer shorts, holding me so close and so tight to her body like she didn't want to let me go, not even for a second. K was stroking my face slowly and deliberately with her right hand. My eyes were closed. Finally, I looked at peace. I could just make out that I was shallow breathing. I knew

I didn't have long to go, and I wasn't fighting it either; I was embracing it because it had been a long time coming.

Watching myself die slowly in the arms of my wife felt more real than life itself. I couldn't quite put my finger on this experience; it felt as if I was really there, watching myself die. I could easily walk around my bedroom and observe me from any perspective. I could pick up and hold any one of my thirty Diesel watches. My watch collection meant so much to me and who I was. The first thing I would put on when getting ready for work was one of my watches, and then I dressed accordingly.

And as I was looking at my watches, I kept wondering, *What is the point of having all these watches? I could only wear one at a time. Who was I trying to impress: me or the world?*

I opened up my wardrobe closet and looked at all my Diesel clothes; I must have spent thousands and thousands on this brand. I loved everything about this brand and what it stood for. I was this brand; I lived and breathed this brand.

Then I had a strange thought: *Why?*

I turned around to face the version of myself dying; I knew I only had a few minutes left.

I stood at the foot of the bed, repeatedly asking myself, *How the fuck did I get here?*

I could not take my eyes off of myself. *Why did I decide to take my own life?* It never once crossed my mind to even think about a situation like this, yet here I was, watching myself die. *Was I born into this world suicidal, depressed, and lonely? Was my decision always inevitable? Or did this just happen to me slowly throughout my life, without me even knowing?*

Then I heard a voice, as clear as if you were standing right next to me. *"Look how peaceful you seem; this is the inner peace you have always been searching for. You will never have to feel any more pain or suffering ever again."*

I turned around, but no-one was behind me, just my reflection in the mirror. So I turned back around and carried on watching myself die.

K was sobbing her heart out uncontrollably; I have never heard anyone cry like this before. I was witnessing the start of my wife grieving as I was dying in her arms. She whispered in my ear, "I love you so much, I love you so much, my beautiful husband. I don't know what I will do without you. You're my everything."

I watched the dying version of myself struggle to open my eyes fully and look up at K. Tears were rolling down my face. "I am so sorry; I am so sorry, I am so sorry, I love you so much, I have had the best eight years of my life. You're the only one who showed me genuine kindness, and I got to experience the purest love ever, something that not many people will ever experience in their lifetime. I love you, my little chicken, so, so, so much. And thank you for letting me be me. I know I haven't been the easiest person to live with and you have not once ever judged me. But I have to go. I can't live with this pain and suffering anymore."

K had loved me regardless of all of my mental health issues; this was true love, and she was my soul partner.

Again, I heard the same voice: *"This is what you have always wanted, and now you're so close to inner peace. K will be OK, so don't worry; she just wants you to be happy."*

I turned around and still, no-one was there; just my reflection staring back at me.

I watched her kiss me on my forehead continuously, watched her tears slowly drop on to my face and run down my cheeks. My wife was holding me even tighter than before; she knew I was about to pass away.

I stood next to my bed motionless, as I watched myself take my final breath, lying in the arms of my wife and looking up at her with tears running down my face. I managed to mouth the words "I am sorry, I love you," one last time before I closed my eyes and sank into her body.

Then came this unbelievable scream, a shattering cry. It was unbearable. I couldn't watch or listen anymore. My wife's world just came crashing down all around her.

I just died, and now she is alone.

Her screams were deafening. I couldn't imagine the pain that she was going through or what she was experiencing; it was like nothing I had ever seen or heard before.

In the Now, tears were streaming down the side of my face. I could feel every emotion that K was experiencing; I was struggling to keep it all together. I needed to leave this painful experience, seeing my wife break down was too much for me. But no matter how hard I tried to open my eyes, I couldn't; I was forced to watch my wife go through all this pain.

My inner voice was continually reassuring me that this was the only way I could be happy and pain-free. I wanted to tell her that this wasn't my fault. *"We have to go; we need to let your wife grieve in peace now."*

I was just about to turn around and leave when I noticed that K seemed to be having second thoughts about letting me go. She picked up her mobile phone and began to dial 111.

In the Now, I felt one of our two cats jump off the bed and run through their play tunnel in the hallway. I watched with bated breath as K placed her index finger on the call button; she was going to save my life. Instead, she paused, looked down at me, and saw for the first time that I was at peace. She kissed me on the forehead one last time, placed the phone back down on the bed, and held me tight and close.

"I love you far too much to save your life. I know how much pain and suffering you have had to endure throughout your life. I just want you to be happy, my beautiful baby, and now you can be with your mum. Deep down, I know this is what you want. Please forgive me, my beautiful husband, but I know you will understand why I didn't call for help." And she held me even tighter, screaming in pain.

My wife selflessly sacrificed her happiness for mine and her heart would always be empty; she would never find happiness again.

In the Now, I was an emotional wreck. My heart felt as it had been split wide open. Yet I was also relieved. I started to shiver, even though it was summer. I pulled another blanket that was hanging off the bed over me and wiped away my tears.

I walked around the side of the bed towards where we were both lying. I couldn't believe she sacrificed her happiness for mine, letting me go to be with my mum and find my inner peace. In doing so, I destroyed the one person who showed me any type of kindness and loved me for being me.

I bent down and whispered into her ear, "I love you so much. I can't believe I was the one who got to marry someone as beautiful as you are. Thank you for letting me go." I gave her one last kiss goodbye on her forehead before I left, so she could grieve alone. Then, I noticed that she had turned around in my direction, looked up at me, and touched her forehead in the exact location that I had kissed in. As if she knew I was right there and that she felt me kiss her.

"We have to go, right now, and I mean now!" my inner voice was screaming at me to leave.

I was seconds away from leaving when a strange thought popped into my head. *How did my wife know the exact location where I kissed her if this hadn't happened yet? How could she feel something in the future at the same time as I observed it in the present? Unless I am observing the present and the future at the same time, but from the perspective of the past.*

But I was also very aware that I was observing this reality from the Now.

How can I be experiencing multiple realities at different times in my life, but also at the same time and in the same location? Fuck, I am already dead? How can I exist after death? You're just dead?

So how come I am experiencing alternative realities simultaneously from the perspective of I-am-already-dead? Something doesn't seem to be adding up. If that's the case, that would mean there is no such thing as death when you physically die? Only Consciousness exists, which means we never die; we are immortal spiritual beings having a temporary human experience. What the fuck, where was this thinking coming from?

"Cornelius, what are we waiting for? We need to leave right fucking now, stop thinking you can work all this out because you can't. You're useless and stupid, remember? All you need to do is walk out of this bedroom, and you will find your peace."

I ignored my inner voice for the first time in my life.

Why is Consciousness observing my suicide? Am I trying to show myself a way to change the inevitable? If that's the case, who is the voice in my head wanting me to commit suicide if Consciousness wants me to live?

That means the voice in my head is the one who's creating reality in the present moment.

We are not creating reality; our beliefs and stories are creating reality.

And our environment is controlling how we think and feel, which in turn creates our experience in the present moment, the fundamental base point for who we think we are.

The more I thought about this situation, the more it was starting to make sense, but I was still missing something. *What am I missing?* I was unable to take my eyes of K, trying to work it all out.

My mind was racing, and something was happening; things were beginning to slot into place. Was I working all this out or was I getting told this? I was so confused.

Then it came to me.

Consciousness is our equivalent to heaven and hell. But in our present reality, this is where we create heaven and hell experiences for ourselves and others, and free will is purgatory. Which means I have the choice of whether to listen to my inner voice and commit suicide, my heaven. In doing so, creating an experience of hell for my wife, as I had just observed. Or I could experience hell and in turn, heaven for my wife.

Suddenly, standing directly in front of me in my wardrobe mirror and staring straight back at me was someone who looked exactly like me but wasn't me. This reflection didn't mirror any of my actions, he never moved once; he just stared directly into my eyes.

I was now observing multiple realities simultaneously from the perspective of my ego.

I could see a future-me who had just committed suicide, lying on the bed.

The Consciousness-me, without a body, looking directly at the ego-me, in the mirror.

Another future-me standing next to my wife, after I'd kissed her forehead.

And the present me-in-the-now as the observer of all simultaneous realities, lying on my wife's bed with our cats in the other room.

The ego-me was looking at the Consciousness-me, wondering what I was thinking.

This is where I confronted my ego. I decided to choose heaven for my wife and hell for myself, regardless of the consequences and the pain I would continually suffer. My wife didn't deserve an experience of hell.

Instantly everything went black, as if someone had picked me up and dropped me in a bottle of ink. I couldn't see anything but blackness, void of all colour.

2

MY EARLIEST MEMORIES

My childhood was definitely not like *The Waltons, The Little House on the Prairie,* or *The Partridge Family,* that was for sure.

I lived in a three-bedroom terraced house with an outside toilet in a small mining town outside Sheffield. I was living with an abusive alcoholic father who would regularly hit my brother Phil and me with his belt, slipper, or hand. My poor mum took the brunt of his violent drunken rage, either trying to protect us or not. It didn't matter. Somehow he would always blame us for his behaviour to justify his actions.

His temper went from zero to a hundred in less than a second, and once he hit top speed, there was no hiding place for anyone. I was always living in constant fear between the ages of seven and thirteen.

One day my dad was outside in the front yard fixing his Ford Capri when I heard a loud scream. Mum opened the door to see what all the commotion was and to see if Dad was OK.

Instead, he ran towards Mum, pushing her hard against the kitchen cabinets, the back of Mum's head hitting cabinet doors. Her back smashed against the overhanging edge of the worktop. Mum gasped for breath, she was winded and dazed. He threw her to the floor, eventually managing to sit on top of her. Both of his hands were around my mum's neck, trying to strangle her. Mum was fighting for her life, but my dad was too strong. Mum was flapping around on the floor, trying to open the cupboards, trying to grab anything to hit my dad with. But he just kept punching her. Somehow Mum managed to free herself and desperately tried to escape on her hands and knees, as she headed towards the living room.

My dad grabbed her feet and legs, pulling her back into the kitchen again. I witnessed my dad trying to rip off my mum's clothes. Again, my mum broke free, kicking my dad between his legs. She was trying to reach the phone when my dad grabbed my mum's head and hair and slammed it into the living room floor, a few meters away from where I was hiding.

Mum noticed me crying and scared, hiding under the dining room table. She shook her head and mouthed, "Don't move." I watched my dad throw punch after punch, until Mum was virtually unconscious. Even then, Mum still had some fight in her; she was frantically trying to get upstairs and away from where I was hiding.

I saw my dad trying to rape my mum, but she wasn't having any of it. She was still trying to fight back, but his anger and rage was something else, there was no stopping him. I was frozen, hand over my mouth, holding my breath, tears running down my face, scared motionless. I started to crawl out, trying to get some help, but Mum knew if Dad saw me, I was next. Again through all this violence, she waved her arms, telling me to stay there and *don't move.*

I could see Mum losing this fight. She didn't have any more energy to carry on or to fend him off any longer. She tried to scream, but with my dad's hands around her throat, no one could hear her. Somehow Mum managed to find something deep down inside her and pushed and kicked her way free again. Mum managed to open the stair doorway and tried to scramble upstairs and away from what I saw next.

Unfortunately, Mum's efforts didn't work; my dad dragged her back down. He had other ideas. He punched my mum twice in the face, and I sat scared under the table, as I watched my dad rape my mum on the stairway right in front of me.

After he was done, he dragged my mum up the stairs by her arms. I heard my dad carry on raping and beating her up; this lasted for about twenty minutes. I just sat under the table in my own pee. I was unable to move; Mum told me not to move, so I didn't.

I heard someone coming down the stairs. I turned away and tried to make myself into a small ball and make myself invisible.

"Cornelius, Cornelius, Cornelius, Cornelius, it's Mum." I slowly turned opened my eyes and said, "Mum am sorry I peed my pants, am so sorry, I didn't mean to, am sorry" and she gave me the biggest hug.

"Cornelius, it's OK, I will sort it, but you need to go quickly, leave now before your dad wakes up. If he knows that you were down here hiding, I'm not sure what he will do, so you need to go and stay with Gail and Scott, I will be over shortly. I need to call the police, and you can't be here, OK? I love you son, but you have to go." I didn't want to leave Mum alone, but Mum convinced me to go.

Mum never called the police that day; I think she was too scared for us all if she did.

During those times, he went in and out of our lives, and you could never tell what state of mind he was in when he did walk back into our lives or through the front door after a night out. Our mother did a fantastic job raising two sons; she was a grafter, regularly working three or four jobs a day and every weekend. She paid the next-door neighbours to look after us when she was offered extra shifts at the local pub.

Whereas my dad, on the other hand, would spend all of his time and money at the pub. We came a very distant third, if that, and heaven forbid if we accidentally woke him up while he was sleeping after an afternoon session. I lost count of how many times my dad hit me with his belt for just being a child and playing with my toys. Most of the time I would play under the bed, as this made it extremely hard for my dad to hit me. Sometimes he didn't even need alcohol as an excuse; he seemed to be angry all the time. I hardly ever saw my dad smile.

I was eight years old when my school teacher told my dad, "Cornelius is having learning difficulties, and he is way behind the other children in his class. Cornelius also struggles to remain focused on what he's doing; we recommend that we hold him back another year."

I felt as though my teachers had already given up on me. During the walk home from school, my dad didn't say anything to me. He offered no reassurance and showed me no love, but as soon as we were home, he hit me with a closed fist for the first time. I took the full punch to my body; I had no idea why he did this. I can only remember the pain. But looking back, I think he was somehow disappointed with me for being slow and not very bright.

When Mum was working, Phil was out with his mates. He was nearly three years older than me. For some reason, I struggled to make any friends, not for lack of trying. But no one wanted to be my friend, so I was always at home, and I hated being home alone with Dad.

***

Mum came home early from work one day. She caught me having a full-on conversation with our gas fire; I had no idea she was standing in the kitchen listening to me. Mum made me promise never to talk to the fireplace again, a promise I kept (he was boring anyway). So I started to have conversations with the kettle, the toaster, and the washing machine. I just wanted a friend, someone who I could play with. I was glad it wasn't my dad standing behind me, that's for sure.

My schoolteachers also noticed that I was struggling to make friends. Most of the time I would just sit in the corner of the playground, wishing I could join in with the other children. But every time I tried, I was told, "You're not one of us." Meaning I hadn't given my life to Jesus.

Miss Stein was a born-again Christian teacher, and all her classes were about the teachings of God and the Bible. If we performed well in her class, we could earn God points, and these points would then be converted into gift points to spend at the local Christian book shop.

There were twenty-three children in Miss Stein's class, and twenty-two of them had given their life to Jesus. I was the only person who didn't. For me, religion didn't make any sense. I kept asking question after question, but Miss Stein couldn't give me a straight answer and sent me out to the hallway to sit on my own as punishment.

The last time I was sent out into the hallway, it was because I asked this question: "Miss, Adam and Eve were created by God, and they gave birth to Cain and Abel. Then Cain killed Abel, who then travelled to a town called Nod, where he married and had children. Who did Cain marry if God only created Adam and Eve?" It was a fair question, I thought, for an eleven-year-old.

Before I knew it, I was back in the hallway. I never believed in God or life after death; death was the one fear that crippled me to tears and most nights I would cry myself to sleep, knowing I would never see Mum again after she died. It was heartbreaking. Miss Stein was the main reason I am not religious or spiritual today.

***

I was super excited for my first day of high school. I was finally in the same school as my big brother, who was in his third year. I still struggled with spelling and writing. Miss Stein called me lazy and a troublemaker in her end of year assessment report. I was placed in the bottom group on my first day. Well, at least I would make some new friends, and I was in the same house has my brother. We were both in Yellow, the other three houses consisted of Green, Blue and Red.

I was so proud to walk into the first house assembly, I couldn't wait to see my brother. When I did see him, I couldn't help but smile and wave to him, but he looked away and didn't acknowledge me.

I sat crossed-legged on the floor in the front row, listening to our Housemaster welcoming us all to our first semester. Once the assembly bell rang, I looked to see where my brother was sitting, but he had already left the room.

During my first morning class registration, I realised I was the only person who had come from my school. Everyone else knew one another; making new friends seemed a lot harder than I thought. I wasn't sure what to do in my first morning break, or who I could find, so I walked around aimlessly in my own world.

All of a sudden, I was pushed to the ground hard from behind. Two boys grabbed my legs and began dragging me on my back towards a metal post; I heard my new school coat rip. I was trying to wrestle and break free, but they were so much bigger and stronger than I was. They spread my legs open on either side of the metal post. I knew what they were going to do, so I used both my hands to try to protect my bits and bobs. Then another lad grabbed my arms and pulled them above my head.

I heard my brothers voice, "Hey, that's my brother, Cornelius."

"Sorry, we had no idea you had a brother?" Just like that, they let go of me and walked away. I had never heard my brother call me by my first name before; that was strange to hear.

I was home about twenty minutes before my brother. I was talking to Mum about my first day and what had happened when my brother stopped those bullies from ramming me against the post. I was so proud to be his brother.

He then walked into our house pissed, off and grumpy. "That's the last thing I ever do for you at school. Just leave me alone and don't ever talk to me."

I had very little to do with my brother through my high school years, only when it suited him.

My first year at high school was so difficult to navigate through; my dad was more aggressive, violent, and angry than ever. I couldn't do anything right in his eyes. I also had a brother who didn't want anything to do with me. On the plus side, I had a baby sister! Called Sharon. Unexpected, to say the least. I loved her from the moment I met her in the hospital. I loved having a baby sister; I had so much love and joy in my heart, and I had a new friend.

Dad decided to go to the pub more than being at home and helping Mum around the house and with my sister. Mum was struggling to cope; she was at the end of her tether; in fact, we all were. Mum tried to divorce my dad for the sixth time; the five previous times, she always ended up taking him back. "I will change, I promise!"

Mum got the help she needed from my grandad, who had moved up from Plymouth and was living on the same street. With the rest of the money from the sale of his home, he paid off our mortgage, which was a massive weight off my mum's shoulders.

Even with the mortgage paid off, it was still going to be extremely difficult for Mum, as a single parent, to raise three children all on her own. Yet she wanted to divorce my dad regardless. However, we all had to be in agreeance if she finally went through with it. But I still wanted my dad in my life; I have no idea why. Maybe because I always believed he would quit drinking and finally love his family. I was the only one conflicted; he promised to change once and for all and to seek the help he needed, even after Mum took him back after his numerous affairs.

Some of my school friends' parents had gotten divorced, and they got bullied more than I did. They were given free school meals, clothing vouchers, and special treatment. I couldn't take any more bullying and beatings. I was just about to say no, but then my sister, who was learning to walk, came bumbling into the kitchen, banging into everything, laughing and smiling.

I also knew once Mum divorced Dad, I would never see him again. I was thirteen years old when I agreed with Mum and my brother to divorce my dad. I never wanted my sister to go through what I went through. In fact, what we all went through; she didn't deserve that sort of life.

Dad didn't take to the divorce well. He went on a two-month-long drinking bender and refused to leave the house. In that time, Mum and my sister went to live with my grandmother. Mum was worried for her life, and we stayed with our grandad most nights, depending on if Dad came home or not.

This was the worst two months ever; the beatings came fast and hard.

I was so scared of going home. I started to hang out with people who were a few years older than me. Plus, some of them had computers, which was so frigging cool; they were like older brothers to me.

***

During my first summer school holidays, I experienced something strange one night. I am not sure what or how to explain it, but the following morning I felt utterly lost and more alone than ever. The following four days I had the worst migraine ever.

Mum was still living at my nan's place when Dad eventually packed his stuff and left, without saying goodbye. I was heartbroken. We were just managing to get by on Mum's family allowance, and everything seemed normal for the first time in well, I can't actually remember, but a long time. Then one day from out of the blue, my brother snapped and punched me for no reason. I fell straight to the floor, lying in the corner between the kitchen sink cupboard and the washing machine. He repeatedly began to kick my head and body. All I could do was curl up in a ball and wait for him to stop. This wasn't my brother; this was more like my dad.

And so it began, all over again.

Six months later, Mum finally returned home. I never once blamed her for leaving us alone with Dad. I was surprised she didn't go sooner. She needed a break from all the violence and the trauma. I also didn't blame my brother, either. He was hurting just as much as me, but he never showed it emotionally, only physically. What do you expect when you have lived your whole life surrounded by hate, violence, anger and me, myself, and I?

My second and third years of high school were no better than my first year. Fifty per cent of the time, I would be sitting alone during my break or at lunch, usually elevated on a grassy bank, observing everyone from afar and wondering, *What is wrong with me? Why am I unable to fit in with any of those groups and why does no one want to be my friend?*

The other fifty per cent of my time, I was either running away from bullies or being bullied and beaten up. It was exactly how I predicted my life to be the moment the divorce was finalised.

Halfway through my third year, I didn't want to be associated with free school meals anymore. I wanted to pay for them myself. I wanted to queue up in the same line as the rest of the people in my year. Pupils who received free school meals were always at the front of the queue, a beacon for everyone to know who the poor kids were, which gave everyone else more ammunition for torment and beatings. There was no way I would be able to survive school living like this. I was in constant fear, always looking over my shoulder, trying to ignore the torment and the verbal onslaught. I couldn't even say anything mean or personal back to them in order to deflect the situation, just in case I hurt their feelings! Something had to change.

I decided to get myself a morning paper route. My brother had one, so it made sense that I had one too. The only paper route available was the one that no one wanted; this paper route was the furthest one away from the newsagents and in the wealthiest areas, but I had no option but to take it. I was delivering all the conservative papers like *The Observer*, *The Times*, *The Guardian*, and *The Telegraph*.

I hated Sundays more than any other day of the week; all the papers came with massive colour supplements, so the paper bag weighed a ton. On Sundays, it would normally take me about two and a half hours to deliver forty-five newspapers. My paper bag was so heavy, I could barely carry it across my shoulders. I had to stop every few minutes and move the bag to the other shoulder.

On the weekends, my brother would always come and try to find me if I wasn't home by 8:30 am, especially after what happened to me one Sunday morning.

I started at 5:30 am, when it was pitch black, wet, and freezing. Ten minutes into my paper route, I was walking up towards a small cul-de-sac located in a housing estate. I distinctly heard someone shouting "Rambo!" from across the road and behind some bushes. I stopped, looked towards the bushes, and shouted "Hello? Hello, is anyone there?"

"Rammmboo, Rammmmmboooo, Raaaaaaaaaaaaaambooooooooooo."

I started to panic; my heart was racing. I began walking a little faster towards the cul-de-sac. I only had two papers to deliver here before I was back walking along the main road. I looked behind me just before I entered the alleyway to the cul-de-sac and saw no one. I delivered those two papers in record time and ran straight back the way I came. As soon as I turned the corner, a man was standing about thirty meters away from me wearing a black balaclava, jumper, pants, and a coat. He was holding a knife in his right hand, and he was on the same side of the footpath that I was on.

I froze instantly, unable to open my mouth to scream for help. He just stood there like the man from the *Halloween* movie, shifting his head from side to side as if he was weighing me up, considering what to do next.

I knew fear all too well, living with Dad, but this was a completely different type of fear. I was shaking uncontrollably, crying without noise, and unable to move or shout out. He slowly started purposefully walking towards me, transferring his knife from one hand to the other.

I had no idea what to do. My mind was blank and all I wanted to do was scream or run back the way I had come, but nothing was working. He was getting closer and closer, until about five meters away from me he stopped, paused, and showed me his knife. I started to pee myself. He then reached inside of his coat pocket and pulled out what looked to be an empty plastic bread bag, placed it over his mouth and nose, and started to inhale whatever was inside the bag. From that distance, I could smell… Mum's Evo stick glue? The one she used to fix the soles on my school shoes. We even had a small red tin in our garden shed.

While he was occupied with sniffing the Evo stick from his bag, somehow I forced myself to shout, "Bro it's me, Cornelius!" The moment the man turned around, still sniffing his bag, to see who I was talking to, I ran straight past him as fast as I could, trying to catch him off guard. Which I did, only for him to take a swipe towards me with his knife, missing my arm by a few inches and catching the side of my paper bag instead. I made it to the main road, where I collapsed in someone's front garden and hid silently, trying not to make a noise by placing my hand over my mouth. I hid there, trembling, until it was daylight, before finishing off my route.

I made my brother promise not to say anything to Mum about what had happened. If Mum found out, I knew that would be the end of my paper route, and that meant back to free school meals. My brother and his friend took turns over the next month to walk me to the cul-de-sac and back to the main road before carrying on with their routes.

A few months later, Mum mentioned that she knew someone from the local pub where she was working who fit the description of the person that I saw. He was arrested for breaking into houses while high from sniffing glue. I never saw Rambo again, so I assumed it was the same guy. I never started my morning route in the dark from that day onwards, making me even later for school.

Somehow, I thought that by not receiving free school meals, the bullying and getting picked on would stop. Not completely overnight, but enough for me to slide through the rest of my school years without drawing too much attention to myself. I would have gotten away with it, but one morning during my paper route, a homeowner opened his front door to collect the paper directly from me, as the newspaper was far too big for his letterbox. To my surprise, his German Shepherd attacked me without warning, first biting my arm before lunging at me as I turned away. I felt the dog's teeth sink into my back as I fell to the floor, not letting go of my coat. I then heard a loud whimpering noise; the owner kicked his dog hard enough for him to let go of me.

The homeowner apologised for his dog's behaviour and helped me up off the ground. I placed my hand inside my jumper and felt blood. I showed him my back asked how badly I had been bitten. "Barely broke your skin, hardly anything there."

I looked at my hand again and it was covered in blood. "What do you mean, hardly anything there?" But he was already inside his house, closing the front door behind him.

Something didn't seem right to me. It felt as if I had been bitten really hard and yet the owner said nothing, so I carried on finishing my paper route. I only had seven papers to deliver before running back home. I was already late, and I couldn't miss class because I had my maths exam that morning.

Mum looked at my back and insisted I should go to the hospital for a tetanus injection and get my back looked at properly, followed by staying at home to rest.

"I can't, I have exams today that determine which group you will end up in the following year."

I wanted to get out of the bottom group desperately, and I studied all year to make that happen. Reluctantly, Mum gave in to my stubbornness, patched me up and sent me on my way to school.

After my morning maths exam, which I believed I did well enough in to move out of the bottom group, I had indoor hockey, the one sport I enjoyed. Midway through playing hockey, I realised I was never going to slide through high school as I would have liked. Lying between my feet was a bloody sanitary towel that had dropped from my back. Everyone pointed and cracked up laughing, including my teacher. The humiliation was just too much, and I ran off towards the changing rooms. What I didn't realise when Mum was patching up my dog bite is that we didn't have any plasters or bandages; she only had sanitary towels, which she sellotaped to my back to stop the bleeding. Well, you can imagine how the next two years of school were for me. Fuck, kids are so cruel; the teachers were no better.

Delivering papers to the wealthiest people did work in my favour, though. Four weeks before Christmas, Mum had about forty Christmas cards left over from the hundred she bought in the last January sales. I asked Mum if I could use the remaining cards. I had a cunning idea.

My idea was simple and based on manners; this approach was new to the paper route industry in the 80's. I sent a Christmas card to every house I delivered a newspaper to and wished them a 'Happy Christmas and Happy New Year, from your paperboy.' I was hoping that all the homeowners would appreciate the effort I put in every morning, come rain or shine, to deliver their paper before they woke up.

The rest of the paperboys laughed. They thought I was crazy. They seemed to think the homeowners could complain to the newsagents, with the risk of being sacked. As they were already paying the newsagents a premium to get their papers delivered, they had a fair point.

Two weeks before Christmas, I didn't receive one card back or any tips. Then with five days to go, one morning I saw an envelope sellotaped to a front door that read, 'To our paperboy, Merry Christmas.'

I took the envelope and opened it around the corner so they couldn't see me. Bloody hell, inside the envelope were two one-pound notes and a Christmas card. This carried on for the rest of the week; in some cases, five-pound notes. And they all wished me a happy Christmas and a happy new year.

Thirty-nine out of forty houses left me either a card, money, or a gift. This was extraordinary! I made over one-hundred pounds in the last week leading up to Christmas. I spent half of my money on the January sales and the other half on presents for the family, especially for Mum. The following year, every paperboy did the same, with similar results.

***

I had a love-hate relationship with school. On the one hand, I disliked everything it stood for; it was no different from a prison. There was a hierarchy and individual groups or gangs within the school walls, teachers became wardens who created their own rules whenever it suited them, walking around with the power to change your life positively or negatively, and they knew it too. People like me just had to get through the entire day, continually looking over our shoulders, walking with our heads down, scared of catching eye contact with the wrong person. But on the other hand, I loved learning, especially anything creative or if I had to problem solve (not so much maths or English).

I moved up two groups after my third-year exams, but I needed to move up another one in my last year if I ever had a chance of going to university. I started to feel a little more confident in myself as that year went along. I was even a little taller now, which helped. I left my paper route and managed to land myself a Saturday cleaning job in a butcher's shop.

I was helping Mum more with raising my sister and around the house. I was still very shy around girls. I never knew what to say. Sometimes I even had girls knocking on my front door, but I was never interested in hanging out with them; I just wanted to stay in and study.

I kept asking myself the same question over and over again: *Why don't I like hanging out with girls and why don't I find them attractive?* It was such a confusing time for me. And my brother didn't help by insisting I was gay.

That was the same year I fell in love with chess. It applied the logical problem-solving side of my personality. Mum was starting to teach me the fundamentals and I practiced against one of my brother's friends. My school even had a chess club; all the smart, attractive girls from my year attended this club. I thought this was a great way to build on my social skills, especially with the girls, and to prove to everyone that I wasn't stupid or thick.

Nervously, I turned up to my first chess club. The tables were all arranged into a large U-shape. Chess club was run by Mr. Pepper, the number one math teacher in our school, who also had the highest IQ of all our teachers.

Mr. Pepper would continuously walk around this U-shape layout, playing against everyone one move at a time, before moving on to the next person down the line.

I wasn't great at chess; I had only just started, but at least I wasn't starting from scratch. Mr. Pepper stood in front of the class and stared directly at me. "Are you lost? This is chess club. This is not for thickos like yourself; you're going to have to leave." Everyone laughed, even the girls I was trying to impress. So I laughed too, a great way to not feel embarrassed and hurt by what he said, just brush it off.

"You're not in any of the top math groups, you're in the bottom ones. There is no way you can play chess, you're not smart enough." To prove his point, Mr. Pepper got me into checkmate in less than six moves; he played against me on a separate table in front of everyone.

I never went back the entire year, so I concentrated on my final year exams instead. We were the first school year in the U.K. to take the new GCSE style exams instead of the old O-levels. They were a mixture of course work and exams. Most of my elective courses were centred around creativity and science. English, written language, and maths were all compulsory.

Based on my mid-year mock exams and along with external moderation feedback, I was only predicted to achieve E's or F's for my final exam results. Only 70% or higher in all of my exams and coursework would guarantee me the C grade I desperately needed, which would allow me to take my A-levels in the sixth form and not re-sit my GCSEs. I was shitting myself; I would need a miracle.

I rarely left my house in the final year of high school. I never attended any school parties or hung out with anyone after school. If I did, it was always on the weekends and only to give myself a break from my coursework.

However, all of my hard work and determination finally paid off. I passed all of my GCSE exams with 1 A, 2 B's, and 5 C's. I stayed in so much to give myself a chance in life. Whatever friends I did make had now dropped out of school in search of work, but, incredibly, against all odds, I had made the lower sixth form with my chosen course electives.

I had been waiting seventy-four days for this moment, ever since I finished my last exam in June.

Mr. Pepper had one responsibility and one job: to prepare us for the outside world the best way he could. But instead, he made me feel stupid, worthless, and useless. So I learned to play chess properly while staying with my nana during the summer holidays. I read book after book on chess, and I even bought myself an electronic chess game with the money from my Saturday job. My manager was also kind enough to let me have some time off after my exams.

I sat back down in the same position as last time and waited patiently for Mr. Pepper to turn up. *Fuck! What the hell am I doing here? This is completely nuts. I am setting myself up for a fall again.* Then I noticed nearly all the girls seemed to have bigger boobs, and everyone looked older, taller, and more confident. They were also wearing makeup. Yet I still looked the same. I was way out of my depth and I needed to leave.

Before I knew it, Mr. Pepper slammed his hand on my desk.

"Obviously, you didn't learn the last time. Chess is for smart people, noughts, and crosses starts tomorrow behind the bike sheds." 'Behind the bike sheds' was a well-known school reference, where all the losers and the no-hopers hung out.

Great inspirational motivator, but he inspired regardless.

I carried on smiling and grinning.

"Why are you still smiling?" He looked puzzled.

"I am smiling because I have nothing to lose, but if I win, you will have been beaten by a, how did you say it last time? Oh yeah, by a thicko."

During my entire time in the lower and upper sixth, Mr. Pepper never once beat me.

***

My first year in lower sixth was all about creating a solid foundation in preparation for my final exams the following year. Life at home was also good, and Mum now had just one job, working in a Do-It-Yourself home improvement centre selling kitchens and earning a good commission. Finally, Mum had money in her pocket.

My sister was growing up fast and starting to become cheekier and a little selfish. My brother had a proper girlfriend now, and the moment he walked through the front door, they went straight upstairs to his room.

Most of the lower sixth had now started to go into town clubbing. I was about five-foot-two and looked fourteen years old; I had no chance, and I knew it, so again I stayed in.

One Friday evening and out of the blue, Brendan, a rich kid from the fourth year, asked me if I could lend him ten pounds. *Strange request*, I thought. *He's rich, what for? When will I get it back?* He then pulled a small brown bottle out of his coat pocket, unscrewed the lid and took a sniff, insisting I did the same. I didn't. He said he needed a tenner so he could buy three more brown bottles before heading off to town later that night.

He then offered me two years' worth of cinema tickets, allowing me to watch two movies per week, every week for two years at our local cinema, where his dad's business advertised. I handed over ten pounds instantly and pocketed the Willy Wonka golden cinema tickets and used them on my date with Gemma.

Gemma was stunning; she was my first real high school crush and the sister of one of the most popular boys in our school. This was my first ever date and hopefully my first kiss at the age of seventeen. I had to play it super smooth; I couldn't mess this up, or I would never hear the last of it.

I arranged to meet Gemma at the cinema, as we were going to watch *Poltergeist II*. During the movie, I held her hand. This was the first time I had ever held a girl's hand and it felt really good.

I wasn't sure if this was the date Gemma had in mind. I didn't know what to do, absolutely no, Scooby Doo. So I just held her hand and watched the movie. I didn't even make any attempts to kiss her. She kept looking over at me, but I smiled and carried on watching the movie. On the bus journey home, sitting on the top deck of the double-decker bus, Gemma seemed so quiet and distant, like she wasn't interested in me anymore.

I didn't know how to tell her that this was my first date and that I was so nervous, without coming across like a right nob-head. I didn't want her brother to know the date had gone badly.

So I leaned in and gave her a kiss just before my bus stop, hoping I could redeem myself. We kissed for about ten seconds before I pulled away and ran downstairs.

Waiting for the bus to stop, I could feel my stomach churn; my nerves were getting the better of me. I could feel I was going to throw up. I just needed to get across the road and throw up behind the wall, out of her line of sight.

But first I had to wait for the bus to leave. I watched out of the corner of my eye as the bus pulled away, and then I waited until the bus turned the corner and was completely gone before leaning against the local dairy wall and started throwing up. I even put two fingers down my throat to get everything out.

That was close!

I had no idea how I held it in for all that time, I thought I was going to pass out. The last thing I wanted was for Gemma to watch me be sick after I kissed her.

Only then I realised that Gemma had witnessed it all from the top deck of the bus; my bus never left. Another bus drove past it while it was waiting at the bus stop and I thought it had been my bus that went around the corner.

I never did get a second date with Gemma, or any date while I was in lower sixth. I was too embarrassed, scared, and shy to go on anymore dates; I felt this one experience was enough to put me off for life.

3

WHY ME

During my first year in the lower sixth form, my Saturday job had now become my part-time after school job. I was working three afternoons a week helping clean down after the day. The other two afternoons, you could find me in the cinema.

I loved going to the cinema; this was my escape from reality. I was still unable to make any meaningful friendships at school or where I lived. So this place became my sanctuary. I was happy and content eating popcorn, slurping on orange Fanta, eyes larger than dinner plates, glued to the big screen, and sitting on the edge of my seat, even on my own.

But that all changed whilst watching *The Rocketeer* starring Billy Campbell and Jennifer Connelly. I was sitting at the back of the theatre on the right-hand side, next to the steps on the aisle, twelve rows from the front of the screen. Halfway through the movie, I noticed another person sitting ten rows in front of me, on the far left near the toilets.

I didn't think twice about this person, I only noticed something was off when I placed my popcorn next to my seat, and now I could see he was a man, sitting in the same row as me, only about eight seats away.

I was starting to feel anxious and my heart was beating fast. I looked over my shoulder to see if anyone else was in the theatre, but I was on my own. I wanted to leave, but I couldn't. I was fixed in place, unable to budge and unbale to speak once again. I was experiencing the same type of feelings that I had on that cold, wet Monday morning a year earlier, confronted by Rambo.

I sat motionless, pretending to watch the movie. But all the time, I was watching this person eight seats away from me through the corner of my eye.

Ten minutes later, he was sitting right next to me, his right hand rubbing my left leg. He was playing with himself and touching me at the same time. He moved his hand between my legs, and tears were running down my face. In my head, I was begging him to stop, screaming at the top of my voice for help, but nothing came out.

He started to unzip my pants. I sat frozen in my chair, unable to turn my head to see what he looked like. I just sat there, telling myself to *get up, Cornelius, get up, get up, get up, get fucking up.*

He climaxed all over himself as he touched my penis.

Get fucking up! I pulled his hand out of my pants, ran towards the emergency exit, and slammed the door behind me. I couldn't catch my breath; my heart was thumping and my anxiety was all over the place. The only place I could think to go was my workplace.

I ran non-stop, without looking back once. The moment I saw the shop, I started shouting for my manager, Robert. He rushed towards me, wondering what all the commotion was about and trying to calm me down so I could explain what happened, but I simply couldn't. I was so out of breath. I was all over the place in a complete mess. I just pointed to the cinema and said that someone had touched me. Robert, Dave, Dennis and Mick immediately ran towards the cinema to see if he was still there, but he was gone. I never went back to the cinema again; my sanctuary was destroyed.

I became very reclused and alone after what happened to me. I wasn't socialising with friends from school anymore. I knew I was alienating myself and becoming very distant, but I had no way to stop it. I was happy to stay in and look after my sister; she was about six years old and so bloody cute.

One night, though, I was dragged along to a lower sixth house party.

All night I sat on this swinging chair, watching everyone else have fun. I wanted to leave the moment I arrived; it wasn't me, loud music, drinking, girls, I was so out of place.

My mind was racing. The number of headaches I was having was starting to worry me, I was popping paracetamol like candy. I just wanted the noise in my head to stop and the headaches to go away.

All of a sudden, this girl sat on my lap, someone who I had seen around the school before. Mia asked why I looked so miserable. *Well, where do I start?* I thought. I just smiled. "Are you enjoying the party?" I asked.

"No, not really, I just came to see what all the fuss was about. Everyone was talking about it today at school." I didn't say anything to her for the next thirty minutes, but she still sat on my lap, watching everyone and occasionally saying, "I'm not hurting you, am I?"

I just smiled and shook my head; I didn't know how to speak to a girl in this way, apart from my first unsuccessful date. My nerves and anxiety were kicking in, and my legs were now starting to shake and twitch. I was trying to calm my nerves down by breathing slowly; I didn't want to show that I was struggling. I could feel myself getting sick again.

I was struggling with my anxiety. I threw up in my mouth then quickly swallowed it back down again and smiled at her as if I was having a good time.

She offered me a beer, still smiling. I shook my head side to side, indicating no. I wasn't sure if I had sick breath or not. Plus, I wasn't eighteen-years old yet. What a rock 'n' roller I was! But I had my reasons; I was waiting for my brother to start drinking first. I wanted to know if alcoholism and violence ran in our family, as I was continually being told it was. "It's in your genes!"

Ten minutes later, I smiled at her and left the party.

I didn't see Mia again for another four weeks until she noticed me waiting at the bus stop outside school one Monday afternoon. She asked where I was going and where I had been. I always kept to myself at school, and once my last elective lesson was over, generally at 1 pm, I would be working at the Butchers shop.

"Hey Cornelius, how are you? I haven't seen you around for ages, I was hoping to catch up with you after the party. I asked around, and no one knew where you were. Did I upset you at the party?"

"No, you didn't upset me at all. I'm not avoiding you, if that's what you're thinking. I'm just not very good in social situations, plus I work most afternoons at a butcher shop in town. I also have a lot on my mind at the moment. Sorry if I gave you that impression."

"I also heard that you go to the cinema twice a week after school and that you have some sort of golden movie tickets that you sometimes lend out. Is it possible for you to lend me those tickets? I am keen to watch *Toy*

Soldiers after school tomorrow; I only need one though, I have no one to go with. Unless you're keen to go, then we can go together?"

Is Mia asking me out on a date or does she just want company? I had never been good at picking up signs, even when a girl knocked on my front door asking for me to come out. Fuck! I hadn't been back to the cinema since the *Rocketeer* movie.

Mia kept on insisting that she wanted to watch the movie. What if it was a date? Then how would I kiss her without throwing up? What if she tried to hold my hand? So much was going through my mind. I blurted out, "Yes, but it's not a date, ok? I need to be very clear on that; it's not a date."

Mia laughed and agreed that tomorrow wouldn't be a date, and that we were both going to watch the same movie, that's all. Definitely not a date, and we shook hands to confirm this agreement.

Mia was waiting for me on the steps of the cinema. I was hoping she wasn't going to turn up. I wasn't prepared for today. I had a shocking sleep the night before, and I was trying to work out why she asked me to watch *Toy Soldiers*. Mia was stunning; she looked like the spitting image of Yasmine Bleeth from *Baywatch* in every way possible. Mia could have her pick of anyone from our school, yet she was waiting for *me* on the steps?

I began to stutter and feel anxious talking to Mia. I felt my heart racing; my breathing became shallow and I was starting to feel light-headed. I really didn't want to go in, but I didn't want to explain why, either. I got myself into a right mess by agreeing to go in the first place.

I slid my golden tickets over the counter for them to be stamped. I bought a bag of Butterkist popcorn and an orange Tango drink and made our way to Cinema 1, the largest of all three cinemas. Mia sat on my right-hand side, near the aisle steps. I took a deep breath as the lights went dim, always looking out of the left corner of my eye. This was the first movie I wasn't paying any attention to, unable to control my right leg from shaking.

I wanted to leave the cinema ASAP. I was starting to have flashbacks and I needed to throw up.

Then out of nowhere, I screamed at the top of my voice. Mia had placed her hand on my knee to stop me from shaking. She knew I was nervous, but that just triggered something else in me. I was fighting back the tears; I was always told that boys don't cry, that it's a sign of weakness. Mia knew something was wrong. I was turning my head to the left every other minute, constantly checking if anyone was sitting next to me.

Toy Soldiers couldn't have finished any quicker; I needed air. We both stood up, and Mia placed her hands on my hips and eased me forward out of the cinema.

***

Mia always stated that from the moment she touched my hips, she knew we would be girlfriend and boyfriend.

Mia was my first love. We were in a relationship for over three and a half years and I loved every second that I spent with her. I was happy inside, something I never thought could be possible.

I lost my virginity to Mia on my 18th birthday, nearly a year into our relationship. As a coping mechanism, I created unbreakable inner contracts, rigorous timeframes, and dates for my life. Losing my virginity was one of them.

Mia and I started kissing on her lounge floor next to the sofa, while her parents and brothers were sleeping upstairs. We had all just come back from attending Mia's grandmother's 70th birthday party. Seeing as it was also my 18th birthday, Mia wanted to have sex. And to give her credit, she patiently waited a long time; one of the many reasons I was head over heels in love with her.

I was so nervous. Mia suggested that we fool around a little before we had sex, a great compromise. I was going to see and touch Mia's boobs and vagina for the first time; this was a big day in the life of Cornelius.

Typically, I started to panic. Mia lost her virginity a year before we began dating, so she was more experienced.

I was kissing Mia when she placed my right hand on her boobs. *Wow, wow, wow, I am touching boobs, like for real.* I was hooked. They were soft and firm and pretty big. I kept thinking, *Wow is this happening?* I mean, I was feeling real boobs for the first time, even over Mia's one-piece white bodysuit. She then asked if I wanted to go further.

Awkwardly lying face down on the sofa, I managed to squeeze my entire right arm down her top, my shoulder resting on the side of her head as she sat on the floor next to me. At one point, I thought I was going to dislocate my shoulder; this was way harder than I had imagined. All I could see was my wriggling snake arm, moving from side to side, making its way down towards Mia's vagina. Bloody hell, who knew bodysuits were so tight?

Finally, I reached my destination. I was touching a vagina for the first time, as if I was trying to guess what sort of present was at the bottom of a Christmas sack. I had no idea what the hell I was doing. Mia's face was also telling me the same story. She asked if I knew how these bodysuits worked. "Yeah, it's like a one-piece bathing suit, innit?"

"Not really, let me help." Then all of a sudden, Mia unsnapped three buttons at the bottom of her bodysuit. I saw the top of my right hand wiggling above her vagina, resembling a lousy puppet show without the puppet. I was totally out of my depth.

Once I pulled my hand back out of her top, I was now in the correct position. We started to fool around and carried on kissing. She began to undo my trousers and slid her hand down my pants. The next minute, I was lying on top of Mia, having sex. I was losing my virginity to someone I was in love with, but I had no idea sex was going to be this painful!

After about five minutes, it was all over. I was no longer a virgin, but *fuck* I was in agonizing pain. I quickly got dressed, kissed Mia goodbye, and left ASAP.

I ran to the bus stop as hastily as possible to check why I was in so much pain. I unbuttoned my jeans under the bus shelter lights. I was still erect, somehow. My penis head was bright purple and swollen, and it was dripping blood; somehow, my foreskin had been entirely pulled back over my head, and it wasn't going back over. Also, my banjo string had been completely torn, which was why I was bleeding so much. I then heard a car pull up alongside the bus shelter and begin to toot its horn.

"Cornelius? Cornelius, is that you?" Someone was shouting my name from the car.

"No, no sorry, my name is Lee, got the wrong guy mate."

"Sounds like you, Cornelius." I was desperate to get my penis in my trousers before I turned around to face who was talking to me.

"What are you doing in there? Do you want a lift home? I am driving past your house on my way home. And who's Lee?"

"It's ok, I'll just wait for the bus to turn up."

"Come on, Cornelius. Or Lee? Get in, it's no issues at all."

Bloody hell, he doesn't give up, does he? Hesitantly I got into his car backwards with my exposed penis covered only by my jumper. I was unable to get it back in my jeans in time.

I sat in the front, holding my breath, eyes fixed to the road and counting down the minutes until I was home— my right hand holding down the jumper covering my exposed penis.

"What you been up to tonight, anything good?"

"Nothing, just hanging out with Mia. Just a normal night in."

Finally, I was outside my house. In my panic trying to get out of the car, I couldn't undo the seat belt with only my left hand.

"Not to worry, this always happens. Let me get that for you."

I will always remember Gary's facial expression. He lifted my jumper to undo the seat belt, and looking back at him was a deep purple, erect, bloody penis poking out of my jeans. He looked at me, then at my penis, and then back at me. You could see he wanted to say something but nothing came out; he just looked dumbstruck. I bet this was the last thing he expected to see on a Sunday night!

I ran inside the house, shouting "Mum, Mum I need your help, something is wrong. I broke my penis!"

Mum took one look at my penis, had a gulp of tea, then walked to the kitchen and grabbed a bar of soap. She rubbed it on the head of my penis and pulled my foreskin back to where it belonged. The soap stung my torn banjo skin and I nearly passed out from the pain.

We never mentioned this incident again and nor did my friend who picked me up; I will always be grateful to Gary for not saying anything to anyone at school. I couldn't take another year of constant piss-taking.

The other painful memory I had was when I walked out of Mia's house after I asked her dad for permission to marry his daughter, only to see her kissing another man in his car. I was in so much emotional pain that I stopped eating for nearly five months. I lost so much weight that Mum had to force-feed me to get me to eat. I was alone and depressed. It took me just over a year to rebuild my self-esteem and get over my heartbreak and finally leave the house. But you never really get over your first love.

I found a new love in my life, called ten-pin bowling. It brought my brother and I a lot closer, too. We even started our own team and in our first season, we won two trophies. I loved bowling so much; it took my mind off Mia. I joined three more leagues that year, a doubles team with my brother called Double Force, and a singles league. I won another eight trophies within my first year.

I was starting to find happiness again; I had a part-time job that I loved, and I had bowling. But if I was alone with my thoughts, that's when I struggled with loneliness and my inner voice the most. There were no league games on Fridays or over the weekends, and during those times I stayed in my room, depressed. I truly wanted a girlfriend, but I had no idea how I would meet anyone. Bowling wasn't a sexy sport, and the people who I bowled with were way older than I was.

My butcher's shop had been bought out by another company, and I was now surplus to requirements. I was very fortunate that Mum knew the manager at our local DIY and garden store. I was a full-time sales assistant in the furniture department and I loved that job. It gave me the confidence to talk to people. Jack, someone I knew from school, was also a department manager. I was starting to feel like my old self again, but that was short-lived. One night I was cycling home, approximately two-hundred meters from home when a young boy came running out from behind two parked cars directly in front of me.

I slammed on my brakes so hard I flew straight over the handlebars and landed on my right shoulder. I slid down the main road in front of an oncoming car, which also slammed on its brakes. I eventually came to a stop with my head directly under the engine.

I was rushed to hospital, as I couldn't move my shoulder at all. Eventually, I left the hospital in a sling. Nothing was broken, but my collarbone was cracked. The following day, I rang work to explain what happened and that I needed to take two weeks off work.

Here's the kicker, the boy's parents were now suing me for the emotional distress I placed on their family and their son, even though he ran out in the middle of the road. I nearly died trying not to hit him, but that didn't mean anything, especially when they could see a pay-out. At the end of the day, who cares about the other person, right?

One Saturday night, I went with Mum to pick my brother up from town; he was on a lads' night out. I knew the bouncer on the nightclub door from school and from where I lived, so I decided to have a chat with him while waiting for my brother to appear. It had been a long time since I had caught up with him. I noticed Jack from work leaving the club, but he walked straight by me, shaking his head. He looked pissed off for some reason.

I returned to work the following week but could only perform light duties. I missed the people from work, so it was nice to touch base after recovering at home, until I was called into the manager's office. "It has been brought to my attention that while you were off work, you were spotted in a nightclub."

I didn't want to lie, so I said, "I wasn't in a nightclub, I was outside waiting for my brother. Mum and I went to pick him up and give him a lift home. I was talking to a school friend, he was the bouncer at the door, so I am not quite sure what the issue is? I didn't go into the nightclub; my arm was in a sling."

"You were spotted in the nightclub. Dancing!"

"What? That's not correct. Who spotted me?"

I was surprised to hear Jack being summoned to the office to explain what took place on Saturday night. I couldn't believe what was coming out of his mouth; he fabricated an entirely different event. I had no idea why he was lying. I was then escorted off the premises.

A few months later, I finally understood why my school friend had lied: there was an internal store job promotion, and he wanted to prove that he was loyal and trustworthy. He got promoted to assistant manager. He threw me straight under the bus for his own personal gain. I was a nobody in his world, even though I had known him for well over ten years. I saw him a few years later, and he didn't even apologise after I brought up his lies. In his head, he justified his actions. He needed that promotion so he could afford a mortgage with his partner.

I was only unemployed for about four weeks; I managed to get another job in another home improvement centre. I was fortunate that I had previous experience working in a DIY store, which landed me the job. I had two store managers: John, the assistant manager who was a lovely family guy with strong principles and ethics, and Chucky, the general store manager, who was a nasty character.

I enjoyed working alongside John. He took me under his wing and sent me on a lot of product knowledge courses, including how to drive a forklift truck. Every night between 5 and 8 pm, I had to restock and face up the front of the shelves and line all the products up with the edge of the shelf, so it looked perfect for the following day. This was boring and tiresome, and the evenings would just drag on. My anxiety was terrible, especially if Chucky was on duty.

I never thought I would ever be bullied again after I left school, but from the moment I started work until the store closed, he was always having a go at me, and always out of sight. Chucky knew I wasn't the most confident person in the world, and he exploited all of my insecurities, precisely like a school bully. If I didn't do exactly what he said, he became nastier, always threatening me with my job. But what I hated the most was his sexual advances towards me and his sexual conversations. Chucky always called me into his office when we worked late together with just the cashier managing the front of the store. After 7 pm we were lucky to get two customers, so he would keep me in his office until closing time. He would always perform random strip searches on me in case I was stealing anything from the store.

I had no idea why he took a disliking to me; he wasn't like this to anyone else in the store. I would sit alone in my bedroom in tears, not ever wanting to go back to work. Still, I needed the money. I need to pay Mum for living with her. There was no way she could run the house and bring up my sister on her pay alone. I wanted to contribute as much as I could to ease her financial burden and worries.

I found myself in a no-win situation again, and with unemployment on the rise in I knew I was lucky even to have a job in the first place.

During my day off, Chucky told all the staff that he was getting relocated to a brand-new store and that John was now going to be our store manager. I couldn't believe my luck; that evil bastard was going to be out of my life for good. But he still had one more trick up his sleeve. He had one month left in my store before he left and he changed my entire schedule to coincide with his.

He placed me on cleaning duties for the entire month and even though I had pulled my back lifting heavy boxes of lawnmowers, he stood next to me not offering to help. Chucky made me work in the area with all of the 40kg bags of dry materials like cement, sand, ballast, and rolls of loft insulation. I had to individually lift every bag and clean them to his liking before placing them back down on a new wooden pallet.

This was a two-person job, but he forced me to do it on my own, while he sat in a chair pointing out my errors. At the end of the night he strip-searched me and patted me down, looking for stolen items. I had never taken anything, not even a bar of chocolate.

He punished me so harshly that I was on the verge of quitting, his leaving gift to himself. He encouraged me to quit, goading me, pushing me and pinning me against the warehouse wall, until he finally left.

One more week working under him and he would have accomplished his ultimate goal. Scott, who worked in the warehouse, knew some aspects about how he was treating me, but he kept quiet. He did invite me out one Saturday into town to meet his best friends, and it happened to be my twenty-first birthday, so I could finally drink alcohol.

4

I SWEAR I WAS A CAT IN MY PREVIOUS LIFE...

I had never been out in town at night before, so I had no idea what to wear. I also didn't want to look like it was my first time, especially since I was meeting Scott's mates. I didn't want my first impression to come across like I was a dickhead. I needed my brother's advice on what I should wear, but he was hardly at home anymore. He had a girlfriend and was with her 24/7. So I asked for Mum's advice instead. Mum was so trendy and stylish for her age, so I trusted her on what to wear.

Mum dropped me off outside The Cricketer's Arms at 7 pm, a pub in the centre of town where I was meeting Scott. I was wearing a grey Debenhams hoodie, dark brown chino pants, and tan boots similar to the brand Caterpillar, but mine were from Jonathan James and only cost me ten pounds. *Wow, I can't believe I am doing this*, I thought as I walked over to Scott, who was waiting for me on a bench just outside the pub door.

I stood at the entrance of the doorway, thinking *I can do this. Cornelius, you can do this!* As I walked into the pub. The interior was dimly lit and all the windows were covered in posters to give it a rock 'n' roll ambience. You couldn't even see outside. The carpet floor was sticky and U2 was playing overhead. Omg it was so loud, this definitely wasn't my type of music. I liked Michael Jackson, Madonna, Roxette, Wilson Philips, George Michael, and Prince.

While Scott was at the bar ordering a drink, I tried to locate his friends. He mentioned that they were already in the pub while I was chatting to him outside. The only people I could see from the doorway were four guys, sitting at a table in the middle of the floor. These guys looked like they had all run into baseball bats or a wall! They were black and blue, with cuts and bruises all over their faces, and all dressed in black, with long greasy hair.

These can't be his mates, I thought. *They must be in the beer garden or something.* I couldn't imagine Scott having friends like these. I don't know why, but they just didn't seem to fit with how Scott came across to me. I mean, Scott didn't have one cut or bruise on his face or long greasy hair, and he didn't dress in black.

I walked towards the bar where Scott stood, and then froze. I had no idea what I was going to order, for some reason it never crossed my mind that I would have to order something to drink. "Oi, what you havin'?" the barman said.

I was about to order my first alcoholic drink. This was a massive moment in my life, one I would never forget. Anxiously, I looked all around the entire bar and said in a confident voice, "Brandy, please."

"What? Did you just say brandy, as in a shot of brandy?"

I had no idea what a shot of brandy was, but I confidently replied back, "Yeah I did, brandy please."

"In a brandy glass?" He cracked up laughing. I had no idea why he was laughing, but I just had my first conversation with a barman. I was so excited, this was all new to me, and we were getting on well. Still laughing, he bent down and pulled a big ass glass from under the counter. It was huge, the size of a goldfish bowl. He then went over to a bottle hanging on the wall and pressed the goldfish bowl against it, which was weird, and then he placed the glass in front of me on the bar top.

Still laughing, "That's one pound fifty."

"One pound fifty? For what?" I could hardly see what I was paying for. This was not what I had imagined as my first alcoholic drink; it was so small. Was I missing something?

"Is there something wrong with your drink, buddy?" He was still laughing. I then realised how stupid I was. *What a dickhead I am, duh.* "Can you fill the rest of the glass up with coke and add a slice of lemon, please?"

"Oh, you're after a broke? That's short for brandy and coke."

"Yes, that's it. I would like a broke, please." I turned away from the bar slowly but steadily and started walking towards Scott, who was now sitting down with the guys who were all black and blue.

I was trying not to spill my broke; it was full to the brim with coke and it also contained two umbrellas, a shiny cherry speared with a cocktail stick, a sparkler, and two straws. The glass was so big that I had to hold it with both hands at the stem. He was pissing himself laughing as he'd handed me the glass. Trying not to spill any of my broke on to my new shoes, I carefully walked along the sticky floor and to where Scott was sitting. All his mates cracked up laughing, and we all knew instantly that I didn't fit in.

Eventually, I plucked up the courage and asked Kermit, one of Scott's mates, why his nose was completely bent the other way. He told me the story of what happened last weekend. All of them had been drinking since 2 pm, and everyone was drunk and high on drugs. Each person took about five E's as they were walking towards The Revolution night club, labelled the biggest nightclub venue in town. Kermit had said to everyone, "The next person who walks around that corner, I am going to punch them straight in the face. I don't care who it is, they are getting a fucking pasting."

Kermit said the next minute someone walked around the corner, he had run up to him and planted a full closed fist and broke his nose instantly. This guy fell to the floor, with blood everywhere.

Kermit then pulled out of his coat pocket a small brown bottle called 'liquid gold'. It was the same sort of bottle I saw five years ago.

While they were telling me this story, he unscrewed the bottle and started to sniff from it, then passed it around to everyone else to have a sniff. Even Scott pressed one nostril closed and inhaled from the other nostril. They asked me if I wanted to try. I was getting a headache from just being in the vicinity of this open bottle. "No thanks, I still got my broke to drink." They all cracked up laughing.

"Sorry, what? You punched someone for no reason at all. What? Are you kidding me, you punched a guy because you felt like it? I don't get that." They all carried on pissing themselves laughing; their faces were bright red like baboon arses. Was I missing something?

Kermit carried on with his story. The lad who Kermit had punched stood up and ran back around the same corner he had come from. Thirty seconds later, about twenty men ran around the corner towards Kermit and his mates. "That's him, that's the one who punched me, he's the one who broke my nose." The lad pointed Kermit out to his father and his mates, who were all out celebrating his son's eighteenth birthday.

They chased Kermit and his mates halfway around town, eventually catching up with them outside the Black Bull Pub. They pinned all of them against the pub wall. Kermit and his mates got hammered that night, and their faces showed it. I can't imagine what their bodies would have looked like. Scott had to work that Saturday, luckily for him.

Even when they told me this story, they were still laughing like this happened every weekend. I was shocked. I asked where the toilets were, and Scott pointed me in the direction.

I never went to the toilet though, I just went out the backdoor and caught a bus home; my first night in town lasted only twenty minutes. I wasn't a fighter, drug taker, or bottle sniffer. I was surprised that Scott hung out with these people on the weekends.

The following Monday at work, Scott asked why I had gapped it. I just said, "This isn't for me, doing drugs and getting into fights. That's not me, sorry."

"Same here, maybe you should give them another go? They will always have your back, no matter what, and if you don't want to do any drugs, they will respect that. I never do Es, and they will never push you into doing anything that you don't want to do. Once you get to know them, they are really good fun, and maybe it wasn't the best timing to meet them. But I can vouch for them, they're all straight-up guys."

Over the next three years, we were all inseparable, going out every night apart from Sundays, which they spent with their girlfriends. Scott was right, I had so much fun. They still had fights and they took a phenomenal amount of drugs. But we all got on so well. They all looked like Hugo Boss models, over six-foot-two, stunning long dark hair, tanned, chiselled facial features with their trademark Diesel style clothes and boots. Girls were all over them; they could have their pick of the crop, and every night they did. I definitely wasn't a Hugo Boss model, not at five-foot-five. I was pale, with a big, broken Roman hook nose with curly hair. But I'd found my tribe.

During those three years in the 90's with the models, our town had fifty-two pubs and eleven night clubs, all within walking distance. Jesters was my favourite place to go during the week, especially on Wednesday nights. This place was renowned as a bit of a 'grab-a-granny' joint amongst the younger generations.

Friday nights we always ended up at Studio 54, the clubbing hotspot, and the Backdoor, which was also part Studio 54. Saturday night was Kingfisher night, a converted former ballroom, dining area and bingo hall. If we went clubbing on a Sunday night, it was always at The Cave, part of The Revolution night club, another 'grab-a-granny' mecca.

Everyone had their routine. We hardly ever strayed from the routine, and to be fair, at first it was awesome seeing the same people every time, a great way to get to know someone. But I wanted to try new bars and at different times. This fell on deaf ears, something the models wouldn't dream of doing. What, change the route?!

When I wasn't out with the models, I was still bowling. I was now the one to beat in all the leagues. I was playing off a scratch handicap of zero when other players were between 10 and 60; this meant I was giving them a 10 to 60 points every game, and we only played three games. Sometimes I would have to catch up on 180 points just to win. I had no real distractions in my life so I could concentrate and spend most of my time fine-tuning my bowling skills at the age of twenty-three. After three years of bowling, I had amassed over a hundred trophies. But I had to give it all up after my first snowboarding holiday.

We all booked a seven-night snowboard trip to Andorra. I was now drinking Tia Maria and coke or Baileys. I still wasn't a fan of the taste of beer and definitely wasn't keen on being drunk, either. I hated going home drunk, especially when I knew Mum was waiting up for me. I didn't want her to be reminded of the days when Dad would come home drunk. I preferred drinking shots rather than bottles or pints of beer. I was consciously aware of being drunk, and the moment I felt tipsy, I just stopped and started to drink coke.

We arrived at our hotel at 11:30 pm, dropped our bags off in the room, and headed straight towards the first bar so we could experience our first nightlife après-ski, as they call it.

Wow, what a first night! I didn't want it to end, it was that good. But we'd all booked snowboard lessons first thing in the morning and the morning was already here. I looked at my watch, and it was 7 am. *How is that possible?* I wasn't even drunk; thankfully, I only drank Baileys. Everyone else looked like shit, though. We ran or staggered back to our hotel room, quickly got changed, and headed back downstairs for breakfast before heading out for our first lesson, which was at 9 am.

By the time I reached the ski lift, I had started to feel a little light-headed. I remember queuing up for the two-person chair lift. I put it down to rushing around that morning with no sleep.

Luckily, I had no one sitting next to me on the chair lift as I headed up the mountain. I was in no state to engage in small talk. There were three of the models in front of me and two models behind me on the ski lift. The higher up the mountain I travelled, the more I felt light-headed. It felt as if I was getting drunk but backwards.

I threw up in my mouth and quickly swallowed it straight back down, my usual trick. My eyes were starting to get out of focus. Fuck, I wasn't feeling good, and at one point I thought I blacked out. You know the feeling when you were at school and you started to drift off, when all of a sudden your head snapped forward, waking you back up? That was happening to me.

Again, I threw up in my mouth, and straight back down it went. I didn't want any of the models to know I wasn't in a good state. I didn't want them to miss their lessons, especially if they had to take me back to our hotel.

***

"Hello, can you hear me? Hello? Hello, can you hear me? Do you know where you are?" That's all I could hear on repeat. When I finally came to, I was in so much pain. My shoulder felt like it was hanging off, which it was; I had dislocated my shoulder, and somehow I had been admitted to the hospital. I had no idea how I got here.

I then heard someone say, "You're one lucky guy; I don't know many people who can survive a hundred-foot drop. Someone must be looking out for you, you lucky bastard. The only reason you are not dead is that we think you passed out during your fall and your body became limp."

He explained what might have happened to me. Since I was drinking all night, combined with the high altitude, this could have caused me to blackout by getting drunk backwards, as I call it. Something along those lines. I lifted the safety chair bar and jumped off about a hundred foot of the ground. I'd had no idea what I was doing. My snowboarding holiday was over in less than thirty minutes.

I take full responsibility for what happened. I had no idea altitude could do something like that. What I couldn't understand was that none of the models came to see if I was alright. They saw me fall from the ski lift and they knew I was on my way to the hospital, but they never came to visit to see if I was ok.

They carried on with their morning snowboarding lessons.

I hardly saw them for the rest of the week, too. They carried on as if nothing had happened. I understand that it was their holiday also. Still, it would have been nice if they'd come back after their lessons to grab me so we could all enjoy the après-ski and salvage some of my holidays, but they never did.

This was my first inkling that they only cared about themselves. I thought I had built a deep friendship with the models over the last few years, but I was kidding myself.

My inkling was confirmed one evening after we had finished playing our last game in a six-aside football league. I was always the substitute. I wasn't great at football, but I enjoyed running around. We sat downstairs in the football club bar, planning our end of the season night out, which was beer, pub, club, followed by a curry.

We were tentatively planning our night out, waiting for Scott to join us at the table; he was the last one to finish his shower and change. I was still wearing my football kit, as I never showered after a game or in front of anyone. The thought alone made me so uncomfortable, and I knew exactly why I felt uncomfortable.

During high school, between the ages of twelve and fifteen, my PE teacher made me strip naked in front of all the other boys after playing football or rugby and forced me to shower first. He would then stand on a bench opposite the showers and watch me. I didn't start puberty until I was about eighteen years old. I had to cover my bits and bobs up and run through the showers. He always threatened me with detention if I didn't lift up my hands and wash in front of him and my entire class.

I don't know how many times I looked down at the floor and cried, my wet hair concealing my tears, while everyone stood and watched, taking the piss out of me for not hitting puberty. It didn't help that I was in a class full of wookiees and bigfoots; I was so far behind everyone else.

What made it worse was that the same teacher forced me back in the shower time after time, even after everyone had finished their showers and were changing into their school uniforms. He just stood there and watched me.

Finally, Scott arrived. We all decided to chip in twenty pounds for our curry night. A few minutes later, my brother phoned to tell me that he had just called off his wedding. He wanted to know if I wanted to go on his honeymoon in place of her. A lads' holiday, so to speak. *Wow, a two-week holiday with my brother, wow, wow, wow, amazing.* I turned to John, who was my general manager at work, and our goalkeeper. He said, "No worries, we can always work something out, you go on holiday with your bro."

I was so excited I was going on holiday with my brother. Instantly, I reached into the kitty to retrieve back my twenty pounds, when one of the models turned around and said, "What the fuck are you doing? That's for our night out."

"Yeah, I know, that's why I am taking my money out. I won't be here anymore. I will be on holiday with my brother that night," I replied.

"I don't fucking think so, once it's in, it's in. You can't just take it back out, that's not how it works."

"What the fuck, didn't you do something very similar last season, and no one complained then. So what has changed now? Ok, if you're going to be like that, then why don't you use my twenty pounds towards next season's league fees? Simple, all sorted."

"I am not sure you're understanding me, that's our kitty money now, it's for us to enjoy beers, club, and a curry. It's not our fault you're going on holiday with your brother. You decided that, not us. Your money is staying in the kitty."

"You can't be serious. How is this fair? Why is it any different from last year? I mean, you're fucking kidding me, aren't you? I can't take my money out?"

I looked at the rest of the team, hoping someone would back me up. Even Scott walked off towards the bar.

"I have known you all for nearly three years, we have gone out every other night, and you're telling me I can't get my money back?"

"No, you can't."

I took off my shirt, shorts, and socks and threw them across the table at everyone. What a complete bunch of wankers. My friendship wasn't worth twenty pounds? I walked just over five miles home that night, pretty much naked. I never saw any of them models again.

***

The holiday with my brother was so good. I had always wanted to go on holiday with him, but I never thought it would ever happen. We had so much fun; I felt I was starting to get to know him as a brother, rather than someone who lived in the same house as me. We slept the entire day and partied until sunrise. I had never seen this side of my brother before; he was so funny. I was surprised we got on so well. We bounced off each other, and the banter was free-flowing. We never once stopped laughing.

He also had a very selfish side to him, which I didn't like. We were continually chasing girls from one bar to another, which was so frigging annoying.

But I understood why. This was the first time in five years he was single, and calling off his wedding at the last minute must have been a tough decision. I had no idea he was that unhappy; he always insisted that his relationship was amazing.

One night towards the end of our holiday, my brother was chatting to this girl in a bar. I felt like a third wheel, so I left him to it and went to buy us entry tickets for the most prominent outdoor night club in Bodrum, Turkey, called Halikarnas. I had been waiting for this night all holiday. When I returned to the bar, he decided to stay another hour and meet me in the club at 1 am at the end of the bar. This was perfect timing, as I needed to go back to our room and change anyway.

"Ok, no worries, I will see you at the end of the bar at 1 am. Please don't be late. You know I hate being on my own, you know I get anxiety being on my own."

"For fuck sake, I said I would be there, didn't I?"

I waited until 4 am. I kept moving from one end of the bar to other, hoping I didn't miss him. The club was heaving and I couldn't relax until he was there. Now I was stressing that he had left and gone back home, and that he was pissed off with me.

I jumped straight into a taxi and headed back to our room. *Fuck, he's not here either*, I thought.

Maybe he's still in the club, I must have missed him somehow? I jumped

47

back into a taxi, paid the entrance fee again, and waited at the end of the bar.

At 6 am, I'd had enough. This wasn't the night I was expecting. I was exhausted and disappointed. What should have been the highlight of my holiday never even happened. I knew tonight was my only chance to experience this open-air nightclub; we were going back home the day after tomorrow.

When I arrived back at the room, he still wasn't there. But five minutes later, he walked through the door and punched me in the face. "Where the fuck were you tonight? I have been waiting in the club all night for you. I thought we were going to meet up there?"

"I am so sorry; I was waiting at the end of the bar as you said, I only just got back myself. I was waiting for you! How did we miss each other?"

"Well we did, I had a shit night, thanks to you," and he stormed off to bed.

The following day I felt awful. I blamed myself for him having a shit night. I tried to make it up to him, but he wasn't having any of it, he just slept by the pool all day. So I carried on reading my book, hoping he would forgive me so we could have one last big night before we went home. It wasn't the night I was hoping for.

About 2 am my brother mentioned he was going home to grab some more money and told me to wait at a bar along the main strip. I was enjoying a JD and coke; I had moved on from Baileys. I was just watching the world go by when a group of lads walked up to me and asked if my name was Cornelius.

"Yes, yes, I am Cornelius, is there something wrong with my brother?" In a split second, someone punched me in the face, knocking me straight off my chair. What the fuck, all I said was my name is Cornelius? I sat at the bar with a towel, trying to stop the bleeding. My nose was broken again.

My brother came over to me and asked what the fuck had happened. I told him what happened and he couldn't believe it. We then headed home. I wasn't in the party mood anymore.

During my first stag weekend away in Blackpool, my brother was trying to be funny in front of his mates and drunkenly told the real story of what happened that night.

In short, the story goes like this: My brother never went to Halikarnas that night. He went to the beach to fuck the woman he had been chatting up in the bar, while I went home to get changed and waited in the night club for him. The guy who punched me in the face was her boyfriend. My brother had told the woman that his name was Cornelius. He also didn't go back to our room to get more money. He went to eat a kebab and hid behind a palm tree a hundred meters away from where I got punched. He watched the whole thing unfold.

He was laughing when he told this story to his mates, who were also pissing themselves laughing.

He'd seen the same woman and six guys walking in and out of the bars looking for him, so he fucked off and left me to take whatever was coming my way, without me even warning me. I also realised that my brother punched me in the room to cover up for his lies and make it believable that he was in Halikarnas. I was led to believe all this time that it was my fault and that I had ruined his holiday.

***

After I decided to walk away from the models, I didn't have any friends to go into town with anymore. Over the next four months, I stayed in with my Mum and sister, playing PlayStation. It had been ages since I hung out with them and I forgot how much fun my sister was. She was so funny, competitive, caring, and she loved me as much as I loved her.

My sister was excited to know what I was going to do for my birthday in two days' time. I loved celebrating my birthday; it was the day I was born, say no more, and that was worth celebrating. But for every year I celebrated, it also brought me closer to the age of forty-five years old.

Forty-five years old was the age I believed I was going to die. Every year since I was eleven years old, I would have a very similar death dream, which always contained the number 45. In my death dream, I was held in someone's arms. I could hear them cry, but I could never see their face. It was like I was the person holding myself in my arms, telling myself that I was sorry.

Anyway, it was just a dream, and I had twenty-one years of celebrating before that day.

I knew my brother would come crashing through the front door.

I could hear his motorbike from halfway up the street; he had bought himself a stunning Honda VRF 400.

"Cornelius, you fancy watching the latest Roy Chubby Brown video with me at Martin's place?" Martin was one of my brother's best friends; his girlfriend was working the night shift tonight.

I have never been a fan of motorbikes; they look so hard to ride. I think this was my brother's third bike in as many years; he loved his superbikes. I was shattered and happy to stay in and play Cool Boarders, but he kept pushing me to go. Reluctantly, I agreed.

I never had any proper biker clothes, so I wore what I was already wearing, a blue T-shirt, tracksuit bottoms, and his spare helmet. We weren't going too far, luckily. Still, I wished I wore my jacket, as it was freezing out and my arms were blue. My brother had a set of full leathers on.

I should have stayed in. The video wasn't funny, just more vulgar than his last video. Not surprising, after all it was Roy Chubby Brown.

Finally, at 11:50 at night, we were heading back home. There was hardly any traffic on the road. Travelling down a long straight road at a speed of 35mph, I could sense the motorbike speeding up. Strange! My brother never went over the speed limit. Still, I was convinced we were going faster than normal. So much so, I started to hold on to the back of my brother a little tighter.

We were definitely going faster than the speed limit. I looked over my brother's shoulder, and we were travelling at 70mph. I began tapping his back and motioning with my right hand, indicating to slow down. Out of nowhere, the bike jumped up to a speed of over 100mph within seconds, and we were fast approaching a corner in the road. There was no way we could make that turn at this speed; we were heading straight towards a wall.

Then his head dropped down between the handlebars, his hand still gripped on the accelerator, and we were now at 120mph.

The bike started to stray into the oncoming road, wobbling from side to side. The bike was about to buckle and flip over. As we approached the corner, two cars quickly swerved out of our way. I felt the air of one car brush past my left knee, missing it by millimetres.

The bike lost full control and the front wheel hit the curb side on. I was thrown ten meters into the air and over my brother's back. My right shoulder, back, and helmet took the full impact against the wall, before I landed and hit the road, hard.

With the velocity of me flipping and tumbling down the road, at times I felt I was airborne, hitting the road hard on impact over and over again before finally sliding to a complete halt, lying face down in the middle of the road.

I could only manage to turn my head a few centimetres to the right, just enough to see my brother lying next to the curb about forty meters up the road. He wasn't moving. I was in so much pain, with no idea how many bones I had broken or how badly I was injured. Out of the corner of my eye, I could see sparks coming from the motorbike as it slid towards me at speed, before hitting the curb and landing on my back.

I wasn't sure how long I had been lying in the middle of the road before being rushed to the hospital. I didn't remember anything after I blacked out. I could only just make out some random voices in the background. I was in and out of consciousness and in vast amounts of pain, but then I felt a warm trickling sensation travel up and along my arm, heading down towards my legs. This warming sensation stopped at my waist. All of my pain was instantly gone.

Within a few seconds, I was wide awake. Unable to breathe, I gripped the side of the bed tight and started to shake it uncontrollably. My lungs and heart felt like they were going to burst into flames. I was rocking the bed more than ever, I wanted to scream but nothing came out; it felt as if I was burning and on fire from the inside out.

The next minute, I was floating roughly nine feet above the ground, looking directly down at myself. *How am I looking at myself? What's happening? This makes no sense. Why am I not moving?* I wasn't even in the same room as before; this room had curtains. *What's going on? Where am I?*

I was observing doctors and nurses frantically rushing around me as I laid on the table. They had no idea what had happened to me or what to do. I watched them performing CPR on me. They were desperately trying to revive me back to life. During this experience, I had no fear or pain, I felt calm and at peace with myself. I only had sadness in my heart. Sadness for my family, knowing I was dead.

I then started to drift towards where my brother was. A couple of rooms down from where I lay. I had no idea how I knew he was there, but I did.

I was so relieved to know that he was alive. I had this overwhelming amount of love for him. I was glad my mum and sister didn't have to say goodbye to us both tonight, that would have been devastating.

While I was observing my brother one final time, I heard a conversation to my right-hand side between a doctor and nurse while they were looking for medical supplies. I also knew that they were still trying to revive me. They hadn't given up on me just yet, which was comforting.

But I was happy where I was. I didn't want to leave, as strange as that sounds. I was so at peace observing the world from this detached, neutral perspective.

The doctor turned to this young woman and asked, "How are the wedding plans going? Are you still on track for Saturday? And what day are you flying out to Zante?"

"I am so stressed, I have so much to do, the wedding cake might not be ready in time, and I have no plan B either. For some reason, I didn't expect it to be this stressful. Zante couldn't come any quicker. Thank god we're flying out the following day," and she started to laugh.

I woke up to a massive gulp of air, eyes wide open, so many faces looking at me, before I passed out again.

When I hear people talk about their near-death experiences, about going towards a white light, saying that you see your life flash right in front of you, I always thought they were so full of shit.

I did see a white tunnel-like light, and I did feel like I was floating further away from my physical body, but I never saw my life flash past me. But then again, I had no idea what the fuck was happening at the time, only what I have described here.

When I eventually came around a few days later, in the early hours of the morning, the first thing I noticed was how dark it was. At the end of the ward, I saw a single downlight shining onto a wall clock that read 3:48. Someone was sitting below the clock at a desk; I had no idea what they were doing.

I looked to my right and left. I was in a row of six beds, all empty. Directly opposite me were another six beds, which were empty too. I was hooked up to four drips and a shit load of monitors.

Was I dreaming? I needed to get home, I knew Mum would be worrying. So I pulled out all the drips, and what seemed to be in slow motion, I watched my blood spill out on these pristine white sheets. I heard a loud constant beeping noise above my head and passed out again.

I woke up again a few days later, in my own room. I was still attached to a shit load of monitors and drips. I was in and out of consciousness for about a week. The only people who came to visit me in four weeks were my mum and sister. Mum mentioned that my brother had a severe concussion after hitting his head on the fuel tank, before falling off the bike. But he left the hospital the following day, only to be readmitted a day later for observational checks. He had no recollection of what happened that night; I was the only one who knew how we crashed. My brother didn't even know he had a brother. It took him a lot of convincing to finally come and visit me four weeks later. Mum explained that I'd had an allergic reaction to Codeine Sulphate, which caused me to have an anaphylactic shock. I was brought back to life with direct adrenalin shot into my heart.

My entire body blistered with pockets of water under my skin, like I was severely sunburnt. The most confusing thing about that whole night was I had no cuts, bruises, or grazes, and all my blisters vanished. I didn't break one bone. It was almost like someone had wrapped me up in bubble wrap during the entire crash. Even my clothes were all intact, not one rip or tear. But I still couldn't feel my legs.

I asked one of the nurses who was looking after me, "Can you please find out if the wedding cake arrived on time?" She looked at me with a blank expression. She had no idea what I was talking about, so I mentioned the night of my crash. "I heard a nurse stressing about her wedding cake; she was worried it wouldn't be ready in time."

I described what the nurse looked like, and she still looked puzzled.

"You seem to be describing Michelle. I can try to find her for you. I believe she's on duty, and you can ask her your question."

Twenty minutes later, Michelle came to visit me; she was exactly how I described her. I asked about her wedding cake and her holiday to Zante. I explained my strange experience, even the full conversation.

"That's impossible, you know that, right? There is no way you could know about my cake. I wasn't in the same room as you, I was looking after your brother that night. But somehow you do? Yes, my cake arrived one hour before the reception party, thank you, and Zante was beautiful." She looked stunned and utterly confused, constantly shaking her head as she left my room.

I lost count of the number of tests I had on my legs, to see if I had any feelings or not. All unsuccessful.

I knew my life would never be the same again the moment I saw my mum break down outside my room window, when the surgeons and doctors pulled her to one side and gave her the news that I was paralyzed from the waist down. The bottom of my spine was fucked, precisely where my brother's motorbike landed on me while I was lying face down in the road.

I hardly ate or spoke to anyone for the next three weeks. I constantly cried, unable to get my head around the fact that I was never going to walk again. The anger I was feeling towards my brother was something else. I blamed him for me being in this state. I was never going to meet anyone now, who would want to date someone like me? I already felt ashamed and embarrassed. My sheets were a right mess. I was unable to pee in a disposable bottle or use a bedpan, and the nurses had to clean me up afterwards. I was a useless waste of space.

***

I was so fucking fed up of feeling like I was a burden to everyone. I decided right there and then that my life was not going to be dictated by negativity, a wheelchair, and years of physiotherapy and constant care. Over the next few weeks I changed my entire thought process.

Rather than being negative and feeling sorry for myself, I started to think more positively, that this was just a setback, not the result. I started to imagine my future as if the crash had never happened, all the things I was going to achieve, the adventures I was going to have, the girls I was going to meet.

I felt so much more positive and happier than ever since the night of the crash.

Then one morning, everything changed. I fancied this young blonde nurse who I got to know very well while she was caring for me. Even in my positive state of mind, I still felt embarrassed when she had to change my bedpan and when my sheets needed changing after I urinated on them.

I sat up, pulled the bedsheets to one side, slid my legs over the bed, placed both feet on the ground, and stood up without any assistance.

I was standing.

I had no idea how, but I was.

It took me over an hour to walk to the toilet across the ward, slowly sliding one foot in front of the other. The nurses looked in amazement; it was through pure will power and belief that I could stand and walk when I was led to believe that I couldn't. Yes, I was fucking exhausted, and yes, I was in pain, but I was walking.

The doctors and specialists had no answers about why I was able to walk. Their rationale was that my spine must have been so swollen that it placed a tremendous amount of pressure on my spinal cord. Their only explanation was that the swelling went down and I got the feeling back in my legs.

This wasn't the case; all I did was change my mindset and outcome. As strange as that sounds, that's all I did.

The next three months I had intensive physiotherapy, and I even returned to work.

One morning, sitting on a bus on my way to work, I thought to myself, *Fuck me, I should be dead, yet I'm not.* I started to daydream about playing in a proper football team like my brother, even going to university and eventually leaving my hometown. I wanted to travel and see the world, do stuff that I never thought would be possible before the crash.

For some strange reason, I was given a fourth chance at life.

Then I kept talking myself out of it. *I can't play football; I am nowhere near good enough to play.* My brother was the footballer in the family, and bloody hell he was an outstandingly fast centre forward who could score and create goals at will. I hadn't played football since I left high school. I wasn't even good enough back then. My teacher used to pay me fifty pence a goal. All I did was goal hang and collect my winnings.

I also thought about attending university, but with no savings or portfolio, and with no idea what I wanted to study, that idea was quickly dismissed.

But I could go back to college and complete a one-year foundation course in art and design and build up my portfolio. That was the most logical idea; it would also give me a chance to save.

Most of the part-time employees who I worked and got on well with were also leaving for University. These guys made my job worth going in for. I couldn't imagine them not being there.

Walking to work, I was still daydreaming, but my constant negative chatter was now overriding my happy thoughts and starting to affect my mood. The closer I got to work, the more negative and depressed I became. I couldn't see a way out, and the moment I heard my old boss Chucky was coming back to manage the store, I wanted to resign instantly. Chucky made my life not worth living with his constant bullying and threats of sacking.

I was starting to have that sick, worrying, anxious feeling of dread in the pit of my stomach, which made me throw up. If I only had the bollocks and some paper, I would hand in my notice that morning.

But this was what I said to myself every day.

Two-hundred meters away from work, I threw up against the wall of the Duck and Pig Pub.

The dread of Chucky coming back to manage the store was too much for me and I threw up again. I also knew Chucky was coming in today to do the hand over with John. I noticed a brown McDonald's paper bag, tumbling along the footpath, twenty meters up from where I was standing. The wind from the passing cars was pushing it closer towards me. It didn't once deviate from the course of its path, no matter how many cars or trucks drove past it; it stuck to the side of the wall like glue. Ronald McDonald was now staring up at me from my feet, as the bag came to a grinding halt.

5

IT CAN ONLY HAPPEN TO ME

I didn't expect a sign from the universe to come in the form of a brown paper bag with a clown-face printed on the front. I have never been a fan of clowns; was this the universe having a laugh at my expense? I ripped open the bag, sat on the wall next to where I worked, and at 8.35 am I wrote out my notice. It was very brief and to the point.

Dear John,

Thank you for giving me the opportunity to work at your store for all these years. I have decided to leave the company so I can enroll in university. Please accept my notice of resignation with immediate effect.

Thank you.
Cornelius

John was terrific, and he didn't once try to change my mind. He understood that I was given the gift of life again. I left my job that morning, walked back home, and told my mum what I had done. I never saw John again.

Mum, on the other hand, was shocked at what I did. She wasn't happy, her main concern was that even if I did hold a degree, I was still not guaranteed a job at the end of the day. Plus, she pointed out that I would have massive amounts of student loans to pay back.

I understood where she was coming from and her concerns, but my mind was made up. If I'd asked for her advice beforehand, I would have never resigned in the first place. I had no savings or money to support me, but for some reason, I had to go to university.

I had no idea how this was all going to work out, and the first semester started in less than three months. Firstly, I had to find something I was interested in, followed by finding a university. Then I needed financial support and lastly, accommodation. Oh yes, I forgot I also needed a quality art portfolio. I was determined to change the course of my life; after all, I was lucky even to be alive.

The first month flew by. I was struggling to find anything that I wanted to study; it was more stressful than I had first thought.

My brother was a little hungover from the night before and running late for his football game. He asked me if I would take his dog Bettie out for a walk. She was a beautiful, loving, brindle Staffordshire bull terrier.

I loved hanging out with her, and it was also an excellent way to clear my mind about me not having a job or degree course with only two months to go; my stress was at an all-time high.

I was lost in thought and on autopilot. Somehow I ended up at my local park, a route I had never taken before. I noticed someone had left a football at the entrance to the park, so I started to kick it around, followed by running straight after it, trying to beat Bettie in a foot race. Which I never won.

It was an excellent way to test out my back and legs after the accident. I felt as if I was the Six Million Dollar Man, one of my favourite TV shows from the '70s. I pretended to be Steve Austin, even making all the sound effects. I loved that show so much, Mum bought me a similar coloured baby blue suit that I wore virtually every day when I was about seven or eight.

I did this for about an hour non-stop, back and forth across the park, until I heard someone shout at me, "Hey fella, is that one of our balls? Does it have The Pheasant written on it?" Which it did, so I walked up towards this guy and handed him back his ball. I asked if his team won this morning, and his reply was, "No, we're shit, but we are always looking for new players, if you're keen?"

"No, I just like running fast, I'm not good enough to play for a football team. I was the one who was picked last at school or they'd even go a player down so they could have rush goalie, that's me." I cracked up laughing.

"That's ok. We are always looking for fast wingers. Most of our players are injured and we're struggling to field a team at times. But if you change your mind, you should come along next week. We meet here around 10 am, no pressure either way."

I walked back home, thinking *Did I just get asked to play for a football side based on me running after a ball with Bettie? That's mad.*

The following week, I decided to take up the guy's offer, and I played the full ninety minutes. I am not sure that would have been the case if they had any substitutes. We lost 3-2. I even knew a few of the players from school; they were a few years older than me, but I knew them all the same. I decided after the game to go back to Pheasant with the rest of the players, the pub they played for, located five minutes from our town centre, for a chip sandwich or two. I was surprised by how much I enjoyed the day.

John the manager and Mick the guy I'd chatted with the week before came up to me while I was eating another chip sandwich to see if I was keen to sign up for the club this coming winter season, starting in two months. "I would love to, but I'm off to University in a few months. Thanks for asking though, and if things don't quite work out for me then yeah, I would be keen to play. I am happy to play for you guys until the end of the season, if needed?"

For the next three weeks, I played as a left-winger for the Pheasant Football Club. I even went out with some of the players on Saturday nights. Damn, if only my town had a university, this would be perfect.

It's funny how things seem to just work out. One of those Saturday nights, and with a month to go before the first semester started, I was drinking with some of the football players in a pub called The Rose. That's where I bumped into Henry, an ex-employee who had also left to go to university.

I liked Henry; he was hilarious and fashion-conscious. The one thing I noticed when I first met Henry was his stunning Diesel watch. I always thought to myself, *One day, I will have a watch like his.* I also loved watches, but these watches seemed to be an extension of his persona or personality. I always noticed how much attention he got when he wore his watches. Plus, they looked so frigging cool. Henry asked if I had found a course or university yet. I replied with a big fat "No."

"You should check out Manchester University. That's where my friends and I are going." That night, he introduced me to his friends; they all seemed relaxed, funny, and down to earth. One of his friends said that they knew someone who had a spare room they were keen to rent out. Five minutes away from their house in a place called Headingly, just outside of the city centre, and walking distance to all the universities. Plus, it was only a couple of hours away from home.

I did consider that university; I even had an interview for a teaching degree, but I never got accepted. Henry asked if I had looked at any courses at Manchester Metropolitan University as they had more creative courses, and he knew I was keen on art. I'd had no idea there was another university!

The following morning, I woke up super excited to look at the course prospectus before getting picked up for a game of football. I noticed that Manchester Metropolitan University was offering a degree in architecture. My dream job, but my teachers had always told me that I was kidding myself and that only smart people become architects. I still phoned up the university regardless, and what do you know, I had an interview that same week.

I caught a direct coach from Town to Manchester; it only took me one and a half hours. But the university was massive, so many buildings spread all over the city. My interview was at 1 pm on level four, but I had no idea which building, and I was so self-conscious about asking people for directions. By the time I found the correct building, I was running late. I wanted to make sure I had enough time to compose myself. I needed at least twenty minutes to try to calm down my anxiety and nerves; they were getting the better of me at this stage.

I managed to find out where my interview was going to take place a few minutes before 1 pm. I was sitting down, trying to keep calm, while at the same time looking through my portfolio and replaying what I was going to say if they ask me why I wanted to study architecture. My mind was all over the place then I heard, "Are you here for your 1 pm interview with Colin?"

"Yes, I think so. I brought along my portfolio as requested." The moment I stood up, all of my artwork fell out onto the floor. I forgot to re-zip my portfolio case; I frantically gathered it all up and rearranged it back into the correct order, moments before Colin interviewed me.

I thought the interview was going well; Colin repeatedly commented on how good my hand-drawn sketches were, which was very reassuring to hear. He seemed to be impressed with what I had done and my positive attitude. But then he asked me a strange question, which threw me totally off guard. "Cornelius, why do you want to be a landscape architect? How can you improve the quality of people's lives based on your own experiences?"

I was thinking in my head, *What the fuck do gardens have to do with architecture? Do we have to design courtyards or roof gardens or something?*

This made no sense, so I asked Colin again to repeat the question, just in case I had misheard him. It was exactly the same question in the same tone. Was I missing something? Was this what the course was all about, having a different perspective on how we saw buildings function? I liked that, and from all of my research, Manchester University was renowned for its creative courses and they encouraged thinking outside the box.

"Well, if I was working in an office environment and there was no park or courtyard nearby, I couldn't imagine eating my lunch five days a week at my desk, staring in front of my computer. I believe this could have an adverse effect on your productivity and also the energy within your office. I think it's essential to eat your lunch away from your desk and in the sunshine. It could be either in a courtyard, a small intimate space, or a large park across the road. This would have a positive effect on your state of being in the office."

I had no idea what I was saying, I was completely winging it, but it felt like it was an honest answer. In my previously workplace environments, I had always eaten my lunch inside, never outside, even on sunny days. All I had was a carpark or the area where people smoked.

"You're exactly the type of person we are looking for in this course, someone who cares about the environment and how people interact with it. I will see you in a month, and I will get our course administration to send you all the necessary paperwork in the coming weeks."

I stood up, shook Colin's hand, and left his office. *What the hell just happened?* I couldn't believe it! I had just gotten into University. *What the fuck, what just happened?* I couldn't contain my excitement and happiness. *I am going to be an architect!* I wanted to phone up my teachers, who told me

I couldn't. I wanted to tell those negative fuckers, "You all talk bollocks, and you're not fit to teach."

Ok, maybe I was getting ahead of myself. I needed to pass my degree first, but still, I had a place, and that was all I needed.

I phoned Henry's mate first to share the good news. Luckily, the room was still available.

I then phoned Mum up. She was so happy for me, but I could tell in her tone of voice that I had a long way to go before everything would work out. This was a demanding profession with long, long hours and was open to criticism. My one major concern was that I didn't have the best confidence speaking in front of people. I was taunted through school regarding my speech impediment and stutter. The only way to overcome this issue was to talk very fast, to get it over and done with.

My brother drove me to Manchester a week before my architecture course started. I had never lived away from home before, and this alone was a new challenge, but at least I knew few people already. David, one of Henry's friends, was kind enough to offer to drive me back home every weekend. He had a girlfriend and he wasn't keen on the student nightlife during the weekends.

Who would have thought it? *Three months ago, I wrote my notice on a McDonald's paper bag, and now I am enrolled in an architecture course, playing football for The Pheasant, and I can still enjoy the nightlife in my home town. Not to mention being at home.* This was my dream outcome.

This dream outcome lasted no more than a week. This was no dream; I was in a nightmare. I had enrolled in a different course completely.

Instead of studying Architecture, I had enrolled in a course called Landscape Architecture, planning through plants, trees, feelings, and emotions rather than engineering, structures, and buildings.

I was so caught up in the moment and fantasising about what student life would look like, I didn't even read the course syllabus and what my first semester covered. All I kept seeing was the word Architecture; I was unable to see the word Landscape, for some reason. I had so much on my mind, it just didn't register.

I was so confident and cocksure that I was studying architecture, why would I doubt it?

What the hell was I going to do now? I told everyone I was studying architecture; I'd fucked up royally. My course fees and accommodation were all paid in advance, so I tried to re-enroll in the correct Architecture course. I even went to meet the head of Architecture for an interview.

Unfortunately, I didn't have a good enough portfolio or a 3D model for him to have enough confidence in me switching courses. I had no other option but to carry on with Landscape Architecture.

My main focus was to get my degree, get a job, and leave. I knew I had no chance of finding a job back home and I didn't want to get trapped in student life, either.

I was labelled a mature student. Even at twenty-four years old, I had zero experience in horticulture. I couldn't even grow cress in a wet paper towel. The last plant I had died, and that was a cactus, which didn't even need watering. The majority of the people in my course had already taken a two-year diploma in horticulture beforehand and they all seemed to know one another, very cliquey. I wasn't expecting that.

I didn't even fit in with the other eight mature students. They all seemed to be relative to the Addams Family. Trying to fit in and find my group was harder than I thought. I only liked a few people in my course. This was going to be a long three years.

I didn't find the course hard, just dull. I had no interest in plants, trees, or any environmental changes.

That first year I had my ups and downs. I slept with one of my housemates and copied parts of her work; she was in the year above me in the same course. She had no idea I did this until she looked through my end of year work. So B, if you're reading this, I am very sorry; it always bothered me that I did that twenty-one years ago, I hope you can forgive me?

I had no enthusiasm for my degree, especially when it came to plants and trees. Every month we had to take a plant ID test. This is where you have to identify individual branches, buds, leaves, and flowers, not to mention correctly spell all thirty plants in English and fucking Latin. Seriously, who uses Latin in today's world?

My spelling was so bad. I had no other option but to copy from her book that she kindly lent me. I had no idea why I was so bad at spelling. I studied all the time, but for some reason, I always had the lowest marks. B didn't deserve that; again, I am very sorry. But on the plus side, wow,

wow, wow, could she kiss. Unbelievable! I still remember that first kiss in the back of the taxi after a Wednesday night out.

One evening, my brother and I went to watch *Starship Troopers* at the cinema. Firstly, it's a cracking film. Secondly, in one scene the two leading stars were getting jiggy jiggy in their tent. The night before the big invasion, they started to kiss before having sex. The only advice my brother ever gave me was based on this film: "If you find a girl who kisses you like that, marry her." That scene will always remind me of her; she set the benchmark. B is in my top three all-time kisses.

I don't have many good university stories, but this is one that always makes me laugh. One night, our house decided to go clubbing and bond after finishing our exams. That night, we ended up at the student bar, which I detested. They didn't play the clubbing music that I liked; they played shitty student music, and at the end of every single night, they played the same three songs in the same frigging order. I called these songs the 'ten to two-er' songs; these songs gave you a ten-minute warning before the lights went on and the bar closed, in order to try and pick someone up before the night finished and you had a cold walk home alone. To this day, I can't bear to listen to these songs.

"Come On, Eileen" by Dexys Midnight Runners
"I Will Walk 500 Miles" by The Proclaimers
"New York, New York" by Frank Sinatra

I was enjoying the night until they played those songs and then I was gone burger, off to get a doner kebab pizza. I still crave Tariq's pizzas; they were the best fluffy, freshly-cooked dough bases, fantastic spicy tomato sauce, grilled onions, jalapeno peppers, and shaved lamb doner kebab, old-school style from a rotating spit. It was only two pounds fifty for an extra-large. I was in heaven.

I was just about to leave when I noticed one of my housemates motioning for me to come towards him. He was talking to this stunning tall blonde. I knew straight away what he wanted. He introduced me to the blonde girl's friend.

I mentioned earlier that I hate clowns; well, her makeup would have scared Pennywise back down the drain. It was just too much. I couldn't get past it.

Andy whispered in my ear, "Can you entertain her back at ours while

I get it on with this bird?" I wouldn't usually say yes, but he pulled out a "you owe me" from a few months ago, so I couldn't say no, could I? We all went back home and those two shot straight upstairs to his room. I was downstairs with Krusty the Clown, making us both a cup of tea. There was no small talk, just awkward silence. She was continually looking at her watch, hoping those two were nearly finished getting jiggy.

At 3:30 am, there was still no sign of them, so she went upstairs, knocked, and opened his bedroom door, only to discover he was getting a blow job under the duvet. She came back downstairs with this sad clown face. I fetched her a few blankets and a pillow, and I went to bed.

Have you ever had the feeling that someone is watching you while you sleep? That night, I did. Standing at the foot of my bed and staring at me was the blonde girl's friend. A cross between *The Blair Witch Project*, Ronald Macdonald, and the girl from *The Ring*.

Fuck me, did I scream! It was like a dog whistle crossed with one of the girls from the *Clueless* movie. It was so high pitched, like *really high* pitched. I thought I was Spiderman at one point, trying to fucking climb the walls backwards and upwards and along the ceiling. She just stood there at the bottom of my bed with a sliver of light coming in from the landing and through the crack of the door frame, perfectly illuminating a small part of her face. It was my worst nightmare come true.

"What the fuck are you doing? I thought you were asleep on the sofa!"

"You want to fuck? I am so horny, and I have nothing else to do, and your sofa is so uncomfortable."

Before I could even reply and get my breath back, she was already naked and crawling along my bed like the girl from *The Exorcist*.

"No, I'm good thanks, and you're pretty pissed, so I'm not sure if that's a good idea. Let me grab you one of my T-shirts, and you can sleep in my bed if you like?" Once I had calmed down, switched my light on, and given her one of my T-shirts, I said, "Look, I have no issues with you staying in my bed, but that's all. Nothing else is going to happen, so let's call it a night, ok?"

I woke up late the following morning. I could feel that she had already left. I was a little relieved about not having another awkward conversation. I turned around, and for the second time in less than six hours, I screamed like a girl again. Andy ran into my room after hearing my scream this time around; he must have been busy still last night. She'd left her entire face imprinted into my pillowcase. Something that resembled a fucked-up panda clown with false eyelashes and red lipstick.

***

My first summer holidays were nothing special. I was just happy that I managed to land a three-month summer job working in a slaughterhouse. I hated this job with a passion; it was 4 am - 2 pm.

I worked with some right nob heads. They just made my job harder than it needed to be. They thought they were being funny, but at the end of the day, they were just bullies.

The job was so labour-intensive. I stood at the end of a twenty-man double-sided conveyor belt, collecting buckets of perfectly cut joints of pork. Each bucket should have weighed about 20kgs. But they kept overfilling them to a capacity of about 40kgs, and I only weighed 55kgs.

They enjoyed watching me struggle, carrying these buckets from one side of the factory to the other. And when I had to walk past them, they tried to kick my legs, seeing if I would fall down under the weight of these buckets. Then I had to run back before the other filled bucket fell off the conveyor belt and onto the floor. Even though they could see I was struggling, not one person helped me.

I got moved around a lot during my first month due to my size and weight. Still, each area had its fair share of nob heads making my life that little bit more complicated than it had to be.

Why can't we just get on with our job and leave it like that? Why do we have to make it so much harder for everyone else? I don't understand that mentality; you're consciously aware that's what you're doing, but you still do it regardless, just to fit in or not.

I only lasted two months.

I received a sign that I should quit. I was working at the top end of the conveyor belt where I had to lift individual 40kg pig legs out of a cardboard box to the height of my chest and carefully place them on top of the pork de-rinder machine. This machine stripped away all of the pork rind from the legs before it was sent down the conveyor belt in order to make the butcher's job easier.

This was the most dangerous job in the factory; these people had to wear chain mail gloves while de-rinding and they were also attached to a dead-stop switch for safety reasons. I was feeding both sides of the conveyor belt. I complained that my back was about to give way and that I needed a break, because I had been doing this non-stop for four hours. The floor manager laughed in my face and pushed me over into the box.

Everyone started to laugh. I managed to get myself back out the box, only for the de-rinder person to unplug himself from the machine and push me back in again. My legs were now flapping out of the box, and my head was covered in blood. Similar to *Carrie*.

"Stop fucking about and go get yourself a clean smock and get back here ASAP."

I was thinking about quitting there and then, but I needed this job. Jobs in town were so hard to come by. I started walking towards the other side of the factory to grab a clean smock, when I heard the most piercing scream I had ever heard. Everyone stopped what they were doing and ran towards the top end of the conveyor belt.

The guy who had pushed me into the box was screaming in agony.

Through all his pissing around and showing off, he had forgotten to clip himself back to the machine, and for some reason, his hands and chainmail were caught in the revolving blades. All his fingers were virtually stripped back to the bone. It was frigging gross.

He was in agony. His screams are what got me the most; it took paramedics over an hour to pull what was left of his hands and chainmail out from the machine. If there was ever a sign to quit this job, that was it. I walked home and never returned.

Somehow the following day, I landed a one-month contract working in the archives of the British Coal for their Subsidy Claims Department, alongside two women. Compared with the slaughterhouse, this was heaven. My job was to sit and wait for a claim to come in, then retrieve a box file from storage and hand it over for one of the women to process the application. It was a shame that it was only for one month. This was my second favourite job of all time.

I was still single and lonely. I had met and dated a lot of girls since Mia, but I could never commit to anyone. I had this awful feeling I was going to get hurt again. So I preferred to have one night stands; at least we both knew what we were doing, and no one got hurt.

Deep down though, I desperately wanted a girlfriend, but because I was unable to commit to anyone. My family were now starting to think that I was gay. It was *gay this* and *gay that*, was I gay? My family knew me the best, but I wasn't attracted to men, was I? Something wasn't right.

During a night out with the Pheasant crew, we all ended up at the Studio 54, my favourite night club. All they played was club classic, the bangers. We didn't give a shit about how we looked, we all just loved dancing. If I was honest with myself, I was always conscious about how I came across and how I looked. A girl walked over to me and handed me a piece of paper with a number on it.

"This is from my friend who is standing over there. She's very shy, but she asked me to give you her number and for you to call her tomorrow. Her name is Sally." Sally was super cute; I thought I had seen her around town before, but I was unable to locate exactly where.

The following day, I decided to call Sally from a red phone box up the road. We had a house phone, but Mum installed her own payphone instead of a standard phone. So by using a public phone, you got more minutes for your pence, plus it was private. When I spoke to Sally, she explained that she already had a boyfriend and she didn't want to cheat on him, it wasn't her style. She apologised for her friend giving me her number. Which I really appreciated.

***

My second year at university, I decided to move in with four guys from my course. Over the first year, we all got on really well; we started to become very good friends. It also made sense that we could help one another.

I was enjoying the start of my second year far more than the previous year. We started to be more creative and focus on problem-solving, sculpture, and narrative.

The energy in the house was good. Student nights were getting better and I finally felt like I was a student, whatever that feels like. I was still travelling back home on the weekends, playing football and going out into town with my brother. I was trying to rebuild our relationship, but it felt more situational than authentic from my brother's side. He was also single, and he needed someone to go into town with. We also had his mate Martin, who was now living with us. He was sleeping in my attic room since I wasn't home during the week, which pissed me off as I had no downtime before I went back to university on Monday.

He'd been booted out of his own home by his girlfriend for cheating on her. She walked in on him getting jiggy in the lounge with another woman. So the three amigos hit the town most weekends.

I was getting a bit bored of hitting the town, seeing the same people in the same bars and clubs. Still great fun nevertheless, but I wanted a girlfriend. I was still feeling lonely, and one-night stands were shit. They didn't give me what I craved or needed. In fact, I had no idea what was missing, but I felt internally lost, with an underlying unexplained sadness, unable to move forward.

During a weekend back home, I decided to buy some new clothes to cheer myself up; I was feeling a little depressed. Walking past a travel agent shop, I noticed the same girl whose friend gave me her number six months earlier, the one who had a boyfriend. I smiled at Sally, and she smiled back, as I carried on walking past the front window. Then I suddenly stopped outside Marks & Spencer and thought *fuck it*, so I turned around, walked through the front door, sat down opposite her and said "Hi."

It turned out to be the best decision I had ever made. She wasn't with her boyfriend anymore, and she was keen to have a date. Sally became my second girlfriend. I also realised where I knew her from; she worked directly opposite where I worked in the butcher's shop. Can you believe that?

6

NEVER GOOD ENOUGH

Life was finally starting to look up. At last, I had a girlfriend who I knew wouldn't cheat on me, and who trusted me while I was away studying. I was starting to enjoy my course, and my brother and I were hanging out more than usual. Not to mention, I loved playing football on the weekends. Life was good.

The only spanner in the works was Sally's family. They just didn't seem to open their arms to me or accept me into their family. Her parents constantly looked down at me, as if I wasn't good enough for their daughter.

Nearly every Sunday, I would spend my entire day with Sally, including having a roast dinner at her parents' house. One of the many reasons I never felt entirely accepted into her family's arms was because they never once asked me to eat dinner with them in the lounge. I had to eat in the kitchen with the dog.

I thought this was strange, but I didn't want to rock the boat because I was so in love with Sally, and I had no idea how I could approach this awkward subject. So I boxed it all up, even though it made me feel like shit. They made me think they always had someone better in mind for their daughter. Ostracizing me was their way of pushing me out and letting someone else come in. But I was determined to make this relationship work; I saw a happy marriage and children with her.

The second year at uni flew by so quickly, it was over before it even began. I was happy and in love, I felt loved, safe, and secure from having Sally in my life. Sally also treated me to some amazing holidays, courtesy of her work discount and commissions. I even got my old job back working at the British Coal Subsidy Claims Department, as they were impressed with my work ethic. They asked if I would like to work there again during my summer holidays and found me a new position in their team, data inputting subsidy claims.

My brother even invited me along to one of his mate's stag weekend do's in Blackpool. There were about twenty people in total. I had no idea what to expect, I had never been to Blackpool, but I was told that what happens in Blackpool, stays in Blackpool. The second I stepped off our minibus, I knew this weekend would be one I would never forget.

About thirty women, all wearing sexy nun outfits walked past me, five of them showing me their boobs.

Fuck me, I thought, *this weekend's going to be amazing and messy, that's for sure,* and it was only Friday morning. One of my brother's mates jumped on my back and said "Welcome to Blackpool, you haven't seen anything yet. Come on, let's get changed and get fucked. Fucking love Blackpool."

Friday night was a complete blur; I have absolutely no recollection of what took place, I didn't even know how I got home. All I remember is that I woke up at about 8 am with two blonde girls in my bed, along with one of my brother's mates. I shouted across to my brother's bed, hoping he could shed some light on how I ended up with three people in my bed.

But I got no answer from him, so I went over to his bed and pulled back his duvet. He was sound asleep, snuggling up to two nuns. That's something you don't see every day, I can tell you. *What the fuck happened last night?* My head was banging and I couldn't remember anything. Then our bedroom door burst wide open and four of his mates jumped on my back again and then started to bounce on my brother's bed to wake him up, all screaming "I fucking love Blackpool, come on let's get back out, its 8 am, we're going to miss the Lounge!"

I sat staring at my full English breakfast covered in bacon grease and fried bread, the room was spinning, and my eyes were sore from the sunlight streaming in through the windows. I looked around and everyone looked hammered. I was feeling so queasy and hungover, I couldn't even manage a slice of toast. I just needed a strong cuppa and four painkillers. If yesterday was anything to go by, I had no idea what today was going to be like. Apparently, it was going to be even better and would involve drinking games.

There was no chance in hell I could play drinking games, especially at 10 am. I was struggling to hold down my cuppa, but I had no frigging choice in the matter, none whatsoever. Whoever lost the first drinking game of the day had to sing in a gay karaoke bar, drink a pint of whatever they ordered in less than two minutes, and wear second-hand shop clothes all day, with no underwear. Fuck me, I lost.

I was in panic mode. I grabbed my brother and pulled him to one side. "There is no way I can do this, can you please explain to your mates that this is my worst nightmare. I don't want to perform in a gay bar with no underwear on."

"Cornelius, there are twenty of them, what do you think I can do? If you don't do this, they will strip you down naked, tie you to a lamppost, cover your dick in ketchup, and watch the seagulls peck at your dick from across the road, I am not kidding you."

"They wouldn't do that, I'm your brother! What about the cops, you can't have your dick out in public, I would get arrested. That's stupid, and my weekend would be over."

"Look at them Cornelius, do you think they give a shit if you get arrested or not, or if your dick drops off? No, it's Blackpool, what did you think was going to happen if you didn't do the forfeit?"

He wasn't kidding either, he was deadly serious; I was fucked. We all walked into a packed gay karaoke bar. I was wearing a floral mini skirt and a see-through white blouse with no underwear. I had to sing Michael Jackson's "Smooth Criminal" while drinking a pint of cement mixer, a combination of Baileys and lime juice, which made it curdle like cottage cheese or wet cement.

I had to down my cement mixer before "Smooth Criminal" had finished, or I had to perform another song with one item of clothes less (and I was only wearing two). I was already drunk and throwing up in the toilets, wearing nothing more than a mini skirt. Somehow I forced myself to down the curdled drink using my fingers as a spoon, just before I finished Salt-N-Pepa's "Push It".

I was in a world of pain and it was only 11 am.

I have no idea how I was allowed to walk into the Tower Lounge bar, located directly under Blackpool Tower. I somehow staggered in with just a mini skirt on. I mean, who lets you into a bar with just a mini skirt on and that's it? And to make things worse, the bar was empty; we seemed to be the first in.

One of my brother's mates suggested that we all order at least four pints before it got packed solid, otherwise it would take ages to be served. I ignored his warnings and staggered off to the bathroom so I could be sick again. But instead, I fell asleep on the toilet.

I was woken up by a woman banging on the side of the cubicle door. She desperately needed to pee. Before I could stand up, she was already sitting on my lap and peeing between my legs while chatting to her friend who stood in the doorway. I didn't say anything. I just sat there. I was so drunk.

I opened the bathroom door and the noise was deafening. *Bloody hell*, the bar was packed solid. I asked a guy dressed in a Spiderman costume what the time was. "1 pm," he replied. I had been asleep for just over an hour, and the bar was rammed. Well, my brother's mate did say it would get busy. I just didn't expect it to be this busy!

I was on the second level, looking over the railing and down towards the dance floor, trying to locate my brother and his mates. Eventually, I spotted my brother chatting to three women on the dance floor. They were dressed up as a sexy angel with wings, a red horny devil, and a care bear. Half the bar was wearing fancy dress costumes, and it was only 1 pm.

From 1 pm to 9 pm was just another blur. By the time we got to a night club, some random woman had lent me her underwear, stockings, and suspender belt to go with my miniskirt; and somehow I had a new white see-through blouse. I looked hot, but not out of place. I had no idea where everyone else was. I was still with my brother and a handful of his mates, so I assumed everyone else had gone back to the bed and breakfast.

I was dancing on a large speaker located on the dance floor with a few other people. I was in my little happy place, not a care in the world. I absolutely love dancing. That's when I noticed this person trying to look up my skirt and grab my attention. Apparently, she recognized me from a bar back in home.

I jumped off the speaker and started talking to her. She mentioned that she regularly saw me dancing in a bar called The Tunnel, which was a converted old train station building. It was the last bar to close in town. If you didn't fancy a night club this was the place to go and it only cost a pound to get in. The queues were massive, but the Hugo Boss models knew the bouncers so we always walked straight in, no matter what time it was.

"I love the way you dance by the way, and I love your style. I always point you out to my friends whenever I see you, but I never dared to say hello. I know I am pissed but hello, I'm Zoe. Do you fancy coming back to my hotel to fuck?" Zoe was very cute and attractive, but she smoked; her breath stank worse than a ten-day-old ashtray. I have never been attractive to anyone who smokes, and there was no way I was going to cheat on Sally. As Simon Cowell would say, "It's a no from me." I got back up on the speaker and carried on dancing.

I realised I hadn't seen my brother for quite some time and I wanted to go back to our room; I was still very pissed and shattered. All of a sudden, from out of nowhere, he jumped on my back. He was in super high spirits, it was nice to see him less tense and more relaxed. "I frigging love Blackpool, and when I get married, I'm having my stag do here, and you're going to be my best man. Anyway, you might not remember, but I was chatting to this girl in the Tower Lounge, and I think she's the one. In fact, I know she's the one."

"Sorry, what? She's the one? What one? Who's the one? You're not making any sense whatsoever."

"The chick in the Tower Lounge, I've just been with her for the last two hours and she's the one. I am so happy you haven't left yet! I wanted you to meet her, seeing I couldn't find you earlier in the Lounge. So wait here, don't fucking move, I'm going to get her."

I waited for about ten minutes, thinking to myself, *He's only gone and done a runner back to our room, so he can fuck before I get back. What an idiot I am, he's so full of shit. The one, yeah, right! No one meets their wife here, I mean look, everyone is cracking off with one another.* Sex was in the air; it was so pungent.

But for some reason, I still waited another ten minutes before deciding enough was enough. I had started to walk towards the exit when my brother grabbed my arm. "Sorry I couldn't find her earlier, but I'd like you to meet her."

You've got to be fucking kidding me, haven't you? Of all the people in Blackpool, my brother introduced me to Zoe, the same person who wanted to go back to my hotel room and fuck. *Come on, she's definitely not the one.*

"Zoe, I want you to meet my brother, Cornelius."

Hmm this is awkward, I thought. *What the hell do I say? I've never seen my brother this happy before, but this isn't the time or place to express my opinions.* So we both awkwardly smiled at one another and kissed each other the cheek before she went back to the bar.

"Isn't she stunning! Absolutely stunning, I am telling you bro, she's the one, I know it. I can feel it."

I couldn't believe he'd introduced me to Zoe as 'the one'. I couldn't get into this with my brother, he seemed besotted already. So I held it in and let this obsession just take its normal course. It wouldn't be long until he moved on and found someone else.

***

With less than two months to go before the start of our final year, we were given the option of which specific area of landscape architecture we wanted to study. We had three options to choose from: urban design, my preferred choice, followed by residential design, my second choice, and finally historic parks, my last choice.

Nobody wanted parks as their preferred choice. Everyone in the class knew which people were going to choose that subject. They were also the last people you would pick for your football team. These were the sort of people that never turned up to lectures, were never on time, and unable to collaborate with anyone.

I got fucking parks, but how? I was in the top five of my class; I was a hundred per cent convinced I was going to get my preferred option. So how the hell did I get parks along with the worst people in my course? Why did all my housemates get their first choice? This made no sense at all; I was livid. In fact, livid was an understatement.

I phoned and emailed the administration, asking for a logical explanation as to why I wasn't given my preferred option, when everyone else had gotten theirs. They never returned my calls or responded back.

I was stuck in parks, totally pissed off even before my final year started. While my housemates were enjoying lectures on urban design, I was in a class listening to why a group of trees was so instrumental to parks. In a class that hardly turned up, I swear it felt like I was getting mentored directly from Colin, the person who first interviewed me two years prior.

The only thing I enjoyed about my parks elective was Colin's perspective on why it was essential to protect our grade one and two listed parks.

To my surprise, over the course of the year, I found a new love for this profession, especially in regard to protecting our heritage parks.

Colin was also the first person who recognised that I had spoonerism and severe dyslexia. Colin had noticed I was missing out keywords and that some of my words where spelled entirely backwards in all of my written documentation.

Of course, I didn't believe him. It was impossible! I was twenty-six years old, and not one of my school teachers had picked up on this issue. Well, that's a lie, they just said I wasn't very good at spelling and I wasn't the brightest child in class, that sort of thing.

So when Colin mentioned my learning difficulties, I needed him to show me. He asked me to read out a sentence from my last essay. So I read out the following: "His minimalist style comprised of grass, water and statement trees and is recognisable the world over and that every tree is purposely planted to provide distinctive vistas." I was word perfect.

He then asked a fellow student to read the same paragraph; they struggled to make any sense of what I wrote. They read out: "His minimalist comprised of grass, water and trees the over world and that tree is purposely to provide view distinctive."

What the fuck! How is that possible? I re-read that sentence again; it read: "His minimalist style comprised of grass, water and statement trees and is recognisable the world over and that every tree is purposely planted to provide distinctive vistas."

I had no idea that this was how I read and wrote. I thought, *If this is how I write, how the hell am I going to get a job if the majority of protecting heritage landscape is comprised of written documentation?* My world came crashing down around me. *Now what?*

Colin's advice was to concentrate on design outcomes rather than written documentation. "Don't worry too much, you will be ok. Trust me, I saw something in you nearly three years ago, even though you came to the wrong interview."

"Sorry, I don't know what you mean by the wrong interview?"

"Yes, you came to the wrong interview. You were never meant to have an interview with me. You took someone else's slot, as they were running late. But I was taken aback by your answer. It's why I fought extremely hard with the other lecturers to have you in my parks group. And here we are, with a month to go before your final presentation. Everything will work out. I hope you don't mind, but I have also arranged for Leeds City Council to be at your presentation; they are very keen to hear about your ideas."

Leeds City Council were so impressed with my presentation that they bought my design concept for protecting the grounds of Temple Newsham while they hosted the V music festival, because Capability Brown designed the grounds which were grade II listed.

I now had a degree in Landscape Architecture, thanks to Colin's mentoring, and he was also instrumental in setting up my first job interview with one of the best landscape consultants in the U.K.

I was stressing out more than usual. It was the day of my interview, and it had been over sixteen years since I last visited London. Staying over wasn't an option, I wasn't even sure why I was going. Being honest, London was too big for me. So the idea of living there was ridiculous. I was humming and hawing about even going to the interview; I had no idea what I was doing.

Eventually, I bought the same day return coach ticket. I figured I owed it to Colin, he pulled a few favours to get me this interview.

By the time I bought my ticket, I had missed my original coach. Now I was running late, very late. The interview was scheduled for 3 pm, and the coach only arrived into Victoria Station at 2 pm, but it also left at 4 pm that same day to head back to home.

I arrived at my interview ten minutes late; not the best first impression. I apologised to the person interviewing me and mentioned that I only had forty minutes. I couldn't miss my coach.

It was a shocking interview. I babbled for over twenty minutes, talking about nothing to do with landscape. I didn't even give him a chance to speak; my nerves and anxiety just got the better of me. The only question I recall him asking was, "Where do you see yourself in ten years' time?"

"Sitting across the table like you are now, giving someone like me a chance." I stood up, shook his hand, and then left.

Two weeks after my interview was my graduation day and the following day, I was going on a two-week holiday with my housemates and two others from the same course. Sally had organised and booked a two-week holiday in Turkey as a surprise and a reward for me passing my degree; she also used her discount for everyone.

Sally even paid for everyone's holiday in advance so that we could all concentrate on our final presentation. All I had to do was collect the money off everyone and pay her back. It was like drawing blood from a stone; they came up with excuse after excuse, happy enough to go out and get pissed every night, but paying my girlfriend back was a different story.

It wasn't a lot either, not for these guys. One-hundred and twenty pounds each, for a four-star resort. It was also Duncan's twenty-first birthday during our holiday, so it was extra special for him. The holiday was exactly what everyone needed. We'd all had a full-on last few months, and this holiday was perfect. For Duncan's twenty-first, I organised a full day of fun, which included champagne, sea diving with unlimited drinks on board the boat, a three-course dinner out, and night club entrance for everyone. And of course, he didn't have to pay for one thing.

It was our treat, all they had to pay was nine pounds. Sally again used her discount to get us the best deals possible, and I really wanted Duncan to have a twenty-first he would never forget.

The entire day was amazing. We had so much fun and we were all in high spirits. Duncan was hammered; we did his twenty-first justice.

Just before we all headed off towards the night club, I asked the rest of the group if they could pay me their nine pounds so I could cover the cost of the dinner and entrance into the night club. Amazingly, everyone started to pay me without me nagging them.

When one of my friend's saw me put some money in my back pocket, they started to question what I was doing. I told them it was the change from my share of the evening and night club entrance.

They not only fucking accused me of stealing their one-pound change from them; now they wanted someone else to handle all the money.

"You got to be fucking kidding me. Are you guys for fucking real? Do you actually think I would rip you off over one pound? When Sally and I organised the whole holiday from start to finish, all you had to do was show up at the airport. Sally even paid everyone's holiday in advance, which was nearly a thousand pounds, and you think I am ripping you off for one pound. A fucking pound?" I angrily replied.

"We saw you put some money in your back pocket."

"Yeah, my own change," I snapped back. I had known these guys for over three years and lived with them for two of those years.

I knew instantly from that moment that I would never speak to any of them ever again. I was devastated and shocked. We went through an entire degree together and they were accusing me of ripping them off.

I was devastated, absolutely devastated, hurt, and betrayed by these people. I thought we were always going to be friends.

Duncan was the only person that night who defended me.

For the rest of the summer, I struggled to get my head around what took place on that holiday. I was so depressed. I also never heard back from the job interview. On top of this, Sally's family was isolating me more than ever. In two and half years, I only sat in their living room once; I had more in common with their dog than I did with them.

I'd set myself a goal of getting a degree in three years, which I achieved with honors, yet I still wasn't good enough to eat in the living room.

I had no positives going for me, so I asked the universe for help.

And three days later, the universe answered: I had the job, even though it was only a one-year work placement. I was over the moon. I wasn't their first or second choice, I was their last choice, but who cares, I had a job.

I was living in a four-story Victorian house, consisting of seven one-bed studios, located in Clapham North and only five minutes away from the Northern line. My new employers helped me find a place to live, which I thought was amazing, seeing as I had no idea what I was doing. I was very fortunate to be living in the attic, too. I only had to share my bathroom with one other person, compared with the rest of the people in the house.

It wasn't great, but it wasn't bad either. I had a separate living area and bedroom, and a beautiful self-contained kitchen. Sally had agreed to move to London once her office relocation came through. This did not go down well at all with her family, and they were constantly putting pressure on Sally to stay.

It was the morning of my first day, and I hadn't slept at all the night before. I was so nervous but also in high spirits, despite being tired. I was now working and living in London, and at the best consultancy in their respected field; this was the happiest I had been in a long time.

I also knew that I had to make the right impression from the start. I got told loud and clear, no matter what, do not be late or don't bother coming into work at all. I knew they were taking a big chance on me, especially with someone with severe dyslexia and after my awful interview.

I had to be in the office at 9 am, so I made sure to leave an hour and a half early.

I finished my black coffee, looked at myself in the hallway mirror, and smiled. Today was my first day of being a landscape architect. Against all the odds, I was finally here. I opened my apartment door, and I was instantly greeted by two naked people fighting on my stairway directly in front of me.

I quickly shut my door again and thought *What the fuck? Did I just see two naked people fighting on the main stairway?* I knew I was tired but really, and I started to laugh. I reopened my door again, thinking I must have imagined it, but I hadn't. There was a naked man and woman actually fighting on my stairs. *What the fuck is going on and how the hell do I get past them? I can't be late, not on my first day.* The man was shouting for me to help restrain her. "I caught her trying to steal my wallet."

But the woman was also asking for help. "He's trying to rape me, please, please help me, he's trying to rape me." I closed my front door again, rubbed my eyes, and reopened the door. *What the fuck do I do? Who do I help? This can't be happening, not on my first day. I can't be late.* My job was on the line from day one. That's all I kept thinking about as I watched them fight and struggle in front of me.

I tried to walk over them; I didn't want to get involved. Any other day, sure, but not today.

"Please mate, I just need you to help me restrain her while the police turn up, my girlfriend is downstairs waiting for them to arrive."

"He's fucking lying, please help me, his mate drugged me last night and I woke up as they tried to rape me, please, please help me."

I was conflicted. *Do I help or not? Is he lying? Or is she lying? All I know is that I can't be late.*

Fuck it, I decided to help the man and restrain the woman from leaving until the police turned up. His story seemed to be more compelling than hers. We were both trying to restrain her for over an hour until finally, the police turned up. I then had to wait another hour so I could give them my statement about what had taken place.

It turned out that the woman had jumped through the bottom

bedroom window while he and his girlfriend were fast asleep. And the moment she was made, the woman ran out of their apartment, took off her dress and underwear, and ran upstairs towards my apartment, crying rape. That was her plan B.

Fuck! By the time I walked into the office, I was two and a half hours late on my first day. This was the worst start possible. In comparison, my interview now looked pretty good. I went to see my new boss, to apologise and explain why I was late. But to be honest, I am not sure if they believed me or not. Or if I had a job at the end of the day.

I sat at my desk, it was now 12:30 pm, and my phone rang. "Cornelius, I have Duncan on line 1." He had phoned to see how my first morning was going. I told him the story of the two naked people.

During my entire time at uni, no one ever corrected me on the words I used or my terminology; I just assumed that we all used the same language. Where I come from, we use the term "duck", meaning a person, thank you, or cheers. For a great example, a checkout assistant might say, "That's fifteen pounds, duck!" Or someone working in a cafe might ask you, "Would you like a cuppa, duck?" or "An egg with that, duck? Or would you like bacon with that duck?" I know we all have our own slang words, but no one ever corrected me on the word "shag"!

"Shag", to me, means mate! You alright there, shag? Fancy a pint, shag? What you up to this weekend, shag? So you can imagine me telling Duncan my story, it was shag this and shag that, here a shag, there a shag, shag, shag, shag and more shag. After about twenty minutes of shagging, I put the phone down, and the entire open-plan floor was deadly silent. My new boss turned towards me and said, "Sorry, Cornelius, but you can't talk to your girlfriend like that, not in this office. It's not how we do things here." I was totally confused about what he meant.

I replied, "Sorry, but I wasn't talking to my girlfriend, I was talking to Duncan, someone who I was living with when I was at uni. He was asking about my morning."

"Oh I'm so sorry, we had no idea that you were gay. But that's ok, Dean on the next floor up, he's openly gay too. Actually, he's one of the company's founding directors, I'm not sure if you met him yet? But maybe you should sit on his floor." I had no idea what he was talking about. *I'm not gay, where did all that come from?* I thought. The next minute, I was introduced to Dean and was relocated to his floor.

Who would have thought that shag means fucking, and not mate!

I loved my first three months working for this consultancy. Everyone was so nice and they even took their time to explain and show me why it was essential to think in a particular way when protecting heritage landscapes. My involvement was mostly at the conceptual level and graphical presentational work, depending which projects I got assigned to at the start of the week.

Everything was working out perfectly. Sally managed to get relocated to a busy office in London. I caught the train back home to help Sally pack the car so we could start our new and exciting life together, living and working in London.

The morning Sally was due to leave for London was awful. Her parents were in tears, begging her not to leave. I sat in the car, unsure if she was coming or not. Her brother was crying, and kept pulling her back into the house to stop her from getting into the car. I could hear Sally's parents saying, "You deserve better than Cornelius; please think about not leaving, you will meet someone else, someone better than him."

I'd always assumed they didn't like me, but I was devastated to hear it for myself. I loved their daughter with everything I had, treated her with so much love and respect.

This was pretty much the icing on the cake. Her boyfriend had a professional career in landscape architecture, working at one of the best design consultancies in the country, and yet I was still wasn't good enough.

Reluctantly, Sally came with me. What a cracking way to start to our new life.

I was always anticipating the day Sally would leave me and go back home to her parents. It was inevitable; her parents made sure we couldn't enjoy what London had to offer. Sally's parents insisted that she phoned home every night between 6:30 and 8:30 pm. The calls lasted nearly two hours, every single night. Not to mention, Sally had to go home every three weeks.

This was my life for the next eight months. Every time Sally returned back to London we always seemed to be more distant. We hardly spent any quality time together anymore, and our sex life was non-existent.

My work placement was about to come to an end, and I had to decide if I was going back to uni to take my graduate diploma. Most design consultancies only hired people with this qualification. But I felt I could learn more working in a design consultancy than going back to university for lectures, plus I had no friends at uni. Not one person had contacted me through the entire year I was in London, apart from Duncan. I don't know how many emails and messages I sent, but all were in vain.

So I sat down with my directors and presented them with a radical new idea: work another year in the office fulltime, and at the same time, complete my graduate diploma, but without attending university for the entire year. This idea also gave me an advantage over everyone else; I would have two years of work experience, compared to everyone else who only had one year of experience. But my fifth-year tutor and the administration board would also have to agree on this idea.

I knew they wouldn't agree with me; my idea implied that everyone in my position could also decide to work an extra year and never turn up to any graduate diploma lectures. Meaning our fifth-year tutors were at risk of losing their jobs.

After three weeks of administration research, I finally found a small loophole in the system. If I paid for the entire course upfront and in full before the first day of term, it would be impossible for the administration to fail me. All I had to do was pin-up my final design, which was a year-long project, before the external examiners started marking, which was at 10 am the day of the exam. The only way that I could fail was either by not finishing all the requirements for the project, or by missing the deadline. Best of all, I had an office full of qualified landscape architects who were all keen to help me.

I was so happy with finding this administration loophole, but this happiness only lasted for a short time.

I came home one evening after work and found all of Sally's stuff packed up; she was waiting for her dad to drive her back home. Any later and I would have come home to an empty house. On top of this, Sally also told me her reason for going back home so often. She was seeing her brother's best friend, someone who her family approved of. Everything made sense, including why we had become so distant. I never saw this coming, not in a million years. Who would have thought Sally would cheat on me?

I had to use all of my holiday entitlements in one go; I didn't want to go back to work in a mess. I didn't want to go back to work, full stop. I was now living in London alone and with no friends. When I did return to work, I threw all that I had into my office work and my university project, anything to take my mind off the thought of coming home that night, knowing she was gone without a trace. I begged her to come back and give our relationship another go, but it was always greeted with "I have moved on and you need to as well; you need to find someone who has the same desires and goals as you."

Easier said than done.

***

While I was on my holidays, so to speak, my office hired four new people, but I only clicked with two of them. One was a year out placement called Oliver; he had a cracking personality, a stylish dress sense, and was very funny. He even looked like Jude Law and I ate lunch with him every day. He loved London, but loved men even more.

The other person was my new boss. I had to report to her daily; she was so calm and professional in the office. However, once we finished work on a Friday, she became an entirely different person. She loved to smoke and party but loved her glasses of wine even more. She reminded me of Dr. Jekyll and Mr. Hyde.

I was starting to find her very attractive, but I wasn't sure if it had anything to do with me being sad and alone or that she was the total opposite of Sally, someone who enjoyed life and London. I didn't even mind the fact that she smoked. I just enjoyed being around her. She made me laugh and made me forget about the pain of not being with Sally anymore.

I remember one evening when we were working on a project together. Dr. Jekyll asked me if I could stay back and work late in the office.

"Unfortunately, I can't, Liverpool are playing in Europe tonight, and I don't miss any games. I am so sorry, on any other night, I would be more than happy to stay behind and help."

Dr. Jekyll demanded that I stay behind and help and said that I was being very unprofessional. Her attitude surprised me somewhat. Was I being unprofessional? I reiterated, "If it was any other night, I would love to help, but I can't tonight. I am so sorry, I really do need to get home before we kick-off, I am very superstitious. But I am happy to come in early tomorrow morning and stay late tomorrow night." I thought this was the perfect compromise. But not to her.

I left the office that evening and went home to watch Liverpool win 2-1. I knew that if I hadn't watched the game, we would have lost.

Straight after the game, I phoned my mum to ask for advice on dealing with Dr. Jekyll. Mum asked me a strange question: "Do you like her?"

"What does that have anything to do with what I just asked you, Mum?"

"Do you though?"

"I don't know, Mum, I am not sure. I do like her, don't get me wrong, but maybe it has more to do with Sally and I, or more to do with me not being alone."

"In that case, make her a cup of tea and apologise to her first thing in the morning."

And that's precisely what I did.

7

EVERYONE HAS A DARK SIDE

Dr. Jekyll discovered the ultimate drug, which could turn him into something else. Suddenly, he was able to unleash his deepest cruelties under the guise of the sinister Mr. Hyde.

I wasn't sure if Dr. Jekyll had a boyfriend or not. She was extremely guarded and very private. She never mentioned anyone in particular, so I decided to ask her out on a date. After all, we were hanging out all the time during our lunch break, along with Oliver.

We arranged to meet in a pub near Victoria Station, a few minutes away from our office. She was working late, so it worked out well. I wasn't sure if you could class this a date or not, it seemed more like a late evening catch up, without Oliver being there.

The evening went by so quickly, but it was nice to have a greater understanding of Dr. Jekyll on a more intimate level regarding her family and friends, and also how she got into our profession. We got on so well that we ended up back at her flat, where we spent the night together. But we arrived at the office the next morning separately. We both didn't want to draw any unwanted attention. After all, our office had a habit of gossip and people creating unnecessary drama.

We could only manage to catch up a few times a week when she was free. Dr. Jekyll had other outside interests, like yoga and Pilates, or catching up with friends. I was happy with this arrangement, as I was still able to carry on with my graduate diploma during the times when I wasn't with Dr. Jekyll. I didn't want to fall behind in my studies.

The more time we spent together, the quicker I was falling in love with her. One weekend, Dr. Jekyll went home to visit her family for her dad's birthday. I didn't realise how much I was missing her. I just wanted to hear her voice. I was feeling a little down, so I decided to call her, but Dr. Jekyll never picked up. After five missed calls, I was starting to worry when I heard no reply.

I laid in bed, worrying if she was ok. Later that night, she phoned me back to apologise for not calling earlier. She had spent the entire day with her parents visiting the Yorkshire Sculpture Park, an open-air gallery in West Bretton near Wakefield.

"Sorry for calling, I got a little worried when I didn't hear back, stupid really, but I missed your voice today, that's all. Just having a sad day. It's raining in London, and it would have been nice to snuggle up in bed watching a movie, that's all."

I could hardly hear Dr. Jekyll, she was so quiet, but I did hear her dad's voice in the background. He was asking who she was talking to. She replied with, "Just a colleague from work, nothing to worry about."

"Look, I will call you tomorrow when I have more time, but thank you for your concern, that's so sweet of you, sleep well."

Tomorrow came and I didn't receive that call. When I saw her at work on Monday, I asked how the weekend was and if it was nice seeing her mum and dad.

Strange, she never answered that question, and she avoided me for most of that day. Finally, she said, "So sorry for not calling on Sunday, I was with friends and I didn't want to say anything to them just yet about us, as they are also landscape architects. Plus, they know some of the people in our office. I hope you understand? I have only been here for a few months, and I am trying to make a good first impression." Her answer made total sense to me, and I didn't think she would lie to me, either. She never once came across as a liar.

We started to hang out even more during the weekdays, but very rarely on the weekends. This was my most productive time to concentrate on my uni work, and I was looking at re-designing Jubilee Gardens, located on the South Bank, directly opposite the London Eye. Jubilee Gardens was a relatively large unused piece of grass, so I thought this was the perfect location for my project. A blank canvas, as you would say.

Most of the weekends, you would be able to find me walking around and observing people on the South Bank, constantly making notes about how people move from one space to another. A big part of my concept analysis and research was understanding and observing the psychology of people's movement.

Why did they walk in that direction or sit down in that location? How come they turned around and decided to walk down a dark, small, wet alleyway that looked and felt unsafe? How come they held their bags closer to them in certain areas but not others?

Why did they pause and reflect in this location and not that location? What was their reasoning? And so on. I loved people watching, and I wanted to understand the why, a vital and key component to my final design. This included my passion for wayfinding, something I was learning about in my second year practice.

My accommodation where I used to live with Sally was coming to an end, and I didn't want to extend it, so I was looking for a new place to live, one that wasn't too expensive. But also, I wanted to live in a nice area with a great cafe culture, so I could observe and watch people, my favourite pastime.

One of my favourite places to visit when my mum and sister came down to visit me was Camden Market. The weekends at Camden were a mixture of colours and personal individuality. It was a collection of handmade and upcycled items and all things creative, not to mention yummy street food.

As much as I loved Camden, I couldn't see myself living there, and I didn't feel I could fit in and belong to the community. No offence, but there were a lot of goth looking people, with piercings and tattoos. This wasn't me, that's for sure. They even wore makeup. Enough said. I really wanted to move there, but it just wasn't in my make-up, excuse the pun. It just wasn't me, no matter how hard I wanted it to fit in.

One evening after work while having a drink in our local pub, which was directly opposite our office, Dr. Jekyll mentioned to me that there was a spare room available in the house that she was sharing with two other people. The location was Belsize Park, a posh suburb and cafe culture haven, not to mention it was a ten-minute walk from Camden Market and a one-minute walk from the Haverstock Arms, a trendy little cozy pub.

Winner, winner, chicken fucking dinner.

The room was tiny, just barely big enough for a double bed and a chest of draws; it was cheaper than my last place, but the utility bills were excluded. But that was ok. I was more worried about living in the same house as Dr. Jekyll, and that I was jumping from one relationship straight into another, without a break.

I mean, I was only dumped a few months ago, and I was desperately lonely and heartbroken. I still hadn't made any friends. I tried to, trust me, but it all just seemed too hard. Everyone was either booked up weeks or months in advance. I knew London was huge, but months in advance just seemed like one-way traffic. Even Oliver was booked up months in advance, and he only lived seven stops down from me in a trendy up and coming part of London. This seemed my best option; I hated that feeling of being alone.

The house dynamics were outstanding, everyone got on so well. I couldn't have asked for anything better, and I even had my own space in the living room for my computer and for all of my uni work.

Oliver was the only person who knew about our relationship, but I still felt that something wasn't quite right with Dr. Jekyll. Something just appeared off; she seemed to be so secretive. But I thought this was just down to me being paranoid, especially after what had happened in my previous two relationships.

I fell in love with Dr. Jekyll hard, fast and very quickly, so I tried to play my emotions down. I was so scared of getting hurt and heartbroken again, but she was so much fun to be around, especially when we were in the pub. Our banter and conversations just flowed and with such ease, compared with Sally or Mia.

Soon, though, things started to go pretty pear-shaped and sour in our house, not between Dr. Jekyll and I, but with our housemates, the Ozzies, as we now called them. Our living conditions in the house were beginning to become very disciplined and with a dictatorship attitude.

I would wake up on the weekends, and find I had all these lists laid out on the ironing board, chores that needed to be done at a specific time, and when we were allowed to have friends or family stay over. We now had to give the Ozzies three weeks' notice for any visitors, when we didn't have to before. I was finding the situation very stressful and strange.

I had no friends, so I was ok, but Dr. Jekyll had many old university friends. I could understand if Dr. Jekyll's friends slept on the couch; that would make the Ozzies feel like their house wasn't theirs anymore. But Dr. Jekyll's friends would always stay over in her room when they came to visit.

So this new structure and system didn't make any sense. I had no idea why all of a sudden this happened, and it started to feel like it was us against them.

One weekend, Dr. Jekyll came crashing through my bedroom door at 1 am. She was absolutely leathered, and for some strange reason, she wanted an argument.

"You don't give a fucking shit about me, do you? You're still thinking about her, why am I not good enough for you? You say you care, but you don't, and you say that you love me, but you never show it."

Where the fuck did all this come from? It was so out of the blue, and I was in shock. I had never seen Dr. Jekyll this angry before, it was scary. I didn't care about her or I didn't love her? I didn't get it! I was madly and deeply in love with her; maybe I didn't show her enough?

"I fucking hate you, you did this to me, this is your fault, why won't you love me?" She kept saying this over and over again. "This is all on you!"

"What is? What's my fault? I am not sure if I understand what you're getting at. Have I done something wrong? I don't understand! I tell you that I love you every day, do I not show you? Dr. Jekyll, what's all my fault? I have been asleep most of the evening. I'm not sure what I have done wrong."

"You did this to me; this is your fault," laughing at the same time.

The Ozzies were out that night, staying over at their friends' place, which was lucky because I couldn't handle them at the same time as what I was witnessing with Dr. Jekyll. I couldn't get a straight answer out of her, nothing she said made any sense.

"You happy now? Is this what you wanted? You did this to me, you did this, it's all your fault, why don't you love me? Why? Why? Why?"

Holy fuck, I was lost, I had no Scooby fucking doo what was happening. I sat on the edge of my bed, wondering if I should phone my mum or not. I decided against phoning for advice, I just needed to calm Dr. Jekyll down.

She was so pissed and so angry, so I just let her vent all her anger on me until she had no more left inside. I took so much verbal abuse that night, I was starting to convince myself that this must have been my fault; she must have had a good reason to be like this.

Did I let anything slip at work regarding Dr. Jekyll and I seeing one another? I had no idea. I was like a rabbit caught in the headlights. I just sat there on the edge of my bed taking hit after hit. Even when I went to make a cuppa, Dr. Jekyll followed me into the kitchen.

"It's your fault."

"You did this!"

"Why don't you love me?"

Eventually, she threw up and crashed on the bathroom floor. I covered her with my blanket as I slept by her side. I was mentally exhausted. I still had no idea where this all came from, but I think I had just met Mr. Hyde for the first time, and he was fucking scary.

The following morning, Dr. Jekyll phoned into work and made the excuse of not feeling well, not that far from the truth. She stayed in bed while I had to go into work. I was onsite with one of my directors, so I definitely couldn't take the day off.

I was still no clearer about what the fuck last night was all about. I tried to broach the subject, but I never got a straight answer, nor did I get an apology or any thanks for looking after her. I was extremely confused. *The girl I am in madly in love with lost her shit last night at me for no reason whatsoever.*

As bad as last night was, I discovered I had a totally new issue to worry about.

I arrived home earlier than normal from the site visit, as I was concerned about Dr. Jekyll; I hadn't heard from her all day. As I peered into her bedroom, she seemed to be asleep, so I decided to work on my uni project, but my computer wouldn't boot up.

I tried over ten times, and still, nothing would start up. *Why was it working yesterday afternoon but not today?* I definitely didn't want to wake up Dr. Jekyll or Mr. Hyde to see if she knew what might have happened. So I rechecked all the wires and plugs, even unscrewed the base unit and checked all the internal components.

Honestly, like I knew what I was even looking for. I started laughing at myself, *what a dickhead, what a total nobhead*, shaking my head and talking to myself. I couldn't stop laughing in disbelief, *after last night and now this?*

I thought I was losing my mind, but then I had a strange thought: *Let's check the security cameras.*

I had no idea if they were recording during the day when we were all at work or not. But then to my horror, I watched one of the Ozzies using my computer yesterday without my permission. Then they turned it off directly from the plug the moment I walked through the gate. *Fuck!*

I checked the last month and the month before that, and every time I wasn't at home, they were on my computer and the moment someone came home, they pulled the plug out of the mains and ran back to the sofa, as if nothing had happened.

I was fucking mortified. They moved their shit out of the living room to create some space for my computer and all along, I thought they were kind, but they had an alternative motive. *Now my computer is fucked, all my work was on that hard drive, and I didn't have any backups or any way to retrieve it.* I was absolutely fucked. Up the creek without a paddle, as they say.

I just had enough with everything; nothing was going right at all. I was losing my mind and my shit, so Dr. Jekyll and I decided enough was enough. The Ozzies were making our life miserable and for what? Absolutely for fuck all. I had never said one bad word against them, and I was just getting treated like shit again.

Against my better judgment, I knew this was a stupid idea, but Dr. Jekyll and I decided to move in together. It was the cheapest way to afford to stay in London and not flat share again.

We were so lucky; pretty much straight away we managed to find a large studio flat, five minutes away from where we were living and in the same suburb, directly opposite another pub called The Richard Steele Pub. It had a similar vibe to The Haverstock Arms, another mecca for celebrities to hang out at.

***

I had never seen any celebrities during my time living in London, until one unforgettable Sunday evening.

It was the evening we had finally moved all of our stuff out of the old flat and into our new one, so we decided to celebrate living together for the first time with a few beers in our new local. We walked across the road to the pub. A nice youngish looking guy and his mate opened the main doors for us so we could enter as they were leaving. "Much appreciated and thank you," I said as I walked straight inside, but then I froze immediately at the entrance of the doorway.

Holy shit, fuck me backwards! Seriously, I just froze in disbelief. I was fixated. I wanted to look elsewhere so I didn't come across as a nutter or a crazy stalker. I tried to move my legs but I couldn't. I was celebrity-paralyzed, struggling to contain my excitement, my heart was racing.

OMG, this was a proper, like proper celebrity and I was only just listening to her album literally five minutes ago. Now she's standing in front of me.

The excitement was overwhelming, I was utterly star-struck. I just carried on staring at her in disbelief, shaking my head, pupils dilated. I was on a celebrity high, and I didn't ever want to come back down.

Dr. Jekyll followed me straight in afterwards.

"Did you see who opened the door for us, can you believe he held the door open for me?"

"What?" I was still frozen, still staring, in her direction and in a flippant way waving my hand, like I cared. "Sorry, who opened the door?"

It was Noel and Liam from Oasis apparently, but all I heard was blah, blah, blah, blah, blah. Standing in front of *me* was Billie Piper, only bloody Billie Piper! How can you top Billie Piper standing no more than three meters away from me?

I was of two minds to run back across the road and grab my album for her to sign; this was a dream come true. Then the ginger guy with the big glasses from the TV show *TGI Friday* came around the corner, and he kissed Billie Piper on the cheek. I was gutted.

I ordered a bottle of beer and slumped down in a corner, looking bloody miserable. I wished I had run over to my place, grabbed Billie Piper's *Walk of Life* album and asked for her to sign it. Gutted.

The following morning, I walked across the road to buy some milk for a cuppa from our local dairy, which was located next to the pub where I saw Billie Piper. I was waiting to be served when I noticed Helena Bonham Carter standing directly in front of me in her dressing gown, looking worse for wear. Or was she already out-out? I wasn't too sure. But I did take note of the items that she was purchasing: one small loaf of bread, one strawberry Chupa Chups lollipop, two refresher lollies, and a pomegranate. Still, it wasn't Billie Piper.

***

Christmas was only a few weeks away, and we had our office work party in a few days. It was fancy dress, and Dr. Jekyll, Oliver and I decided to go as characters from the *Star Wars* movies: Leia, Obi-Wan, and I was going as Luke Skywalker.

I wanted my first Christmas with Dr. Jekyll to be special, one that we would always remember, so I decided to paint something from my heart rather than buy her a present.

So, while Dr. Jekyll was out celebrating Christmas with friends, I decided to stay home and finish off my painting. It also helped with my anxiety and stress levels. I still had no idea what to do regarding losing all of my uni work. There was no way I would be able to stay in my present employment, as they only took on post-grad students. So this was a welcome distraction task.

Our Christmas party was exceptional. I was having so much fun, I didn't want the night to stop. It was a great feeling to be part of something special; we had a fantastic work environment, and I couldn't be any happier.

I was a little tipsy when one of our directors and his long-time partner followed me into the toilet. I thought nothing of it. As I tried to leave, my director stood directly in front of the door, blocking my exit; he wouldn't let me pass, while his partner stood behind me.

I asked politely if he would move out of the way, but he refused. Instead, he reached between my legs, touching my penis while his partner started to place his hand down the front of my pants. I could feel him getting hard and aroused.

I stood motionless, tears running down my eyes. I was shaking. Both of them were fondling me. "Please can you stop, please, I am begging you, please stop, I am not gay."

"Have you ever been with a man before? You might like it. There is nothing wrong with trying. Why don't you come back to my place? We can smoke some weed, do some coke, and just have some fun?"

"Please can you stop, please."

But they wouldn't stop. I wanted to shout, but again, I was unable to. Then my director went down on to his knees, grabbing my penis with both hands. He was going to place his mouth around my penis while his partner's penis was pressed against my backside; he was trying to force himself in. This was the beginning of being raped during my office Xmas party.

Just then, Oliver started banging on the door, wanting to come in, "You ok? Dr. Jekyll and I are going to a bar in Kings Cross; we just wanted to see if you fancy coming along?"

Somehow I shouted "Yes, yes, yes, I'm just washing my face!" I turned to my director, "Please, I want to leave," tears streaming down my face. I was trying to keep it all together, but I could feel I was about to pass out.

Eventually, they let me out.

"You ok? You look very pale."

"Yeah sorry, I just threw up, and these two were just helping me sort myself out. Do you know what, I think I'll give the pub a miss tonight, if that's ok? I think I have had a little too much to drink tonight. I am not feeling great at all. I'll just get a taxi home and see you both tomorrow."

I ran down the stairs, but I was stopped just before I bolted out of the building. Our receptionist, who saw that I was shaken up and upset, gave me her number and said to call her if I needed anything. I gave her a hug and a kiss on the cheek, said thank you, and left.

I never said anything to anyone regarding what happened to me at the Christmas party. After all, he was a director of the company and I needed this job. Plus, who would believe a year out student?

I just wanted be home with our white Christmas tree, beautifully decorated, standing in the corner of our living room. It was my beacon that I was safe and secure, while I tried to heal internally once again.

***

I left London a day before Christmas Eve, so I could spend a day shopping alone with Mum in Nottingham. I was going to tell her what happened at my office party, but every time I tried to approach the subject, I changed my mind at the last second.

Mum knew something wasn't right. I was too quiet for this time of year. I just wanted to stay in and be around my mum. I think she also thought it had something do with Dr. Jekyll and I, so she never really pushed the subject. She knew that if I wanted to talk, she was always there.

Dr. Jekyll and I didn't leave London on the best of terms either; she accused me of cheating on her with our receptionist. She'd watched our receptionist give me a hug and her number from the top of the stairs where our office party was held. I had no idea she was watching me from the top of the steps.

I tried to explain that nothing was happening. Still, she wasn't taking no for an answer, and I wasn't sure how to tell her about what happened in the toilets. So I tried to convince her otherwise, that nothing had happened between us. I wasn't even in the mood to finish off her painting, so I went out and bought her a pair of earrings instead.

We tried to see each other over the Christmas break, but it just didn't seem to work out. I phoned many times, but it always went straight to voicemail. I only heard back when she decided to call me. I assumed she was still angry with me, even though I wasn't sure why.

When I got back to our office, I decided that I needed to move from my director's floor to another floor; my excuse was to seek alternative experience.

I only had five months before my university deadline, and time was against me. At least the Christmas break gave me time to think about the best approach regarding my university work. I realised that everyone was going to present their university project work in some sort of cool rendering and graphics software, which we were all exposed to in our year out.

I had no time to rebuild my 3D CAD model and get it all graphically rendered again, so I decided that I would play to my strengths and hand draw everything. This approach would give me a fighting chance to finish my project before our deadline on June 8th at 10 am.

I was burning the candle at both ends once again, but I was optimistic that I could actually pull this all off. That was before Dr. Jekyll started to become very ill all of a sudden. She was going off her food and didn't feel like she wanted to drink or smoke. She was losing weight and always very tired. I was worried; I had never seen anyone get dramatically ill this quickly. I had no idea what was wrong. Then it all became clear, crystal clear: Dr. Jekyll was pregnant.

I had no idea how she got pregnant; I thought we were always careful. I knew there were a few times around Christmas when we weren't too careful, though.

I was in shock; I had no idea what we were going to do, or how we would manage. I didn't expect to be a dad a few months after Christmas, but I was, and I had an overwhelming feeling of love and happiness. I was going to be a dad!

Well, I thought I was, for all of about thirty minutes. Dr. Jekyll reassured me that the baby wasn't mine. Which was impossible. *How can that be, unless she's been with someone else?*

"What do you mean the baby isn't mine, of course it's mine. I mean, it's not like you've had the chance to fuck someone else behind my back, is it? Is it? Is that what you have done, you've been fucking someone else behind my back? How? That's impossible; we live together. You told me you loved me. You're not making any sense. Have you fucked someone else behind my back? You haven't. Have you? Please don't say that you have? Please."

Dr. Jekyll reassured me the baby wasn't mine, because she had been fucking two other guys while we had been together. And while I had been with Dr. Jekyll for over six fucking months, living with her for two of those months, she never used protection. What the fuck!

But the story gets better: they weren't just drunken one-night stands, oh no, she was in a relationship with both of them. But how? We worked and lived together; this made no sense.

I didn't understand what she was saying and why she wanted to hurt me. Was this all about her perception of me having a relationship with our receptionist? Was this my punishment? I was heartbroken; I wanted the world to swallow me up and never let me return.

How could I not see this? How did I not pick up on the signs? And more to the point, whose baby is it then?

She started to confess that she had been seeing Bill, her ex-boyfriend, every time she went back home to visit her mum and dad. The person I heard in the background who I thought was her dad was in fact Bill. I even made him breakfast when he came to visit Dr. Jekyll one weekend, when we were living with the Ozzies. He didn't just stay in her room; they were fucking right next door to my room.

Ted was the other guy. He was someone who Dr. Jekyll had been working with in her old design practice. The main reason she started working in my office was that they didn't want anyone to know about their relationship, seeing as he was her director. So while I was painting her Christmas present and doing my university work during the weekends, she was catching up with her director at his apartment.

I had no idea what to think. I kept replaying the same shit over and over again. *How can I be so blind and stupid? I trusted her and this happens again, I have been cheated on.*

I asked how she knew the baby wasn't mine. Dr. Jekyll kept apologising and reassuring me it wasn't mine, and that she had made a stupid, stupid mistake.

I didn't know what to believe; I was hurting like I had never hurt before. I started thinking, *Is this my fault? Was I so desperate to be loved and not alone, that I just ignored all the signs, even though they were right in front of me?*

Dr. Jekyll convinced me so much that I wasn't the father, I even started to feel sorry for her. Bill and Ted piled on so much pressure for her to carry on with their relationships, otherwise they would ruin her career; she felt so trapped. The moment she fell in love with me, she wanted to end both relationships, but they wouldn't let her.

I had no idea what to believe. One week, I thought I was going to be a dad, and now I am helping Dr. Jekyll to have an abortion. I even went along to the clinic to support her through this difficult decision. I was mentally fucked; I wasn't sure whether I was coming or going! I wasn't even sure if I was in a relationship or sharing a relationship. I just sat in the waiting room, head between my hands, constantly thinking, *Have I just aborted my child, without me even realising it?*

The thought of that alone was too much. I was starting to lose my shit. I wanted to go into the room and shout "Stop!" until we officially had a DNA test, but I was too late.

Dr. Jekyll walked out of the procedure room as if nothing had happened, and we went to grab a coffee and a bite to eat. All the time I was wondering whether it was mine or not and what the fuck had just happened. Dr. Jekyll could see I was hurting and so confused, but she kept reassuring me that she had spoken to the actual father, whoever that was, and he was happy with her decision. I didn't know what to think; I was like a fucking zombie.

Dr. Jekyll left her job a month later and quickly found another one. I was still working there and it was a miserable two months before my university deadline. I had fallen well behind; with everything that had been happening, my project took a back seat. I was unable to concentrate and I had no motivation whatsoever.

I honestly thought I was going to be a dad, and now I had no idea if I would ever get the chance again.

I had no money and still no friends. Dr. Jekyll convinced me that we could still make our relationship work, despite everything, and that it was worth fighting for. She even showed me text messages stating that she had ended her relationship with Bill and Ted, so I decided to stay.

I also quit a week later. My heart wasn't in it anymore and I hated going into work and seeing him there, pretending as though nothing had happened during our office party. I was unable to shake off the horrific memory and the thought of what could have happened.

So I spent the next two months 24/7 trying to finish my post grad. If I didn't pass my course, I would struggle to find a new job. I was so stressed about the possibility of leaving London that I slowly stopped eating. I was too worried to eat and unable to sleep with constant reoccurring nightmares of being raped.

***

It was the morning of my deadline, over seventy-two hours since I had any sleep or food, and the clock had ticked down to 0.00. I had no more time left; I now had to get to Manchester before 10 am, not a minute later. My fifth-year tutor Daniel had decided that my work was going to be one of the first to be moderated by the external examiners, even though I had to travel up from London. I had a feeling he wanted to prove a point and make me an example of bucking the system, even though I had emailed him asking to be moderated last to make it less stressful. Surprise, surprise, he never once replied back.

Nothing this morning was going to plan. The Northern Line was delayed, and now my train from London Euston to Manchester was over an hour delayed. All I could do was stare at my watch. Time was ticking away from me; I was still thirty minutes out from arriving into Manchester, and forty minutes before my deadline. This gave me only ten minutes to race across the city.

I looked at all of my work one last time. I felt so proud of what I had achieved, despite everything that had happened to me in the last year. I was trying to calm my anxiety and remain positive. One moment I was laughing and the next I was crying; I was unable to control my emotions. This carried on for the next thirty minutes. The train came to a grinding halt and shocked me out of whatever I was going through. I now had a ten-minute foot race from one side of Manchester to the other, so I could pin my work to the wall on time.

I had no energy whatsoever, and my legs felt like they were made of lead. One hand was carrying my portfolio and the other hand was trying to gesture and stop oncoming cars from hitting me. Cars were tooting their horns and I was trying to dodge people as I ran down the streets. I could have just sat down and laughed if this wasn't so serious. It felt like I was in a romantic comedy, trying to stop my best friend who I was in love with from boarding her plane. But this was real life, this was happening, this was no movie. And as funny as it seemed, it really wasn't funny at all.

Constantly looking at my watch, *Fuck I need to make this. Come on Universe, please help me out, please,* I kept saying to myself, continually looking at my watch. As I ran up the steps of my university, I heard dong, dong, dong, and that third dong was the moment I realised that I had failed my course and missed the deadline.

I sat down on the steps outside Manchester University in a flood of tears. I had convinced myself I could do this. I had believed in myself so much that whatever life threw at me, I knew I could still do this. I then felt a hand on my shoulder; it was Colin.

"Cornelius what you are doing sitting here, why are you not pinning your work up? You did finish, didn't you?"

"Yes I did, it's right here, but I missed the deadline. Administration and Daniel made it very, very clear that if I missed this deadline, they would fail me. Daniel wanted to make an example of me and close the loophole that I found in the small print regarding me working full time and not turning up for any lectures. He didn't want to open the door to everyone doing the same thing as me."

Colin helped me to my feet and we both walked to where I was supposed to present my work. It was now 10:20 am. The external examiners were now moderating another student. I pinned up my work, regardless. No one knew what I had gone through this last year. I never spoke to anyone from my degree course or from the guys who I used to live with, even though they were also doing the post grad. I had the impression that they thought I believed I was better than them.

I stood back and admired my sheer determination and hard work when all of a sudden, I noticed that I was the only one to produce hand-drawn graphics and illustrations. Everyone else had stunning full-colour 3D renders. I was blown away by the standard and quality that they produced, yet mine had an artistic impression. A softer side, should I say a more relatable feel, not so much in your face. Regardless of the outcome, I achieved exactly what I had set out to do.

Then I heard a voice coming from behind me: "Excuse me, is your name, Cornelius?"

"Yes, it is. I am so sorry for running late, but the train from London Euston to Manchester was delayed, so again my apologies, and thank you for being so patient."

"Oh is that Jubilee Gardens? I live about ten minutes away from there. Please talk me through your project."

The lesson to be learned here is never to give up; you just never know what the universe has in store for you.

I passed my post grad qualification and they closed the loophole.

***

The next few years, my relationship with Dr. Jekyll was hard work; she was still drinking and smoking, which in turn caused more arguments, which also brought out Mr. Hyde. I also realised that the night I first met Mr. Hyde, when he barged into my bedroom, it wasn't about me; it was all about her relationships with Bill and Ted, and she reflected all her shit on me rather than them, a kind of mirrored reality.

I was still in love with Dr. Jekyll, but I had now started to develop major trust issues and was starting to become very jealous. I was never quite sure if she was still seeing Bill or Ted or not, but I couldn't carry on living in fear, so I decided to start trying to trust her all over again. "Let me prove to you how sorry I am and that you can trust me again." she pleaded, "We all make mistakes, so, please, let's move forward in a positive, happy way."

Just as we were making headway in our relationship, I received a call from my mum. She phoned me at my new place of work, as I wasn't answering my mobile phone. She was in tears. I had never heard my mum cry. She was our rock and our glue, and now she had been diagnosed with cancer!

For the first time, I had no response. I was speechless. I mean, what do you say to someone when you learn that they have cancer? I felt dead inside and slipped into my zombie state, dead from the inside. I broke down, unable to say one word back, tears rolling down my face.

I got up, left my desk, walked past my director, and walked home. I don't even know how I got home. I was on autopilot, crossing roads without even thinking or looking; I was lucky I didn't get hit. Mum had cancer, and there was nothing I could do help her.

Mum was diagnosed with throat cancer on the left-hand side of her mouth and along the length of her tongue. And to make matters worse, I was still living in London, so getting up to see her was very costly, and my salary wasn't that great.

Dr. Jekyll wanted to settle down in London and buy a house, but I still felt restless and unsettled; I was never quite sure where I stood with her. She wanted to prove to me that we had a future and that I could trust her, and buying a house was her way of showing me her commitment and trust. But all I could think of was what my mum was going through.

Whenever I could afford to travel back home, I would I want to be with her all the time and also try to forge a loving relationship with my brother. For some unknown reason, he didn't want one, even though I made every effort to have one. He was so self-centred and selfish, making it very difficult to build any type of brotherly connection. He also had just bought a house and was investing in his fiancé's hair salon, so he had no time for me.

Between the months of June and August, I had so much going on. I was a walking zombie and my mind was mush; everything was spiralling out of control. Mum was going to have her operation to remove her tumor. My brother was getting married and having his stag do in Blackpool. I was his best man. Dr. Jekyll and I were finalising all the paperwork for a house in Battersea Park, London.

I was continuing to have doubts regarding buying a house with Dr. Jekyll. Her drinking wasn't getting any better, and the following morning apologies were starting to become the norm. I had no idea what was happening. I didn't have any control of my life, and I had no idea how to take it back. My brother's stag do was awful. All weekend, he kept provoking me for some reason. He kept insisting that I was gay, and I enjoyed cock, constantly putting me down in front of his friends. But as long as he came across as the funny one, he didn't care about my feelings.

I hated it when he kept going on about me being gay. It was all the time, and my sister didn't help either. I remember one time, the first time I had seen my dad in fifteen years. My sister had invited him to her eighteenth birthday, I believe they kept in touch with one another, but it was always on his terms. Over that same period of time, he consistently phoned Mum when he was drunk, begging her to take him back. Always with the same promises—"I promise to stop drinking, I promise to pay child support, I promise to get some help"—those types of empty promises.

When I eventually met my dad that night, I didn't have anything to say to him. I was also mentally shattered and I had just travelled up alone from London, leaving Dr. Jekyll back in London.

My brother and sister introduced their respective partners to my dad, when all of a sudden, my brother and sister started to look at one another, repeating the same sentence over and over again.

"You tell him."

"No way, you tell him."

"Nope, you tell him."

Pissing themselves laughing, I just stood in the middle of them both looking at them from side to side, while I was also facing my dad. I had no idea what they were going on about.

"Ok, I'll tell him then."

Dad replied, "Tell me what?"

"Cornelius's gay!"

My dad stared at me. He didn't say a word, he just turned around and walked towards the bar. He ordered four whiskies and three pints and downed them all in less than two minutes. He walked back over to where we were all standing and said, "What a disappointment you are. I knew nothing would come of you. You're no son of mine." Then he sat down somewhere else with more beer.

All I have ever wanted from my dad was his love and for him to be proud of me and I turned out to be a disappointment. All night I was told to 'cheer up, you're spoiling your sister's birthday' when inside I was broken.

This wasn't just a one-off situation. The first time I introduced Dr. Jekyll to my brother and sister, they both said, "As nice as you seem, there's no point in getting to know you, no point at all. Cornelius's gay and we are just waiting for him come out." I felt sorry for Dr. Jekyll. She was trying to make an effort and wanted to get to know my family, and that's the first thing they say to her.

So the night of my brother's stag do, I was fed up with his gay remarks, especially in front of his mates. I decided to whisper something into my brother's ear. I'd had enough of what he was saying. It wasn't funny anymore.

The next minute faces surrounded me, all looking down at me and asking if I was alright. My head and jaw were ringing. My brother had given me a full right-handed closed fist uppercut, lifting me totally off the ground and over the dance floor handrail. I landed straight on the dance floor.

My mouth was bleeding and my jaw felt like it was dislocated. I started to gently move it from side to side to see if it was still in place. Fuck, that hurt; I'd never felt a hit like that before. It came out of nowhere. His mates gave me a hand to get back to my feet.

"What the fuck did you say to your bro? He's fucking fuming and he's just been escorted out of the night club."

"I told him the truth, and he didn't like it."

"What, that you're gay?"

"No," I started to laugh in pain. "No, am not gay. I told him that Zoe picked me first when we were in Blackpool, and she wanted to go back to her hotel and fuck; he was my sloppy seconds, so to speak." I deserved that punch. It was a long time coming, but it was worth it!

But I wasn't that arsed; whatever I was feeling was nothing compared with what Mum was going through with chemotherapy. Mum looked like a shadow of herself, unrecognizable. She didn't have any of her spark or zest for life. I wasn't sure if she would ever get it back, nor did we know if the cancer was in remission. Everything was a waiting game; a slow, cruel waiting game.

***

Against all the odds, Mum beat her cancer.

I was also now a homeowner, and I had been living with Dr. Jekyll for nearly a year. Our relationship was really good, and for the first time, we had a good foundation for moving forward.

But that happy state only lasted for a short time. Most of the times I had no idea what time Dr. Jekyll or Mr. Hyde was coming home, or in what state. I felt sorry for our neighbours; they could hear everything. We were like the neighbours from hell. We never got invited 'round to anyone's place, and why would we? Dr. Jekyll and Mr. Hyde were so unpredictable.

What looked promising at the start was long gone. My relationship was now starting to mirror my mum and dad's relationship, with Mr. Hyde taking my dad's role. I was reliving the same pattern, unable to get out of it and unable to make it work. I was exhausted from the constant arguing and trying to keep the peace.

I kept thinking to myself, *Am I the common denominator? Her reason and excuse to drink?* I was still in love with her, despite the drinking. When she wasn't drinking, she had a cracking personality. Her dry sense of humour and quick wit matched mine. We bounced off each other, and at times, the stress of our relationship seemed to fade away. But those were short-lived moments. I wish I had happier memories, but you only recall the ones that affect you emotionally or physically, the ones that hurt you the most. These are the memories we keep and can't seem to shake off.

Despite all the shitty memories that I had with Dr. Jekyll, my best memory came when we were living in our new house on the evening of 25th May, 2005. A night I would never forget, and it didn't even involve her. Liverpool was playing in the champions league final against AC Milan.

I now had a full-on scruffy curly ginger beard. I was way ahead of my time, way before it became all the rage with the hipsters. I wasn't able to go to any project meetings. I looked like a homeless person, but I didn't care, especially when it came to Liverpool and my superstitions.

On the 15th of September 2004, my director asked me to have a clean shave for tomorrow's project meeting, which I was happy to oblige; I was never a fan of looking scruffy. That same night, I was working late in the office, and Liverpool was playing Monaco in the champions league. I set a new personal best for cycling home. I'd never missed the start of kick-off, but I knew I needed to have a shave. I hated having a shave before I went to sleep, as I always had razor rashes and my face always itched, no matter what aftershave balm I used.

Then I heard the Liverpool anthem "You'll Never Walk Alone" and I knew that kick-off was imminent. I looked at myself in the mirror and thought, *Fuck it; I'll shave after the game.* I ran into the living room, grabbed Chenzo, my little beanie bear who I had had since I was with Sally. I held him during every game. I was so scared of putting him down; I thought it might change the outcome of the game.

That night we beat Monaco 2-0, and I convinced myself because I didn't have a shave that was what won the game, so I made the most life-changing decision I had ever made when it came to Liverpool FC. I decided to ignore my director's request and not to have a shave until we were knocked out of the competition. My decision didn't go down very well in the office, and my director was pissed off. He didn't even let me go to the project meeting, but I didn't care.

Now I know what you're thinking, that I was bat shit crazy, that I wasn't the reason why we made the final in Istanbul. But the universe works in mysteries ways, and I am totally convinced I was the sole reason we did make the final. Depends on how you look at it.

Ok, so we were down 3-0 at half time. It wasn't the result I was expecting. I needed to do something, and I needed to do it quickly if we had had any chance of lifting this trophy.

Dr. Jekyll was upstairs on the phone talking to her mum. With five minutes before the second half started, I did the unthinkable: I had a shave. And it was a dog's arse shave at that. All I'd had was an old rusty blade and no shaving foam. This needed to happen.

I ran back downstairs just in time for the start of the second half, with numerous amounts of toilet paper stuck to my face. I looked like a bloody mess. Incredibly, we pulled it back to 3-3. The unthinkable had happened; we were level at the final whistle, and we were going into penalties! Ok maybe Rafael Benitez, the Liverpool manager, had something to do with our sensational comeback and that he changed the team at half time, but that was only ten per cent. My face was the other ninety per cent.

Dr. Jekyll was just about to step on the living room floor when I shouted "Nooooooo! Wait, you might change the game if you touch the floor." I was the only one who was in the living room watching the game, not including Chenzo. I thought she might jinx the penalties outcome, so I carried her into the garden and asked her to stay there until we won. Only then was she allowed back into the house.

It was the greatest night of my life. I single-handedly won the champions league from my living room by having a shave, and no one can tell me any different.

The next morning, my new-cut face didn't go down very well in the office, but who cares? We were five-time winners. I also never went to a meeting for at least another six months.

***

During that same summer, my brother invited me to Blackpool once again. One of his football mates was also getting married, and this just seemed to be the perfect excuse to let my hair down and have some fun. I'd also grown my ginger beard back. I looked pale and ill without it, but in a more manageable hipster-type look.

I worked a few late nights in the office in order to take Friday afternoon off so I could travel directly to Blackpool from King's Cross Station. I knew I was running late, and I had already made arrangements to meet my brother in a bar at about 7:30 pm along with his mates.

When I arrived in Blackpool, I quickly jumped in a taxi to the pub where I was supposed to meet my brother. The pub was packed solid and everyone seemed to be staring at me, looking me up and down. I felt so paranoid. I just put it down to my style; surely Blackpool hadn't changed that much?

A week earlier I'd gone clothes shopping in Camden. I'd wanted to buy something trendy to wear in Blackpool—something upcycled, nostalgic and retro; my type of style. I'd always felt I was on point when it came to style and what felt comfortable to me.

My grandad was my style guru and inspiration; he'd always looked so dapper. I was so proud to hang out with him, walking around in town with him. He just had that style. He always wore smart shoes and a three-piece suit, shirt, tie, and a fedora or trilby hat. He never went out of the house without a watch, either. My grandad reminded me of the 1930's era, and this was the style I was drawn to the most, even though the majority of style for going out in town came from four shops: Top Man, Burtons,

River Island, and Debenhams. Or if you had the money, you could shop at Flannels, the trendiest clothes shop at the time, located in Nottingham. You were able to purchase name brands like Hugo Boss, Lacoste, Ralph Lauren and Stone Island, with those awful arm badges.

Eventually, the clothing market became flooded with Benidorm or Turkish fakes. And apparently, everyone had a real Ralph Lauren or Stone Island jumper; *yeah right!* And let's not forget those fake Rolex's and Tag watches.

I saw one of my brother's friends, and the first thing he said was, "What the fuck are you wearing? Fancy dress isn't till tomorrow night. Is that what people are wearing in London? Thank fuck I don't live there. Anyway, your bro is over in that corner talking to some chick." He pointed in that direction while he was cracking up with laughter. I wasn't surprised by his reaction; after all, he was wearing a pastel pink Ralph Lauren shirt.

When I finally found my brother, he also had a strange reaction to what I was wearing. "What the fuck! Fancy dress isn't till tomorrow night, didn't you get my text? I sent it last week." He pissed himself laughing, and then turned around and carried on chatting to this woman.

"I'll get myself a drink, shall I?" I said in a sarcastic way and headed to towards the bar. I made a quick stop at the bathroom. I was paranoid and I wanted to check myself out; was I missing something? Then it hit me.

Fuck me, what am I wearing? I looked ridiculous; even I would have stared at myself walking into the pub. I looked like a frigging leprechaun. I had only bought a green velvet three-piece suit and a white 70's shirt with big collars. It didn't help my cause that I had a full-on ginger beard and was wearing a green fedora hat.

I swear it looked black in the shop, and even when I got changed at my bed and breakfast before I saw my brother, it looked very black. How the hell did I get this so wrong? Did I pick up the wrong clothes? Then I started to crack up. It finally hit me that when I was shopping, I was wearing my transitional glasses and everything looked black at the time, not green.

But in the pub, the glasses had turned clear. Staring back at me in the bathroom mirror was a five-foot, six-inch leprechaun. *This is going to be a long night. What a dickhead.*

It wasn't the best Friday night in Blackpool. The moment we all walked into a bar, twenty minutes later, we were necking our drinks and en route to another bar.

I didn't understand why we were in and out so fast. They all seemed to be on a mission to get hammered. To me, it felt like we were just chasing someone or trying to meet up with one of my brother's friends, seemingly always missing them. I was getting fed up with this in-out-and-walk-to-a-new-bar attitude, so I asked one of my brother's mates, seeing as I had hardly spoken to or seen my brother all night. And when I did, he never gave me a straight answer.

Everyone seemed so pumped up, energetic and very talkative, they seemed completely different compared with all the other times we had been to Blackpool. I couldn't even get a straight answer from them either; they seemed to be on another planet. I couldn't put my finger on it, and I had a feeling I didn't fit in, either. What a disappointing night. I eventually went back to my room shortly after 1 am.

The following morning during breakfast, I noticed everyone was so quiet. There was no banter at all, which was odd. They also looked like they hadn't slept for a week. I just put it down to too much drinking and dancing. I wasn't even sure what time my brother came home, either.

The weekend's fancy dress theme was superheroes. The groom and his best mate were dressed as Batman and Robin, a similar look to Del and Rodney from the classic TV show *Only Fools and Horses*. We were all dressed normally for the day.

They'd had no idea at all that my brother and the rest of the football team had all gone shopping with the groom, and that they'd all bought fancy dress costumes. So when they came running down the stairs and ran outside onto the street for their big Batman and Robin entrance, they looked stunned. No one told them it was just those two wearing costumes, and now we were out-out. There were sixteen of us, including Batman and Robin. I knew today was going to be a fun day, but my lesson from my previous Blackpool visit with these guys was don't play drinking games.

During the day, it was one laugh after another for the entire day. Tower Lounge was packed solid as usual. Everyone was in high spirits, but my brother seemed to be miles away.

My brother was divorced, something I'd only found out about after my mum told me. I'd had no idea. I'd had an inkling that his marriage wasn't going to last too long; they didn't seem to have that long-lasting spark. And she was a little bit of a nutter, too.

A few months earlier, with a different woman, my brother had also become a father to a beautiful baby boy. I had been really happy for him; he'd seemed to have found someone nice to settle down with.

I walked over to my bro and sat down next to him, jokingly saying, "You texting another woman?"

He got so angry with me, "What the fuck has it got to do with you anyway, who I text?" he snarled back at me.

"You're kidding me, aren't you, you're not actually texting someone else, are you? You just had a baby."

"What's it got to do with you, what I do?" he replied. I had heard that tone before, so I stood up and left to find someone else to hang out with.

Saturday had a similar feeling to Friday, as we were moving from bar to bar. Again, it seemed like we were looking for someone. I was the type of person who enjoyed the atmosphere of a few bars rather than many; I was getting pissed off with all this walking. I didn't want my head to be snapped off again from my bro, so I asked one of his mates, "Why are we walking all the time?"

He also snapped at me, "Ask your bro, he's the one that has been chasing this chick all over Blackpool."

That can't be right, I thought, so I decided to find my brother and confront him about what his mate had just said. He'd had no idea that I was behind him, listening to what he was saying earlier to his new girlfriend, the mother of his newborn son. "I love you so much, and please give my little one a big kiss from me. I am so proud of you; I can't wait to see you tomorrow."

After listening to his phone conversation, I was convinced he wasn't chasing anyone around Blackpool. So I gave my bro a big hug and told him I missed him and I loved him, and I went to buy him a drink. I came back from the bar, and he was gone. His mates said, "We're off again, best drink up." I left both drinks at the bar and left too. I knew they wouldn't wait, and I didn't want to neck both bottles.

I was glad that we all made it to a night club. I thought I could finally relax and enjoy some dancing and not worry about anything else. That is, until I asked one of my brother's mates if they had seen my bro. I hadn't seen him at all since we arrived at the club.

"Your bro left with that chick about an hour ago, the one he's been chasing all weekend. But he made us swore not to tell you, he knew it would piss you off if you found out. Anyway, we are all heading back to our room, we're going to calling it a night."

It was 4 am, after all. I was fucking fuming, what the hell was going through my brother's mind?

I got back to my room, and my door was locked. I tried my key, but that didn't seem to work. Something seemed to be blocking the key from the inside. I knocked on the door, and I got no answer. Then Batman ran up the stairs and tried to barge the door open with his shoulder, but he bounced straight off the door and back down the stairs.

We all just cracked up, pissing ourselves laughing. I mean, he physically bounced off the door and onto the ground floor. Some Batman he was. But he was ok. He mentioned that my bro was in the room with that chick.

I was fuming. *How the fuck can he do this, after what I heard him say to his girlfriend earlier?*

I then noticed near another door there was a bucket filled with some type of water, fried chicken bones, half-eaten burgers, etc. It smelled and looked minging. I started banging on the door, demanding that he open it. The moment the door opened, I was ready to throw this entire bucket all over him for lying to me and wasting my entire weekend. I was that disappointed with my bro.

I'd had fucking enough of his behaviour. The door slowly opened, and I threw the entire contents of the bucket towards my brother, but I banged my arm on the door frame the moment I launched the bucket, which changed its direction. I totally missed him and accidentally threw it on the woman instead.

Everyone outside the door started to piss themselves laughing, but my brother was fuming. I apologised to the woman, but no apology would have made this situation any better, especially when she had a piece of chicken skin sliding down her face, and her naked body was covered in this wet stench.

My brother jumped off the bed and tried to land a few punches to my face. I had never seen him this angry before, yet he was the one who was cheating. His mates eventually broke up our fight, and he walked the woman home. giving himself time to calm down. Hopefully, he would realise that he was going to make a massive mistake if he did sleep with her and that I had his back.

Still, I wasn't sure what mood he would be in when he did get back, so I slept in one of his mate's rooms, just on the safe side.

All of a sudden, I felt my windpipe collapse in on itself. My eyes instantly opened upon impact. I was gasping for air, but no air was coming in. Then I felt another sudden force to my face, I heard my nose crack, tears streaming from my eyes.

My brother was standing above me with both hands gripping the top bunk for extra leverage, as he repeatedly stamped on my throat and my face. I was in a world of pain. I couldn't breathe or see, my head was pounding, and all I could do was curl up in a ball. I thought that he wasn't going to stop, that he was going to kill me.

One of his mates jumped off the bed and tried to restrain him. "What the fuck are you doing? That's your bro! You're going to fucking kill him if you carry on." He then pushed his mate to one side.

"I don't fucking care! No one tells me who I can and cannot fuck."

He then managed to land another three or four kicks to the side of my head as he was being restrained. I nearly blacked out, but he didn't stop.

He wanted to destroy me. I have never seen rage like this before.

Another one of his mates heard all the commotion and ran into our room, trying to help restrain my brother. He was like a man possessed; screaming at the top of his voice "No one tells me who I can and cannot fuck! No one! You're fucking dead!"

He managed to shrug off both his mates. He was relentless and determined to kill me that morning.

It took five of my brother's mates to drag him out of the room, kicking and screaming.

"You're going to kill your brother if you carry on like that!"

"I don't fucking care—no one tells me who I can and cannot fuck!"

I extended my stay in Blackpool by an extra three weeks after that horrific morning. I was incapable of moving. I was in so much pain. I knew my face was fucked; I just didn't realise how bad until I saw my reflection in the bathroom mirror.

A few days later I was unable to recognise myself. I was in a right fucking mess, unable to fully open my eyes, cuts and bruises all over my face and body, struggling to breathe with a crushed windpipe. Having two broken ribs made it no easier. And my nose was broken again.

I didn't want anyone to ask me any questions about what happened, so I used my entire four-weeks holiday entitlement, making an excuse to my boss that I needed to look after my mum, so no one saw how broken I was, inside and out. I just couldn't get my head around why my brother wanted to kill me that morning.

It couldn't be just because I had stopped him from fucking a random woman. That made no sense to me. I have never seen anyone this angry before. Something had changed. I had an idea, but I knew he would never tell me the truth.

I still believed I did the right thing that night. But his mates weren't that convinced, and said I shouldn't have gotten involved.

Using the excuse to look after my mum didn't go down very well with Dr. Jekyll or Mr. Hyde. The moment I stepped through my front door, I took more physical and verbal abuse. It was never-ending.

***

Six months later, I hadn't heard anything from my brother since the fight in Blackpool, not even an apology. Not like I was ever going to get one either, but still, I hoped.

My relationship with Dr. Jekyll was still not good, and I was starting to see more and more of Mr. Hyde. I was so embarrassed; our poor neighbours—every other weekend they could hear us argue. I just couldn't understand why she couldn't stop drinking and build a solid foundation to move forward. Something had to give!

We both decided maybe another fresh start away from everyone was the best way to save our relationship. Perhaps me more so, but it wasn't a bad idea at the time. A lot of people had gotten married or tried to start a family to save their relationship; a new start made a lot of sense.

The only issue was our fresh start was in New Zealand, on the other side of the world. Dr. Jekyll had applied to work at Manukau Council, and was offered a position along with a three-year working visa. I was also granted a three-year working visa, but I figured it would be best to apply for jobs once we arrived in Auckland, making the interview process easier.

We still had a lot of organising and sorting out before this opportunity became our reality. We both had to pass police background and medical checks and find an established estate agent to rent and manage our property while we were away for the three years.

I was excited, apprehensive, but most of all, scared shitless of leaving my family behind. Mum had always encouraged me to be independent and think for myself. Most of all, she wanted me to be happy. I had always wanted to try something new, something a little different, maybe a little adventurous. I just didn't expect it to be on the other side of the world.

Mum had two quotes when I was feeling down and lost: "I just want you to be happy, no matter what anyone else tells you. You create your own happiness, not anyone else, this is your life to live and enjoy." and "Worry when I worry, and I'm not worried."

Mum used both quotes the day I told her I was leaving for New Zealand, one of the hardest conversations I had ever had with Mum. I knew she was devastated. Even though I had lived away from home since I was twenty-four, moving to the other side of the world was a little too far for her. I promised her that no matter what happened, we would treat those three years as our around the world holiday adventure. We could meet halfway for some much-needed mother and son time.

My brother, on the other hand, wasn't so supportive. We still hadn't sorted out our differences since Blackpool, and now he was laying the guilt trip on me by saying, "Thanks for leaving me to look after Mum, thanks for that. I will never forgive you for leaving our family. I can't believe I am the one who has to look after Mum while you fuck off and enjoy yourself."

I wasn't surprised by my brother's outburst; obviously, he was still angry with me, but Mum had only just turned sixty-two and I was only away for three years, if that. It never made sense to me why he said that, but then again, he was only looking after himself.

He wasn't one for seeing the world unless it had bars, nightclubs and girls, his type of culture. And to be fair, I also admired this about him. He always knew what he liked and I couldn't fault him.

Me, on the other hand, I was still searching for my happiness. I had no idea what my calling and purpose was in life. I followed everyone else, hoping something would shout out to me and stick; something had to be better than the life I had dealt with so far.

The day before Dr. Jekyll and I were due to fly out to New Zealand, we had an enormous argument about me getting work and how I would be able to support myself or pay my share of the mortgage. I didn't have much savings and I also never felt it was our house. Always a fifty-fifty share, but Dr. Jekyll never reassured me when times were tough that she had my back.

I sat outside in our communal garden, starting to have second thoughts. I just wasn't sure this was going to work. I really wanted it to, but for it to work, we could only take Dr. Jekyll; Mr. Hyde had to stay behind. I was leaving my family for us, and I gave up so much. All she had to do was give up the booze.

I was lost, and with four hours before we drove to the airport, I decided to call my family. I wanted to hear their honest opinion on what to do. But I never heard back from anyone, so I took it as a sign to get on the plane and create a new life for Dr. Jekyll and me.

As soon as the plane was speeding down the runway, I immediately started to have a panic attack or a moment of clarity. *What the fuck am I doing? This isn't my dream or my adventure. I got bullied into this with the promise of a fresh, new, loving start. And because I was so scared of being alone, I just went along with it, when I should have said something. But I also didn't want to have to deal with Mr. Hyde either.*

As the plane banked to the left in the direction of New Zealand, I realised that I had just packed up my entire life for Dr. Jekyll's dreams and adventures, and I had no idea why I was even with her.

Fuck, now what?

8

AUCKLAND WASN'T LONDON THAT'S FOR SURE

When we touched down in Auckland, New Zealand, the City of Sails, the first thing I noticed was how blue the sky was. It was the bluest of all blues, truly stunning. We had arrived at the height of summer, with no visible clouds in sight.

But it should have said "Auckland, City of Grey." I couldn't believe how grey the city centre was. No matter where you looked, everywhere in the Central Business District (CBD) was grey, or shades of grey, hardly any green spaces or trees.

I don't know what I was more disappointed with: the fact that the CBD was so small and completely vehicle landlocked, that the city started to shut down during the week at around 8 pm, or that the city was so grey. Auckland's waterfront had gotten get a slight facelift when they'd hosted the America's Cup back in 2003, and the waterfront viaduct area was born: a mix of bars and restaurants overlooking the marina.

And once you'd walked up and down both sides of Auckland's main street, called Queen Street, or veered off to High Street adjacently opposite, that was basically it. My town centre seemed bigger than Auckland's CBD. It's funny how internet photos always seem way better than in real life. I blame photoshop.

I left London to move **here** *with Dr. Jekyll for her new job? What have I done?*

Dr. Jekyll and I needed to find somewhere to live, so one day we caught a ferry to a place called Waiheke Island, roughly thirty minutes from the CBD. It didn't take us long to fall in love with this village-style island neighbourhood. The views towards the city were breathtaking; this place had such a good vibe with its colourful villas, quaint little streets, and an eclectic array of cafes, bars, restaurants, and beaches within walking distance. Waiheke Island had a similar feel to Belsize Park during the weekends. We instantly knew that this was the perfect location to start our life in New Zealand. I could easily imagine myself commuting by ferry with the sun on my face, the wind blowing through my hair, drinking a coffee, or as they say, a 'flat white'. I was in love.

Waiheke Island became our new home; we found a stunning two-bed villa right in the heart of the village and only a ten-minute walk to the ferry terminal. It was perfect; all I needed now was a job.

Dr. Jekyll settled into her new role very quickly and was enjoying the new challenge. I, on the other hand, was already missing home. Auckland just didn't have the same feeling as London. Nevertheless, I had interviews with all the leading design practices, and with my experience, I could have worked anywhere.

But after much deliberation, I settled on a smaller practice, which was not as well-known as the others. Still, they offered me the role of lead designer for a brand-new urban park, which was part of a huge urban regeneration development. The only issue with working for this design consultancy was that the office was located two hours away from Waiheke Island.

I sure know how to pick them, and I definitely didn't make it easy for myself. I was up at 5 am so that I could catch the ferry at 6 am to the city, then catch the 6:45 train, followed by a twenty-minute walk to the office.

This was my routine for the best part of a year, as I didn't have a driver's license. I'd had no need for one, especially living in London. Plus, Dr. Jekyll and I had made a sustainable commitment to only use public transport and not add to the ever-growing congestion. We stood by our belief that all cities needed to be walkable and not dominated by vehicles.

In my previous employment, I was fortunate enough to have worked on some very high-profile projects, which were miles ahead in terms of innovative thinking compared with the designers in Auckland. Auckland had virtually no public transport infrastructure, making our decision not to have a car all the more challenging, but somehow we were coping.

My expertise was in conceptual artwork, narrative and telling the story, not to mention detailed design and construction details. And from my experience, if you were not sure about how to construct your design, then you might struggle with your overall budget, timeframe, and initial

117

concept when presenting to your client. I have always believed that unless you know these things, there's no point presenting in the first place; you will never get the desired outcome.

The first five months were extremely tough, especially being in a new country. Dr. Jekyll had started to make some friends, whereas I found myself struggling to make friends again. Although one time we did get invited to a house leaving party by the same people we had just bought bedroom furniture from.

But it went pear-shaped very quickly: within an hour of arriving at the party, I was completely drunk. I didn't realise that I was drinking 80% rum with my coke. I needed to get home fast, as I wasn't in a good place; I just needed my bathroom.

The moment we got home, I quickly ran into the bathroom and instantly threw up. I had hardly ever got drunk, maybe only once in the last five years. I had always hated the feeling of not being in control, and I hated being sick.

After I threw up, I curled up on the bathroom floor next to the radiator with a warm towel over my body.

All of a sudden Mr. Hyde was screaming and yelling at me for being pissed!

"You're fucking useless at drinking. You have ruined my day. You know how much I wanted to get pissed and now I can't. You're an absolute waste of fucking space and I wish I hadn't come to New Zealand with you."

Mr. Hyde started kicking me in the back, shouting "Get up, get fucking up, you're a useless fucker. How dare you get pissed like this, how dare you ruin my day, what am I going to do if you're like this all day? Fucking useless you are, pathetic little boy."

I had no idea what I had done wrong. I had just got drunk very quickly without realising it, and all I wanted to do was come home and sleep it off. But Mr. Hyde had other ideas; she was trying to drag me out of the bathroom by my arms and into the hallway.

"What have I done wrong? I just want to sleep, why can't you let me sleep?"

"You've ruined my day. I was enjoying myself, and now we're here. This is all your fault. You're fucking useless."

The next minute, I felt something land on my face; it was a torn-up photo. Mr. Hyde had started ripping up all of our holiday photos and throwing them at me while I was still on the floor, continually screaming, "You're fucking useless, a fucking stupid twat, I fucking hate you."

Our fresh start had only lasted five months.

At least work was going well, and I had my initial design concept signed off by the client, including all major stakeholders. The next step of the process was the construction and engineering drawing and designing the retaining walls for the two main stormwater ponds. I didn't want to pick any off-the-shelf, same old retaining walls that were being used all around Auckland. Those types of retaining walls didn't fit in with my overall concept, and, after all, I was hired based on my expertise.

We started to go to our local pub more and more. I even started smoking, even though Mum had won her battle against throat cancer. Mr. Hyde had introduced me to smoking, convincing me it would help me relax, seeing I was missing home more and more. Eventually, it became the norm every time I had a beer.

On the plus side, my office had relocated into the CBD, and my daily commute was now thirty-five minutes instead of two hours. I was delighted with this outcome. The office was located in a historical heritage building, with original brick walls, large sash windows, and existing wooden floors. My desk even had views out to the city.

Even better news, Mum decided she would fly over for a three-week holiday in November. But Dr. Jekyll wasn't too happy with that outcome, since I would be spending most of my holidays with Mum.

When I handed in my holiday request form, I was told that I wasn't entitled to any paid holidays within my first year, even though I had already accumulated three weeks during that year. Apparently, this was part of New Zealand's Holidays Act of 2003. I explained that my mother was flying over and that she had already purchased the tickets as a surprise, so I asked if it was possible to have fewer holidays the following year.

The answer was a sharp *NO!* so I had to take unpaid leave, which didn't go down well with Dr. Jekyll either, as I still had to pay my share of our U.K. mortgage. I asked if Dr. Jekyll would help me out for the month Mum arrived, but I got an unexpected *no* from her, too.

***

I was very apprehensive, and I was starting to have that churning feeling of dread in the pit of my stomach, when you know the shit is going to hit the fan. I was waiting with bated breath, knowing Mum was about to walk through the arrival doors. As soon as she did, I gave her the biggest hug ever; I desperately needed that.

I think it lasted for about two minutes before I spotted my sister walk through the doors, too. I had no idea at all that she was arriving. I was in shock and totally surprised; I was waiting for Cilla Black to appear next with her catchphrase, "Surprise, surprise." I had no idea at all, and I couldn't have been happier. This got a total opposite reaction from Dr. Jekyll; she was not pleased one bit.

Jetlag and the time difference hit my mum and sister like a truck. They would both sleep for the entire day, and then be wide awake during the night. I think my sister struggled the most. She was always hungry in the middle of the night. This made her unbelievably grumpy for the first two weeks, which I totally understood; it had been a massive shock to my system, too.

I decided that we should all take the Overlander train, which left Auckland and arrived in Wellington, the capital of New Zealand.

It was a twelve-hour journey through the countryside, but we soon realised that we should have driven or flown down. The scenery was all the same, nothing really to look at. It was a real disappointment, as they had advertised it as something else. Not the start we were hoping for.

But wow, Wellington was stunning; it had everything that Auckland didn't have: a fantastic waterfront, loads of funky bars, shops, restaurants, open spaces, and best of all, you could walk from one side of the city to the other. We were all in love with Wellington. All the tourist books referred to windy Wellington, but when we were there, all we had was stunning sunshine, which was also deadly. I kept telling them both to please use sunscreen, preferably factor fifty. But they wanted to get a tan, so my advice fell on deaf ears.

The first time I realised New Zealand's sun was lethal was when Dr. Jekyll and I had sat down on a bench in Waiheke Island looking out towards the city, both of us with high hopes regarding our work and our relationship. I was wearing shorts and a T-shirt and fuck me, did I burn! The sun was ruthless, unforgiving and brutal; if you didn't wear sunscreen factor five hundred, you would burn like you'd never burnt before. I now realised why New Zealand doesn't have poisonous snakes or spiders, or in fact, anything at all: they all fucked off because it was too hot.

I had been in so, so, so much pain, I had to keep bottles of aloe vera in the freezer. My legs were the colour of cooked lobsters, and my face was like the Red Skull from the *Captain America* movie. I had to sleep standing up and I was popping pain killers like they were Smarties. The pain had been unbearable. Even the slightest of breezes felt like Freddy Krueger was knifing my legs and peeling the skin off of my face. I am not even exaggerating. If you ever decide to visit New Zealand in the summertime, mistake me not, this is real. I had stayed out in the sun for no more than ten minutes.

But Mum and my sister both insisted that they would rather go back to the U.K. with a tan than wear sunscreen, saying that they always go red before they go brown. I am not sure it's worth the pain, to be honest, but you can only advise.

Mum kept persisting that Dr. Jekyll and I should move to Wellington. Unfortunately, if I wasn't already living and working in Auckland, I could easily have seen myself staying there to live.

The first few days in Wellington were amazing; even Dr. Jekyll was enjoying herself. But then I received 'the call' from my director, ordering me to get on a plane right that minute and head back into the office; some of my drawings needed to change ASAP.

I had left explicit instructions to my team and my director that we didn't need to send any drawings out until I had got back from my holiday. I had forwarded her the client's email before I left, saying that he was happy with this decision, and he signed it off.

But my director had other plans. She went through the entire set of draft concept drawings and noticed some spelling mistakes that I had to rectify ASAP, regardless of whether I was on my holiday, even though anyone from my team could have changed them.

I had that sick feeling in the pit of my stomach, constantly churning more and more. The worry and anxiety were starting to flood my body. I tried to reassure her that I could do the edits before I sent them out in a few weeks' time, or that someone from my team could do them if it was that urgent. Which it wasn't, so I was really confused about what was going on.

I hated the fact that I was now worrying about my position in the company; this was entirely out of the blue. *Something has happened behind my back. Now I am in the firing line, and I have no idea why. It can't be for a few spelling mistakes on hand draft drawings?*

This was very alien to me. I was used to working in collaborative teams, and when someone went on holiday, we all just got on with it and helped out. Also, these were draft concepts that didn't need to be sent out for another three weeks.

But my director had other ideas; she wanted to send them out that day, which made no sense to me. I even said, "Please check your email, the client is happy for us to send them out when I get back."

It's amazing how one phone call can turn a fantastic experience into a pile of shit. I was really worrying. Mum could see how concerned I was by my face and body language. I was showing signs of stress. I really needed a cigarette more than ever, but I didn't want my mum to know I was smoking, so my anxiety and stress where sky-high.

I tried to explain again to my director that I didn't need to come back to Auckland merely for text amendments, but she wasn't taking no for an answer. I was on the phone for over an hour trying to convince and explain that this could all be done when I returned to the office, but then the phone went dead. She had hung up on me and didn't take any of my calls afterwards.

I had no idea what to do, as I had never been in a situation like this before. I had worked over sixty hours per week for nearly a year, never asked for any pay raises or time off, and out of the blue, she turns out to be another fucking Mr. Hyde.

I decided to carry on with my holiday with my family, rather than fly back for some text amendments, but I ended up regretting that decision. The next two weeks were dreadful, and my director's behaviour caused me was so much anxiety and unnecessary worry. I was being bullied, and I was unable to eat or sleep for nearly two weeks, playing over and over again what I had done wrong. I was constantly worrying about my job and I dreaded going back.

When I did return to work, my director didn't speak to me for over two weeks; I felt I had to be on my best behaviour and that my job was not secure anymore. I still had no idea what that outburst on the phone was all about. I wanted to be reassured that my job was safe, but I always got, "I'm not talking to you right this minute, go away."

Even Dr. Jekyll was worried about me keeping my job. I asked for her advice, which was "This is your shit to sort out. You have done something and you're not telling me what, so how can I help? You're lying about something."

I wasn't lying about anything; I had no Scooby Doo idea what I did wrong. So I just kept my head down until it all blew over.

I had needed Dr. Jekyll's advice on what to do next and the best way to manage this situation. I was so miserable, I dreaded going into work. I had no idea what to expect anymore. My anxiety and worry had now started to keep me up most of the night, and I looked like shit the following morning.

Dr. Jekyll and Mr. Hyde offered me no advice. They both decided to blame me instead, saying that I had placed Dr. Jekyll in this position regarding my situation, and she was concerned it might come back to bite her.

I just didn't know how to take my mind off of everything that was happening around me. My boss was now bullying me daily, always threatening me with my job if I didn't do this or that.

Dr. Jekyll and I had started going to the pub every other night. It was a bad idea, but at least it took my mind off of what was happening at work. Maybe someone there could offer me advice. After all, we were starting to make some friends. Difficult not to, really, seeing as we were now classified as locals. I only drank four bottles of beer, and then I was more than happy to go home, cook dinner, and snuggle up on the sofa to watch some shitty TV.

Mr. Hyde, on the other hand, loved the conversations at the pub, only leaving when the pub closed, generally at 12:30 am. She would rather sit outside in the freezing cold winter air, smoking and drinking sauvignon blanc like it was water, followed by rum and cokes.

I was in total conflict about what to do every night. *Do I go home and wait for Mr. Hyde to walk through the door or do I stay?* I had lost count of how many times I kept saying to Mr. Hyde, "Fancy going home and having an early night?" But the answer was always the same: "One more, then home." But then it was one more, followed by one more, followed by…

I tried to talk to Mum about the situation I was in, but I never got the answer I wanted, mainly because I didn't tell her the full story. I just didn't want her to worry any more than she already did, living this far away from me. But mums always seem to know that something is wrong, just by your tone. No matter how hard you try to cover it up, they just know.

***

I knew my time was coming to an end at the consultancy. I had spent twenty-two long, hard months working on this one project, and we were only a month away from getting it all signed off and able to start construction.

My director stomped over to my desk and started aggressively prodding my chest with her index finger—actually prodding me and pushing me back in my chair—as I was trying to stand up.

"This is all on you. Don't bother coming in tomorrow if you can't get these retaining walls signed off today."

Her aggressive, angry, explosive behaviour came from out of nowhere. I had never seen any of my previous directors behave in this manner before, and now I was confronted with pure anger. Just when I thought our working relationship was back on track; it was only the day before that she had bought me a flat white and a muffin and to told me to take the afternoon off for all my hard work.

"Can you just please stop prodding at my chest and calm down? What's my fault? What's happened?"

"Well, I just got off the phone with the engineering consultants regarding the stormwater retaining walls that you designed and reassured me that they could get constructed. He says no engineering company in New Zealand will sign off on your drawings, and we have to get them signed off today, no excuses!"

Let's just put the above statement into context. The idea was simple, so I thought. We would use 600mm x 450mm empty hessian sacks, filled with 40kg of wet concrete with a drying strength of 65MPa, dropped on top of steel rebar. Very similar to the ones at Vimy Ridge, a famous WWI battlefield in 1917, just a few miles from the city of Arras, France.

Canadian and British forces used sandbags as their retaining wall structure for their own trenches during attempts to place mines under the German trenches. To this day, they are very evident and still standing, ninety years after the battle. They built these trenches in a frigging war, during a war!

"You led me to believe that these retaining walls could be constructed, and now my company will be a laughing stock if we can't get these drawings signed off. So sort this out right now or fuck off back on your boat to where you came from."

"Can you please stop prodding me, I don't like it. And let me try to get to the bottom of this situation, what you're saying is the total opposite to what the lead engineer said last week when I presented our drawings. They seemed very happy with them."

"Just sort it out," she said, with another prod.

"Will you please stop prodding me, I don't like it. I just need to be one hundred per cent clear: are you telling me that one of the most renowned engineering companies in New Zealand can't build a sandbag retaining wall in 2008, when armed forces during World War One did? And this was my fault, why?"

"Yes, it's your fault, so sort it now," she said with one final, hard, aggressive prod.

I spoke to the lead design engineer later that day regarding my director's concerns. He had no idea what I was talking about and signed off on all of the drawings the following morning with no issues. Again, I had no idea what I did wrong or why she attacked me the way she did.

A week later, sitting at my desk with my headphones on, I was hoisted entirely out of my chair by the scruff of my neck, or should I say by my shirt, and dragged away from my desk by my director's husband.

"What the actual fuck?!"

"You're coming with me *now*. I am taking you personally to the AA centre to get your driving license. You're going to learn how to drive, and I am going with you to make sure you do. I am so fed up with you not having a driving license, so you are coming with me."

"Can you get your hands off me please, and are you serious? Are you dragging me to the AA to get my license? And again, get off me and stop dragging me across the room."

I moved his arm off my shoulder. "You're kidding me, this is how you treat your employees, grabbing me by the scruff of the neck and marching me off to the AA centre?"

"Yes, you're coming with me to get your license," and he started to grab my shirt collar again.

"Can you take your hands off me? Please, I don't deserve this, you are treating me like a criminal."

"I am giving you one month to get your driving license; otherwise, you're fired." He eventually took his hands off me and walked out of the room.

I was livid and so angry. I was being overworked here, and for all the effort I put into this place, I was shit on their shoes. I was bullied through my entire school life, bullied and sexually abused in my job at the DIY store, abused and molested in my first professional job, and now I was being verbally and physically assaulted in my workplace environment in New Zealand.

Again I needed an escape plan, ASAP.

That evening at the pub, I wanted to explain to Dr. Jekyll why I had been feeling so down and so distant, and what had been happening at work. But I didn't know how to approach the subject. I had a feeling I was going to be blamed. *"You're talking shit and you're making this up. This didn't happen, there's no way this happened. You're about to be fired, aren't you? This is your way of convincing yourself and me that it was their fault. And they're right: you are to blame. You don't have a driving license. In fact, come to think about it, I have to drive you everywhere. For once it might be nice if you drove instead of me."*

Just as I had thought, Mr. Hyde blamed me for all the issues I was having at work and offered me no advice. She just insulted and blamed me instead.

I had no other option but to look for employment elsewhere; they made me feel like I was worthless. I was starting to feel depressed, and some days I didn't even want to get out of bed. But every day, Dr. Jekyll was continually reminding me that I had to pay half the mortgage and she wasn't going to help me out.

Then out of the blue, I was given an opportunity from the artist that I had been working so closely with on my project. She wanted my help to build and launch her new art studio. Without hesitating or consulting Dr. Jekyll, I said yes; anything was better than where I was.

My off-the-hip decision didn't go down too well with Dr. Jekyll. I was now starting my second job in two years, and she saw this as a failure, rather than supporting me.

With my new contract signed, I was dreading this part the most. I had never wanted to leave, but I had no other option as I was being bullied, verbally and physically, out of my job. Now I had to tell my boss I was leaving. This wasn't going to go down well.

I knocked on her door and politely asked if she had a few minutes to spare. I wanted to get in and out as quickly as possible with no dramas. I just hoped she would see me handing in my notice as being the best thing for us both of us, rather than taking it personally.

"I just want to let you know that I am giving you a month's notice. As you're well aware that the situation in the office is not healthy, and I can't see any way of resolving our issues. I don't want to go into the details; we both know what these are. I just want to say thank you for allowing me to work in your company, and I will make sure that I hand over all up-to-date work so you can sign off on all the drawings, so there is no loose ends or surprises. And again, thank you."

Given these estranged circumstances over the last few months, I thought I came across as calm and to the point, even though I was shaking inside.

My boss didn't say one word. She just sat behind her desk, giving me an unbelievable death stare. Fuck me, I had never seen anyone look at me in that way, it was so intense. I didn't know what to do or say. I was unable to read her, and that scared me even more.

She just sat there. Tick tock. Tick tock. Tick tock. It was so still in her office. She didn't say a word for about two minutes; she just kept staring at me. Then, all of a sudden, she started to hyperventilate and bang loudly on her desk, quickly opening and closing her eyes while clutching her chest.

She started to scream at me, "I'm having a heart attack. I'm having a fucking heart attack. You did this! You did this to me! This is your fault." She fell, crashing hard against the floor. Her chair smashed against the wall behind her, and everything on her desk spilled onto the floor and into the air.

She was lying on the floor, still clutching her chest.

"You did this."

I had never seen anyone have a heart attack before apart from in the movies, but something was telling me this wasn't genuine.

What I was witnessing seemed to be something out of a B-movie; it was shocking acting. I sat in my chair, fixated on my boss rolling around on the floor, watching everything unfold. *Is this really happening?* She was still moving from side to side, pointing her finger at me from the ground with every other roll, "You made me have a heart attack; this is your fault."

I looked over my shoulder and into the central part of our office, hoping someone else could see what I could see, but everyone else was just doing their own thing. Was this a prank, was I getting pranked?

Is this really happening?

This was so bizarre. I needed to leave.

It was really hard not to laugh at this point, and I really wanted to so bad. I was cracking up inside. "Are you going to accept my notice or not? I need to grab some lunch."

She suddenly jumped back on to her feet. "You can leave right now! Don't come back. And don't expect a reference either."

***

Thankfully, I had a job to go to straight away. I was really enjoying my new role and direction. I had always had a passion for graphic design and brand strategy. So much so that during my spare time, I was working on my own project: a new innovative way to sell or rent your home.

I had always been outcome- and solution-focused, with an eye for finding a niche in the market. The idea I was working on was called Text-Agent, an information delivery system providing property information and photos directly to your phone via text message.

Most New Zealand homeowners advertised their property through local and national papers or via real estate companies, which at the time was the only way to sell or rent your property. I was working with another person on this project. We had it all worked out, a super strong brand and the technology to boot. Nothing like what we were proposing or building existed in New Zealand at the time.

First-generation iPhones had only just hit the market, and they were very expensive to purchase, so most people in New Zealand were still using older phones. Located at the bottom of the property description would be a six-digit number. Anyone who was interested in that property could text the number and within less than a minute, they would receive photographs of what the property looked like externally and internally, including relevant information; all downloaded straight to their phone.

This would save people so much travel time, as they would already have an idea of what the house looked like and whether they were interested or not. Dr. Jekyll and I had spent so much time traveling and looking at homes the first two weeks in New Zealand, and it was a nightmare. So I knew I was on to a winner.

After coming back from lunch, I noticed that my computer was on and my Text-Agent folders were all open. I thought this was strange, so I waited until my boss came home and told her what had happened. She looked at me worryingly. "You're describing something my husband came up with a few weeks ago; I think you have your wires crossed."

"No, I can assure you, I haven't got my wires crossed. Can you please go and ask your husband to come to the office? I need to know why my personal project is open on my computer."

"He's not here, he's having a meeting in the city with the owners of Trade Me and *New Zealand Herald*, regarding his idea."

"Firstly, it's not his idea and secondly, are you fucking kidding me? He's gone to Trade Me, New Zealand's very own version of eBay, pitching my idea of selling and renting a property via the phone?"

At the time, Trade Me only sold other people's items. I was so fucked off. I had spent the best part of two years working on this idea and her husband stole my idea and passed it off as his own!

"There is no way he would do that. He's not a thief, and I resent the fact that you're even accusing him. You're out of order, I think you should leave."

Then all of a sudden, that thieving fucker walked through the office like nothing had happened.

"Can you please ask him about his idea? I am not leaving till I get an answer, and that's final."

"Sweetheart, can you explain your idea to Cornelius? He says it's his concept and I'm not happy he's calling you a liar."

"I haven't got time to talk about anything at this moment in time, especially if he's calling me a liar. He just needs to go; he's not welcome in our house anymore."

"I am not leaving until you tell me why you went to Trade Me. What was your meeting about? You have stolen two years' worth of ideas and passed it off as your own. You come across like you're this creative musician and you're just a fucking lying thief. What was your meeting about? If you're not man enough to admit you're a liar and a thief, then you're no man at all. Selling other people's creative ideas and passing them off as your own. Fucking pathetic."

He finally snapped, "Whatever you do in this office belongs to us, not you. So what? I went on your computer and took your idea. You were working on our time, not yours, and if you call me a lying thief again, I'm going to fucking hit you."

I looked at my artist friend, hoping she would back me up. But, no surprises here, she didn't; she sided with her husband and asked me to leave.

I left that night and never returned. I had been in my new role for just over four months.

The following year, Trade Me Property was launched, now New Zealand's most significant online buying and renting property database. Text-Agent never did take off, but I believe the idea to sell and rent your property on Trade Me was born from what we created and what he presented on that day.

I had never come across people like this in my life. Those who just take, take, and take, with no remorse, and sleep so well at night. They have no idea how this affects people who work so hard to make a life for themselves. That fucker had stolen two years' worth of hard work, and he and his wife somehow justified that this was ok.

I was now unemployed again and Dr. Jekyll and Mr. Hyde weren't happy, to say the least. I tried to explain what happened, but they weren't having any of it. "This always happens to you; it's never your fault, it's always someone else's. How come this never happens to me? It's always you. I'm fucking sick and tired of your fucking excuses; man the fuck up and get a job ASAP or else."

I thought that Dr. Jekyll and Mr. Hyde might be right; after all, maybe this was all my fault. Why did these incidents always seem to be happening to me and not anyone else?

I couldn't understand for the life of me why I was unable to keep a job for more than a few years. I had always been fully committed to what I did, and I work hard. I never gossiped or created any office drama. But these things kept following me around.

Was I too trusting or just gullible, an easy target? Should I act like everyone else and take, take, take and fuck everyone else? The only person who seemed to be getting fucked was me. But to screw people over, lie, cheat, and stand on anyone who got in my way just wasn't who I was. But maybe it should've been.

I love this saying from the movie *Layer Cake*, starring Daniel Craig:

"You're born, you take shit, get out in the world, and take more shit, climb a little higher, take less shit. Till one day you're in the rarefied atmosphere, and you've forgotten what shit even looks like. Welcome to the layer cake, son."

Is this a true reflection of how life is?

I needed to find another job ASAP; otherwise, I had no idea what I would do. Our three-year working visa was nearly up, and Dr. Jekyll wanted to stay beyond that and become a New Zealand resident. Over the next few months, I struggled to find a job. For one reason or another, no one was looking to hire me, and I was running out of money. We were spending every night drinking and eating in the pub. Finally we had started to grow a network of friends, a welcome relief from the stress of finding a job, but this wasn't the solution.

Luckily, I managed to find a new job working at another design consultancy. One morning I was drinking a flat white in my local cafe located in Oneroa, the main town centre on Waiheke Island, when I met Dave, who at that exact moment was looking to hire a landscape architect to help expand his company. I got the position right there and then. What were the chances of that happening? I was on cloud nine. I was employed as an associate within the company, supporting both directors.

Frank had a brummie accent and seemed very knowledgeable, to the point where he always knew more than everyone else. He even labelled himself as the best landscape architect and architect in New Zealand, even though he had no qualifications in either profession. We all know those sorts of people, right?

There was nothing he couldn't do, except turning up to meetings on time. He was the Yin in the office.

He loved day drinking, but he loved the sound of his own voice even more. He was always right, and you were always wrong. During one project meeting, Frank decided to show off how amazing he was. He wanted to prove a point that designers like himself created urban environments and that he designed everything from door to door.

He addressed me as a gardener in this meeting, someone who makes 'his' spaces look pretty with plants and flowers. He didn't even address me by my professional title. Yet, he wanted me to help build a landscape architecture team within his company. I felt sorry for him in a way; he needed validation by undermining me in front of his clients and the project team.

Dave, my other director, seemed like a decent family guy. He swore by his principles and morals; he was the balance within the company, the Yang. It wasn't hard to see why everyone liked him, myself included. He always had my back and promoted my ideas and visions.

In my first year, I secured over seven-hundred thousand dollars' worth of new work, built a successful team consisting of four landscape architects and two graphic designers, and we were winning project after project. Still, I wasn't sure if Frank was happy with this outcome.

I was astonished one night when Frank knocked on my home door. He was on his way back home from drinking in the city and he wanted to personally thank and congratulate me for all my hard work over the last year. Frank handed me a small wrapped present and asked me not open it until Christmas morning. He blew me away with his kind gesture; I hadn't expected anything. I thanked him and closed the door.

I was struggling to figure out what he had handed me; it was no bigger than a cork. I couldn't wait a week. I needed to find out what he had personally bought me, right there and right then. I unwrapped his present and, fuck me, why would you even bother? This was an insult; he had only wrapped up a pair of headphones, the kind you receive for free when you purchase a new phone.

I was gob smacked. I didn't know what to expect, but I hadn't expected a handful of scrunched up headphone wires wrapped in a white napkin. Once my team returned back to work after the holidays, I asked if they received anything from our directors for Christmas. I was so curious to know.

I wished I hadn't; I was shocked to learn that Frank had given the latest iPod to everyone else—even the part-time landscape architect, who had only been with us a few months.

I just didn't get it. Why would he do this to me? What was his angle? Was he threatened or jealous about the amount of work I brought into his company? It didn't make sense.

I felt this was a personal slap in the face, and I had that same feeling that my time was up yet again, but Dave reassured me this wasn't the case.

I would have been happy with a genuine handshake or a pat on the back saying, 'good work and thank you for all your effort.' I wasn't expecting any gifts, but some sort of authentic gratitude would have been nice.

Later that year we moved into the city, and our new office window faced directly opposite my old boss's window, the one who had faked her heart attack. *Great.*

I had a bad feeling about this year. Something was off, something was happening behind the scenes. Frank and Dave were hardly in the office, and I wasn't being kept informed about what was happening, like I had been the previous year. For some reason, Frank wasn't talking to me anymore. I had that feeling in the pit of my stomach again of never being quite sure where I stood. All I could do was deliver on our projects.

Eventually, I found out what all the secrecy was about: Frank and Dave had brought in a third director, Geoff. He was the head of finance and operations, and it didn't take him long to stamp his authority throughout the office. In a few short months, Geoff had successfully created a negative working environment, which contributed to increased stress and illness. He introduced tighter deadlines, increased our billing hours to over ninety-five per cent in a forty-hour working week. Lunch breaks were non-existent.

On top of that, I was ordered to bring in an additional twenty-five per cent more work than the previous year, about a million dollars' worth of work. Ethan Hunt from the *Mission Impossible* films would have struggled to complete this mission. Geoff wasn't even prepared to listen to any compromises and never took no for an answer; I had no room to breathe.

Due to the amount of stress I was now under at work, coupled with one of New Zealand's coldest winters in years, I was struggling to breathe. I was exhausted, feverish with chills, suffering from chest pains, and continually coughing up an abnormal amount of phlegm. I became seriously ill overnight, and was rushed to the hospital with pneumonia.

But this didn't stop Geoff the Dictator from trying to order me to work from home just so I could hit his ninety-five per cent target. I was off work for over two months, and once I got the all-clear from the hospital and the doctors, I wanted to go back to work ASAP.

Unfortunately, I was unable to resume my position within the company. I learned I was under an internal investigation for not hitting my targets, even though I had had pneumonia. They were also looking at restructuring the company and discontinuing my position. I wasn't even allowed to enter the office or the building until this was all resolved.

I was continually phoning the office and Dave, but no one wanted to take my call. I just wanted to go back to work. I was so fed up with all the bullshit. I caught the ferry, marched straight into the office and demanded answers. Geoff looked me in the eye and said "You will never return back to work as long as I am here, that I can guarantee. And if it was up to me, I would have fired your fucking ass two months ago!"

"Two months ago? I was fighting for my life with pneumonia."

"Not my problem, so fuck off out of my office."

I was sacked later that day, with no explanation. I tried to call Dave but he never returned any of my calls, texts, or emails. I couldn't believe this was happening to me again. I had pneumonia, I was lucky to be alive, and I was sacked after everything I had done for this company.

I phoned Dr. Jekyll at work immediately. I needed her advice; I was shaking and in shock, and I was also shitting myself about what to tell her. I wanted to meet her at home, away from everyone else, but she knew something was wrong and wanted to meet me in the pub that night.

I was in no position to argue so we sat away from everyone while I explained everything. It didn't take long until I met Mr. Hyde that night. "You're fucking useless, absolutely fucking useless. How many jobs is it now, three? And guess what, you're the common denominator in all of this. How come I can keep my job, and yet you have so many issues?"

"You saw how ill I was. I was unable to get out of bed for over six weeks. You think I wanted this to happen? Can you for once see how I am not at fault here? I had fucking pneumonia, *pneumonia* for fuck sake! How can you call me fucking useless when I had pneumonia? Where is your heart, your compassion? I am your boyfriend, and you're treating me like shit, and I'm to blame?"

"You do know that no one will ever employ you; you're unemployable. You've burnt all you're bridges. Even I wouldn't employ you. You're a fucking liability."

And on and on it went. The more she drank, the more I was verbally abused; even the people sitting around us had now moved away. I stood up to leave and the next minute I was told, "You're not going fucking going anywhere until I get to the bottom of all your lies. You were not sacked for having pneumonia, you were sacked for something else. You can't be sacked for having pneumonia, so what is it? What have you done? What are you not telling me?"

All I wanted was a hug and to hear the words "It will be ok, this isn't your fault; we will get through this," but I was dreaming; that was never going to happen. I wasn't standing for anymore of her abuse, so I walked home, empty and depressed. I knew Mr. Hyde would stay. Maybe that was for the best; she could now slag me off behind my back. But I also knew the nightmare that came from leaving her at the pub on her own.

I'm not sure what time it was when I heard Mr. Hyde stumble through the door, maybe around 3 am, two and a half hours after the pub closed. I had no idea where she had been, but I did have an inkling.

I pretended to be asleep. I knew what was coming; you couldn't stop it; you could only delay the inevitable. I had tried many times, but was always unsuccessful. I wished I wasn't in love with Dr. Jekyll. I'd thought about leaving her so many times, but I had no idea how to. I felt like my mum, trapped and imprisoned in a relationship that had no love, no respect; only anger, violence, and abuse.

"Wake up, you lazy fucker, I know you're not sleeping. You think I'm stupid, you don't think I know when you're pretending to be asleep? Get up, I need to tell you something; I need to let you know where I have been tonight. You did this to me, this was your fault, you made me do it. Get fucking up. Get out of bed. We need to talk."

Mr. Hyde looked in a right state, pulling the duvet away and grabbing my arm, trying to drag me off the bed, but I pulled the duvet back over me and told her to sleep it off.

"You're too pissed, and you know I hate it when you get like this. I don't understand why you always attack me when you're pissed, you weren't like this yesterday."

Mr. Hyde grabbed the duvet again and threw it on the floor.

"I fucking hate you. I wish I had never met you. I should have stayed with Bill and Ted; I'm glad I fucked them both behind your back. You don't deserve me at all. You have no idea how to treat a woman properly. You're thick as fucking pig shit, fucking useless. I'm leaving you tonight. I'm going back to fuck Burt again—yes, you heard me—I fucked Burt tonight. You made me do this. You made me fuck him. I hate you so much," and then she grabbed her car keys.

Mr. Hyde was in no state to drive. She was struggling even to stand straight. There was no way I could let her drive. *Arghhhhh what the fuck, why are you doing this to me? Why?* I knew if she drove off, there would be a good chance she would hurt herself, if not kill herself. I quickly stood up and started to get dressed.

I heard the engine start up, *Fuck me, she's out of control, why is she punishing me, why can't she just stop fucking drinking and concentrate on our relationship? What the fuck do I do? Fuck, fuck, fuck, I can't let her drive, she's going to kill herself.* I ran out onto the road and she drove straight into my legs. I instantly buckled under the impact, my head hitting the car bonnet before I crashed back down to the ground, my head hitting the road.

I was in so much pain. My knees were fucked, and I felt blood dripping from my head. I managed to get back to my feet and smashed the driver's window, trying to grab the car keys.

Mr. Hyde kept hitting me in the face. I was begging her to stop. I was trying to save her life, but she was so angry. She didn't care. I managed to prise the driver's door open, and somehow, through all the hits I was taking, managed to grab the car keys.

"You're not going anywhere, you're too fucking drunk and angry. Please, please let's go inside; the neighbours heard all the arguments and have come out to see what's happening. Please, I'm begging, please let's go inside, please, I love you and I don't want you to do anything stupid."

Eventually, I managed to get her back inside the house. I also managed to convince my neighbours not to call the police. I made the excuse that she received some awful news from the U.K., and she didn't take it very well.

I made an excuse for her behaviour, but it was the correct call at the time. I was bleeding heavily from my head, and my legs and knees were severely bruised and heavily cut. I had no idea how I manged to even stand. I was fucking shattered, but she was alive.

I managed to calm her down, and eventually she fell asleep on the sofa. I stayed awake until the sun shone through the windows, sitting in the lounge and keeping an eye on her just in case she wanted to drive again.

During that time, I made the professional suicide decision to sue my former employees for unfair dismissal. I knew I was never going to be employed again in New Zealand, but after last night, I had nothing to lose. Ever since I had moved to New Zealand, I had been treated like a criminal, bullied, physically and verbally abused, and had concepts and ideas stolen from me. These people had no conscience at all, and enough was enough.

I was advised many times from the people from the pub that this was a stupid idea. Still, I didn't care; I thought mediation would be the most sensible approach, as I wanted to find an amicable solution.

My anxiety was through the roof, and I had no idea what I was doing, but I knew that these fuckers couldn't treat me like this. They couldn't get away with it. It wasn't fair.

My experience in New Zealand had been awful, definitely not the fresh start I was hoping for, but I had no other option but to stay. I had no plans for what to do next, win or lose!

Mum knew something was up. I stopped making my weekly phone calls home, and they became once a month calls. I didn't want to lie to her and say everything was OK.

My solicitor had drawn up a final settlement agreement if we won. I wasn't that bothered about the money. But in my employee contract, it had stated that I wasn't allowed to work for anyone or myself for six months and not within a 20km radius.

The door of the meeting room opened, and Frank, Dave and Geoff walked through with their solicitor and sat directly opposite me. I was fucking shitting myself; this was happening, this was real.

I explained the correct version of what had happened, including a written statement from my doctors, outlining that I had a chest infection that turned into pneumonia. I went on and explained the conversations I'd had with all three directors, followed by showing them printed emails and text messages stating I just wanted to come back to work, and asking why I wasn't allowed.

All three directors denied these allegations and the evidence I presented. I looked across to Dave, begging him to tell the truth. I was fucked if I wasn't able to work, and he was the only person who'd heard the conversation I had with Geoff. "Please Dave, I am begging you to please tell them what you heard regarding Geoff wanting to sack me when I had pneumonia. Please, please, if I can't work, I am not sure what I am going to do. You know what you heard—you were right there."

"I heard nothing of the sort. I wasn't there, sorry. I wish I could help, but I can't. These allegations didn't take place."

"What? You were right there—you stood right next to me. Why are you lying? Why are you doing this? I won't be able to work for six months—I won't be able to pay my mortgage, and I won't be able to get my New Zealand residence. Please Dave."

Dave said nothing more. The man who lived his life through principles and morals, and who I thought had my back, wasn't a man at all. He was a lying coward with no backbone; he would rather see me deported and out of work than do the right thing.

I looked towards Frank, hoping he would prove me wrong, hoping that he would say something, but he also looked away, out towards the sea. This was his company, and he had a responsibility to his employees; he was no man either. I finally turned to Geoff.

"Well done, you must be so proud of yourself, making sure your dog pack all sticks to the same story. How do you sleep at night when you know the truth and you're just lying? How can you all sit around this table, and not one of you has the balls to tell the truth?

"You all come across as big men, but you know what? You're no bigger than me. You're small and pathetic. You're all bullies who manipulate the truth to save face, convincing yourselves this is what happened, believing your own bullshit. No one respects you; you don't even respect yourselves. You're all living a complete lie, and that's sad.

"This is your one chance to let go of all the guilt and finally set the record straight and tell the truth: you wanted to sack me even though I had pneumonia. Well done. Your children must be so proud of you. What great examples you are: take, lie and ruin other people's lives, just so you can feel righteous. You're all full of shit. What a joke, I feel sorry for all your children. You're all fucking pathetic, absolutely pathetic."

Geoff bit.

"I'm glad you're not working, and you know what else I'm happy about? No residence for you. We don't want you. No one does, so fuck off back to where you came from. So what if I ignored all your calls and deleted your emails from our system; you deserved to be sacked. I wanted to get rid of you the moment I became a director. I don't know why, maybe it's the way you look or that fucking stupid accent you have. I knew if I increased your percentage, you would buckle under the pressure, just as I predicted.

"And the moment I heard you had pneumonia, and you couldn't bill at ninety-five per cent, you were worthless to me. If you think I am hiding behind these two, you got a lot to learn, little boy.

"And how fucking dare you criticize me for being a shit father? You have no idea what the fuck you're talking about. I am more of a father than you will ever be. So, you want to hear the truth, do you? Yes, I did say I wanted to sack you, and I did that same day."

Their solicitor placed his head into his hands and slumped back into his seat; he knew we had just won. It was like a scene from the movie *A Few Good Men*. But it wasn't over just yet; my solicitor took me to one side and asked me what outcome I wanted.

"I need to work, that's all I want. I have to be able to work."

"Do you trust me to get what you need?" I did.

All three directors then continued to refuse the next four written final settlements and the pay-out sum. Even though I had won, they still wanted to stop me from working. Unfucking believable. They still wanted to punish me, and this was their only way. So they kept exercising clause twelve on page eight. I was not permitted to work for six months. Every time my solicitor presented them with a new settlement, they just looked at that clause on page eight and the last page with the final settlement pay out sum.

On the fifth version of the settlement, all three directors signed the agreement without hesitation after we all agreed on the final pay out sum, which was only four months of my salary. Geoff and Frank started laughing and congratulated themselves. Dave didn't even glance in my direction. I stood up with a massive grin on my face. I was shaking, but I didn't want anyone to know this; I just needed to go outside and breathe.

Just as I was about to leave, I heard Geoff say, "I have no idea why you're grinning to yourself. You think I am arsed about the money? It's fucking peanuts to us, so fuck off back to the U.K. You're a fucking useless cunt. Good riddance."

My solicitor turned to Geoff and Frank. "My client won't be going back to the U.K. anytime soon! He's able to work for any design consultants or himself starting tomorrow; you signed away contractual clause twelve on page eight. If you don't believe me, take a look for yourselves." My solicitor took out clause twelve on the fifth version of the settlement; they had only looked at the final pay out sum. I looked Dave dead in the eyes and shook my head.

"'I live my life through morals and principles', yeah right! you keep telling yourself that."

9

THE BLACKEST OF OCEANS ON THE DARKEST OF NIGHTS

Even though I had won my unfair dismissal case, I still lost! Because between them all, they had mentally broken me. I was so exhausted from the whole process and what they had put me through for absolutely no reason, apart from that they could. Eventually, after six months, I concluded that the only person I could trust to treat me sincerely was myself.

After four years, Dr. Jekyll and I had to move out of our rented accommodation because the original homeowners were keen to move back to Waiheke Island. We were lucky that the house next door came up at the same time we had to move out; all we had to do was throw our furniture over the fence. I was lucky enough that this rented accommodation came with a granny flat located at the back of the garden; this became my new office. It was also the same year that we finally became New Zealand residents.

I loved detailed design so much that I spent the following two years as a construction specialist consultant on an initiative to help shape New Zealand's first technical specification—a professional working document and guidelines for construction consistency. By the end of the project, we had a comprehensive specification document that was coherent and accurate, allowing our public spaces to be constructed with much more accuracy than before, improving the design outcome.

Still, I started planting the seeds of self-doubt, and began to question my abilities. Was Dr. Jekyll and Mr. Hyde right? Because all she did was blame me for all the issues I had with my previous employees. "It's funny how it's always you as the common denominator, no matter where you work. You decided to go on your own, not me."

Every time I approached the subject of needing her help, it was always greeted with a solid no. All I wanted was to be introduced to her design team, but Dr. Jekyll and Mr. Hyde was happy to watch me struggle from the sidelines. "If you could just keep your job for more than a year, you wouldn't be in this mess."

Dr. Jekyll could have easily helped me out, but she chose not to. I was trapped in a vicious cycle; she was more concerned about how this could reflect badly back on her rather than supporting me, her boyfriend.

After two years of knocking on a hundred doors, my first significant design break came when I was commissioned to design a brand-new public space, located in 'South Auckland'. I was honoured and humbled at the same time for being able to work on such a transformational project.

The timeframe was so tight, and I had to get my design signed off by Iwi, the Māori nation; Auckland's mayor; city council; and the community; then constructed and opened, all within a year. The challenge ahead of me was enormous, but I knew I could deliver this $1.5M project within that timeframe. The biggest challenge was the removal of all ten parking spaces; Aucklander's love their parking spaces so much, I can't even express it in words.

After four months, and with the help of my project managers, we knocked it out of the park; my design was signed off in record time. The only issue was that shortly after the design was signed off, my new budget became $1M. And the design could not change.

I had less than four months to complete the full set of working drawings and detailed designs, and I had to find a way save $500k. I worked out that if I changed the depth of all the foundations that the paving sat on and increased the size of the paving units, I could save around $300k. My other saving cost was to initiate a completely radical new tactile paving idea, like the one I saw on a project called 'More London' located on the South Bank.

New Zealand would then have its first shared space, including a brand-new way of introducing tactile paving, rather than the yellow or silver dots that we usually see at pedestrian crossings.

It was opened on time, and I saved the $500k needed.

I thought this was the start of my career in New Zealand, but then all individual surrounding councils amalgamated into one Super Auckland Council. Most of the existing council employees either got relocated into new departments or had to reapply for their old positions.

Change was coming, including an influx of overseas U.K. designers straight off the boat. Unfortunately, that meant most of the contacts I had been building up relationships with had now all moved elsewhere.

I was back to square one, looking for any scraps of work to keep me going.

Dr. Jekyll was headhunted during this challenging period, and she decided to take a more senior role within a well-known established engineering design consultancy, leaving her Manukau Council position. She was now my competition.

The good news was that the U.K. mortgage interest rate fell. We were starting to build up a nice nest egg of rental income, and I felt the pressure lift a little regarding the mortgage repayments. I just wished Dr. Hyde would stop drinking so we could build a strong relationship foundation and move forward. It had been over a year since Dr. Jekyll and I last slept together. I felt the respect she had for me fading fast, but I was still determined to make this work. I know, hey? Crazy!

Looking back, I realised I should have never left the U.K. I was being held hostage in my relationship—with no real friends, as she kept pointing out to me—apart from the people at the pub. I was lonely, depressed, withdrawn. I felt ashamed, guilty, worthless, insignificant, unloved, and most of all, trapped in an abusive, controlling relationship. I was so far from home.

The mind games Dr. Jekyll and Mr. Hyde played were next level shit that I had no idea how to handle. Mr. Hyde stated many times that no one would have me, that I offered nothing to anyone, and that I was lucky to be in a relationship with her.

She was so good at convincing me that I started to think maybe she was right; perhaps this was the best I was ever going to get, and without her, I would be nothing.

***

I still hadn't patched things up with my brother. He never texted me to see how I was. It was always me texting him. Always one way, and the same went for my sister. I loved them so much, yet, I got nothing back, not even a 'how are you?' text. I thought of going back to the U.K. and starting all over again.

I was so overwhelmed that I was beginning to spiral out of control. The voices in my head were getting louder, more cynical, and I was listening to what they were saying. And more importantly, I was doing what they were saying; I had no way to stop the noise.

I headed to the pub for a drink and to see who was there; anything to take my mind off of what was going through my head. I sat downstairs next to the bar in the 'locals' corner with a bottle of Stella. A new friend who I met about four months ago was also sitting at the bar. He introduced me to his sister called K and then continued talking to his girlfriend. I was so nervous talking to K. Not because she was so attractive; I was more concerned about what Dr. Jekyll would say if I got caught talking to K, because Dr. Jekyll was also on her way to the pub from work.

Without a doubt, I knew Mr. Hyde would appear later that night, looking to start an argument in the pub followed by further verbal abuse when we got home, out of sight. I strategically positioned my bar stool so that I could talk to K and look over her shoulder through the pub window. This way, I could observe when Dr. Jekyll was crossing the road, heading towards the pub, which would then allow me enough time to shift my position to look like I wasn't talking to K on my own.

K asked me if I preferred living in Auckland over London. For the first twenty minutes of meeting K, I moaned about missing London so much and how shit Auckland was. I realised that I hadn't once ask K any questions about herself.

K worked at private hospital in Albany, located in North Shore, as an office administrator. Outside of work she volunteered at a cat rescue and sanctuary, helping cats that have been neglected. She'd also lived and worked in London for over two years. However, when her work visa ran out, she'd come back to Auckland to live with her mum while waiting for her boyfriend's work visa to Australia to go through. They'd both discussed moving to Sydney as soon as it did, and it was in the process of getting approved.

I asked K which area of London she worked in. "Mainly Old Street," she said.

"I know Old Street; I don't know how many times I walked up and down both sides of the street on the weekends, looking for Jamie Oliver's Fifteen Restaurant."

I had always loved Jamie Oliver, ever since I first saw him on the *Naked Chef* cooking series, which appeared on TV in 1999. I always craved Jamie Oliver's lifestyle, especially the rapport he had with his friends. My sister would buy me his latest cookbook for my birthday, without fail.

I had admired Jamie for what he was trying to achieve with Fifteen, and I had always wanted to eat there as a way of paying my respect back to him for his efforts to help troubled teens, but the waiting list was like nine months long. Dr. Jekyll was never keen. Instead, she would rather spend her money on wine than eat somewhere nice.

K replied, "Wow, that's so funny, I had also been trying to find the location of his restaurant, too." We both cracked up laughing.

"How can it be that hard to find? I also heard that his steaks are amazing. Maybe it just wasn't meant to be! I think the food is the thing I miss the most about London, not that I went out to eat that much. I especially miss a good curry. I love curries, but the ones in Auckland aren't the same as home; they all seem too sweet, and they aren't that hot either," I responded. "I really love curries, but in Auckland, I have struggled to find anywhere that tastes like home."

I remembered that my obsession with curries had started in my early twenties after a night out with the models. Somehow, I'd ended up in the local curry house and I had never eaten curry before, so I took their advice on what to order. I had a Kingfisher strong beer, three papadums with all the condiments, a garlic naan, and a chicken jalfrezi.

It was an unbelievable mouth-watering flavour bomb of aromatic, layered spices, tender pieces of juicy chicken breast fully submerged in a thick, reddish-brown curry sauce. I was like the little girl in *Goldilocks and the Three Bears*, except my first curry wasn't too sweet, and it wasn't too hot either. It was absolutely perfect, served with a bowl of aromatic, fluffy white rice in little copper bowls. I was in heaven, and no matter how full I was, I was still optimistic about finding one last piece of chicken hidden in all that sauce at the bottom of the bowl.

We'd never really had Indian spices in our house when we were growing up. Our dinners mainly consisted of meat and two veg with

Bisto Instant Gravy. Not that I will ever complain—Mum's dinners always tasted fantastic. On infrequent occasions, Mum would make the best BBQ Chinese pork spareribs. I had eaten many ribs in my time, and nothing had ever come close to her sauce. It always won, hands down.

I also never shared my food, either. During my first proper date with Dr. Jekyll, we'd gone to the Freemans Arms, a pub in Hampstead. I had just finished eating scampi, chips, and peas: one of my all-time favourite meals. When I noticed on the dessert menu that they had profiteroles, I was so down to order them, and asked Dr. Jekyll if she would like a dessert.

She replied with, "No, I'll order another glass of wine instead."

So I ordered my dessert and within five minutes, I had seven beautiful golden brown puff choux pastries, filled with vanilla cream, and capped with dark, glossy chocolate. I was in heaven.

I was just about to pop the first one whole into my mouth when Dr. Jekyll reached over the table and tried to grab one.

"What are you doing?" I said in a sarcastic, dry tone.

"I want one now, and you have seven of them, if that's OK?"

"Sorry, that's not ok. I asked if you wanted a dessert, and you said wine is your dessert of choice. I already mentioned why I don't share my food, but this is who I am. I'm sorry."

"It's just one profiterole; surely I can have at least one?"

"I am sorry, but I don't share my food with anyone, and you know why I don't share. I am just not used to it. Ever since I was little, whatever was on my plate was mine."

Dr. Jekyll wasn't very impressed, but neither was I about her reaching over and assuming she could just take one without asking. Looking back I think that was the first night I'd witnessed the emergence of Mr. Hyde—

"Well you're more than welcome to come to my mama's house, and I am happy to cook you a curry. It might not be the same as the ones you had back in the U.K., but I definitely don't add sugar, and I can make it as hot as you like. It's up to you, but the offer is there."

I couldn't get my head around what I had just heard, so I didn't say anything for about ten minutes; I merely sat at the bar drinking my beer, baffled and confused.

This was the first time in my entire life that someone had shown me any type of kindness, without seeming to want anything back in return.

Why would K offer to cook me a curry?

I didn't get it, it made absolutely no sense. I didn't share my food. I never shared my food.

I was desperately trying to figure out what her angle was, her end game. But K seemed honest, sincere, straight up, and genuine.

Nothing was falling into place. Dr. Jekyll refused to even buy me a coffee when I'd accidently forgot my wallet one day; I remembered watching on while she drank hers.

My mind was working overtime; my emotions and feelings were scrambled. Logic wasn't working. Nothing was working. People don't just offer something for nothing in return. Not in my world.

Had that been a lie I had been led to believe all my life? A lie I had never thought to question, until now?

My body was trembling; inside I wanted to cry, scream, and shout.

I was so upset by K's offer, but I had no idea why. I felt like I was having an internal panic attack.

That was the first night I realised something was wrong with me. Something was off, something was really off. That night was the first time that I'd glimpsed my future—and that scared the fuck out of me—but the worst part was that I just sat there drinking my beer, smiling and behaving like nothing was wrong with me.

***

Over the next few months, Mr. Hyde came out more and more. The arguments were now escalating rapidly. They'd also started to intensify, and I was terrified of both Dr. Jekyll and Mr. Hyde.

With them, you had no idea where you stood: one minute everything seemed OK, we were laughing, and then the next minute Mr. Hyde wanted a full-on argument about why I hadn't gone downstairs to get her another glass of wine, or worse, even dared to suggest going home early.

Sorry, but no curry in the world was worth the wrath of Mr. Hyde, so I never took up K's offer.

Auckland Council had become the largest single-handed client for commissioning design projects, I was repeatedly told, time after time. Unfortunate for you if you didn't have a track record or any collaborative experience.

Let's examine Auckland Council's Catch 22 project procurement process: I had to provide three or more completed projects over a specific value, they had to be projects for design services, and I couldn't use any projects from previous design companies or any projects from the U.K. They had to be specifically in New Zealand.

I needed to be part of a design team that already had a record of accomplishment, just so I could be in their procurement database. So unless you were already in the top ten preferred design consultancies, you were fucked!

I also founded a world-first urban design social network for everyone with a committed interest in the built environment. I created an information hub devoted to tracking emerging, innovative designs, and sustainable trends in the built environment.

I was getting an average of 22,000 hits per month. I had all the best resources and expertise from around the world at my disposal. How could I not break that top ten with what I was proposing?!

Dr. Jekyll wasn't interested in what I was trying to achieve; she was more concerned about who to tap up using her old council contacts to bring in new revenue for her new employees. I asked Dr. Jekyll for her help so that I could get my consultancy off the ground, but her response was always, "Someday."

"Someday I am going to cook you dinner."

"Someday I am going to stop drinking."

"Someday I'm going to help you."

"Someday I am going to respect you."

One day, I'm going to leave Dr. Jekyll and Mr. Hyde.

***

I wanted to treat Dr. Jekyll with a nice dinner out, and I was so excited to share all my hard work over the last five months. I wanted her to be proud of me and what I was trying to achieve. Despite all the setbacks I had encountered in New Zealand, I wanted to show her that no matter how hard I got knocked down to the ground, I got back up on my feet again even stronger, more determined, more focused. I wanted to prove to her that I wasn't useless or stupid.

We didn't end up going out for dinner. That night, she wanted to meet me in the pub straight after work because she wasn't having a perfect day.

My night took a back seat; it was all about Dr. Jekyll. So we sat outside on the veranda upstairs, under the heaters like every night.

I wasn't in the mood to drink, so I started to roll Dr. Jekyll a Port Royal as I watched her down the first of many glasses of wine. I knew Mr. Hyde would show up, sooner rather than later. We were sitting down with the regular drinking crew, and I was bored out of my mind listening to the same "stimulating" conversations that we'd talked about the previous night and the night before that. It was the same shit every night; it was monotonous.

"I would definitely fuck her, I would totally fuck that one as well, and her friend, but in the ass." Whenever someone new entered the bar, stimulating as they were, I just bided my time to throw my two cents into this world-changing conversation. "I have a question: what happens when you're out in the city, and you meet this stunning woman in a bar, you both also took MDMA that night, and you're in a loving, happy, sexy mood. The next minute, you are both in a taxi heading back to her place.

"She then asks you to make a couple of drinks while she takes a shower. Ten minutes later, she opens the bathroom door. In the moonlight, all you can see is her six-inch black stilettoes, an unbelievably sexy three-piece combination of black soft floral lace and an erotic wet look lingerie. Emphasizing her perfectly sculptured breasts, but cleverly concealing her nipples, complete with a matching suspender belt hugging her curves tight. Your eyes slowly glance over her legs. She's also wearing soft, shiny black stocking and suspenders, with a perfectly matching G-string.

"You can't believe your luck, you think you've hit the jackpot tonight, but then you notice she's wearing a black, nine-inch strap-on dildo, and she wants to fuck you in the ass. Would you let her?

"I mean, if you can fuck her in the ass," I nod in the direction of the woman he was just talking about, "then surely she can fuck you in the ass?"

I was just stirring the pot, but also it was a valid question.

"What the fuck are you talking about? Do I look fucking gay to you? You want me to whip out my cock and show you that I am not gay?"

That sentence alone says it all. So I stirred the pot once again.

"Wait a second; you're saying that if she fucks you, you're gay?"

"Yeah, I am!"

"But you said last night that your favourite porn scenes are the close-up ones when all you see is dick and pussy. In these exact words, 'when I watch those scenes, it always makes me want to cum harder!' So, when you're in that state of flow, intensively fixated on watching cock and you are just about to cum, how is that less gay than a chick wanting to fuck you in the ass? You're knocking one out while looking at cock."

You could physically see and hear his cogs turning. Everyone around the table was pissing themselves laughing; even the next few tables who overheard the conversation also started to snigger and laugh. It's incredible to witness how some people have so little respect for one another, but when you turn it around on them, they don't like it?

"You're a fucking idiot, that's what you are, a fucking idiot. I am not staying here to be fucking laughed at." So he stood up and left.

I turned towards Mr. Hyde, hoping that she would back me up regarding objectifying women, but she didn't say anything. She sat there and necked down her wine; she hadn't been too impressed with what I had said, and I didn't know why.

Eventually we all headed downstairs. I still wasn't in the mood to drink, and I was anxious, apprehensive, worried, and nervous, all at the same time. I had a bad feeling about tonight. My stomach had started to churn. When I felt these emotions, I knew something terrible was going to happen; my anxiety was rising.

I wanted us both to go home the moment we left the veranda, but Mr. Hyde had other ideas. She wanted to stay and carry on drinking. I was torn on what to do: stay and monitor her or go home and leave her there and hope for the best.

There is nothing worse than your partner putting you in those no-win situations. I knew a big argument was coming, but I had no idea how it was going to start, what it was about, or how it would finish. But I knew it was going to happen. I hated the feeling of the unknown. I just wanted it to be tomorrow already, but my tomorrow was always the same. That argument was going to happen, regardless of whether it was tonight or next week.

So I decided to stay and try to manage the situation. I was on damage control; I stood at the bar, watching Mr. Hyde finish off her third bottle of wine. When she was on to her fifth rum and coke, I even asked the duty manager to cut her off, but this fell on deaf ears.

I don't know how many times I had asked Mr. Hyde to leave with me that night, but the answer was always the same, "One more, then we will go." But one more always turned out to be another one, then another one, then another one.

It was 11:30 pm. Mr. Hyde was outside drinking and smoking; I stood at the bar, having a full-on internal battle. I was kidding myself, there was no way I could control tonight's outcome nor could I persuade Mr. Hyde to come home with me. She wanted to stay all night. During my inner battle, I saw K and her brother walk through the front door; this was the first time I had seen K since she offered to cook me a curry, about eight months ago.

But then I noticed that everyone in the bar started staring at her, they were scrambling over one another all trying to look at K's boobs. She was wearing a low cut jumper, not too low, but low enough. Their behaviour made me feel so uncomfortable that I took off my scarf and placed it around K's neck, to cover up her cleavage, without her even asking.

"Thank you; I did feel as if everyone was staring at me, even walking up the stairs into the pub. Dr. Jekyll looked me up and down. I did ask my brother if this top was ok to wear to the pub, and he said yes."

I could hear the wolves licking their lips, smelling that fresh blood had just walked into the pub. My actions did not go down well with Mr. Hyde, the moment the news reached her outside. She stormed in and immediately had a go at me for giving K my scarf, even though I explained my reason; my reason wasn't good enough.

K asked me if I was staying for a drink. "Unfortunately, I can't, I need to get Dr. Jekyll home, she's had a shitty day, and she's so pissed." But Mr. Hyde was now at the bar ordering yet another drink, all the time looking at me with such disgust. "Ok, I can stay for one, but then I should go."

I stayed for a bit longer than I thought I would because I was chatting with K about movies, but all the time I had one eye on Mr. Hyde. I wasn't fully engaged with what K was saying; in the back of my mind I was working out the best strategy to get Mr. Hyde home. Finally, at 1 am, I managed to convince Mr. Hyde to come home with me, just after she had another go at me in front of everyone for giving K my scarf. She needed to make a point and she needed me to be provoked. I just ignored her; she wanted a fight and I wasn't going to give her one.

I was now in the familiar 'unknown-known space'. This is the space where you're always walking on eggshells, and on super high alert, knowing that one wrong word could provoke or trigger a full-scale argument. I was just about to leave the pub when K stopped me and handed back my scarf, once again saying thank you. I couldn't even smile back; one misplaced smile could trigger the argument. I slowly escorted Mr. Hyde out of the pub doors, my right arm holding on to her waist and pulling her back towards me, my left hand on her stomach, trying to give her stability. But once we stepped out onto the street, the cold air kicked in and all of a sudden it hit Mr. Hyde hard, she was all over the place, unable to walk in a straight line.

"Get fucking off me, I don't need your fucking help. I bet this makes you feel so fucking righteous, not drinking 'cause you have to get up for work tomorrow. You're so full of fucking shit. You're fucking useless, you know why I haven't had sex with you? You fucking repulse me, you're so fucking unattractive, even your girlfriend doesn't want to have sex with you. It's why I fucked someone else as well when I was in Queenstown, and he knew how to fuck me, hahaha."

Mr. Hyde was now in full antagonizing mode, trying to get me to bite, trying to get me to argue. Mr. Hyde needed her fix, her drug, but I didn't bite, I just needed to get her home.

"This is all your fault; you made me like this. You're fucking useless, no one wants you, and no one likes you. Even your family doesn't want anything to do with you. Everyone in my office thinks you're a fucking joke. Nothing will ever come of you, and everyone knows what a useless fucker you are. The reason why I never recommend you to any of my council contacts is because I know you will let them down, and everyone will point the finger at me."

I tried to ignore the onslaught of insults, still trying my hardest to keep her standing up straight to get home. But the insults kept on coming, and they were relentless, one after another. "I know something you don't. I have been keeping this quiet all the time, and I am so glad I did it." Mr. Hyde was now trying a new approach; she was now firing insults based on the past. "If you only knew what I did. Do you want to know? I took something from you years ago, all you need to do is ask. Go on, I dare you to ask me what I did. I am so glad I did it now, right under your big fucking nose".

We were halfway home, only about another two-hundred meters to go, but I still didn't say a word. Inside, I wanted to know what she was going on about. What did she mean by So glad I did it? My mind was racing, but I knew this was what Mr. Hyde wanted. This was the emotional and mental abuse that she craved. And I still didn't bite, I was fighting to hold her up, fighting my feelings and now I was fighting my inner voice. *Just ask her, you're dying to know, you need to know, you have to know.*

But I stayed silent. She pushed me to one side, trying to take a swipe at me, but she fell down instead, slumped in the middle of the road, still the insults carried on.

"I even fucked three of your friends from the pub. They all think you're a fucking joke. They also know how to fuck me; it's why I love to fuck them. It's why I sucked his cock in the toilet tonight when you were in the pub, right under your big nose. He finger-fucked me, too, and you shook his hand. We both laughed at what a twat you are."

I finally snapped when Mr. Hyde slumped down in the middle of the road. I turned to her and said, "I wanted to take you out for dinner tonight. I wanted to tell you my plans, and I wanted to show you my new office. I wanted you to be proud of me. I don't understand why you are with me if you hate me so much. I don't get it. I have done everything for you, I have been there for you. Why you are like this? I don't get it, but I am still here trying to pick you up off the floor. Trying to get you home. All I ever wanted from you was to love me and be proud of me." I kept repeating myself because I didn't understand.

I walked away and left Mr. Hyde sitting in the middle of the road, tears running down my face. *I've had enough, I deserve better than this.* But now I had given her cause for the unknown to happen at home. Fuck, I was so disappointed with myself, fuck, fuck, fuck, hitting the side of my head, fuck. Telling my inner voice to be quiet, *'now look what you have done.'*

I could still hear the barrage of insults from behind my back, fuck Mr. Hyde was relentless, my head was all over the place, I was in a mess, my inner voice was also telling me, *'she's right you know, everything she said is true, she even sucked your friend's cock tonight, but who did she fuck? Ask her, what's the worst that can happen, just ask her.*' I had no way of stopping this voice, either. I just wanted it to all stop, swallow me up and stop. I couldn't take it anymore.

Mr. Hyde was not giving up; she always had to have the final say and she still wanted to punish me, hurt me, and destroy whatever self-pride I had left. I could hear her walking down our street towards our house, calling me a useless fucker. I was struggling to open the front door because my hands were shaking. When I did finally manage to open the door, I headed straight towards the spare bedroom and immediately closed the door behind me. I sat down on the floor with my back against the door; I just wanted this night to be over.

Then all of a sudden, I heard the front door crash open, banging against the wall and knocking the picture frame off, crashing down to the floor. I had the image of Jack Nicolson from *The Shining*: here's Johnny! "Where are you, you little fucker, how dare you fucking leave me sitting in the road, where are you, useless fucker?"

I didn't say a word, but Mr. Hyde knew where I was. She continuously banged loudly on the door, kicking the bottom and trying to force her way in. Eventually, I had to open it, just so I could get her to stop. "You're not fucking sleeping in this room tonight, no fucking way you are." She pulled all the sheets off the bed. "I haven't finished with you yet! you're a wanker, a fucking wanker, and do you know the reason why no one likes you at the pub, and why you can't make any friends, and why your family doesn't care about you? 'Cause you're a fucking useless wanker."

I managed to barge past her, trying hard not to say anything back. She was so pissed; I had never seen Mr. Hyde like this before, and it scared me. I just had to keep my mouth shut and take it all; I had a horrible feeling that this was only the beginning. Mr. Hyde's anger took me back to my childhood, when my brother and I would sit at the top of the stairs outside the bathroom, listening to my mum and dad argue. The verbal abuse was also relentless, followed by violence. It always started when alcohol was involved, especially when my dad drank too much and was unable to control his anger.

It broke my heart to hear the violence downstairs, Mum pleading with my dad to stop hitting her. But he never did, the rage took over, destroying everything in its path. We were too young and too scared to go downstairs.

I sat there with both hands over my ears, head between my knees, crying and scared, when the downstairs door opened.

We would both immediately scramble to our room and pretend to be asleep, hoping that this was the end of the argument. But it was usually my dad going to the toilet then heading straight back downstairs to carry on where he left off. I never understood why he got like this, and why I lived in a house full of violence. Mum always made excuses for his behaviour. "You know what your dad's like when he's had one too many, nothing to worry about." But the truth was that I was always worried.

One time the violence was so bad I thought my dad had actually killed my mum after another drunken argument. We were both suddenly woken up in the middle of the night, with the loudest crash coming from downstairs. We both sat at the top of the stairs, listening to the familiar sound of violence and abuse. Dad was pissed off that Mum was having a good time talking to her friends in the pub, while my dad fell out with everyone else in the pub. My dad was very argumentative and always had to be right. And Mum didn't back him up on his point of view.

Suddenly without warning, the stair door crashed open. Mum tried to run upstairs, kicking away my dad. She waved her arms to us both. "Get into your room!" she screamed. We were petrified. The violence and abuse were similar to what I had witnessed a few years earlier; Mum again was in serious trouble. We both stood in the doorway of our bedroom, watching the violence unfold, hoping one of our neighbours heard all the noise and hoping they would call the police. But they never did. My brother continually told me, "It will be OK, please don't worry."

The fighting escalated and moved away from the stairway and intensified into the bathroom; Dad was out of control. Then all of a sudden, it went quiet. We both tentatively walked towards the bathroom and peered in. Dad had both his hands around my mum's throat; he was strangling her over the bath and Mum had no fight in her at all. Her neck and head were hanging over the inside of the bathtub and her body was lying on the floor next to the toilet. Dad was standing directly over her; he was determined this time to finish the job. I stood on the landing, peeing my pajamas. I was so frightened that I couldn't move, I just stood there shaking and watching my father kill my mother, and I knew we were next.

Then all of a sudden, my brother pushed me out of the way, and I hit the floor hard, with my head banging on the side of the bannister. He ran straight into the bathroom and started hitting my dad in the face, screaming at him to let her go. The knock to the floor shook me up and I followed my brother's lead, trying to loosen my dad's grip on my mum's throat. Mum wasn't moving anymore, it wasn't working. But then he instantly stopped strangling her and let go.

I looked up; my brother had hit him over the head with a vase of some sort. "Mum, Mum, Mum, wake up, Mum, please wake up, Mum, Mum, please, please wake up, please."

My brother and I gently lifted Mum's head away from the edge of the bathtub; her neck was black and blue, cuts and bruises all over her face. I was unable to hold her, and she slumped down next to the toilet. I carried on shaking my mum, trying to wake her up. "Mum, Mum; please wake up, please, we need you, I need you to wake up, Mum, please, please wake up," tears running down my face, eyes blurry, scared out of my mind, "Mum, please, please wake up."

Mum slowly opened her eyes and gasped for breath. We helped her stand up and get her to our bedroom. We all sat on my brother's bed, Mum still shaking from this horrific ordeal, hugging us both. That was the first time we stood up to my dad, and the first time I saw my brother cry. We never saw my dad after that night, until he eventually returned home three months later.

"I am so sorry; it will never happen again, it's the drink, you know what I am like when I drink too much, I need help, I promise I will stop." It was always the same excuses. Mum always had to make the same call: take him back, or risk something worse. She still took him back, with the same broken promises. This merry-go-round carried on for many years, he never stopped drinking, the violence never ceased either, and things got worse. I then turned my back on Mr. Hyde, and I started walking down the hallway towards our bedroom.

"Where the fuck do you think you're going now?" she screamed at the top of her voice. "You're not fucking staying in my room, you can think again, fucking useless man, you know why I fucked behind your back? 'Cause you're a weak, pathetic man, fucking useless. You can't even hold down a job for more than a year before you're sacked and then you blame everyone else, fucking useless." Mr. Hyde then grabbed a photo frame and threw it at me while I was walking away, missing my face by mere inches, hitting the corner of the hallway door and smashing on impact, glass cutting my face.

"Don't you dare fucking turn your back on me!" She threw another picture frame, which hit me in the head. I fell to the ground, straight away touching the back of my head to see how bad I was cut. I was a little dazed. I refocused and stood back up; cup after cup was thrown at me, still I didn't say a word, still trying to stay calm in all this chaos. I tried to suppress all the anger that I had inside of me, holding and fighting it back. I wanted to react just as severely as what she was dishing out.

I kept telling myself, *This is what she wants, she needs to justify her behaviour and her drinking, she wants to blame me for her being this way, just like my dad. She needs confrontation and a fight.* I turned around and walked towards Mr. Hyde, heading into the garden. Mr. Hyde grabbed my arm to stop me from leaving, but I shrugged her off. I was looking for any type of resting place to gather my thoughts, but she had other ideas. Something smashed directly in front of me, and I felt the air move past my face, white shards of clay hitting my face. Mr. Hyde had thrown our handmade teapot.

I stopped, turned around, and looked at my girlfriend, tears and blood running down my face. I had never seen Mr. Hyde this angry before. I stood there, shaking my head in disbelief that this was all happening. Dr. Jekyll was unrecognizable that night; I was even struggling to see Mr. Hyde. This was Mr. Hyde's Hyde, if there is such a term. The onslaught of abuse started to ramp up even more than before, if you can believe that. Still, I didn't bite. Mr. Hyde kept on goading, pushing, and provoking me; she was coming at me from all angles.

My hands started to form fists, body trembling, anger and hate starting to rise. I could feel I was about to lose my shit and just let go. *'Don't just stand there you fucking useless cunt, tell her exactly what you think, fucking push her around, see how she likes it!'* With everything going on, I was struggling to block out my inner voice. 'Don't let her win, don't give in, she needs you to react, she needs you to hit her, and the moment you do, you lose.' *'He's already fucking lost, stop being a fucking pussy, stand up for yourself, hit her fucking back, hit her, hit her, hit her.'*

I was fighting more with myself, and she knew it. She could see that I was struggling to hold back the anger and the hate, she could see it in my eyes; she knew I was about to bite. Then she stopped. and grinned at me; I noticed her body language change, it became more relaxed, the tension dispersed. Mr. Hyde knew how to break me, but instead of breaking me, she milked the fact that she knew and I didn't. So she just stood there in the middle of the kitchen at 3 am and grinned at me before she unleashed hell.

"I am glad I aborted your baby, you would have made a fucking terrible father, just like your dad. And you know what? You deserved everything you got when you were sexually abused and raped, and I am glad it happened to you because I fucking hate you so much." "What the fuck are you talking about, you're making no sense at all. What do you mean, you aborted my baby? You said it wasn't mine, why are you saying this now? That makes no sense, why would you say you're happy for me to be raped and abused? You're pure evil."

Rage and anger were running through my body. I was trying to work out what the fuck she was going on about, nothing she said made any sense, but I had this uncontrollable urge to grab her and push her through the fucking wall and into the lounge. I wanted her to feel the full force of my rage. *Do it. Kill her, she deserves it. She aborted your baby, stop fucking around, you pussy, go on do it. Strangler her like your dad did with your mum.* My inner voice was taking control I kept banging my hands against my head begging it to stop. "Why would you say you aborted my baby, I was with you when you had the abortion. You reassured me it wasn't mine, now you're saying it was mine?" Mr. Hyde stood there, not offering any explanations to any of my questions. She just grinned and smirked, again like she knew something I didn't.

My inner voice kicked in, '*You sat outside in the waiting room while she aborted your baby, your one chance of being a dad, and she took it all away from you and then went and had coffee as if nothing had happened. Do it, what are you waiting for?*' I wanted to scream so loud; I was in so much pain, and my head was spinning. I wanted her to feel the pain I was in; she aborted my baby and never told me, who fucking does that? "I don't know what's worse, saying that you had an abortion or that I was raped. You're full of shit, you're trying to get me to hit you, that's all your doing. You're full of shit, you're a nasty piece of work, fucking nasty, do know how fucking sick that sounds? Do you? Answer me, for fuck sakes. Do you? Why won't you fucking answer me?

You're fucking sick in the head, seriously you need help. I think I'd know if I was raped or sexually abused, you're fucking sick, that's what you are, fucking sick. I feel sorry for you, I really do. You know what's even worse, saying that you're happy I got raped, what is wrong with you? Who says that? You're glad that I got raped and sexually abused?"

I laughed and made a sniggering sound, "sexually abused and raped, yeah right; full of shit, I would have known if that happened to me or not, I would have to know if that happened to me, how could I not know?" I kept replaying the same sentence, repeatedly, why would she say I was sexually abused and raped? I would know if I was abused and raped.

"It's just not true, that never happened to me, so whatever you're trying to do isn't working, your mind games aren't working, you are just a sad, vindictive, manipulative, angry, evil, pathetic drunk, plain and simple and you know it." "Omg, you actually don't remember, do you?" she started to laugh. "This is even better than I expected; you honestly don't remember anything? Well, well, well, let me enlighten you, shall I?"

The night you found out that I was fucking Bill and Ted behind your back, in the middle of the night, you said this shadowy figure with no face tried to suffocate you with the duvet. You were unable to move or speak while you were lying in bed next to me. After the shadowy figure left, you were sitting up in bed, crying, shaking, and petrified, almost white. You said during this horrific experience, you had memories that you were sexually abused and raped between the ages of seven through to thirteen, and you said this was the second time you had seen the shadow man."

She started clapping and laughing and said, "Oh well," with a grin. Something that Mr. Hyde said rang true, regarding the shadow man with no face. I was trying to rack my brains on this shadow man. Then I started to shake, and I remembered when I saw the shadow man.

I was in my bedroom lying face down on my bed, feet hanging over the end of the bed, touching my bedside cabinet, head turned to the left-hand side watching American Football, which was being shown on Channel Four. The San Francisco 49ers were away, playing the New York Giants in the playoffs. I was struggling to stay awake, but I forced myself to stay up to watch the game. I didn't want to go to sleep, for some reason. All of a sudden, I felt my bed move as if someone was trying to climb on top of it. Then this someone slowly crawled up my back one hand at a time, pushing me down into my mattress until he reached my shoulders. My back felt like it was being crushed, unable to breathe.

I tried to turn around to see who this was, thinking it was my brother playing a game with me, but I was paralyzed, frozen and unable to move. I was so scared and fearful that someone was going to kill me. I tried to shout out to my mum for help, but I couldn't, nothing would come out, I was unable to speak, tears running down my face. Still watching the game and pinned to the bed, fully conscious, I noticed through the reflection of my TV screen, a shadowy figure with no face pinning me to my bed, staring directly at me with one hand over my mouth. I felt a warming sensation trickle down my leg; I looked down at the floor and realised that I had just pissed myself. I knew instantly the exact date this took place. It was during my first summer school holidays. I remember waking up the following morning with a massive migraine. That was the day I got raped for the very last time.

"Ah, how cute you pissed yourself," Mr. Hyde started to laugh. Something was wrong; I started to feel dizzy, the kitchen slowly started to spin, I could feel myself wobbling, I was struggling to breathe. I then hit the floor and blacked out.

I woke to find myself floating face down in an ocean that looked pure black before I realised where I was, a massive wave came crashing down on to my back; my heart was in my throat. The sheer power and force pushed me down under the water, and very quickly, I was held there under terrific force, being tossed around like a rag doll in a washing machine. I desperately tried to swim to the surface, trying to catch my breath, but then a second wave began to lift me out of the ocean, and then it started to pitch. I knew I was going to get slammed again. I was back under the water in a giant violent vortex; I was completely disorientated, my ribs felt like they were getting ripped out.

This second wave kept me under for even longer; I was getting annihilated, in this intensely dark, vociferous, frightening, unpredictable washing machine, and my lungs were bursting. I frantically needed air. Once again, I tried to swim to the surface and, as soon as I took my first breath, I was immediately hit by another gigantic wave, knocking all the air out of my lungs. I was fighting for my life; this ocean was relentless and without mercy. I took hit after hit; the impacts felt like a truck was continually hitting me. I was constantly getting squeezed; I had no idea if I was upside down or doing somersaults. Then the waves stopped, I was exhausted, I had nothing more left in me, I just floated face down, like I was when I woke up.

Then came the freezing cold rain and hailstones the size of golf balls. Thunder echoed throughout the dark sky. I was trying to tread water, arms above my head trying to protect myself, cut and bruised from the hailstones. I wasn't able to see past more than five meters, everything was black, but this blackness had a familiar feel about it, like I had been here before. But I had no idea how I got here, either. I was unable to carry on treading water; I just wanted to close my eyes. I was in an inhumane amount of pain, internally and externally. I had nothing more to give, the water was so cold and so black, I closed my eyes and decided to let go, slowly sinking to the bottom of the ocean.

I had no idea how far I had sunk, but then abruptly, I hit the bottom of the ocean, hard. Suddenly my eyes were forced open from the impact, and I looked around and saw nothing but black. *But I have been here before, how do I know this place?* Then something sharp and hard hit my back. I turned around and saw a single black box starting to float towards the surface. I watched the box gradually float past me. *I have seen this box before! I know this box, but how?* And then I realised why this place was familiar and why I had seen the box before.

FUCK! I had to stop that box reaching the surface. Then overarching fear kicked in. *That box cannot make it to the surface, no matter what.* I tried to grab the box, but every time it was in arm's reach, the box just seemed to carry on floating up towards the surface, millimetres away from my grasp. No matter how hard and fast I swam, it was always out of my reach. I knew exactly what was in there, and why this place looked so familiar. This is where I buried my memories when I was thirteen years old, what was in that box was pure hell.

The moment I reached the surface, I frantically started looking for the box so that I could sink it again, but I couldn't locate it. I was treading water, alone and scared in the dark. Then I was on my hands and knees in my bathroom, the door half-closed. The landing light was off, the living room light shone through the single pane of glass, illuminating part of the stairs. Just below our painting of a cutter ship in the night time waters hanging on the wall, I had someone's cock in my mouth, and he was stroking my head. He was wearing scratched black Doc Martins boots and black ripped jeans. Every now and then he would lift my head up so he could see me sucking his cock. *Fuck, I know this person, what the fuck, this makes no sense.*

The next minute, a massive wave grabbed me and slammed me against some rocks, my back cracked, my head felt like it had split open, the pain shooting through the entirety of my body. I started to scream out in agony before crashing back down into the ocean. I opened my eyes and saw my box smashed open, floating on the surface. I suddenly came to, still lying on the floor in my pee. Mr. Hyde was standing above me, kicking me, shouting and screaming, telling me to get up. I had no idea how long I had been like this, but by that time, Mr. Hyde had smashed all of my family photos.

Enough was enough. I stood up and grabbed her wrists, holding them up above her head, trying to restrain her. All the while, she was continually spitting in my face and trying to kick me. "You fucking deserved being raped, you deserve everything you get, how does it feel to suck another man's cock? Your family was right, you're fucking gay, if you suck cock and take cock, your fucking gay."

I ignored what she was saying, focused on restraining her by pushing her into the spare room where she could do no damage to anything else. I threw her onto the bed, and I begged and pleaded for her to stop.

Then another memory came back. "Fuck me, you're hard; you like boys? It's ok; I like boys as well. See, my cock's hard, too. That's why we get on so well. It's ok to be hard. Let me have a look at how hard you are."

As I was bent over the sofa, he inserted a marker pen inside of me, at the same time touching my penis and testicles. I told him to stop many times, that he was hurting me, but he just kept inserting the marker deeper inside. Gritting my teeth, trying to hold back the tears, I closed my eyes and hoped this would be over soon.

Then I heard someone trying to open the front door; I could hear the keys.

In his sheer panic of trying to pull up his trouser, he pushed me out of the way, and I went tumbling over the sofa landing on the floor. A sudden pain rendered me motionless; the marker pen was now fully inserted. Blood started to drip onto the white carpet.

"Now look what you have fucking done. How am I going to explain this to my mum? She's going to kill me." Then out of nowhere he punched me. I felt a sharp crack; my eyes filled up with water instantly.

"We can say you accidentally banged your nose on my knee, playing around on the floor."

I apologised to his mum for ruining her carpet and left immediately. I could feel blood dripping down my leg as I hobbled home in pain.

What the fuck, I know this person too. Nooooooo. I crashed to the floor. I was finally broken. She opened my puzzle box of childhood memories where I was molested and raped for over five years, from the age of seven through to thirteen. Just to win an argument.

I was completely destroyed. I had buried everything the night the shadow man first appeared. No wonder I felt utterly lost and more alone than ever.

All of a sudden, there was a knock on the door. Red and blue lights were streaming through the bedroom. I opened the door and was immediately pushed back against the wall.

"Hands behind your back, sir."

"I haven't done anything wrong; my girlfriend is pissed and totally out of control, she's the one you need to arrest, not me!"

"Hands behind your back."

I kept saying, "I haven't done anything wrong, why are you arresting me?"

"We saw you through the window, and you were fighting with your partner. That's why we are arresting you, hands behind your back. This is your last warning; I won't repeat it again." While I was getting cuffed, I heard another police officer saying to Mr. Hyde, "You OK, ma'am, did he try to hurt you in any way?" "He went crazy, he smashed up the house, and you can see what he's done to my wrists. He just threw me down onto this bed, I was so scared of what he might do if you hadn't turned up when you did."

The neighbours had heard all the shouting and screaming, and the house getting smashed up and called the police. I was handcuffed and escorted into the back of the police car; I will never forget the look Mr. Hyde gave me as she peered through the gap of the front door when I was driven away, that fucking smirk. I never did make it to the police station, nor did I get charged. Later that night, I was dropped off at a friend's house under strict conditions that I don't go back home until the following morning.

I later learned that men cause most domestic violence in New Zealand and what they did was to take me out of the equation, regardless of who was right or wrong. But they didn't need to handcuff and march me out to their car with all our neighbours watching. For over twenty-three years, I had no idea that I was raped or sexually abused until tonight, when Mr. Hyde opened my box. I returned home tentatively the following day; I slowly opened the front door to find our house completely smashed up. I walked into our bedroom and found Mr. Hyde sound asleep on the bed.

I was cleaning up the mess when Mr. Hyde came into the kitchen and told me to leave it, she would tidy it all up. She kept apologizing for last night, saying that she needed help with her drinking. It was the first time I heard her say she needs help! But I wasn't sure if she meant it or not, it had a familiar notion to what my dad used to say.

While Mr. Hyde, carried on tidying the house up, I went for a walk to clear my head. I needed a plan, I was so miserable, lonely and utterly lost. I had now been with Mr. Hyde for over nine years. I deserved to be happy, and I needed time to heal before I could move on with my life. "You cannot heal in the same environment that made you sick," something Mum always said, but I never really understood what it meant until now.

I realised that if I wanted to be happy, I had to change my environment and that happiness comes from within. So I decided to leave Dr. Jekyll and Mr. Hyde once and for all. But I didn't want to just up and leave; deep down, I knew she was never going to get the help she needed on her own if I just left her. I was worried about her mental state, and regardless of how someone has treated me, I have never been that person who turns their back on someone when they needed help. I wanted to leave my relationship on the best possible terms. I knew what Mr. Hyde was capable of doing and I wasn't mentally that strong either. I had no other option but to stay in this destructive environment knowing that if I stuck to my plan, I would finally escape this prison.

I had a solid two-year plan. The first year, I would move into the spare room and out of our main bedroom because I wanted Dr. Jekyll to know that help was just down the hallway when times got tough, while she was seeking help and advice regarding her drinking and anger issues. In the second year, I would move out of the spare room into my place but still in the same suburb as Dr. Jekyll, just in case she still needed help, and eventually, move out of that suburb altogether.

It was a lengthy plan, but with Dr. Jekyll's manipulative ways, especially considering that we were in the same professional industry, not to mention her drinking issues, I didn't want her to do anything stupid or cause me any more grief. I detailed and planned everything, right down to specific dates. For this plan to work, no one could know what I was doing, so for the next two years, I had to pretend to be in a happy relationship with Dr. Jekyll, convincing our friends and those in our shared profession. But inside, I had already left her, and I just needed to catch up to that reality.

I chose to sacrifice two years of my life, whatever that looked like, so I could be free of Dr. Jekyll and Mr. Hyde and give myself a chance to find happiness. I knew this was going to be tough; I just never realised how emotionally tough this plan was to execute; no matter how well you plan something, reality keeps on going. The thought of living on my own at the age of thirty-eight and starting again, after ten years, was causing my anxiety to spike even though, in reality, that situation was actually two years away.

I had no work or money, but if I was going to heal and pull off this two-year plan, I needed to find work ASAP. I was also concerned about what people were saying behind my back. The village drums were already beating, and word got out overnight regarding my arrest. Still, no one bothered to ask me what had happened; they drew their single-sided conclusions.

You have to realise that you will become the villain in someone else's story, even if you think you're doing the right thing. You can't control the narrative of the other person. I knew I would come off worse than Dr. Jekyll because her network was vast, layered, and reached many parts of New Zealand.

10

WHO AM I?

I needed my mum more than ever, so we decided to have a three-week adventure in Vietnam, followed by two weeks in Thailand. I decided to throw whatever energy I had leftover into organizing this adventure with my mum, and all Mum had to do was get to the airport on time and meet me at Singapore Airport. I arranged it so well that our planes landed in Singapore within thirty minutes of one another. The night before we were due to fly out, I informed Mum that you couldn't import any cigarettes into Singapore, it was law.

I am not sure how many times I mentioned this to Mum, but when I met her, she had over forty packets of cigarettes hidden in her suitcase. I had no idea she did this until we were escorted and held in customs. I was so disappointed that she ignored my advice and chose to take the advice of an eighteen-year-old duty-free checkout assistant at Gatwick Airport, who told her, "Of course you can take cigarettes into Singapore."

Let me be clear that you can't, learned through being held in customs for over five hours and threatened to be deported on the next available planes. After customs officials disposed of all of my mum's cigarettes, they then asked again, "Do you have any more cigarettes hidden in your suitcase?"

Mum was not in a good mood and snapped back, "NO!" Even I was taken aback with her tone. We were eventually let off with a warning, after hours of negotiating and apologising to officials. When we finally reached our hotel room, Mum started to empty her coat pockets and, fuck me! There were only another ten packets hidden in her coat. I was fuming with her; she had no idea at all how close we were to not even having an adventure, and yet she seemed not too bothered about it at all.

"Cornelius," with a quick snap of her tongue, "I didn't come here to be told off by you, the officials asked me if I had any more cigarettes in my suitcase, and I said no, which I didn't, if they asked if I had any in my coat, I would have said yes, but they didn't, so leave me alone."

I had no answer.

We had one full day in Singapore before we flew out to Vietnam later that evening, I wanted to take Mum to the Sing Tel, Singapore Formula One (F1) racetrack. Mum loved F1 racing, it was like my love of Liverpool. Listening to Mum talk about F1 as we walked the course, this experience had already made up for the loss of her precious cargo.

I watched Mum's face light up when she sat down on the floor in pole position, raising her right hand in the air with a single-digit pointing to the sky, indicating number one; I could have watched her all day. She was so excited to be here. My sister had taken her to a few F1 races in the U.K. to experience first-hand the noise, and thrill of F1 racing and to watch her hero, Lewis Hamilton.

But we couldn't stay out in the heat for too long, the humidity was intolerable. I was praying, hoping, and wishing that the weather in Vietnam wasn't going to be anything like this; otherwise, our five-week adventure would be unbearable.

Thankfully when we arrived later that evening in Ho Chi Minh City, previously known as Saigon, the weather was a little more bearable. OMG, the number of scooters on the roads was something else; no description or photos can describe this experience, apart from experiencing it for yourself. I had never seen or heard anything like this before. Hundreds and hundreds of scooters all tooting their horns; it was suffocating and relentless.

Our adventure started in Ho Chi Minh City, and we had seven days to explore this city and the surrounding places, including the famous Cu Chi tunnels. But first, we had to cross the road, and I had no idea how. We both stood on the edge of the curb, holding hands and waiting for the right moment. After twenty minutes, we both realised there was no right moment. We were playing a real-life version of the popular app game Crossy Road.

"Why did Mum and Cornelius want to cross the road? To sit in the shade." No joke. We held hands, looked at each other, and I said, "They will move out the way for us, we just need to keep walking straight and stop only a few times if we have to." Mum was not at all impressed with my plan, and to be honest, neither was I. We'd been watching other people cross the road for hours, sitting at a bar in the heat and trying to work out the best strategy. The most glaring thing we noticed was that the scooters seemed to move out of your way, or they tooted their horns. But none of them was walking across the road with my mum, either.

So we took a leap of faith and slowly inched our way into the middle of the road, with a strategy of stop, go, and dodge. Eventually, we crossed the road to the shade. The relief that ran through my body was extraordinary, but that only lasted for a few seconds. Mum realised that she had left her camera in our room. You think that after sitting at the bar for over two hours, she would have remembered? So I took another leap of faith and went back across the road to grab her camera.

I returned to where Mum was sitting under a beautiful shaded tree with my life still intact, thinking, *At least I don't have to do that again anytime soon.* That is, until Mum mentioned that she forgot the SD card, which was in her other bag in the hotel room. This was a joke. Again, reluctantly, I crossed the road and retrieved the card. I crossed that horrific road five times and Mum never took a single bloody photo all day. This is what I loved about my mum, you couldn't get angry with her. She had so much good intention but her execution was shocking, and you couldn't help but just laugh.

During this adventure, I also wanted to experience ocean canoeing, especially around Ha Long Bay. Still, Mum wasn't keen and opted out and there was no way I could convince her otherwise, so I decided to canoe alone. I went up to this guy and asked how much would it be to hire a canoe for three hours.

"Sorry, your mum needs to come with you," he replied.

"What, my mum needs to come with me? I am thirty-six years old; I think I am more than capable of canoeing on my own. I really don't need my mum holding my hand, that's for sure," I sarcastically replied.

Again, "Sorry, but I can't let you go canoeing without your mum; your mum needs to come with you." I rubbed my face and looked over to my mum, who was sitting down on this makeshift floating barge with a cuppa, watching the world go by.

"Sorry, I don't quite understand, why does my mum have to come with me? I more than capable of doing stuff on my own. Again, I am thirty-six years old. I really don't need my mother; actually, it's the other way 'round, my mum needs me more. So what you're saying doesn't make any sense." Annoyed and dry was my tone this time.

He looked at me again, in a stern voice, "I can't let you go out canoeing without your mum. I only have a two-person canoe, and your mum needs to be with you to balance it out; otherwise, it's really difficult to paddle. So you really need your mum."

Ohhh, sheepishly looking down, avoiding all eye contact, feeling like a fucking dick head, I slowly trudged off in the direction of my mum. I sat down and told her what the man had said. Mum just cracked up laughing, continually repeating the words over and over again, "You need your mum to go canoeing, your mum, ha-ha, your mum."

When Mum and I laugh simultaneously, we have a very unique laugh; a cross between Muttley the dog from the cartoon *The Wacky Races* and some random northern accent. It was so distinctive, so loud, and very unique. After about an hour of laughing, Mum grabbed my hand and said, "You owe me big time for this," and marched me over to the man with the canoes.

"I am Cornelius's mum. I will go canoeing with him."

He also pissed himself laughing; I was too embarrassed even to look up and acknowledge him.

Because Mum helped me out with canoeing, I agreed to watch a ladyboy show with her in Thailand. So we ended up in Pattaya to watch a ladyboy show. I wasn't looking forward to the show; I didn't understand Mum's fascination with ladyboys. I wasn't keen on watching Thai men dressed up in women's clothes, but I had seen drag acts on T.V. before, so I had an idea of what to expect.

Also, being called gay for most of my life, the last thing I want to do was watch a Thai drag show, but I did reluctantly agree to go. Mum was super excited, and I now understood why! She'd been watching a reality TV show back in the U.K. about ladyboys and she was fascinated by them. Thirty minutes into the ladyboy show, I turned to Mum and said, "When do the ladyboys come on? I think I will go get a drink and let you watch that part, to be honest, it's not really my cup of tea."

Mum looked at me with this funny expression, "What are you going on about, son? This is the show!"

"I think you got this all wrong Mum, that's not possible. All these women have boobs, and they don't look like any drag acts that I have seen. Are you sure we're watching the right show?"

"Yes, son, this is the ladyboy show; this is what they look like."

I carried on watching the show, still not convinced that these were actually men. After the show finished, Mum wanted to do a meet and greet and pose for photos. I was even more confused because they all spoke with beautiful, light feminine voices, and I could see that they had real boobs. Shaking my head in disbelief, I still wasn't convinced. I was more confused than ever, but Mum kept reassuring me and insisting that they were, in fact, men.

This is not what I expected at all; in fact, I had no idea what to expect apart from the image of not very funny drag queens. They were really attractive, to the point where I found myself being attracted to them.

The following day, I was laying on the beach, playing *The Legend of Zelda - Links Awakening* on my Gameboy. Mum was bored and went to get a relaxing massage instead.

I was trying to wrap my brain around the fact that all the ladyboys had feminine voices, were beautiful and stunning to look at, and they seemed to have real boobs. But they also had a penis. What was more confusing was that I was really attracted to them. That was the first day I questioned my sexuality. *Am I gay?* Were my family right all along, did I not want to admit that I was gay or was this way of thinking connected to what I had just learned regarding my past?

Since that night horrific memories had come flooding back. I didn't want to close my eyes or sleep, so I forced myself to stay awake for as long as possible. Some days I stayed awake for 48 hours straight. Only exhaustion made me sleep, and that was only for a few hours. I was struggling and I knew it.

My inner voice was now starting to convince me that I was gay all along; why else would I find ladyboys attractive? *'Just admit it, you like men, you like cock, you always have since you were seven years old, why else would you suck men off? Admit and come to terms with your sexuality.'* STOP telling me what to do, leave me alone! I started banging the side of my head, letting him know that I am not happy. Stopping just before Mum came back from her relaxing massage.

She wasn't impressed at all with the massage; they bent her this way and that way, pulled and pushed, twisted and turned every part of her body and then sent her back to me grumpier than when she left. She was so pissed off; she didn't really speak to me for most of the day.

That night, I lay in bed, still thinking about my sexuality. How could I be gay, don't you have to be attracted to men to be gay? And yet they didn't look like men, they looked female. I was in a constant battle with myself, trying to understand these new emotions and feelings. I couldn't be gay or bi, I wasn't attracted to men. Yet I was attracted to ladyboys, but they were men. I was desperately looking for answers. It made no sense. I then started to fantasize about having sex with a ladyboy. I was so lost I had no idea who I was anymore, and I just wanted to cry.

Then all of a sudden, Mum shouted, "Cornelius, Cornelius, Cornelius! Wake up. You won't believe this, but a miracle has happened."

"What are you talking about, what miracle?" Slowly opening my eyes, "What is so important that it can't wait till morning?"

"Listen to this," Mum read aloud half a page from her book to me.

"I have no idea, Mum, what you're going on about."

She read another paragraph. She was like a kid on Christmas morning. "Cornelius, Cornelius, Cornelius, I can see! I don't need my reading glasses anymore."

"What do you mean, you can see? Of course you can see."

"No, Cornelius, I mean, I can actually see. Do you think that massage fixed my eyes? I am not wearing my reading glasses. Look, they're on the table. But I can read perfectly."

And again, Mum read another paragraph from her book. I sat up and saw her glasses on the table. I was watching her read; she now had my attention. Mum's face was just beaming from ear to ear.

"Cornelius, a miracle has happened to me today, a bloody miracle. I don't need my glasses! Can you Google or find out if massages can heal your eyes?"

Mum carried on reading without her glasses word-perfect; I was perplexed. Was I dreaming or was this a real miracle? Even I could see that she didn't have her glasses on. I had honestly never seen her so excited in my life; then I had a thought.

"Mum, are you wearing your contact lenses?"

Mum looked and thought about the question. Her reply said it all, "Oh Cornelius, I am, I forgot to take them out earlier." And queue the Muttley laugh.

We pissed ourselves laughing. We just couldn't stop laughing and eventually went to sleep about 4 am. We kept replaying the same stupid miracle over and over again.

But a miracle did happen the following morning. Whatever they had done in yesterday's massage, Mum was able to walk, up and down steps, pain-free. Mum broke down in tears; she had a new lease on life, she had been struggling with her left hip for over ten years and this morning she had no pain.

During the last five days in Thailand, we hired an English-speaking guide, and she was so informative and knowledgeable, we had so much more respect for Thailand's heritage and culture. I think this was the first time Mum noticed that I wasn't happy in my relationship with Dr. Jekyll. She saw that I was flirting with our guide, who was also paying me some attention, and this felt good, especially after what had just taken place a few months earlier. Mum kept encouraging me to give her my mobile number, seeing as I was staying in Bangkok for an additional two nights before flying back to New Zealand. She was keen on me hanging out rather than staying on my own.

After saying a difficult goodbye to Mum at the airport, I got a message from our guide, asking me if I was keen to meet up later that night. So I texted back with a yes, seeing we'd been flirting with one another over the last five days.

I was just about to grab a taxi when she texted me and cancelled. I was gutted; it had been so long since someone just wanted to hang out with me, and I also fancied her. I texted back and said, 'no worries at all' and headed back to my room. I received another text shortly after saying she was sorry for flirting and leading me on, and also that she felt embarrassed that she had lied to me.

I asked her what she lied about. 'I am ladyboy, and I wasn't sure how you would react if you found out later tonight.'

'Later tonight?' I texted back.

'Yes, when we go back to your hotel! I really fancy you, and I want to stay over.'

I never did catch up with her; I stayed in my hotel room for those two days. I was unable to leave. I had mini panic attacks. I kept replaying the last five days. I was flirting with a man, and I didn't even realise? How did I not notice that she was a he? She didn't even look like a he. What would have happened if we did go out, and we did kiss or as she said, went back to my hotel for sex? I was still confused. How can you have sex with a ladyboy; isn't that gay?

But also, she found me attractive enough to want to have sex with me, and that thought alone was really nice. I even questioned those feelings. I didn't get it, why was I attracted to ladyboys, what was it? Was I gay? Was this the reason why I struggled in my relationships, why they always seemed to leave me? Was I attracted to men without realising? Could I even have a relationship with a ladyboy, even if I found her attractive? How would that work? It can't, it's impossible; she had a penis. *If I had any type of sex with her, I would be gay, and everyone would be right. But I find women attractive, not men.*

Once I started, I was unable to stop. *What would I do if a woman walked out of the bathroom, but instead of a strap-on, she had a penis? Was that no different than a strap-on? Would I find that attractive? If so, that means I am gay. Or is a ladyboy different because he was a she, and I saw her as a she, not a he?* I was thinking about the movie *Silence of the Lambs*; did he want to be a ladyboy too, or was that something else altogether?

I just couldn't stop questioning myself. *How can I be gay? I fancy women, not men. But I fancied a man as a woman, so that means I must be gay. What was I missing?*

***

I spent nearly a year questioning my sexuality after my Thailand revelation, along with having flashbacks of my childhood. These memories and thoughts alone took all of my time up, as I was struggling to understand who I was.

Had I lived an entire life without being honest with myself, lived life through lies and did things that were expected of me rather than what would make me happy? And why didn't I want to believe that I was gay? Or was it just to spite my family with *I told you so*? Would my relationship with my brother be any different if I was gay? Would I be any different to who I am if I was gay? Was there a way of being with a man and not having sex?

I felt like I had cheated myself out of life, and this confusion wasn't helping my mental state. My inner voice constantly told me that I was gay, *'And you like men, you just need to admit it.'* Did I change my whole persona based on lies and stories to keep me in the majority rather than the minority? *How can I be attracted to women and ladyboys when I know a ladyboy is not a woman but in fact, a man? So I must be gay!*

On top of all of this, Dr. Jekyll and Mr. Hyde didn't get any help as promised. She was still getting pissed and still mentally abusing me and blaming me for her shitty life.

I felt like something was about to give; I had no idea who the fuck I was anymore; my entire life had been a lie. I'd had a hell of a year. I needed to go home, I needed to talk to my mum about how I was feeling. I wasn't in a good place, and I thought I was stronger than this. I thought I could execute my two-year plan but getting my head around my sexuality and my childhood memories had brought me to a breaking point.

I was mentally and physically shattered. By the time I got back home, I had so much running through my mind. I just wanted to be a couch potato, do nothing and think of nothing, but I still wanted to go out into town. It had been ages since I had last gone out with my brother at Christmas and New Year. And this was my favourite time of year. Town was packed and everyone was in a good mood.

The factories broke up early on Christmas Eve and everyone headed straight into town, wearing some sort of Christmas decoration or mistletoe. Everyone was out; the largest and most popular bars were like nightclubs, even at 1 pm. New Year was no exception, either. Thousands of people all in fancy dress, night club tickets all purchased well in advance.

If you didn't have a ticket, there was no way you'd be getting into a club. It was mental, but a good mental. My brother and I were always part of the fancy dress club, too. Even better, on 5th January, Mansfield was hosting Liverpool in the 4th round of the FA Cup. It was only an hour's drive away from Mum's place. As soon as I found out the unbelievable news, I went straight to the internet to look for any unsold tickets that I could purchase. I went on every website I had ever used to get tickets for Liverpool games.

I couldn't find any tickets at all, so I tried Craigslist. I'd never used this website before, but a guy was selling four tickets for the game. I emailed my sister, who was living just outside London at the time, to see if she wanted to come with me. My brother wasn't that keen, as he was a Manchester United fan, so it was a *hell no!* from him.

I emailed my sister, explaining that the tickets were a hundred pounds each and that I would need the money ASAP when she came up on Boxing Day with her new boyfriend in tow.

I emailed many times, expressing that this might be a scam and continually asking, "Are you sure? I have never used Craigslist before, but the photos the guy sent me look genuine." My sister replied back, "Yes, 100%. And can you get one for my boyfriend too? I want to surprise him and treat him with the tickets."

"Are you sure?" I replied. "The tickets will cost me three hundred pounds, and there's no guarantee we will get them. I just want you to know this before I buy them."

I was happy to accept a loss of a hundred pounds, but I wasn't sure my sister was that willing to do the same. But she told me to go ahead and buy them. I was so excited and felt that this guy was genuine; we texted and emailed one another regularly. I deposited the money into his bank account, and he assured me that the tickets would arrive overnight.

Overnight became over a week and still no tickets; and worse, no response from him either. I was totally scammed, but I was even more gutted that I wasn't going to see Liverpool. My sister drove up as promised on Boxing Day along with her boyfriend. He was a lot older than I expected, I think fifteen years older, and he had two teenage daughters. I was taken aback a little; my sister didn't mention the age gap or the two teenage daughters he had. I imagined what my sister would be like if they got married and she became a stepmother. I have to be honest, it made me laugh, thinking of my sister telling two teenage girls to tidy their rooms and do homework; none of this ever applied to my sister when she was growing up. My sister lived in a world of chaos and mess. No clothes ever went in the drawer or were hung up. My sister dreamed of having a walk-in wardrobe, but I didn't expect that walk-in wardrobe to be her bedroom floor. And not to mention, when she came home from school or work, clothes would just be flung everywhere, with an attitude of *I'll do it later, I just got in.*

Her mess drove Mum up the wall; Mum was so house proud. Walking into the living room, all you could see was my sister's clothes piled up on the chairs. So yes, it made me laugh to think that she would ask her stepdaughters to tidy up.

I didn't mention that we got ripped off over the Liverpool tickets until they arrived on Boxing Day, and regretfully, I had to ask her for the two hundred pounds.

"I am not paying you two hundred pounds for any ticket. We didn't receive them; how can you expect me to pay for something I haven't received?!" This response shocked me to the core. I sat looking at her and her new boyfriend in utter disbelief; I had no answer to this.

"I emailed and texted over twenty times, saying this might be a scam, and you asked me to purchase them regardless. So what you're saying is that I am three hundred pounds down, and you're not going to pay me back for your tickets? Rather than me losing a hundred pounds, I am now being scammed by you as well?"

"I am not paying for something I haven't received; it's unfair of you to ask me for the money back."

"But I would only be losing a hundred pounds, except that you asked me to purchase another two tickets. I kept saying there was a chance we might get ripped off and you said purchase them anyways. So, to be honest, it's only fair that you pay for your tickets; otherwise, I am three hundred pounds down." I looked at her boyfriend and he sheepishly looked away.

My sister was wearing the trousers in this relationship, it was evident to see. "I am not paying you back, end of."

I looked for reassurance from my mum and brother, but I got nothing back from either of them. They were both happy to sit on the wall, when clearly and morally I was in the right, having given my sister many advanced warnings to pull out of participating in purchasing the tickets. Neither of them said a word. I was fucking fuming. How many times do I have to be ripped off over money from friends, and now my sister was doing the same? Even her boyfriend didn't offer to pay for his ticket. Was I wrong to ask for my two hundred pounds back, or was my sister just happy for me to be ripped off for the full amount? I was so fucking confused about what was unravelling before me.

I mean, if I had asked a friend of mine to purchase the tickets knowing there was a risk, there is no chance in hell I wouldn't pay him back. After all, I had asked him to do so on my behalf. Was I actually missing something? I had just witnessed the ugly side and a totally different perspective of my sister. Was it always there or had it only shown up for the first time when it came to money?

I didn't want to believe that my sister, who I helped raise all those years, would turn her back on fundamental principles and morals. I thought she would have learned her lesson from the incident with the police when she was twelve years old, but I was wrong. I should have known when it comes to money with my family, but I never learn. I always wanted to believe they were like me, somehow. I recalled how during a tenpin bowling league game, Mum had phoned the bowling alley, asking me to come home straight away. "Drop everything and come home, no excuses. The police are on the way."

Mum accused me of stealing a twenty-pound note from her purse. I can't tell you how many times I said to Mum that it wasn't me, it was my sister, but all the time she kept denying it. My sister was happy for me to take the blame. I begged her to tell the truth, but she refused.

Only when the police came knocking on the door—Mum's way of teaching us a lesson on stealing and the trouble you can get yourself into—did my sister eventually confess to taking the money without asking. I wasn't that arsed about my sister stealing the money, but no words could describe the sadness that I felt inside, knowing that Mum thought I was capable of stealing over my sister. I hoped that was the first time and the last time Mum would ever doubt a word I said.

It's also a memory I can't shake off, either. I just can't seem to let that one go. I think that was the first time I realised that greed could make the most beautiful, loving person so ugly, with no morals. *If I can get away with it, I will, and fuck everyone else.* I was so hurt by my sister, by her deception and moral betrayal. This was the first sign, when I knew we were going to go our separate ways.

All my sister had to do was to apologise and pay the money back. But she didn't. In her head, her decision was justified, and there was no way I could ever change her mind. She had no remorse or empathy about how her actions would affect me. As long as she looked good and came out on top, that was all that mattered.

Her attitude was something else. This wasn't the sister that I knew; something had changed, something wasn't right. I didn't recognise her at all. Was I to blame for her change? Because we weren't as close as we used to be before I moved to New Zealand.

Her anger was similar to my brother's when it came to me moving away, because they had to look after Mum. I never went out over Christmas or New Years, either. My brother had decided he wanted to work over the holidays, bragging about how much money he was earning rather than spending time with his brother when I needed him the most. I only saw my niece a few times as well.

I'd flown across the world to spend time with them, my family, costing me thousands of pounds. And I got an unbelievable amount of shit from Mr. Hyde in the process, as she stayed back in Auckland. But they didn't even give a damn. They were so self-obsessed and so wrapped up in their own lives, that I wasn't even on their radar. They never once asked how my life was.

Dare I say it, I was actually looking forward to going back to New Zealand. With only a few days before my flight home, Mum and I had decided to go to shopping in Sheffield. I was planning to buy a brand-new summer wardrobe to take back to New Zealand. Our summer was winter in the U.K., and the clothes in the U.K. where amazing compared with the styles in New Zealand. You'd have to experience it rather than me expressing it through words. It's a shocking and dreadful experience; no colour and only one style: Kiwi.

After a full-on day of shopping and feeling like Julia Roberts's character in *Pretty Woman* (the scene where she says, "Big, big mistake!"), we headed home on the train. It was packed solid, hardly a seat to spare. I was talking to Mum about where our next adventure should be, when out of nowhere, I was punched full-on in the face by a guy who had been watching me while I was checking destinations on my phone.

"Give me your fucking phone, you cunt!"

Dazed, confused, disorientated, and before I could even focus on what the fuck had just happened, I was hit again, but this time twice as hard as before, breaking my nose. I had no idea where these punches were coming from; all I could hear was, "Give me your fucking phone, you fucking cunt."

I heard my mum asking for help: "Can someone please help my son? Please, can someone help my son?!"

I was blinded, tears streaming down my face, unable to see. I was hit again and again and again, punch after punch. It felt like I was getting punched by two people, but I had no idea from where. I covered my head with my arms and tried to see through my watery eyes, blood streaming down my face. I was unable to stand, getting annihilated in my seat. If I wasn't getting punched in the face, I was getting hit in the back of the head.

Again, I could hear my mum. "Can someone please help my son?!"

No one responded.

Everyone looked down. Even the people sitting across from us didn't help.

The next thing I could feel was that someone else was trying to grab all my bags. Were there two people or just one? My eyes were still blurred, but no help came, and this was a packed train. Mum tried in vain to help me, but she wasn't that successful.

"Please, can someone help my son?"

Still, no help came.

I managed to compose myself and open my eyes. A six-foot tall white guy, wearing blue tracksuit bottoms and a white T-shirt was raining punch after punch, and his girlfriend was punching me from behind. I struggled to get a good look at her, but I could hear her voice saying, "We've got to go, our stop is next." They were opportunistic thieves, trying to get what they could before they got off at their stop.

I was taking blow after blow to the head; if it wasn't from him, it was from her. Still, no one helped. I managed to stand up and fend him off but was unable to fend her off at the same time. My mum tried to grab the man and restrain him; a seventy-year-old woman trying to fight off a six-foot man, and no one batted an eye. He was too strong, and he pushed her hard back into the seat, flicking a lit cigarette on to my mum's clothes. Mum desperately tried to find where it landed so she could put it out.

I shouted, "Can someone just fucking help me?!"

Still, no one helped.

Eventually, the train came to a sudden halt. I managed to hold on to all my bags and fend off those two fuckers, moments before they both jumped off the train with nothing in hand, the door closing behind them. I slumped down in my seat, fucking exhausted, one eye completely closed, my nose broken, my face battered and bleeding, and no one even looked up to ask how I was.

I felt so sorry for Mum that day; she witnessed two people hitting her son from all angles, and no one wanted to help. But they were more than happy to watch, ignore, and I even saw a few people record the incident on their phones. So they can share with their friends, upload to social media just to get a fucking like for social validation, rather than help. The fact is, if something like this happened to them, they would be the first to complain to the papers and upload their faces to social media, playing the victim.

The word "karma" comes to mind. Is this the Universe's way of saying that there are lessons to be learned from your actions? Who knows? But my observations about the world were starting to change. Was I right to ask my sister for the ticket money in a self-obsessed world, where social validation seemed crucial to happiness and getting a Like was more important than helping another person? Was it really her fault or was I always in the minority?

***

That first year, living in the spare room was psychologically tough. I didn't expect it to be this hard. I had no idea what to expect, to be honest; I had never felt more alone or more depressed. I knew it wasn't helping my mental health issues; I kept going back and forth. Was this the right decision after all, to stand by and help someone when all I get in return was mental abuse?

Maybe being in an abusive relationship was more comfortable than being alone. Perhaps that's why people stay in those relationships, even when their friends tell them to leave, that they deserve better, that there's plenty more fish in the sea. But we just ignore them, even when they're right.

For me, loneliness was far worse than my depression, even though it was part of my mental health issues. Knowing that no one loved me or wanted to be my friend was a terrifying experience of solitude, isolation, and separation from the world. A constant barrage of negative thoughts: *What is wrong with me?*

Yet, Dr. Jekyll was doing great in her new position and she seemed happier than ever. However, I was more depressed. How was that possible, shouldn't it be the other way around?

Work didn't come easy for me; no matter what new doors I was opening, they were closing just as fast. So I decided to go in a new direction. I had an idea that I had been working on and researching for some time now. I had been noticing a growing trend in online bespoke T-shirt designs and that the majority of the market was in Asia, Australia, and New Zealand, with the leading online company offering a two-week delivery timeframe.

This got me thinking, what if I was able to offer an alternative to what's already out there? The concept was similar to purchasing limited edition artwork. But this was artwork you could wear. Each T-shirt would have the individual number printed on the label inside; when we hit two hundred and fifty, that was it. No more printed, no matter how popular they were. All of our T-shirts would be made from organic cotton, printed and dispatched within two days; no one was offering service online at the time.

To make this work, I needed help; people who I could trust with this concept, had the same amount of energy and passion as me, and most of all, could see this taking off, especially in New Zealand. This was my baby; I poured everything that I had into the business. I knew I had to drive this forward, so I enlisted some phenomenal artists from all over the world, designed a leading brand, and we were backed by a great story of why we were doing this. The second director was responsible for production and distribution; the third director was responsible for sales.

With no landscape projects and building up our online T-shirt brand, I was allowed to teach landscape construction at an education campus where they offered short courses, certificates, diplomas, and degrees which were all employment-focused.

I had an exciting and inspirational idea to help third-year Landscape Architecture students understand what it would be like to work in a design consultancy and on a real-life design. I would showcase the practical side of our profession rather than the theoretical side and teach the students that all design decisions need to be justified. This initiative would run for twelve weeks, in parallel to a real-life urban design and city regeneration project that was being undertaken with Auckland Council. It was vastly different from anything that had previously been taught. No more pie in the sky ideas, no more bullshit concepts; if you're going to get into this profession, let's make sure you're armed and well prepared for the real world. Like Colin did for me. This was my chance to say thank you.

Lecturing was my only source of income and a welcome relief, even if it was a small monthly amount. I absolutely loved being part of something exciting and new, especially in the educational sector. I was so happy to give back to the students and the profession. It also seemed to help to slow down the constant barrage of negative inner voices.

I managed to convince some of New Zealand's leading designers to be part of an external design panel, and I persuaded them to offer free mentoring to our students. When I was asked to see the head of the department regarding this new initiative, I assumed it was going to be positive. So I was surprised to learn that other lecturers had voiced their concerns and pushed back on this idea; they were not keen on potentially teaching real-life design scenarios. They seemed happier to carry on regurgitating the same course structure year after year.

These concerns completely threw me off guard. I thought the students' education came first, and that our job was to give them as much practical information as possible. I had no idea that I was upsetting the apple cart.

I was burning the candle at both ends, and in the middle of it all, Mr. Hyde was starting to get more and more stressed at work, which led to her drinking more, and more abuse followed. I sank all my savings into the T-shirt business, pulling out all the stops to make it happen. Still, with me being so occupied with teaching, the other directors hadn't contributed to anything. Even the director in charge of marketing couldn't be arsed to promote our brand. We had thousands of flyers printed, to be dispersed around the city and the universities; he decided to throw them away and met his mates in the pub, instead.

When they weren't in the office working on the brand, they were in the pub. One day, I overheard both of them talking when they thought no one was around. They said that all of the money from the account was gone. I'd sank everything I had into this business; I had known these two guys for over five years, and I never expected this. At the same time, the other lecturers were not happy with the positive student responses to our new design initiative. They didn't want to change what wasn't already broken, and I knew my time was coming to an end when two things happened.

At the end of the year, I attended a University Christmas party. One of the course lecturers was utterly pissed out of his head, another drinker who couldn't handle their alcohol, constantly insulted me in front of my students. He talked about my failing design consultancy and kept questioning who I was and my sexuality. He made me feel so small in front of the students. He was so embarrassing that the students begged him to stop, but he wouldn't. The only way for this to stop was to leave my own professional institute's party.

The students and I complained about his behaviour that night, but the head of the department dismissed it immediately, and no action was taken.

I was never asked back to lecture again, unsurprisingly. I had wanted to teach students what I was taught at University: that with hard work, passion, and thinking outside the box, you can succeed. I never saw or heard of one lecturer disrespect another in front of their students. Yet, all of this happened to me as a lecturer.

Finally, after one year to the day, the date I had originally given myself, I left Dr. Jekyll, after ten years. Even though I was only living five minutes away, I was finally free. As crazy as this sounds, no matter what happened between us, I still wanted to remain friends. I still loved Dr. Jekyll (not so much Mr. Hyde), but I wasn't *in* love with her.

I was now living on my own, starting again from scratch in a country that never quite worked out during those eight years; a country with over four million people. Why did I struggle to make one single friend? I started to question everything, even the point of living, my first suicidal thought. *Why is my life this hard? Why do people treat me so badly? What do I do to piss everyone off and for them not to like me?* When all I had was love in my heart; I had so much love to give, I just had no one to give it to.

My mental health was getting worse; I was unable to leave the flat for over six months. I started to drink and smoke heavily, taking the odd trip to the supermarket for more beer and ordering takeout, alone and bored in my new place. I was constantly reminded by the hundreds of empty beer bottles on the kitchen floor that I was alone in this world and I would be better off dead.

In the first six months of living on my own and suffering from chronic loneliness, not one person rang, texted, or came to visit me. Even though I thought I had a collection of Jamie Oliver-style friends from his early days on the Naked Chef.

I gained 10kg in weight, and on my 5'5 frame, I looked so fucking ill. It wasn't hard to see why no work came my way; my energy was shocking and so negative. *Who would want to work with this type of negative energy?* I kept saying to myself, or maybe it was my inner voice. I had no idea anymore who I was, in a world of darkness and bleakness, with no light ahead.

My body felt old for the first time; the only thing that kept me going was playing football and managing my team on Saturdays. I loved playing football with the team. My days of running around were long gone, but it got me out of the house once a week.

Dr. Jekyll only came to visit me once in those six months. Even though I was there for her for over a year, she couldn't even take the time or effort to see if I was alright. I was suffering chronic insomnia, eventually getting some sleep around the 5 am mark.

I kept thinking, *Did I make the right decision to leave her? Is this my karma, did I have to learn a lesson? If so, what is the lesson?* I was more miserable than when I was actually in a relationship with Dr. Jekyll; I contemplated many times getting back with her and trying again.

Mum always said, "We can't live with each other, and we can't live without each other." She was right, maybe I did make a mistake. Plus, we still owned a house in London.

I kept replaying all the hurt, all the tears, and all the pain that I had suffered during my time with Dr. Jekyll and Mr. Hyde. Did I really want to go back to something that took me years to escape from, just because I was lonely? I knew I wasn't mentally strong enough for the emotional abuse that comes with Mr. Hyde. That one thought kept me from picking up my mobile and making contact.

I was now seriously starting to contemplate suicide. I had no happy childhood memories left, they were taken from me on that cold, dark night; I had not heard from my brother or sister for over a year; I wasn't sure if I was gay, straight, or bi. The fact that Mum was still alive was the only reason stopping me from taking my own life. I couldn't do that to her, no matter how much pain and suffering I was in; she didn't deserve that.

I had nothing; I was nothing, and I had no idea who I was anymore. I just wanted to drink myself to death.

11

THE TEXT MESSAGE

The following morning I woke up with the hangover from hell at about 10 am. I had a shocking night's sleep; every time I woke up during the night, my inner voice was already there. I thought it would turn off when I fell asleep, but I got that wrong! You can't escape, it is relentless, consistent, and always on. A constant merry-go-round, and one you can't get off of.

I stumbled out of bed at 10:30 am, eyes half-open, my head thumping. I went to the bathroom, had a pee, walked to the kitchen, and made myself a shitty instant coffee. Then I walked to my living room, opened the outside door, rolled a port royal, and slumped into a wet, cold chair to check my Facebook account. No new friend requests. I opened my football and tabloid apps, kidding myself that I had a genuine interest in what was happening in the world around me. I checked my messaging apps, hoping someone had an actual interest in my life, but nothing; I was operating on autopilot.

Add driving to work, sitting down at my desk, talking to the same people about the same shit they watched last night on TV, desperately waiting for five o'clock to arrive. Then heading to the pub, I would sit down, talk about fuck bollocks all, or sex, head home half-pissed, get back into bed, continue checking all the different apps (something might have changed in the last ten seconds), maybe watch something shitty on my phone, notice it's now 6 am and hope to get at least an hours sleep. This was my life, day in day out, nothing ever changed.

I wondered if I even had the energy to venture outside my front door to pick up some milk. *Fuck it can't be arsed.* I smoked my port royal. The thought alone hurt my head, so I took a warm gulp of shitty instant black coffee, finished off my port royal, and stared at my phone. With a mindless blank expression, I hoped something would pop into my mind, so I could convince myself that I had an interest in something. But the truth was, I had no interest in anything. I just needed to get through this day and head back to bed, so I could wake up tomorrow and do exactly the same shit that I was doing today. And do you know the worst thing about having chronic depression? People expect you to behave as if you have everything under control.

Just then, a text message came through.

'Hey you, I had a dream about you last night, it was very surreal. There was a knock on our front door, so I went downstairs to see who it was. I was in my dressing gown, but I wasn't wearing anything underneath. I opened the door, and you were standing there.'

I re-read the message repeatedly; I had no idea who this was from. I didn't have the number saved into my contacts, and I didn't recognise the number either. I didn't reply straight away. I thought someone was playing a joke, or worse, it could have been one of Dr. Jekyll's friends; this was a bizarre text message. I rolled another port royal, walked back to the kitchen, made another shitty coffee, and sat back outside, still wondering who the fuck this was. What a strange text message to receive without a name or an initial attached to the message.

I tried to rack my brain: *Who would send me this random message?* I wasn't sure a typical 'who is this' reply would be the right approach, or even engaging in a conversation as if I knew this person. Coffee in one hand and port royal in the other, I sat there staring at my phone, which was now resting on my lap. *Which approach do I take?* I took a deep long hard drag of my port royal, another gulp of coffee, and I replied with: 'Wow, that's interesting. I wonder what that means?' I thought that was a great reply; respond with an open question. Hopefully, more details on who this could be would follow in the next text message.

'Well, it's obviously about you,' was the reply. *Fuck, that didn't work!*

I replied with 'Actually, it's more about you, you're the one who had the dream about me. And do you know why you dreamt about me?' I was now on a fishing expedition, searching for any clues about who this could be, but there weren't any. It was a bloody text message, even Sherlock couldn't figure out who I was texting. Another text message popped up on my phone.

'Well, last night, I wrote down on a piece of paper ten attributes that I wanted to find in someone, placed it under my pillow, and I asked the universe to help me find that person. And I dreamt of you.' *Fuck me, I still had no scooby-doo who this was, but the dream must be significant enough for this person to text me.* I was so confused. I genuinely wanted to ask who this was, but now I worried that this person figured I knew them, and I had gone too far down the rabbit hole to text back, 'I'm sorry, who is this again?'

My phone went off again, and another text message came through. 'And my new braces are cutting into my gums, so I am feeling sorry for myself.' Braces, who the fuck do I know who wears braces? I had no idea who this person was, and I was fucking clueless. I replied, 'ouch' with a sad face emoji.

My phone went off again; two sad-faced emojis and a crying emoji came straight back, followed with 'sorry about the dream text, I didn't mean to freak you out btw.' Another text message: 'I didn't think you would mind, but I haven't seen you for such a long time.'

For such a long time! Who is this?

The only person who I hadn't seen in such a long time was K, but the last I heard of her, she had a new boyfriend and was moving back to Australia. Another text message: 'hope to see you around -K,' followed by three smiley face emojis. *Fuck me; it was K who had been texting me!* I finished my Port Royal gulped downed the last of my shitty coffee. I was stunned that it was K!

I stared at my phone blankly, unable to type anything. I had no idea what I was going to reply back with, so I rolled another port royal and smoked it super quickly as my anxiety roared at full capacity. I typed 'You fancy meeting me once you've finished work? We could meet up at the North Head,' with a smiley face emoji. I closed my eyes, thought about it for a few minutes, and pressed send, clenching my teeth. I wasn't sure what I was expecting back in return; I was just happy to be having a conversation with someone, even if it was via text message.

K replied instantly. 'I am not too sure, what about Dr. Jekyll? I don't think she likes me, and I don't want to cause any trouble?' I replied straight back, 'Why don't we meet anyways, and I will tell you about Dr. Jekyll and me, and why you haven't seen me around the pub for ages!'

'Ok, I will see you at the entrance of Oneroa Beach at 4 pm.' *Fuck, now what?* I didn't expect K to meet me, I was totally unprepared.

I was worried all day about what to say when I saw her. *Do I tell her the truth or not?* I mean, I had only met her a few times, but if she asked the universe to help her find someone, that didn't seem like she had a boyfriend at the moment.

4 pm came around so fast; I was so nervous that I had butterflies, something I hadn't felt since I was sixteen years old when I kissed Gemma on the bus and immediately threw up. I walked about ten meters through the entrance of the gates when I saw K jump off a grassy bank and onto the path, which was heading down towards the beach. She was full of energy. I wasn't sure if she always had this much energy or if it was just nervous energy; I had only ever seen her surrounded by people at the pub. Nervously I said, "Hey, how are you? How was work?"

"Yeah, not bad, not bad at all. I'm pretty tired if I must be honest, I left my house at stupid o'clock this morning." I looked her up and down; she was wearing a pair of black Converse high tops with white soles, tight-fitting dark jeans rolled up to above her ankles, and a black Guns N Roses T-shirt. The first thought that popped into my head was *Wow, she has tiny feet.*

"I can't stay long; I have to get back and help Mum out at home." I just smiled and said, "No worries, I have to get back too," which I obviously didn't but I didn't know what else to say. Omg! I also realised she wasn't wearing a bra; how did I not notice that first? As we walked along the beach hearing the waves crashing against the rocks and stopping every now and then, I wasn't sure if I should bring up the fact that I was no longer in a relationship with Dr. Jekyll and Mr. Hyde. I was about three months away from completing my two-year "leave Waiheke Island plan" for good.

But I told her anyway because I had nothing to lose, and I didn't want to lie to her. So when she did eventually ask me about my relationship, I told her the truth. K looked genuinely surprised by what I told her because she had no idea I was ending my relationship with Dr. Jekyll. I wasn't in love with her, but I did care enough to support her through her drinking and anger issues. I didn't go into too many details; I wasn't sure if it would help or hinder, so I just elaborated more on my two-year plan. The time quickly came around when K had to head off back to her mum's.

I walked K towards her car and watched her drive off. While walking back to my place, I thought to myself, *Maybe I should have asked her out, or is it too soon? Or should I stick to my plan and wait three more months?* Playing it super cool and aloof, I texted her as soon as I got back home. I figured the fifteen-minute rule was long enough not to look desperate. I asked if she wanted to watch a movie sometime soon, keep it casual, and go as friends. K replied later that night with a 'Yeah; I'd be keen, let me know when?'

Still playing it super cool, I replied instantly with 'How about next week? One-word response: 'Sweet,' with a smiling emoji. Fuck, I had no idea what was on at the movies. I quickly checked. *Yessss. Pacific Rim* was playing, and I really wanted to watch this movie. I am a massive Godzilla fan, and this had monsters and transformer style robots; what's not to love, right?

I waited a few minutes, and texted back, 'Sorry, was cooking dinner and I forgot to text back. Pacific Rim, 4:20 pm,' with smiling emoji. That was a total lie, who cooks dinner in three minutes? Apart from 3-minute noodles, which I actually did make in the end. *Damn, I'm shit at flirting and being cool. It's been over ten years since I asked someone out on a date!*

'Yeah, sounds good, but I have not heard of that movie before, so I'll take your word that it's good. And what did you cook in three minutes?' puzzled and laughing emojis. *Damn, I think I've been rumbled already.* Our movie date couldn't come around quick enough. But the issue was that I wasn't sure if it really was a date or not. I mean, I didn't actually specify that it was a date, but I convinced myself that if it wasn't, K would have said something. I was just surprised that K actually turned up!

We were halfway through the movie when K needed to use the bathroom, so she got up and left. There were only three other people in the cinema, five including K and myself. K came back, and I watched her walk up and down the steps numerous times. Was she looking for me? I mean, I was sat on the end of the aisle, four seats in from where she was standing. And yet, K walked down the steps towards the screen and sat four rows in front of me, watching the movie on her own.

What the actual fuck! I didn't get it; she's now watching the movie on her own? How strange. I was so perplexed; I had never been in a situation like this before. I kept thinking, *We were just sitting together five minutes ago, and now we're sitting separately?* I didn't know what to do or how to resolve this. Did I give out the wrong vibes? Should I get up and sit next to her? What the fuck would you do in this position? It was one of the best movies I had watched so far that year. Sat on the edge of my seat, mouth wide open in awe, unable to breathe. It was so tense; this was a great movie, but one hell of a shit date.

When the movie finished and the lights went on, K turned around and smiled. I just sat there thinking, *What the fuck? This is crazy.*

"How come you watched the movie down there on your own?"

"I couldn't find you, so I thought I would watch it regardless."

"I was sitting right here, like four seats in, how come you couldn't see me?"

"How come you didn't say anything? You could see me looking for you."

We both had good points, but I think K's was more valid. I definitely could see her walking up and down the steps looking for me, but nothing came out. Maybe it had something to do with my past? Afterward, we went to get something to eat, and we started chatting about our respected families; I wanted to know as much as possible about K. As it turned out, we both had shitty alcoholic fathers. Who would have thought we would bond over our dads' drinking issues?

I didn't see K for a few weeks after our non-date date; I was trying to get a tender out to win a design project, which I got invited to tender for. Yes, that's right, you read that correctly: I was invited by Auckland Waterfront to submit a proposal to re-design a small existing public space, and the project manager was the same one I had when I was working on my urban space first project. He was now in a position where he could choose who he would like to tender, and he was also part of the tender panel that awards the project. After many phone calls, he reassured me that Auckland Waterfront was looking for fresh, new creative designers, and that he wanted to work with me again. They didn't want to be seen giving out work to the same old consultants.

After three years of knocking on doors, I finally had an in; my proposal was airtight. We also had to provide additional methodology on how we would collaborate with an artist who was based in America. I assembled a really experienced team, and our methodology was on point. I even had someone in our team who was based in America and who could collaborate with the artist in his studio. Our price was even more competitive; it was tough to see how we wouldn't win. I poured over 120 hours into this proposal, and I even paid a professional writer to proofread the whole tender and double-check everything. I was in super high spirits.

I got a call a week later: "Sorry; unfortunately, you weren't successful this time." I asked how many points away I was from the winning bid. "I am sorry, we're not allowed to give that information out." I then asked who won the project, and can you believe it, for all of my efforts and the constant phone calls asking me to submit a proposal, it went to the same consultants that he told me he didn't want to give the project to. I was devastated; words couldn't describe the feeling of failing again. I was encouraged from the start to go for this proposal, only to find out later that they needed to secure five consultants. Otherwise it was going to be an open tender, and that would have delayed the start of the project.

I was the fifth and final consultant. I was never going to win this project, it was always going to be the same consultants that they had used on the rest of the waterfront, they just needed the process to look transparent. The only feedback I received was that they had concerns that they haven't worked with me before. About a week went by since the disappointment of not winning this project and I really needed some company. I wasn't in a good place, so I started walking towards the pub, to see who was there. It had been ages since I last went, but then my inner voice kicked in.

"Maybe Mr. Hyde was right, you are fucking useless, and no one wants to work with you. So why don't you get pissed tonight? It's not like you have work tomorrow; in fact, no one wants to work with you."

I had been really struggling recently with my inner voice, but I didn't want K to know how bad it was. If it wasn't for her always texting to cheer me up, offering advice, telling me that I am good at what I do and that all I needed was just a break, I don't know what I would do. Loneliness is one of the saddest feelings I have ever felt. The first time I met K, she mentioned that the people who I associated with at the pub weren't really my friends, and they didn't care about me. I had to give it to her, she told me how she saw it; no playing games with this one, that was for sure.

She fucked me right off with that comment, though. I had known this group of people for over seven years, and she said they didn't give a damn about me. Deep down, I didn't want to hear the truth and I didn't want to believe her. But she was spot on. No one texted me, no one came around knocking on my door, and I was never invited to anything, not even for a beer. K's comment that day continually played in my mind on a loop. *Was I just somebody who was always at the pub? Someone to have a beer and a laugh with until their actual friends arrived? Was I that blind, or was I so desperate to fit in, regardless of what they thought about me?*

I walked up the stairs to the veranda, where we all usually sat. Halfway up, I could hear everyone laughing; nothing seemed to have changed. In fact, Mr. Hyde and I seemed to have been replaced by another young English couple. I sat down amongst them all with my Stella, and all I got was a "Hey you, where you been, we haven't seen you around for ages," that sort of shit.

The conversations were still the same old regurgitated chit-chat: sex, sex, and more sex. Nothing had changed in over nine months. I tried starting a decent discussion about an article that I had read some time ago regarding breastfeeding; it was on the front cover of Time Magazine: 'Why attachment parenting drives some mothers to extremes.' So my conversation started like this, "Hey guys, here's a question: when did society dictate to us the appropriate age to stop breastfeeding and why are mothers always made to feel like shit when they're breastfeeding in public?"

It was greeted with deft silence, followed by a single response: "Say that fucking shit again, I am not kidding, I will knock you the fuck out." "What, the article about breastfeeding?" "Yes, I am not fucking kidding, say that shit again, this is your second warning. I will knock you the fuck right out, no one here wants to talk about that shit." *Wow.* All I wanted to do was have a stimulating conversation, not too far from their original topic of sex. Well, it still had the element of boobs in it at least. But they would rather talk about objectifying women and about the size of their cocks rather than have an intellectual conversation.

Something was amiss here. Rather than argue or get knocked out, I stood up and headed downstairs, hoping that I might see K. She mentioned earlier in a text that she might pop in with her brother later. Then all of a sudden, someone shouted, "Hey, it's your round next!" and I was bombarded with drink requests. "No worries, let me go grab someone first,

193

to take down the order while I nip to the toilet." I never went to the toilet; I walked down the stairs and straight out the pub's front door.

I have never been back since, and I have never spoken to anyone from that night either. I walked away from seven years of what I thought was friendship, only to realise that I was a nobody to them in the first place. I also never heard from one single person either, out of thirty people who I had known for over seven years. These same people who came over to my house for BBQs and parties, and I was a shoulder for them to cry on. I supported them and offered genuine advice when no one else would. I even built a business with these people and not one person ever wondered what happed to me that night when I never came back from the toilet. You'd think someone would send a text to see if I was ok.

I felt distraught. Maybe the voice in my head was right all along, had I just wasted seven years on these people? I thought they were genuine friends. No one told me for the last seven years all I had been doing was making situational friends who would drop me like *that*! A click of their fingers when something better come along. I wish someone would have told me sooner, making friends is harder than you think. I had three months to go before I left Waiheke Island.

Dr. Jekyll had started seeing someone else, and I was genuinely happy for her and relieved that she wasn't my problem anymore. K was now living in Mt. Eden, another Auckland suburb about a five minutes' drive from the CBD. She had moved out of her mum's place and scored a fantastic one bed flat. I was still trying to find a somewhere new myself, but nothing was coming up in the areas that I wanted to live in or that I could afford. I definitely didn't want to flat share, that was for sure. The perfect solution would be for me to live on the same block as K. We would both have our own space, and we could just hang out whenever we liked. It would be the perfect situation. Even though we had only been texting for a few months, I really liked her.

Ten days before I had to move out, I received a text from K. She was sat on a bus on her way to work when she noticed a two-bedroom apartment on her block through the Trade Me app; she was also looking at places for me. It was only three doors down from K's place. She sent me the link ASAP and within the hour, I had signed the contract. I mean, what are the actual chances of that happening?

Ok, it was a little more pricey than what I could afford, and the apartment wasn't as nice as K's, but who cared? I moved out of Waiheke Island the exact same day that I had predicted two years earlier. I found the first three months strange; one of us would walk to the other person's apartment, have dinner, maybe watch a movie or play cards, and then head back home afterward. It was so surreal, but it was exactly what I needed; I knew I wasn't ready to rush into another relationship. The more I was getting to know K, the more I realised how amazing she was. She never took any bullshit, she was always straight up with what she wanted, kind-hearted, caring, and bloody hell was she ever funny, super quick-witted, sarcastic, dry, mixed in with a little bit of cheekiness and best of all, no fucking drama. She was no Dr. Jekyll and Mr. Hyde; that was for sure.

I knew I had found someone special the moment she told me why she was late coming home from work. During the day, she had been sorting out some stapled documents when a random, not fully closed staple pricked her finger. So she decided to go through over a five hundred separate stapled documents to make sure that this didn't happen to anyone else. How rare is that? She cared more about someone else pricking a finger than being able to get home early. That same night, she asked me what my childhood was like. I sat her down and bravely opened up again. I trusted her, and I believed that she would not use my past against me or hurt me in any way.

I also mentioned the last time I was raped as a thirteen-year-old boy. I still have no idea by who, the only thing I can recall from that horrific memory was hearing some random rap song in the background when all this took place. I even opened up regarding the inner battles that I was having in terms of having sex now that my box is open, I felt dirty, ashamed, guilty and disgusting. I was unable to re-connect with my body, and I didn't want anyone to touch me. I didn't want to touch myself either. Every time I tried new memories would begin to emerge, and then I would start to shake and throw up in my mouth; the stress and the emotional pain my body was experiencing were too much. I also mentioned to K the issues I am having regarding my sexuality and that I am attracted to ladyboys, and I have no idea why. That was the first time I had cried in twenty-three years; I completely broke down and it was also the first night K stayed over. She hugged me all night and didn't let me go until the morning; I didn't want her to let go, either. A year later, K and I moved into our first place together, in Mt. Roskill, about twenty minutes from the city centre. It was a perfect split-level house. I lived downstairs most of the time, I had my own lounge, bedroom, and bathroom, and K lived upstairs where the kitchen and the main living room was.

K also had a bedroom and a separate bathroom; all we had to do was walk up or down the stairs in the same house, a huge upgrade from Mt. Eden. Having my own space was perfect, a little unconventional but it really worked for us. I had my own space to heal in; my memories were starting to come back in dribs and drabs ever since Dr. Hyde opened my box.

I read somewhere that every time we bring up a memory, we take that memory out of our memory bank, observe it, and then distort it by several small factors. These factors include schemas, source amnesia, the misinformation effect, the hindsight bias, the overconfidence effect, and confabulation. Then we put that distorted memory back into our memory bank, so our memories might not be an exact record of what took place. We can even convince ourselves of something that wasn't true, something that creates persistent negative emotional thoughts that we bring to our present, continually replaying and believing these false stories on a continuous loop, 'This happened to me, and this is why I am like this.'

I was living in constant fear of these new memories. I had no idea when they would pop into my head and how bad they were. But the moment I identified them as a new memory from my past, no matter how big or small they were, I sank them straight back down to the ocean floor. I didn't want to relive one second of my past, especially with my state of mind. I was scared shitless of what they might reveal if I did piece together the full memory. So this time I made sure the boxes were harder to open up. I called these my Hellraiser puzzle boxes, a considerable upgrade from my original puzzle box.

K quit her job as a scheduler to work for herself, running a small fresh-squeezed juice bar in the city centre, not too far from my office. The juice bar wasn't the best location because she was surrounded by other leading juice bars, but instead of using pre-made juice, every juice K made was made right in front of your eyes. You saw exactly what you were drinking, no hidden surprises. That same year, Dr. Jekyll got engaged and I was really happy for her. I didn't want to throw away ten years, despite how bad they were, so we were trying to keep our relationship alive.

I was also collaborating with a well-renowned architect regarding the possibilities of upgrading a small town centre urban space. Auckland Council design team presented us with a concept idea based on a project that was built in the U.K. a simple, hardwearing, and flexible urban space located in Clapham London.

This concept would be the catalyst for upgrading the urban space and the surrounding environment and it was also the same project I worked on in the U.K. I mean, what were the chances of this? They wanted a similar concept and I was part of the design team that delivered the project. We both spent about a year working on a feasibility report and possible alternative design upgrades with minimum disruption to surrounding local businesses. Our feasibility report was hailed a tremendous collaborative success and was signed off and commissioned as a combined project, securing funds for over $2M.

We were both quickly commissioned again to produce another feasibility report, but this time for mainly upgrading the existing Auckland laneways system. We knocked that one out of the park too, and we were strongly advised to build a team to deliver and construction both projects.

We had already spent nearly two years understanding the needs of the communities, securing all the necessary funding via our reports and designs understanding the council's clear outcomes, and we built strong relationships with the local community and within the council. I lost both tenders again. Their feedback was, "We haven't worked with you before on any other construction projects." So what was the point of tendering? Both projects were awarded to the same design consultancy.

Not to be awarded any of these projects, words can't describe that feeling of *Now what? What's the point of even trying when it just goes to the same set of consultancies?* People who make the decisions and are in a place of power have no idea how they make us feel when we try so hard, and they encourage us like we have an honest chance of winning, only to be knocked back down to the ground. I genuinely don't understand their rationale. What's the point in encouraging you to tender, if the excuses will always be "we haven't worked with you before?" Then how can you ever win a project?

I took about five months off from work due to my depression and suicidal thoughts. I couldn't get out of bed again. No matter how hard I tried to make something happen, I was consistently knocked back down, and I was finding it harder and harder to get back up and try again. We also sold the juice bar, as K had to take time off to look after me. I was slowly feeling that I was having a mental breakdown; I just needed to be with my mum again, and I decided to cheer myself up with our next adventure in America.

I have always wanted to visit the U.S., and my ultimate dream was to cycle the West Coast of America, I planned this dream trip for nearly two years when I was living in the U.K. I loved the Tour De France and cycling; I loved the feeling of just me and my bike. My journey would start in Vancouver, Canada and finished in Las Vegas. The same year I planned to cycle the West Coast was the same year Dr. Jekyll, Mr. Hyde, and I flew to New Zealand.

Maybe I could do something very similar with my mum, minus the cycling. A three-week adventure, followed by one week in Las Vegas, where Mum would meet K for the first time. Our American adventure was the best one yet, it had everything. I had never laughed so much in my life. Mum was again on point, and the moment I greeted her at the San Francisco airport, I was already dreading the time when I would have to say goodbye. We packed in so much, from staying in San Francisco and touring Alcatraz to visiting the world-famous San Diego Zoo. While we were there, we also visited the RMS Queen Mary, a retired British ocean liner, which Mum used to work on in her twenties.

We went to the Hollywood walk of fame, noticing at one point seven different Spidermans all posing for tourist photos. We both thought Hollywood was very disappointing. Not sure what we expected, but we did expect it to be better! We had some fantastic conversations and some not so good, but Mum was starting to feel her age on this trip. She had just retired from work after twenty-two years at the same company.

The company gave her two options: take redundancy and a $10k payoff or stay and be relocated. I knew Mum would struggle with being at home; in her words, "I would just sit there waiting to die." As much as Mum was getting older, she also needed to work. Not for the money but to keep her going, belonging to something. I offered to pay Mum $10k a year so she wouldn't have to worry about money, and she could get a part-time job. She still felt that she had a lot more to offer this world. After all, she was only in her early 70's.

But my brother and sister convinced her otherwise. I never understood why they persuaded her to retire; my brother said it was $10k in the bank, but I was happy to pay that amount every year, so it didn't make sense for her to fully retire. But they did an excellent job convincing her otherwise.

Mum was way more negative on this adventure compared to the other ones. She always talked about her death and funeral, which songs she wanted to have played, the clothes she wanted to wear when being cremated. These conversations were hard for me to hear, and the fact that she wanted to be cremated was difficult to swallow. The day Mum received the sad news from her brother that her mum had passed away in a tragic house fire hit her hard. She kept envisaging how her mum died and how she was alone when she caught fire.

Mum never went back to her original childhood home ever again after the funeral, not even to visit where my Nana was laid to rest. My greatest fear is death by drowning, ever since my schoolteacher stood at the side of the pool, watching me struggle to swim and then placing his foot on top of my head and pushing me down under the water. I started to have a panic attack when I couldn't touch the bottom of the pool, and I was unable to breathe. I swallowed so much water that my lungs filled up and he eventually pulled me out of the pool. When he noticed that I had stopped flapping my arms in the air and sank to the bottom, he performed mouth to mouth to revive me.

I was seven years old, and his rationale was that this would make me become a stronger swimmer. Even though I live near some of the most stunning beaches in New Zealand, I have been in the sea no more than five times, and only if I can touch the ground.

Mum always said she never wanted to be cremated. I think the image of her mum on that day was just too much. We all thought she wanted to be buried, even in her will it said for Mum to be buried in her local cemetery, where we all grew up. But she also hated the thought of worms eating her as well, even though she didn't want to be cremated. Catch 22.

But during this adventure, she opened up more to me than ever before regarding her funeral. She persisted that she wanted to be cremated, she also had the idea that her ashes could be compressed into a diamond and used in a pendant or ring. She loved that idea, but she was a long way off, Mum was fighting fit. So I was constantly trying to re-focus the conversations on the positives of life, not the negatives, which was very strange, as Mum was never a negative person.

What was very noticeable to me when I went back to the U.K. a few years before, was how much doom and gloom was on T.V. Everything was just so negative and so cynical, and Mum watched endless amounts of reality T.V. I am not saying I was blind to all of this because I wasn't; I also watched my share of reality T.V, streamed from the U.K. to New Zealand. I was a big fan of *Geordie Shore*, which reminded me of my university days to some extent.

K hated the fact that I was watching people getting pissed and having sex on T.V, so she introduced me to one of her favourite reality shows, a very different type of reality show called *Survivor*, hosted by Jeff Probst. I binge watched all the seasons, totally intrigued about the social aspects of this game show. But the direction of the show changed when we were introduced to Boston Rob in Season 8. The show took on a totally different direction to the previous seasons, which was intriguing. And when Russell Hants appeared on Season 19, it took on a completely different direction altogether, with so many blindsides, betrayals, and finding idols. All good fun, until Jeff says, "The tribe has spoken."

This was such an unbelievable reality show, I felt so connected and so hooked, not sure why, but something resonated with me. I also used to be a massive fan of soaps, Mum's number one TV programs. We were never allowed to talk while her soaps were on, and if we did, the volume went up. A good portion of what we watch today is bleak, fearful, dark, miserable, violent, disturbing, celebrity, and sexually driven reality programs. And we call this entertainment?

We watch these programmes as a way to relax after a hard day's work, trapping us in a perpetual cycle of having the same types of conversations, day in day out with one another or within. I had some fears while thinking about travelling around America or South America. I was so worried about being robbed and beaten up again, especially because it was just my mum and me. I had never been fearful of travelling, but at that time I was.

Mum always looked forward to our adventures, something that

gave her happiness in a world of gloom and despair. If I didn't organise these holidays, I am convinced my brother and sister wouldn't have done anything either. To my sister's credit, she did organise many long weekends away for Mum, especially in Europe. But my brother couldn't even be bothered to take his daughter round to see her grandmother or take her out for dinner.

One evening, coming out of the underground in LA and traveling up the escalators after arriving back from San Diego, I thought I heard someone getting mugged at the top of the escalators. I turned to Mum and mentioned what I heard.

"Mum, for fuck sakes, keep your head down, and as soon as we get off the escalators, turn right not left." Mum was Mum, looking everywhere but down, saying "Who's getting mugged, Cornelius? I can't see anything."

In a stern voice, "Mum, for fuck sakes, head down and don't say anything. I think I can hear someone asking for their wallet and watch to my left, so head down and turn right, please."

Again, "Who's getting mugged Cornelius, I can't hear anything, are you sure?"

We got to the top of the escalators, and my mum shouted "Cornelius, Cornelius, Cornelius, that guy is getting mugged with a knife; you were right!"

The guy with the knife heard my mum and looked straight at us, trying to weigh us up, Mum walked quickly to the right as instructed. I stood my ground and stared back at him, not moving, just staring. I was taken back to that morning of my paper round. But this time I walked forward towards him, as much as I was fucking shitting myself, and my nerves, anxiety and my adrenaline were through the roof, no one was ever going to make me feel weak and vulnerable like that morning. So I walked towards him, slowly telling my mum to carry on walking in the opposite direction, I wouldn't be far behind.

The guy just stood looking at me and squaring me up and down, then he turned and ran away. I wasn't sure why he did that, but I am also not sure which was worse: the potential of being mugged again and getting stabbed, or getting a right old bollocking off Mum, for doing something so stupid or brave, depending on the perspective. I like to think I was a bit of both, and I like to think that that evening, no one else got mugged by that guy. These are the memories that made going away with Mum so amazing.

Las Vegas, though, was something else, and I had one night with my mum in Vegas before K and Mum finally met for the first time. I had never seen anything like the strip before, and I was even more surprised that it wasn't what I had expected. I always had in my mind what I had seen on TV, a rough and seedy stripper spot full of stag and hen weekends, yet it wasn't anything like that. The streets were packed full of people, all in high spirits, the hotel lights, the glamour and the glitz, not to mention inside the hotels. I was blown away, something I thought I would never experience in my life; it was purely magical.

Every hotel had a different theme, not one hotel was the same. The casino noise was exhilarating; I was hooked within minutes. I love Vegas. I hardly ever gamble, but Mum and my sister had come to Vegas a few years before. They only played the 1c slot machines and Mum said you got free drinks when you were playing the slots. I wasn't that convinced that she was telling me the truth until I was asked what I wanted to drink. Mum ordered a pina colada and I a rum and coke, and off the host went. Five minutes later, we were toasting one another. We tipped the host for her troubles, and twenty mins later we had another round in hand.

What the actual fuck is this place? I thought. *And why have I never been before?*

I was pretty tipsy after about five rum and cokes, so we went outside and watched the world go by. I looked at my watch and it was 4 am. *How is it 4 am, I am not even tired.* Mum explained some strange theory she had watched on T.V. *Las Vegas Uncovered* or something like that, where they pump the casinos with oxygen so you don't become tired. I never checked if this was true or not, I just loved listening to her crazy theories, right or wrong. But we did have to get some sleep, K was arriving in the morning for her two-week holiday, and I was so nervous.

12

MUM MEET K. K MEET MUM

It was the morning of K's arrival in Vegas. I was feeling nervous and anxious, and I was trying to reassure Mum of why I fell deeply in love with this beautiful fantastic person, especially after my relationship with Dr. Jekyll and Mr. Hyde. I was explaining to Mum the three different depths of love, and why this love was so different.

See, your first love happens to you at such a young age. However, eventually, you grow apart as you both want different things in life. When you get older, you look back and think, was it even love? Nevertheless, the truth is, it was to you back then. It was love, or what you knew love to be.

Your second love is the hardest one, and the one you get hurt in. This love teaches you many lessons in life and makes you stronger. This love also includes great pain, lies, betrayal, abuse, and unbelievable inner damage. However, this is the one where you grow. In this love, you realise what love is actually about, and what love is not. You will also know the difference between who is kind and who is not, and how we sometimes become closed off, careful, cautious and considerate. You also know precisely what you want and do not want.

The third love comes to you blindly, with no warnings. It creeps up on you without you even noticing. You don't even go looking for this love. This love comes to you. I could put up any number of walls I wanted, but K always found a way to break them down. I found myself caring about K without even trying. K also looks nothing like my 'typical type' either; far from it. Every day, I get lost in her beautiful brown eyes and transported to another world when I hear her amazing, infectious laugh.

In K, I see the most beautiful, loving person in my entire life, despite how she sees her imperfections, flaws, and defects. I am unable to conceal anything from her. K always knows what's on my mind, deep down I knew that I wanted to marry her and to start a family, but I had always believed that marriage and children were never going to be part of my life, so I convinced myself precisely that. Every day, I thank the universe for guiding K to me. I had waited for over thirty-eight years to have one true friend, but in K, I found my best friend, my one true love, soulmate and my Princess Bride.

Oh, and I also didn't mention to my mum that K was Indo-Fijian, something I was always worried about, because of where I was brought up. I think the first brown person I ever saw was from the local curry house when I was twenty-one years old. I also never saw a black person in real life until I went to university. To be honest, I don't think I ever saw colour in anyone, including K.

But Mum was from the old school of thinking generation; I was ten years old when Mum advised me that if I ever had mixed-race children, there would be a good chance they could be bullied. I didn't think my mum's thinking was that much different from anyone else's in the early 80's. I think that's why my type has always been white English-Rose curvy girls. With not having many influential people in my life to offer me any type of advice, my mum's advice was the one I listened to the most and took to heart.

K is going to do her fucking nut in with me for writing this part in the book. Still, it's true; with all her amazing qualities, I also fell deeply in love with her boobs. I have never to this day seen boobs like hers before. She first showed me her right boob during one summer evening, walking along the beach.

K has unbelievably soft but firm natural teardrop perky c-cup boobs, nipples always erect, like on a cold winter's day, perfectly aligned to 45-degrees. The best way to describe K's nipples is that someone meticulously placed a perfectly formed small chocolate Malteser, laid flawlessly on a beautiful chocolate Cadbury button, surrounded by golden caramel. I was immediately transported back in time to when I was eighteen years old, when I saw a real boob for the first time. I think I have always remained eighteen-years-old when it comes to K's boobs, constantly wanting to touch them, with a permanent smile of wonderment on my face. Sorry sweetheart, love you, but it's true, xxx.

As I was explaining the qualities of K to Mum, minus the boob reference, I didn't even notice that K was standing about two meters in front of me, waving her arms in the air like a madman. I didn't even recognise her at first. K had a new holiday haircut; it was super short with shaved back and sides.

K's hair was a lot longer before I left for my U.S.A. adventure with Mum. This style was radically different to what I had been used to, she looked even sexier than before. "Wow, wow, wow, you look amazing, love your new style."

"Mum, meet K. K, meet my amazing Mum."

Mum's face was an unforgettable picture, she looked so surprised and also blown away at the same time. While K hopped and skipped towards the luggage carousel, Mum punched the top of my right arm. "K is beautiful; you've done well there, son." I laughed, but deep down I also couldn't believe how lucky I was, either. Our first night in Vegas, Mum was so eager to take us both to experience Fremont Street. This world-famous venue is home to one of the largest closed-canopy L.E.D. screens in the world, about 500m in length, an orgasm of live music, bars, restaurants, casinos, entertainment, and street performers.

The moment we turned the corner onto Fremont Street, I couldn't believe what I was witnessing. It was a kaleidoscope of sound, colour, and happiness. I was unable to process it all. I was bewildered, like the first time I saw David Copperfield make The Statue of Liberty disappear, or when he walked through The Great Wall of China. My eyes were wide open, unable to blink. I didn't want to blink in case I missed something, I was absorbing everything in. I never want to leave this place, and it was only 5 pm.

I loved being a child again, even at forty-two years old. I think we all forget what it's like to be free and innocent, enjoying one long, hot, summer *Goonies* or *BMX Bandits* adventure with your best mates. Creating your reality and letting your imagination run wild, pretending to be whoever you want to be, free from any rules, free from any worries. This is how I saw Fremont Street, through the eyes of a seven-year-old boy. I thought Blackpool was good back in my heyday, but Fremont was on another level. We both didn't know where to look, and I could tell on my mum's face that she was so happy to see me this happy.

We both decided to grab a drink; I ordered a rum and coke and K ordered a rum and ginger beer. Even to this day, we still call our homemade cocktails 'Fremont's'. Ironically, we ordered our drinks from the D-Bar, part of The D Las Vegas Hotel and Casino, which opens up onto Fremont Street. Three stunning half-naked women were dancing on top of the bar. This good looking bartender grabbed two plastic pint cups, filled the bottom of the cups with about five ices cubes, then he just Fremont free poured rum to the top of the cup, followed by a small splash of coke for me and two splashes of ginger beer for K.

I had two of these free pour drinks during the evening, K had one. I felt very drunk after my first cup, but the second cup, fuck that hit me hard. I knew I was getting drunk but didn't want Mum to know.

K mentioned she wasn't feeling the effects of the Fremont free-pour as much as I was, and she headed towards the bathroom inside the main entrance of the D casino, directly opposite to where we were watching a live band.

I love watching Mum people watch. I always get a tap on my shoulder, followed by, "Look Cornelius, look over there! And look over there!" But this time, I was unable to focus on who Mum was even looking at. I had heard this term many times, but I had never experienced it myself until now: I had double vision from drinking. Mum said to me, "Cornelius, I missed you so much, come and give your mum a hug, it's been ages since I last saw you," followed by how much weight I had put on since the last time she saw me. This was what I loved most about my mum. She said precisely what was on her mind but with no attachment to it.

I stood stationary and blurry-eyed, trying hard not to sway and give any signs that I was drunk as a skunk, looking towards Mum, but I wasn't sure which Mum I should hug. I just stood there and kept smiling, hoping the right Mum would embrace me instead.

"Cornelius, come and give your mum a hug," she said again. I tried to close one eye, hoping that this would sort out my double vision and give me clarity on who I should hug. *Fuck, which one is the real Mum?* They both looked the same, and I had no point of difference or anything to compare with. I started to rub my eyes and blink quickly, continuously looking at the ground and away from Mum's view.

I took a big gulp of air, tried to focus on the job at hand, internally saying, *I've got this, I just need to open my arms out more and hug both mums.*

Hopefully, she won't know that I am pissed and with double vision. I was just about to take my first step towards hugging my mum, when Mum noticed K had been gone for over forty-five minutes. What the fuck!

All this time, I had been standing there, trying to work out which Mum was real for over forty-five minutes, without even realising K wasn't here. Shit, panic kicked in. If I had double vision, then what was K dealing with? Then all of a sudden, K was walking towards me with this almighty relief on her face and gave me a massive hug and a kiss. "Shit! That was scary," she whispered in my ear while she hugged me.

"What happened, did anyone touch you? Are you ok? Where's your wallet"? I was bombarding her with so many questions. "I am ok; I got unbelievably lost in the casino. I came out of the toilet, turned right, and then all of a sudden, I had no idea where I was, where to go, or how to get out. I have been walking around the casino looking for the main entrance for ages. Then I started to panic and started worrying about how to get back to our hotel."

"Why didn't you ask anyone for help?" "I was convinced I knew where the exit was, and then all of a sudden I was back at the bathrooms again, so I sat down and waited for you. But you never came, so I got back up again, turned left, and the next minute, I was lost again. I found the bathrooms and sat back down and waited again, and still, you didn't come."

"Well, while you have been trying to get out of the casino, I have been trying to work out which one is Mum since you left. I have double vision, and I didn't want to hug the wrong Mum and fall flat on my face." I have never laughed so hard in my life; we both just pissed ourselves. Fuck me, those Fremont free-pours were something else! After we finished laughing, I said, "How the hell did you manage to get out of the casino then?"

"I have absolutely no idea; I was walking and walking and then all of a sudden, I saw you and your mum. I was so relieved that you hadn't left yet."

"Wait for a second, how come you couldn't see us?" and I pointed directly to the bathrooms; they were right in front of us all along. "How did you not see the main entrance? I mean, you can't miss them, they're right there." We just pissed ourselves laughing again. I always wondered what my poor mum must have thought about us both that night.

They say what happens in Vegas, stays in Vegas, but not this night. This first night in Vegas was something else. During our first week, we all had so much fun. Mum and K got on so well, she could easily see why I was so in love with K. K never once changed her personality, style, or self to appease my mum; everything was so effortless, fluid, and natural, even Mum was starting to fall in love with her.

One late afternoon, we were all in the swimming pool (shallow end, of course) when K got out and moved all of our belongs to another lounger facing the sunshine. No one asked her to do this, she just did it. Mum turned to me out of earshot of K and said, "Son, if you fuck up just once with K, she will walk, and you will never see her again. She loves you that much, and she doesn't deserve to be hurt." This wasn't my mum giving me advice, Mum was telling me the truth.

My brother, on the other hand, was one of those people who thought that the grass is always greener. And now with the ease and accessibility of social media and chat apps, you don't need to fuck someone else in today's world to cheat on your partner. Just by texting in secret, hiding your phone, turning off your chat apps, or even turning on airplane mode, you have already cheated! Fucking is just the conclusion. I had never heard my mum say anything like this to me before, never mind swearing. It was so direct, a chilling warning not to fuck up.

I got out of the pool, walked over to K, and gave her a hug and a kiss and said, "Thank you for being you." When Mum gives relationship advice, I take note. But sometimes you're not always correct, hey, Mum!

The week with Mum went so fast that I really didn't want to say goodbye to her at San Francisco airport. This holiday adventure was so different in so many ways, but all I wanted was Mum's approval of K, which I got on so many levels and so many times. K and I flew back to Vegas to enjoy the final week of our holidays, soak up the sunshine, eat more amazing food, and experience what Vegas was all about.

I mentioned earlier that I never wanted to get married, but K was the exception. I would be crazy not to, and I am not crazy! The thought of having the same surname as K made me feel complete and whole. I know it sounds absurd, I know it's only a name on a piece of paper, but to me, it meant so much more.

Therefore, after another fantastic night out, we decided to get married in Vegas the following year. I just needed to save up and fly back to the U.K. for Christmas, so my brother and sister could finally meet K.

In addition, my sister had had her first daughter the previous year, and she would be one year old at Christmas, so this would also be the first time I would get to meet my new niece. It was a win, win situation. One of the most fundamental problems you can have when your family lives on the other side of the world is planning your holiday around other members of your family, especially six months in advance. It had been seven years since K had left London and we wanted to make sure we both had a shared experience of London for ourselves before we spent time with Mum. She loved London at Christmas also.

Mum was struggling with retirement. She was bored shitless sitting at home, watching doom and gloom T.V. My brother hardly ever went round to see her, and my sister had just become a mum, so she felt very alone. Our weekend phone calls were getting more and more negative as Mum was more cynical. And she would moan about everything and anything; the only positive thing in her life was that K and I were flying back for Christmas. However, organising what to do was proving harder than I initially thought. My brother and sister were non-committal towards anything that I suggested, and I suggested many things that we could all do as a family.

I wanted to at least organise something for Boxing Day and New Year's. Still, no one wanted to commit to anything, and I should have listened to K, they just weren't bothered about seeing us. I am not sure why I never wanted to listen to this advice. In the back of my mind, I wanted that statement to be wrong, more than anything. I kept telling them both that we had to book hotels, transport, flights, etc. in advance to make sure we got the best possible deals. It wasn't just me coming home, I also had K.

Travel costs had now doubled in price and even when I explained all of this to them, it was ignored. I was making all this effort, and I was getting nothing back in return. I asked my sister if we were going to celebrate Emma's 1st birthday. Surprisingly, she said no! Shall we do something for Boxing Day then? That was also a no! I even suggested taking my brother's daughter out to a pantomime, and his response was a no! Jane had already seen *Aladdin*. Ok, let's try a pantomime in Sheffield. Too far, was his reply.

Excuse after excuse from both my brother and sister, and all I wanted them to do was meet K and spend some time with their brother. It had been three years since I last went back home, surely it couldn't be this hard to organise a few days with your brother and sister? The stress of organising my trip back home brought my depression back on, but this time I noticed something unfamiliar, I was now struggling to get out of bed. I couldn't get my head around why both of them didn't want to see me or meet K.

I started to pile on more weight, dark circles were constantly under my eyes, my skin looked dry and old, and my hair was getting greyer by the week. Add this to the stress that I was already under, with hardly any work coming in, and it was all getting a bit too much for me. I kept crying into K's arms, "Why don't they want to see me? What have I done wrong?" I could understand why my sister wasn't that arsed, after the football tickets rip off. However, for my brother not to make an effort was baffling to me. When I approached him on the subject, he said, "I have no idea what I am doing over that time, that's why I can't organise something now." But in reality, he was hoping something better would come up.

I was too blind to see this or I didn't want to believe that I was surplus to requirements and that he didn't want to see me. But when you love your family, you still hang onto the possibility of hope all the same. But in return, I only got sadness. In fact, in the last three and a half years, I must have texted my brother over three hundred times first to start a conversation. He only texted about ten times to see how I was, or when he needed something from me.

I texted my sister about a hundred times, to see how she and her little new arrival were doing. Even though she ripped me off, I still tried to make an effort, but I never got one back. It was always one-way traffic. Again, I wish I had listened to K regarding that they weren't that arsed about seeing us; I also didn't want to let Mum down either, she was so excited to see us. I needed a backup plan. I had already paid the full amount for the flights all upfront, and I needed to make sure that our trip back home was not wasted, after all. With none of them wanting to do anything with me, I planned our holiday without them; it included dining out at Jamie Oliver's Fifteen, finally. We wanted to watch some west end shows, especially *Wicked*, we both wanted to watch that show the most. I also booked a high tea experience at the Shard.

K had never been ice skating before, so I organised that experience as a surprise for her. I also had a plan to secretly propose to K, even though we both agreed that we wouldn't buy a ring or even propose. Just because society expects you to buy a ring when you propose, it doesn't mean you have to! This didn't go down very well with my brother or sister. Funny that they couldn't be fucked to sort out their shit to see their brother, but they had an opinion on me not buying an engagement ring, go fucking figure.

My proposal idea was to take K to watch her first Liverpool game at Anfield against Leicester on Boxing Day, seeing no one wanted to do anything that day, and propose to her there. I thought if I got permission from Liverpool Football Club, I could propose to K standing on the pitch an hour before kick-off. Nothing too flashy, no cameras and no cringing moment in front of millions of fans around the world. K would kill me, that's her worst nightmare.

Nope nothing like that, walk through the tunnel and ask her to marry me, plain and simple. Combine the two loves of my life in one place. I even organised seven nights in Amsterdam over New Year's. I adore that city and everything it has to offer. I had visited Amsterdam so many times when I was researching for my final degree project; I loved the people, the museums, the galleries, the restaurants, the red-light district, and I also fell in love with their cafe culture.

It would be rude of me not to say hello once again, and K loved their cafe culture too. My brother still wasn't bothered about doing anything for New Year's, and my sister had already booked her tickets to watch darts at Alexandra Palace. It would have been nice to be invited, seeing as I love darts too. But I also made sure I had five days to spare after we came back from Amsterdam, just in case my brother and sister eventually wanted to meet up before I flew back home.

With only a few weeks before we were due to fly back to the U.K., my sister decided to celebrate her daughter's 1st birthday after all, which fucked me right off. I had been trying to organise seeing everyone for over five months, and now she had moved the goalposts at the last minute.

She was asking me to change all of our travel arrangements and our accommodation, just so I could spend two hours with my niece. Only two hours mind you, not a minute more, as I was told. Back in August, I asked my sister if we could stay at her place for the weekend so we could catch up, but the answer was no, her partner's children were visiting that weekend and the following weekend. Funny, I never gave my sister any dates for staying over at her place.

I even asked if she was willing to bring Emma into London, since she only lived about thirty minutes away. It would be far easier than changing all of our travel arrangements, seeing as we were all going back to Mum's on the same day as Emma's birthday.

I phoned my sister and said, "Why can't you bring Emma to see us? It would be an absolute nightmare if we all came to see you. We would have to drag four suitcases during Christmas morning rush hour, from Belsize Park on the underground via the Northern line to Euston Station. We would then have to catch a train from Euston Station to Luton, followed by a taxi from Luton to Harpenden. Then back to London, Kings Cross St. Pancras Station, onwards to Sheffield, and then another train back to our local town, followed by a taxi back to Mum's house. Mum can hardly walk due to her bad back, and you're expecting us to do all this traveling so I can spend only two hours with my niece and all in one day? When I asked you in August if you are doing anything for Emma's 1st birthday. Do you think this is fair when it only takes you thirty minutes to get into London and we can meet you anywhere?"

"Cornelius, London is too loud for a one-year-old, I'm not talking about this anymore," was her reply.

"Sorry, I'm not sure if I understand what you are saying. How is London too loud when you took Emma when she was six months old to Silverstone to watch a Formula 1 Grand Prix Race? I don't get it." "If you want to see your niece, then you're going to have to come to me, and you only have two hours anyway, so it's up to you."

"Ok, what about when I come back from Amsterdam, would that work?"

No reply! My sister had hung up the phone. K just said it straight, "She doesn't want you to see your niece, you have tried for five months now and this is what you get. I am so sorry sweetheart, but she doesn't." I just broke down in tears. "I don't get it, I want to see my niece, and this is how hard she is making it, I don't get it at all, I just don't get it."

We finally landed at Gatwick airport for the start of our Christmas holiday; I was feeling depressed, flat, and apprehensive. I had made this twenty-four-hour trip to see my family, and I had no idea if I even would. K and I were so frigging jetlagged. Our first full day in London, we booked

Wicked, which, to be honest, was far too early, but we wanted to cram in as much as possible.

However, ten minutes into the show, I was starting to nod off; my head was beginning to drop forward and then suddenly I was awake again, struggling to keep my eyes open. I turned to K, and she was already asleep! What had we done? We both wanted to watch *Wicked*, and we were both struggling to stay awake. I woke K up, and she was all over the place, struggling big time to keep her eyes open.

We both managed this on/off routine for the first half. I had no idea where we were in the story, I just kept nodding off and then reawakening once my head snapped forward. We went to the bar and ordered three cans of Red Bull, hoping this would kick in for the second half, but it didn't. K had a great idea, she suggested that we sniff some Vicks vapor rub that was in her pocket to keep us awake. I am not sure if this actually worked, but I was high as a kite, taking a hit up my nose every two minutes and then passing it over to K to do the same. We repeated this process for the whole of the second half, and when our heads did that snap drop when we fell asleep, we would take a bigger double sniff.

When the show finished, I turned to K, and we just started hilariously pissing ourselves laughing, we were high as a kite. We were having our very own theatre rave, minus the ecstasy. I kept thinking what the hell were the people thinking who sat behind us. Every time we nodded off, we woke back up and sniffed Vicks vapor rub. I swear, they thought we were vapor junkies, it was the most surreal theatre experience I have ever had, and we still don't know how the story started or ended.

During our first week in London, the stress of trying to organise seeing my family had taken its toll, especially on my chest. I was starting to show early signs of pneumonia. Which developed into nasty chest infections, to the point where we were both admitted to Royal Free Hospital in Hampstead. I had a bad feeling, seeing my mum. I just felt like something was wrong, and it was. My sister had gotten to her first regarding why we couldn't see my niece, saying that she tried to make all the effort. Still, I wasn't willing to budge on my plans, and I was selfish? I decided to explain that this wasn't true, but for whatever reason, Mum didn't believe me. It felt like déjà vu.

I kept trying to reassure her that I honestly wanted to see my sister and my niece and that I texted her with many options when I was back in New Zealand. Still, I never got one reply. Same with my brother, he went M.I.A. too, hardly saying anything and confirming nothing.

K was right; we shouldn't have come to the U.K. It was clear they didn't give a flying fuck about K or me. I argued and argued with Mum, which I had never done. I wanted her to trust and believe me, yet she wouldn't. I read out the text messages that I sent both of them and their reply, and still, she didn't believe me. Mum had no idea what this was causing me internally, not being believed, when we came all this way. None of what my mum was saying made any sense to K or me.

I felt so sorry for K; she was caught up in a massive family feud, when all she wanted to do was pack her stuff and go back to New Zealand. It had gotten that bad. Again, I tried to reassure Mum, and even K kept saying, "I am not sure why you're not believing your son, but you're breaking his heart in front of me. I have no idea what you're doing, but he's telling you the truth, he's tried everything possible to meet up with both of them, but they don't want to hear it for some reason."

Mum phoned my sister to sort who was lying once and for all. My sister said that I was lying, and my mum believed her again. I had no idea what the fuck was going off, but I couldn't put myself through all of this. My body was so fragile, and now my inner voice was telling me, *You're useless, even your family doesn't want anything to do with you; even your mum thinks you are lying. No one wants you here, including your mum. No one wants you; no one loves you.* I could feel I was starting to have an emotional breakdown.

"Why do you think Cornelius is lying? All he has ever done is take care of you and show you love, when your other deadbeat of a son, who lives two minutes away, can't even pop in for a cup of tea to see how you are? Your daughter has always been vindictive and manipulative, you know it, you told me in Vegas what she's like. So why are you choosing her side on this? Cornelius has read you the text messages, and still you don't believe him; you can see it's killing him."

Then my mum showed me a text from my sister. It was the text that I had sent her, but the end of the text was perfectly cropped off, and missed the 'let's try to catch up after I come back from Amsterdam' part! Then my mum angrily snapped, "If I don't believe your sister, she won't let me see my granddaughter, and you live in New Zealand. Then who do I have?"

Finally, the answer.

Mum chose to believe my sister regardless, and the arguments got so bad that on Christmas Eve, K and I had to stay in a hotel; in fact, we stayed in the same hotel until we went to Amsterdam. Christmas dinner, Mum didn't say a word to K or me, it was the worst possible homecoming. My brother was no better, he was having a go at me for traveling to Liverpool to watch the game. He was so pissed off that we weren't doing anything on Boxing Day.

My sister had only organised a buffet on Boxing Day without telling me, and now I was the selfish one for not going. Even though everything was planned for me to propose to K at Anfield and I only found out this was happening over Christmas dinner. The morning of the game, I tried to box up all my feelings regarding my family and sink them into my ocean. Today was such a special day. Still, with everything going off, I overlooked that no trains were running on Boxing Day, and time was not on my side if I was going to pull this surprise off.

We quickly ran to the coach station, and we were lucky enough to get the last two seats for the direct coach to Liverpool. Then the coach took a detour, stopping off at Leeds coach station, due to a faulty engine. The next coach to Liverpool was running about an hour late, due to motorway traffic. I was not in a good mood. Everything I had planned was not going to plan, and I had no idea what to do, so I decided to Uber from Leeds to Liverpool. I sat in the back seat, numb and disappointed. I knew in my heart that I had missed the chance to propose to K at Anfield.

The only shining light was that we got there before the start of the "You'll Never Walk Alone" chorus a few minutes before we were due to kick-off. I wanted K to experience this unbelievable atmosphere and why I love this football club so much. We had travelled from the other side of the world for this game, and we were stuck in fucking traffic on the motorway. Now we were even going to miss the start too; this was a complete disaster, everything that went wrong had gone wrong.

We took to our seats twenty minutes into the game. I had paid a fortune for K to experience Anfield, and this was no experience at all, a complete fucking disaster. This holiday was a disaster, but least we had

Amsterdam. We had about three days back at the hotel before we flew off, and I asked Mum for the money that I had lent her while she was in America. She promised me that she had it and, with the hotel bills mounting up, I had started to run out of money.

Mum didn't have the money. Well she did, but it was her retirement money, and my brother said not to give it to me as I could afford it. His words, "If Cornelius and K can fly over to the U.K. and spend money on hotels in London, trips to Liverpool, and the seven nights in Amsterdam, he can afford it. You need it more!" I was never going to ask my mum for the money, but I had just spent over a thousand pounds on hotel bills because K didn't want to stay in the house, as the atmosphere was awful and Mum and I were still arguing about all the lies.

My brother decided that he would work again over the holiday period, bragging about how much he was going to earn again rather than being with me and trying to get to know K. However, I really needed the money. The tension was not good, Mum already had high blood pressure, and this situation wasn't helping. Still, I didn't cause it, this was all my sister's doing. All she had to do was admit that she lied and just say sorry. But I knew this was never going to happen, based on the football tickets last time.

In fact, I never heard my brother or sister ever apologise to me, regardless of whether they were in the wrong. I even tried to explain to my brother one last time about how manipulative our sister is, but all he said was, "I'm not bothered. We know what you're like, you're full of shit." My brother and sister have absolutely no idea what I am like or who I am. That sentence means, *'I am so full of shit myself, I am selfish, I lie, I cheat, I do whatever I want and I don't care who I hurt in the process as long as I get what I want.'* But because my brother and sister think that we are all cut come from the same cloth and we have the same genes we must be the same.

We flew to Amsterdam two days before New Year's Eve. I sat on the plane stoking K's thumb for the whole flight, my anxiety was sky high tears running down my face. All I wanted was my brother and sister to meet K before we got married. I had another bad feeling the moment we landed. As soon as we got to the hotel, my phone went off. My brother had phoned, shouting at me, calling me "a cunt, a fucking wanker, fucking useless. What sort of brother do I have, you fly all this way, and you don't spend New Year with Mum? You're a selfish fucker, you're no brother of mine. Mum is completely stressing out regarding you asking her for your money, and you can fucking afford it if you're in Amsterdam."

I was hit for six, I was a fucking cunt for doing something for myself when no one wanted to do anything, not even my brother was doing anything for New Year's. He lives two-minutes away and he was staying in, but I was a useless cunt for trying to salvage what I had left of this shocking holiday.

"Stop asking Mum for money, she doesn't have it, and if she did, you can afford it," which I couldn't. I said to my brother, "When you lend Mum a tenner, you want it back the next day, and you can afford it." "What's it got to do with you if I can afford it or not? You're fucking useless. You've haven't helped at all, she's on blood pressure tablets because of you and your lies, and you have ruined Christmas for Mum and all of us, I will never forgive you for this."

I was all over the place, shocked tremendously. I had tried so hard, and yet I was the villain. I wasn't in the mood to show K this fantastic city, we were now starting to argue. K was over all of this shit. I was lost and I still had this awful chest infection, struggling to breath, my chest was getting tighter and tighter, my stress levels where a real cause for concern regarding my health. I was replaying all of what had happened, wondering whether I was the reason for all of this. Was I selfish, was this my fault?

I texted Mum so many times to apologise, but I got nothing back. She was devastated by what occurred, but I still couldn't get my head around it all. I had no idea how to rectify this situation. K was so miserable; I was in so much pain. This pain cracked my heart open. I had never felt anything like this before; Mum turned her back on me, like everyone else in my life, and I had no idea what do to next. I boxed up all of these feelings, and sank them down into the ocean, trying to make the best of this holiday with K.

It was New Year's Eve and we had booked a restaurant to celebrate in. Still, I was only just managing to hold the box under the surface of the ocean with my hand; the storm was coming. I knew I was in trouble, I had so many visions popping into my head from my past. I was so sad, struggling to hold down my emotions. Walking back to our hotel, with such dark sadness in my heart, when we both then heard fireworks go off in all directions, and we stopped on a little canal bridge. We both looked towards the night sky; it was New Year's Day, but I was not in any mood to celebrate. K held my hands and told me to look at her.

"Saweets, I love you, and I want to be with you, not your family. I love you, you're my everything, you're such an inspiration for what you have gone through. I don't know anyone who has gone through this amount of pain and I know no matter what life throws at us, as long as we are together, we can do anything. So will you marry me?"

13

ALONE

I flew back to New Zealand heartbroken. I didn't make peace with my brother or sister, and to be honest, I didn't expect to either, but I did expect to make peace with Mum. I neither slept on the plane nor watched a movie; I just sat in my seat feeling numb, replaying everything that happened in my head.

Why did I need Mum to believe me? Why was it so important to me? I just couldn't let it go. I needed to be right, but so did my sister!

Deep down, I believe Mum knew the truth, but she chose to ignore it. But why? She didn't want to believe. Christmas was a product of pure manipulation.

"We hurt the ones we say we love the most, but as long as we always look good and are never seen looking bad, that's all that matters. We are still going to hurt the ones we say we love."

My depression was the darkest it had ever been; I was starting to get some seriously negative thoughts. However, I pushed them all aside and decided to focus again on re-branding my business instead, because I didn't want potential new clients to see me as a one-man band.

All I kept hearing repeatedly were the jungle drums beating down hard. One time, I was presenting evidence in a council hearing, representing my client on a sensitive development project. His development infringed on Council planning rules, which in turn could have had a harmful visual impact on the environment, especially from obscuring local resident's views.

Before they made any decision on granting planning consent, we had to present our evidence to an independent hearing panel.

Even after successfully winning this planning application, the director of the architects company who I collaborated with said to me in a lift full of highly respected council managers, "You're so fucking stupid; you can't speak a word of English. No one can understand a word you say. I am so surprised that you even got this project. I would rather have worked with a monkey. They can speak better English than you. You're just a small one-man band, and you won't be anything bigger than that."

Everyone in the elevator laughed with him. Even though my work and evidence were so important in gaining planning consent for his project, I was still made to feel like I was nothing.

No one corrected him either. I just looked straight at the ground, holding everything in and praying that the doors would open. I was hoping that someone would say something in my defence, but he was part of the old council boys club, and they all thought it was ok to personally attack someone who clearly struggled with anxiety and reading out loud.

"It didn't mean my work was shit, and I wouldn't even be presenting my evidence and saving your fucking ass if you could actually fucking design a decent development and respect the planning rules. Your design is no better than a five-year-old child's drawing. But no, it just means fuckers like you consistently put people like me down, and you expect us to just fucking take it. So you can fucking show off in front of your friends? Congratulations for putting me down, I hope that makes you feel better about yourself, you fucking cunt!"

That was what I wanted to say, but I couldn't. I still wanted to be seen as a professional, regardless of the personal insults.

This was just one of many personal attacks that I had to endure, and I wanted to prove to everyone that I wasn't just a one-man band, so I decided to re-brand again.

We moved into the CBD and found a work-to-live apartment, the home upstairs, the studio downstairs, all connected via an industrial looking staircase. It was perfect. Instead of spending three hours a day driving, it now took me five seconds to get to work. I even asked K to come and help me set up some new document templates and project data sheets, including managing the studio whenever I was attending meetings.

I designed the studio space exactly how I imagined it to be, and best of all, I got to work with my best friend every day. K always said I was the boss downstairs, she was the boss upstairs, and once we closed up for the day, no work talk. Most of our talking was about our wedding and what we wanted to experience. We didn't just want a day to remember, we wanted an adventure to cherish, and our destination was Las Vegas. I was burning the candle at both ends, again but one end was far more exciting than the other. I was going to marry my best friend, the one person who had shown me nothing but a hundred percent pure love.

Never in my wildest dreams did I think I would even have a friend—never mind a best friend—and I got to marry her as well. My only wish was that Mum would answer her phone. But I knew she was hurting, and that was because of me. Fuck, why did I have to be right? Why could I just not let things go?

I texted her every other day, apologising for my part at Christmas, hoping that my mum would pick up the phone. And one day, she did.

It was so good to hear her voice at last; even though I could still hear the tension, at least we were talking. Mum also said, "If everything gets too much for you, there's always a roof and a bed here. No matter what your brother and sister think, you're still my son." Just to hear her say that I am still her son was a massive relief. We never spoke about what happened at Christmas, but then again, our relationship was never the same either.

I had just hired two new employees, and they both fitted in well. My new contacts were giving me work, and they introduced me to more of their connections. After seven long hard years, things were starting to look up at last.

K spent a lot of her time designing her wedding outfit, a fantastic gold, sporty, short jumpsuit with a beautiful lace jacket. I had a bespoke shirt and waistcoat, and some of K's jumpsuit material was sown into my shirt.

Our wedding adventure was all but finalised; we just had to decide what our wedding song would be when we walked down the private Bellagio courtyard steps, right next to their world-famous fountains. And to make it more romantic, I booked a night wedding, too.

For once, something was working out this year. I was feeling happy, the happiest I had felt in a long time. Then in the middle of the night, I got a text message from my brother: 'Call me.' I panicked and my heart started to race. Something was wrong. I phoned straight away.

"Is everything ok?"

"No, Mum is in hospital. She's in an induced coma. We're not sure what's wrong, just waiting to hear back from the tests," he said.

K sat next to me; she immediately knew something was wrong. Tears started running down my face, and I could barely string two words together. "Mum is in a coma. She's in a fucking coma. Was this my doing? Did I do this by putting too much stress on her trying to get her to believe me? My mum is in a fucking coma, a fucking coma, K. Why couldn't I just let things go, why did I need Mum to believe me so much?"

It was all too much for me; I replayed every scenario over and over and over again. *Did I do this, did I put my mum in a coma?*

Over the next few months, Mum remained in an induced coma. She was diagnosed with acute pancreatitis, which can make your pancreas vulnerable to bacteria and infections, and requires intensive treatment and surgery. She was in serious trouble.

An early symptom of pancreatitis is continual lower back pain. Mum had had back pain for over a year. Still, she hadn't seen a doctor. I'd even asked my brother to take her, but it was always, "Yeah, maybe next week when I have time."

Work again was put on the back burner. I was too worried to work and blamed myself for her being in a coma. I was a complete mess again.

Then with one month before our wedding, I got another text: 'Call me.'

It was amazing how I always had to phone my brother; he didn't even want to use his phone credits to call me. I had to go home. I got the earliest flight back to the U.K. via Manchester airport. I just dropped everything I was doing at that time. I knew K was more than capable of looking after the studio project deadlines because I had no idea when I would be back.

Mum was in Queens Medical Centre in Nottingham. I said to my brother before I left New Zealand, "I will have to stay at Mum's, seeing that I don't know when I will return."

"No you fucking won't be staying at Mum's, end of!"

"What! Are you serious? I can't stay at Mum's, why?"

"You're not fucking welcome, Mum said so at Christmas."

"What, that can't be right. I have been speaking to Mum since the end of January, and she said I am welcome back anytime. And where else will I stay?"

"Not my issue, that's your problem. If you want to see Mum, sort out your own accommodation. You're not staying in Mum's house, and that's final." There was no point arguing, not while Mum was this ill. She was out of the coma, but it wasn't looking good.

I landed at Manchester airport, stressed and tired. I got to the hospital, and the first thing my brother said was, "This is all on you, and don't even start with your sister. You haven't been here, and we have had to deal with all this on our own. You don't even have a say."

I wasn't sure how many times when Mum was in a coma that I would say "I can come home and help out," but I was ignored. I hugged my sister, but I got nothing back, not one word. I tentatively went to see Mum lying in bed, but it wasn't my mum. I couldn't recognise her, she looked so frail, so old and so pale. She also had to have a tracheotomy for her breathing while she was under the induced coma. She was unable to speak, she just looked at me, and her eyes said it all: *I am going to die.*

I just couldn't hold it in anymore and let out the loudest cry ever. My heart just broke, what was left of it was nothing more than shattered pieces. I had no way of fixing my mum. I gave her a coming back from war hug, and I never wanted to let go. I was too scared of letting go. Mum was the person I relied most upon in this world, and now she was going, and I couldn't stop it from happening. And making matters worse, my brother and sister blamed me for Mum's condition, that was crystal clear, and they made sure I was aware of it as well.

I managed to find accommodation that was five minutes away from the hospital, costing me over a hundred pounds a night. That was the closet one I could find, and yet Mum's home was less than forty minutes away. My brother and sister didn't only blame me for Mum's condition, they punished me for it too, while they took no responsibility for their actions. It was all too easy to blame someone else, and that someone was me.

The ward staff were fantastic; they gave me a bed in her room, and I slept next to Mum most nights, holding her hand. I was in a complete state of shock that my mum was dying, and everyone I knew blamed me for this. All I wanted was to be loved by my brother and sister, but they wouldn't even give me that, not even now when I needed a hug the most.

I missed K. I wasn't coping at all, the voices in my head were getting louder and louder, and the negative thoughts were becoming so overwhelming that I started to let them in. I had no strength in me to fight them off, and for the first time, they were winning. I had fought off so much pain in my life, so much trauma, and I had managed to get back up whenever I felt down, rather than staying down.

I had no strength left in me to fight. I had tried and tried to make something of my life, and yet I got nothing back in return, apart from unbelievable pain. No one gave a damn about how my life turned out, as long as they got whatever they needed to satisfy themselves. We have gotten so caught up in our own selfish lives that we can't even be arsed to care about anyone's problems anymore. If it doesn't affect me, then it's not my issue. I tried to box everything up and sink it into the ocean, but my thoughts and emotions were spilling out faster than I could fill them up.

Then another memory came back, and I was unable to ignore it. I was in my neighbour's living room lying face-up on the sofa, naked. I didn't recognise this woman who was penetrating me with her fingers while her mouth was around my penis. Another man was fucking her from behind. He was telling her what do to me. They were both getting off molesting me. She wanted to know what an eleven-year-old tasted like. He then forced my head in-between his girlfriends' legs where she held my head with both hands, directing me on what to do while he bent me over and raped me. She wanted to experience me licking her pussy at the same time watching her boyfriend climax inside me.

The voice in my head said, *"Cornelius, your pain will go away. Just let go; you will not have any more pain. I guarantee you, no more sorrow, no more hurt; you will be with your mum soon. You know what you need to do? Just do it. I have been here many times to advise you: let go and be with your mum."*

I held my mum's hands, looking longingly into her eyes, and I knew this wasn't what she would have wanted for me. I just wanted the voice and all my pain to stop. I looked at my bottle of painkillers and started to cry; I needed the voice to stop.

Just as I was about to pour the pills in my hand. My phone went off; it was a text from K.

'I am so sorry I am not with you, be strong baby, please be strong. I need you back here with me, ok? I am lost without you, and I love you so much x.'

I was so torn between being with Mum or living my life with K. I spent four days constantly thinking about what to do.

I gave Mum one last hug, kissed her forehead, told her how much I loved her, and most importantly, I thanked her for being my mum. I walked away from her as she laid in bed, and her eyes said it all again: *Goodbye son, I love you.* I couldn't hold back my tears; I knew my world would never be the same again. I knew that was the last time I would ever hug my mum.

I now had to get back and be with K. She also needed me, and if I am honest, I needed her more. I managed to land back in New Zealand two days before our scheduled flight to Las Vegas. Before I left, I had organised with the ward staff a live stream of our wedding on her iPad. I wanted Mum to at least see her son get married and be happy. Mum always said, "I want you to be happy, no matter what." Happiness is different for everyone, and I also needed inner peace just as much. Our wedding rings that K designed were finally ready, a few hours before we flew out. It was so close that K's mum, who I call MJ, bought us new wedding rings just in case we didn't receive ours in time. She also organised a beautiful celebration reception when we got back.

MJ wasn't just going to be my mother-in-law. She was already a mum to me, and it wasn't hard to see where K got her kindness and love from, her mum had it in bag loads. I thought K had a massive heart, but MJ's was about a hundred times bigger, and never once did she ask for anything in return. I admired her so, so, so much. She was in her early seventies, working close to twelve hours a day, five days a week, and looking after cardiac patients as a nurse, which she had done all her life. No matter how tough her day was, she always had a smile on her face whenever K and I visited her at home once a week for dinner. She made the most amazing curries or Sunday roasts. Nothing was too much, and I loved how she called me her son.

Her kindness just radiated out, and if the world had more MJ's, or even five percent of her heart and her love, this world would be a better place than it is today. But what broke my heart was that her two sons didn't want anything to do with her. One was living in the same house as her, and the other moved to Queenstown over twenty-five years ago to be with his chosen parents, whatever that means.

MJ lived for her work and the people she worked with. She was so loved at Auckland Hospital. All the doctors, surgeons, nurses, and administration staff called her MJ. This woman was a one-off, a rare find in a world of apathy.

The day we flew to Vegas, we checked all of our suitcases in, but we decided to carry our wedding clothes on board the aircraft. We went through security control and then sat down at a table while waiting for our terminal number and boarding call.

While waiting, we decided to have a rum and coke. I phoned Mum's hospital, and they had moved Mum into another facility; they were optimistic that she was going to get better. Our plane was ready to board. I turned to K and asked, "Where are our wedding clothes? They're not on the trolley"

"What, yes they are, aren't they?"

"No they're not, where the hell are they?"

I started to panic. I had the perfect vision of our wedding day, in which we would start by drinking a glass of champagne, then order room service as we got ready, followed by walking hand in hand along the casino floor, wearing what we had designed with the noise from the casino playing in the background. Then, we would wait at the top of the Bellagio steps to get married.

But now, this vision might not happen, and I was starting to lose my shit. We had no idea where they were. We had walked through the border control, sat straight down next to the trolley and had two drinks. No one sat near us, and we'd never left, either. Then it hit us, *Fuck!* We'd left them where we filled out our departure cards.

We had moved our clothes to the table to get our passports from our hand luggage but never placed them back on the trolley, and our plane was leaving in 30 minutes. K was super calm. "If we don't have our wedding clothes, we can get married in something else; it doesn't matter to me."

"It bloody matters to me. We need to get them back." I told her my vision, and how I wanted it to happen, no if's or but's, it had to happen. It was the only silver lining I had focused on while I was going through everything with Mum. I did not want her to see me not wearing my wedding clothes. It wasn't happening, it just wasn't.

We told security what happened, and they eventually located our clothes in an off-campus secure lock-up. Seeing that we had just left them on the table, they were treated as suspicious packages.

This facility was 20 minutes away from our terminal. K was continually reassuring me, "It's ok, your mum will understand, it's just clothing sweetheart. What matters is that we are on that plane and we are getting married."

Then the airline began paging us on the airport intercom. "Mr. Wilson and Miss Phillips, please make your way to terminal eight, everyone is waiting for you."

Time was ticking, and now we had become "those" people. I hated those people! And now we were them. But I stayed put, trying to control my anxiety by breathing in and out, and trying to remain focused.

Again, the announcement went out, "Mr. Wilson and Miss Phillips, everyone is now waiting for you and we would like to take off." I stayed put. I was not leaving without my wedding clothes; I was just not.

"This is the last and final boarding call for Mr. Wilson and Miss Phillips, we have completed our final checks, and everyone is waiting for you."

"Saweets, we have to go, we can't miss this plane."

"I am not leaving; I am not getting on that plane without my vision intact. It's not happening."

But K was right, with everything that was going off around us, we just totally forgot to pick them up. Slowly I walked up the gantry towards the door when I noticed it was bouncing. I turned around, and someone was running up with our clothes. *Fuck me, fuck me, and fuck me!* The relief in me was something else, this looked like another scene out of a rom-com movie, but it was our rom-com movie. We could not have cut this any finer. Ten more seconds, and the door of our plane would have closed, and we would have started to move.

Sometimes, watching a movie, we think to ourselves, *Really? Does that actually happen?* This experience has proven to me that it actually does.

Our wedding took up three weeks. The first week was our stag and hen week, but just the two of us. It was all about fun, fun, fun, and we stayed at The Paris Hotel. The second week was our wedding week, specifically the 27th of August, which was our wedding day, and we were staying at the Bellagio. The third week was our honeymoon, and we were staying at Treasure Island, and that was also all about fun, fun, fun.

One of the main reasons we decided on the 27th of August was that

Britney Spears was still playing at Planet Hollywood and I could get tickets. I really wanted to see her, and Jenifer Lopez a week later. Our three weeks were centred on magic shows, music concerts, and food. Mum had brought us up watching David Copperfield and magic, and K was a fan of David and magic, too. Where in the world do you ever get to see David Copperfield live and get married in the same week? Only in Vegas.

Vegas was just breathtaking. No one could understand why we would want to spend three weeks there. We always got a 'most I could do is a weekend' attitude, but not us. The food was terrific; words cannot describe how good the food experience was. Every night we ate at a different world-class restaurant, and we did whatever we wanted without care.

On the 24th of August, I got a text from my brother: 'Mum has passed away at 8:04.'

A fucking text message. A fucking text message.

My world was over, I had just lost my mum, I was alone in this world and all I got was 'Mum has passed away at 8:04.'

My brother and sister, including their partners and my mum's sister, were all around her bed when she passed away. They had gotten the news earlier that day that she wouldn't make it past today. But I wasn't even given a chance to say my goodbyes like everyone else. My brother's excuse was, "She wouldn't have recognised you or your voice."

They all said their goodbyes, and when the fuck did he become a specialist on what she could or could not hear or see? All they had to do was put a phone to my mum's ear, and she would have heard my voice. Instead, she didn't hear me at all, and I knew in my heart that Mum would have wanted to hear my voice.

When I heard the news, I just had pure fucking rage and anger. They stole from me my last words to my mum. They took that away from me. They made a collective decision for me not to say my goodbyes, and they took it all, for what, for fucking what?

I broke down. Mum passed away three days before I got married. What was meant to be the happiest day of my life had now become a constant reminder of being alone. There was no happiness; I had none to give any more. I just wanted to curl up in a ball and go to sleep. I was so alone in this world, and Mum was the main reason I was still here, the main reason I had kept fighting and hadn't given up.

K said to me, "Go home, say your goodbyes, we can get married next year." I lost count of how many times she asked me to go home and postpone our day.

I tried to work out how I would get home and how I could organise K's journey back to New Zealand. I had so much to organise, and yet, the anger inside me was out of control. I kept thinking, *they knew, and I didn't, they knew, and I didn't. They said their goodbyes and I couldn't, I couldn't, I couldn't.* And the more I replayed these words in my head, the angrier I became.

I had never had a fight in my life, I had never struck any man, and yet, I couldn't resist the urge to punch my brother in the face. And I wasn't going to stop there, nothing was going to stop me, no matter how hard he tried to fight back. I was fully ready for this battle. No matter how much pain I was in, I was going to get back up and hit him again and again and again. Nothing was going to change my mind with how much anger I felt. He deserved everything that was coming to him, and no one was going to take that away from me. Violence was coming, it wasn't going to stop, and I was not even sure if I would ever see K again.

I made the hardest decision of my life, one that I will never ever get back. I decided to stay back in Vegas and get married for three reasons. The first reason, I was in love with my best friend, and I really wanted to be her husband. The second reason was what my mum had always said to me, "I want you to be happy, that's all I have ever wished for you." And the first reason made me happy. The last reason was I knew I was going to fight with my brother and anyone else who got in my way. My mentality was like the John Wick movies, but all combined. I would have killed my brother that day.

I knew this was going to happen, and I also knew that this was not what my mum would have wanted. I had lived with violence all my life, and this is not how I wished to pay my respects to Mum. That was the primary reason I stayed, and I would have to live with this decision for the rest of my life.

The evening of my wedding was such a bag of mixed emotions: happiness, sadness, loneliness, joy; it was wave after wave. My inner voice was constantly telling me, '*What a useless son I was, all this time your mum looked after you and you couldn't even say goodbye; you're a selfish cunt. What a disappointment you turned out to be."*

I just wanted Mum to be here with me, giving me her worldly advice, but I knew it was never going to happen. I tried my hardest not to show K my sadness, but I also wanted to honour Mum too, so I decided to wear her little gold watch she'd bought from Argos many years ago. We walked across the casino floor, and it was exactly how I had imagined it. But with sadness in my heart.

Walking towards the Bellagio steps, hand in hand with K, admiring how beautiful she looked, and I still couldn't believe that this person wanted to marry me.

Standing at the top of the Bellagio courtyard steps, I was holding K's hand and waiting for our wedding song to be played, which was Calvin Harris and Rhianna's "This Is What You Came For".

I tried to contain all of my emotions and thoughts. If only Mum could have held on for another three days, she would have seen me get married.

Then I heard Elton's John "Your Song" playing in the background, which also doubled as one of Mum's favourite songs, and one that she wanted at her funeral. I turned to K and said, "Is that my mum's song playing in the background? I think I am hearing things."

K gave me the biggest smile. "No, saweets, you're not hearing things. Your mum's song is playing in the background, and it's coming from the fountains. Your mum is here watching."

K was right; the Bellagio fountains were dancing to my mum's song at that moment. I became lost in my thoughts, a unique mixed feeling of loneliness, sadness, and happiness.

Then our wedding song came on.

I walked down the steps, constantly glancing in K's direction and for that a small period, I had uninterrupted happiness in my heart. I chose happiness over sadness; Mum would and did approve of my decision, and that day will always be the happiest day of my life, and the saddest.

Because I wanted to be involved with organising Mum's funeral, even from Las Vegas, I phoned my brother continuously over the next few days. I wanted to be included in all the preparations for her day because I was excluded from everything else. They ignored everything I said and told me lies after lies, just so they could have their own story to tell everyone,

one that made them look like the hero and painted me as the villain. The biggest joke was on my mum's coffin. They had a photo of Mum drinking a can of beer, a fucking can of beer, and yet alcohol ruined her life. They even ignored all the ones I sent of her on her trips around the world, in favour of her drinking beer.

I wanted to write a eulogy, but why bother. "They were not going to read it out." It was like I had just been deleted from their lives. My short-lived wedding bliss was exchanged for full anger and rage again. I couldn't understand why they did this. I had every right to be part of her day, and they decided yet again that I wasn't worth it.

We came back from Las Vegas married, and as amazing as it was, slowly, sadness started to creep back in. Then it hit me hard; I would never be able to hear Mum's laugh ever again. The realisation of *I have no Mum at the end of the phone* started to kick in.

As soon as I realised these negative thoughts, the quicker I moved them to a new box and sank that into the ocean. I didn't want to believe that Mum was gone. I didn't want to let her go; I wasn't ready to let her go. Mum was such an influence in my life, and I wasn't sure how I would cope without her. It had never dawned on me that Mum wouldn't be here. I think death was the one fear I suppressed the most; in fact, I think we all do, knowing that we are not going to live forever is our biggest fear.

Having a family is one of the main things that we think guarantees us some sort of legacy that will change the world, for better or worse. Even as a young boy, I would cry myself to sleep, continually thinking about not being here, and that no one would show up to my funeral. I know it's a morbid thought, but it's true. No one wants to die alone and be forgotten, and if that's the case, why are we here? What is our primary purpose in life? I was becoming so obsessed with suicide and death. I had nothing else but blackness running through my body no light, whatsoever.

I kept imagining my life without K. If she was dead, how would I cope? What would I do? This new fixation had started to consume most of my thoughts. Then I started to question why I got married to K, why would I put myself through this pain if K died. *Surely, it's easier not to be in love, so you don't experience pain and loss.* I started to imagine the police knocking on my door, telling me K was dead. Darkness was all-round me. The loss of my mum was so crippling that being in love and loving someone was starting to make no sense to me.

I started a downward spiral of imagination, and I couldn't stop these negative thoughts. It was almost like I was reprogramming and preparing myself for sadness and loss. I wasn't enjoying married life anymore, and that was a strange feeling. I felt more at home in my head than being present.

My negative inner voice was now taking control of what I was thinking and feeling daily; I had let it in and now it was here to stay until it had enough. I was so in love with K that it brought me more sadness than happiness. I tried many times to stop the negativity, yet I always found myself coming back to the notion of a phone call or a knock on the door, telling me that K was dead.

It was all-consuming. Love wasn't what I needed; I needed pain and sadness so I could feel alive. The first year of being married and balancing work was one of the hardest I had ever encountered. I would go to bed at 5 am and get up at 7 to open up the studio. Then I would wear a happy mask and pretend that everything was okay, pretend that life was good, and pretend that Mum was still alive.

I wasn't sure what grief was or how grief worked, but I was unable to let Mum go. I really wanted to, but my inner voice was telling me to take the pain, soak it all up, that it was good for me, something we could use later. More childhood memories were starting to come back in bigger waves. In those rare moments of not being sad, visions of what had happened to me came flooding back.

I started to hear voices and remember names, where I was and what happened, and it was getting too much for me. TV was becoming harder to watch. Everything seemed to remind me of my past, and I was struggling to shake it off. So I started to self-medicate to numb the pain.

On the flip side, Dr. Jekyll and I were in contact; we started to have a really good relationship. In fact, it was becoming better now than it had been when we were together. We would try to regularly catch up for dinner or coffee when she was in Auckland. I even flew down to see her when life was getting also tough for her, especially when I received a phone call from the hospital in the middle of the night. Mr. Hyde had got so drunk that she slipped and smashed her face on the curb. She was lucky not to have been killed crossing the road. I had promised her that no matter what was happening in my life, I would be there for her.

I flew back to the U.K. for the anniversary of my mum passing away. I hadn't spoken to my brother, and I had not heard anything from my sister, but I had a feeling that something was off. I was right. Between them, they had decided to change the resting place for Mum; instead of being laid to rest according to her will, they decided to move her without asking me.

This became known when I said I was coming home to pay my respects. I also wanted to sort out Mum's house, but this was all taken care of months before. I wasn't even thrilled with the valuation of Mum's house, and I said we should hold off for more, but they didn't listen. I tried to phone Mum's solicitors, and I realised that they had changed her solicitors and all the names of the deeds. Her house was supposed to be shared between the three of us, yet I had signed no paperwork, and they wouldn't even tell me who Mum's solicitors were or who was in charge of the will. I was excluded from all these decisions again.

My brother said, "You will get your share. Stop going on about the fucking solicitors; it's got fuck all to do with you. Stop causing us grief, you're not here."

"But it does have something to do with me. I am Mum's son. Why are you doing this? What have I ever done to you guys?"

"Mum would be here if you didn't come back and give her grief at Christmas. It's your fault we don't have a mum; you always have to be fucking right." I had no words to say back; I always thought that they did blame me, but I was hoping that they didn't. But they did. My brother never wanted to listen to my side of the story, and my sister had gotten in there first.

I laid down next to Mum's resting place, talking to her, and I was asking for some advice on what to do with my brother and sister. I was looking up towards the sky, which was covered in white clouds, no blue sky in sight. And then, the clouds opened up into a heart shape and the most stunning blue shone through directly above me.

I quickly tried to grab my phone to take a photo to show K, and then I realised that I didn't need to take a picture, I didn't need to prove anything to anyone. I knew what I had just witnessed, and I knew I had to make peace with my brother.

That afternoon in Sheffield, I went to eat at TGI Fridays, one of Mum's favourite places to eat. I texted my brother and told him how I was feeling, how lonely I felt, that I needed help, and I wasn't coping very well. I told him about having negative thoughts, my fear, and I just wanted my brother and sister back in my life.

It was such a long text message. I was trying to explain how both of their actions made me feel and how they treated me; I wanted him to see it from my perspective. I sat in the far corner, away from everyone in a flood of tears. I just wanted to be loved, and I just wanted him to say, "I love you. I am sorry for treating you like this." I would have just been happy with four words, "I love you, Cornelius," and I would have forgiven him for everything he had done and hadn't done. He replied with, "Go fuck yourself and die. We don't want anything to do with you!"

I knew what I'd seen in the clouds, and I knew what it meant. I texted again and again and again, hoping that he would say what I wanted to hear, but it never came. I lost count of the times I tried to reconnect. My relationship with my sister was over. Even when I saw her at the hospital with her daughter, I was never introduced to my niece. It was like I didn't even exist and there was no point; they would never be in my life again. I knew I lost her forever that day. Even though I texted her, I never got one reply back. My brother texted me one night, 'Our sister wants nothing to do with you ever, so stop texting her.'

K phoned about thirty minutes after I left TGI Fridays. Her Nani had passed away. She asked if I could fly home for the funeral; she needed my support. Nani passed away the same day Mum was laid to rest, exactly a year to the day.

I flew back to Auckland, still in shock from all the events that happened to me in the U.K., and straight into Nani's funeral. I didn't even have time to breathe or compose any of my thoughts, I was just on autopilot. I boxed all my pain and emotions and again buried them in my ocean.

My wife needed me, and I had to be her husband and best friend. This was a sorrowful time for our family, and more so, for MJ, who had just lost her mum, and I knew that feeling very well. What I didn't understand was that her eldest son decided that he wasn't going to attend the funeral. It was the toughest day of his mum's life, and the day she needed both her sons the most, but he made a conscious decision not to fly an hour and twenty minutes to support his mum.

I couldn't get my head around this. He was always in contact with her, but he'd never made an effort to see her when he flew to Auckland, never made that extra effort to take his mum out for dinner or even give her a hug. I thought to myself, *Your mum is alive today and she needed you, and you can't even be arsed?* His excuse was that he couldn't get the time off work, and he had already said his goodbyes twenty-five years earlier, when he left to live in Queenstown. He couldn't even give himself half a day off.

The day of the funeral, still unable to grieve for my mum, I sat next to MJ. She was crying her heart out while holding my hand tight, but I knew the hand she wanted to feel was her eldest son's hand.

September was such a hard month for me emotionally, unable to deal with my loss. I felt like I was a zombie, not even knowing what I was doing from one minute to another. I was so grateful that we had our little fur baby to show us both love and compassion when needed. Princess Zelda was a beautiful golden Burmese female cat. I wanted to witness K with a little one, so we made a very conservative effort to have Zelda. K spent two years researching which cat breed would suit us best. I was a cat lover and K was a dog lover, and a Burmese breed had both dog and cat-like traits.

K was so nervous about looking after Zelda when I was away that I could feel her anxiety. She didn't even know how to pick her up. But the most amazing thing occurred while I was away in the U.K. Instead of K looking after Zelda, Zelda looked after K. Zelda was the one who would crawl up to K and sleep on her chest until she woke up the following day. Zelda followed her all over the house and even into the studio. Zelda made sure, no matter where K looked, she was always in her view.

However, I struggled to bond with Zelda. She never really came to me, never snuggled up, and every time I went to pick her up, she would go off in another direction.

I didn't mind this at first, but then I started to think, 'even Zelda doesn't want to be with me'. I never really said anything to K, but I was really struggling with suicidal thoughts, and I was pretty sure I had prostate cancer; I was bleeding heavily from my backside. I just wasn't in good shape and I knew it, I felt like I was dying and rotting inside. I knew something wasn't right with me and I could feel a considerable change happening. I was piling on the weight, and my energy was getting zapped; I was either emotionally drained, or I was physically tired. I kept thinking of the number forty-five in my dreams. Every morning I placed on my work mask, went down to the studio, and again pretended everything was ok.

I even carried this work mask over to Australia. I had made contact with two amazing entrepreneurs, Andy and Soul. their company was one of the fastest-growing architectural drafting companies in Australia. We were always in communication and talked about the possibility of flying over and discussing the potential of being partners. I saw a fantastic opportunity. Rather than continuing to rely on landscape work, I could see an architectural element to my portfolio.

Their business model was about efficiency, professionalism, experience, quality, and affordability, not to mention the timeframes they could deliver in. These two young guys had created an unbelievable platform, something that would work perfectly in New Zealand. I took two very good business friends, who I had been working with for the last two years, over to meet them as well. They had no idea why I was so excited. But it soon became clear.

Generally, in New Zealand, if you wanted an architecturally designed home, the cost of a fully completed set of drawings would vary typically between six to twelve months, and the price could be between $55 - $100k, depending on experience and the amount of work needed. These guys could provide better quality designs for a fraction of the cost and complete the work in twelve weeks. They had built a cloud-based architecture team consisting of over two-hundred architects, engineers, surveyors, and inspectors.

In all my time as a Landscape Architect, I had never seen a business delivery model like this. And at the heart of their model, their target audience were the mums and dads of this world: ordinary people earning average wages. I introduced my business friends to Andy and Soul.

When Andy explained how their business worked and how it could be implemented in New Zealand, I saw my business friends' mouths drop. They had just witnessed the start of a new era in architectural drafting. I could hear the cogs ticking; they were working out the best way to bring this model to New Zealand.

After months and months of communications, I was only a few weeks away from launching this new era. I had a stream of projects that would kickstart this all off. We all left their offices in a massive buzz. We knew we had something special.

I walked over with drinks in hand, ready to celebrate the start of a new partnership, when one of my business friends turned to me and said, "Where do you see yourself fitting in with all of this?"

"Huh? Fit in, well, I would be running the delivery section and operations. The question is, what do you guys offer me? I mean, you've never met Andy or Soul until today, and now you're asking me where I fit in, that doesn't make any sense. Why are you asking me, what the fuck is going on?"

"Well, while you were at the bar, we both got talking, and we want to hear your pitch. We want to know why we need you."

"What the fuck are you both talking about, why am I pitching to you guys? I thought this was a team effort, we have collaborated on so many projects in the last two years, and now I have to pitch to you guys? What the fuck, you are not making any sense."

"Well, we don't need you, if we are to be honest. You got us here, and now we know how it works."

"You are fucking kidding me! I have done all the hard work, and now you're cutting me out, just like that? I am not worth knowing, and I am just kicked to one side, is that what you're saying?"

"In short, yes. We have more contacts than you, we can launch our own architecture drafting company tomorrow using their architects, and we can add their service to our own company. I am saying we don't need you. Thanks for the contact, but we will take it from here." I was mortified. I'd introduced them to Andy and Soul, and these two motherfuckers had come to my wedding celebration, and now that I had shown them a fantastic solution, I was dog shit on their shoe. Even when I got back to Auckland, they wouldn't answer my calls. Suddenly with no warning, I found I had been kicked off all the projects I was working on with them, replaced by other consultants. These two fuckers had taken my idea and then got me kicked of all their projects for their own fucking greed.

What sort of world do we fucking live in? Seriously, they would rather line their pockets over friendship?

The only thing I had going for me was our cruise ship holiday, which was fourteen nights to New Caledonia over Christmas and New Year. I just needed a break; I had just had enough. I was running on empty, still unable to grieve, with no contact from my family. I was even more depressed. It was crippling me.

I seriously started to think about a date to commit suicide. I had no way out of the thoughts and the loneliness in my head. I was so ill inside, still bleeding from my backside, and had also found a lump on my testicles. I didn't have any more plans, and I had no light at the end of the tunnel. In fact, the tunnel was black, and the holiday was the only thing that was keeping me going.

The cruise was terrific; whatever happened on the cruise, stayed on the cruise. K really enjoyed cruising; emoji face with hearts and peach is all I can say. We got back from the cruise, and for the first time, I suffered the holiday blues. I had never felt like this before; combined with already being depressed, the situation was unbearable. I don't think I even managed to get out of bed for about three months, and then I had to make a tough decision to let my employees go. I couldn't function on a daily basis, never mind on an hourly.

My depression and suicidal thoughts were just too much, and my health was getting worse. In less than three months, I had piled on about 10kgs. I didn't feel attractive, my self-esteem was zero, I couldn't get myself out of this slump, and I didn't have the energy even to try to help myself.

K tried everything, but my energy was so low. Even though I put my Husband mask on every day, deep down, K knew I was struggling.

Then the big one came.

14

HELL IS COMING

The Inland Revenue Department (IRD) came banging down my door, chasing me for $300k in unpaid back taxes. Which couldn't be right, all of my taxes were up to date. I had all the paperwork to prove it. Well, that was what I was led to believe. Every time I rebranded my company, I'd closed down all of the business that I had set up and asked my accountants to do what they needed in regards to my taxes.

Yet, for some reason, the IRD were asking for unpaid taxes from eight years ago. *I mean, what the fuck!* I didn't even have a business eight years ago, and yet here I was, trying to work out what was happening. All my taxes were entirely up to date and employee taxes were all up to date, yet the IRD included the last three years as well. *What is going on?!*

I wasn't the savviest businessperson; I relied heavily on the people around me to help me out, but for some reason, I still owed $300k. I hired new accountants to help me sort this out, as I was unable to locate my existing accountants. Still, they couldn't work out where this $300k came from. I tried to talk to the IRD, and I got nothing; they were not interested in anything I had to say. Also, during this period, every project and every client had stopped giving me work. My income dried out instantly with a big bang overnight. And I only had enough money in my account to keep us afloat for another three months.

I phoned all my existing clients, but not one person returned any of my calls. I phoned the consultants that I was working with on my projects, and they also didn't return my calls. Something was fundamentally wrong with this picture. But I had a backup plan. My idea was first to pay the outstanding amount to the IRD on the advice of my accountants, and then look into where the $300k had gone and sort it out from there.

239

One thing at a time. I phoned Dr. Jekyll and said, "I would like to sell our house now." We had a separation agreement drawn up three years earlier, which allowed us to give each other a first option of buying our share off one another before considering selling via an estate agent. I also had over fourteen years of my share of the rental income in our house account. I knew I had enough to cover this, or at least make a sizeable down payment in good faith while trying to find the underlying cause of this issue.

I came off the phone shaking and confused. I had told Dr. Jekyll what was going on with the IRD, and that I needed at least the rental income to make a good faith payment while she considered buying me out or selling the house. She told me, "It's not a lot, and you are not going to like the answer to why."

"What? No, I have worked it all out, and I know how much I should receive. All the rental income is in our house account, I haven't taken anything out, so if you can please transfer that money, I will be really grateful."

"It's not how much you think it is. Once we have paid the mortgage, taxes, and paid the estate agents, we don't actually get that much anymore, so please prepare yourself."

"Prepare me for what? I know how much we get per year after we've paid everything out, we both have the same amount of rental income. You're actually not making any sense. Can you please just send me the bank statements and I will check it myself?"

"Talk to my solicitor," was her response.

"Your solicitor, what the fuck do you mean, talk to my solicitor? You're not very clear in what you're saying, why can't you send me the house accounts? In fact, I will go online and get them myself."

"You can't. They're not in that account anymore."

"Yes, they are, we have a signed separation contractual legal agreement saying all monies should stay in that account."

"You're not going to like what you find. Talk to my solicitor," was her response, and the phone went dead.

I was trembling with worry and I wasn't sure if I was going to pass out or not. I turned to K, and said, "I think Dr. Jekyll has taken me to the cleaners regarding my house and that I don't have any money to pay the

IRD. She said I won't like what I will find and to talk to her solicitors."
"What does that mean?" K said worriedly.

"I have no idea, but she alluded to the fact that the money that was in the house account had been moved to another account, and I don't have any access to that account, even though it stated in the separation agreement that it stays in that account. I think she's used all of my rental income as part payment for her Auckland house deposit."

I had money and a house, yet I couldn't do anything. This made no sense. So I texted Dr. Jekyll, one after another, 'I need answers, please pick up the phone. I think I might be in trouble if you don't help me.'

'I need to pay the IRD in good faith a down payment while I sort out what's happened to my taxes. Please pick up the phone.'

She texted back, 'Talk to my solicitors, fuck!'

I knew I was in trouble, and the only person who could help me was Dr. Jekyll. Had I been blindsided for over fourteen years? Was this always her plan—find someone so low to manipulate, then take it all and leave me with nothing?

I tried not to let it worry me too much. I had the money tied up in a house, and I had a perfect accountant helping me sort out why the IRD was after that amount.

I even had taxes owing from the T-shirt business I set up with my friends. I had assumed this was all taken care of way back. Well, the IRD must have made a mistake. I left this all to my accountants to sort out. We had just moved into a new place that was forty minutes north of Auckland, and I was sharing a new studio with my closest friend, George. I had known George for over four years, when I was the manager of an Over-35football team called 'Plan B.'

I loved everything about this team, the players, the dressing room banter, the end of the year weekends away. But we did have some people on the team who consistently made excuses for not having a beer after the game or were unable to attend training during the week. My philosophy was, 'if you don't turn up for training, you're not starting', so I never started them. Thankfully, they all pissed off and set up their own team. It also meant that I could bring in some new faces and new talent; George was one of them. We just hit it off from the moment he turned up for try-outs.

I'd managed Plan B for 5 years. We won three league titles and two cups. I was hard but fair, but the last year of managing Plan B was my toughest. I'd never told anyone about my depression or suicidal thoughts, and I always had my manager's mask on. I also didn't let them into my life either, to be fair.

I couldn't understand why I was playing football when all I kept thinking about was my mum buried in the ground, rotting away; football had no meaning to me anymore. My head and heart weren't in this anymore, and my weight and fitness were gone. I used to be a quick centre forward, but with all the weight I had piled on, and how heavy my bones felt, I wasn't even fast enough to run past a tortoise.

I remembered this one moment as if it was yesterday. Bruce, the ex-Plan B manager and who I took over from, slid in a perfect through ball for me to run on to and I was clear on goal, but I just stood still, watching the ball go past me, and I did not even attempt to run for it. I just let it go past me. I thought that exact moment, *Fuck this, I'm going home*, and I subbed myself out of the game and drove home. I knew I was done; I had nothing more to give, and all I wanted to do was crawl into bed and cry.

Driving back home via the motorway that day was the first time I thought about closing my eyes and putting my foot down. I knew right there that I was more than capable of suicide. I couldn't shake off the vision of the last time I got raped; it just wouldn't go away. Suicide was the perfect answer.

∗∗∗

We went to watch a musical with K's orthodontist, Maggie. They both seemed to fancy one another; Maggie was polyamorous, so it made sense to me that we opened up our relationship. This was something K and I had been discussing for a few years, especially with K's condition and what I was going through. K and I had been on some fantastic dates in the past, our relationship and love for each other was so strong that jealousy never reared its ugly head. We both enjoyed getting ready together, and we were so excited to meet someone new for the first time, especially someone keen on dating a married couple. Polyamory was all new to me, so I was trying to get my head around it all and how it worked. We also met Maggie's girlfriend for the very first time that night. Her girlfriend, for some unknown reason, didn't take a shining to K or me.

I think she was jealous of their close friendship, which was very confusing to me as they had been in a polyamorous relationship for over seven years, and she had many lovers.

The show was a disaster. The sound quality was awful, and you couldn't hear a word they were saying. What a disappointment.

All of a sudden, halfway through the show, I was unable to move. Tears started to run down my face, and my legs started to tremble uncontrollably. I started to pee myself. I had no idea what was happening. I felt like I was having a stroke, I was unable to speak. I looked at K, hoping she would notice me and try to snap me out of whatever I was in. That night I was transported back to when I was thirteen years old.

The musical played a song by Grandmaster Flash— "White Lines"— and I found myself in a bedroom. I wasn't sure why I was in this room. I couldn't make out whose bedroom I was in, either. I just knew it wasn't mine. I could hear "White Lines" playing quietly in the background, coming from a tape recorder on repeat. Then someone turned it up louder. I tried to find out who this was, but my head was forced into a pillow, so I was unable to see who it was.

I heard this person's belt fall to the ground, I heard him unzip his jeans or trousers, with one hand still firmly pressed to my head and forced into the pillow. I tried desperately to turn around, but he just pushed harder on the back of my head, forcing me deeper into the pillow. I was now struggling to breathe. Then my jeans came off, followed by my underwear. He inserted what I believed was one finger inside me, could have been two. He kept pushing harder and harder, trying to force his way in. I was trying to scream, trying to resist, until I could resist no more. I knew I was being raped, and there was nothing I could do about it. He then pushed his penis inside of me, thrusting as hard and as fast as he could. One hand pressed my head while his other hand held both my arms behind my back, and all I could hear was the song "White Lines" playing in the background, over and over again. I was not sure how many times it played or how long I was raped.

"Saweets, you okay? Saweets, saweets," I heard K shouting at me, grabbing my knee to stop me from shaking.

I snapped out of this trance, looked at K and said, "This is the rap song that I heard playing in the bedroom over and over again, when I was raped for the last time. The night of the shadow man." We were both stunned. I was visibly shaken from this ordeal, from this memory.

What the fuck has Dr. Jekyll done?

I was unable to control when these memories would enter my head. I didn't want them, nor did I ask for them, yet they were here to stay, and that I was sure of. I just wanted to go back home, but I also didn't want anyone to know, so I quickly put on the Fun Cornelius mask, and we all headed home.

Nothing came from that evening either, with Maggie and her girlfriend, and I was grateful for it. I wasn't in the right headspace, even though Maggie was; she was keen to have sex with K. But fortunately for us, her girlfriend was in no shape at all; she was absolutely fucking leathered. So much so, that as soon as we got back to our place, ran to our bathroom, threw up in our sink and just left it there and went home. Classy chick.

We never heard from Maggie again.

***

Moving away from Auckland and sharing an office with my best football mate was just what I needed. I didn't want to be on my own. I needed friends around me more than anything. The thoughts were overtaking every little decision. K was also in the office too, and our tri-working relationship was in full bloom; it was banter, banter, banter. It was the main reason we moved out of Auckland and up north, so we could be closer to our friends.

K and I also made some good friends via my hairstylist called Norman, a 6'7 Scottish gay bear (his words, not mine) and he really knew how to cut my hair well. We actually all got on so well that we were starting to be invited to his parties and events, and we were introduced to more of his circle of friends, mainly gay guys and a few straight women. I had met Norman via his best friend, whom I had met on Tinder. K knew I was on Tinder; she was sitting right next to me 99% of the time, and I never once lied to her if she asked what I was doing on my phone or who I was talking to. I was so lonely in my head that I would just chat with anyone. I would always be open, honest, and upfront that I was married, full transparency.

She mentioned that her best friend was a hairstylist and I needed a haircut. The last time I'd gotten a haircut, I showed the stylist my typical style, but what she did was not my usual style, more of a peanut cut. I paid anyway, as we do. This Tinder connection was also keen on dating K and me, but when we started a three-way conversation, it became very evident that the attention was all on herself. She needed the attention more than I did, and again I was unmatched without explanation. Not that I needed one, but after a few months of chatting and her consistently making excuses to meet up for a date, it would have been nice, that's all.

But she did give me her stylist's number, so it worked out well in the end. One of the issues of not living in a live-to-work apartment was that Zelda was home alone. She was such a social little cat. It was breaking our hearts knowing that she was all alone. So we got another little fur baby, a chocolate Burmese called Link. We named them Zelda and Link after the first-ever game I completed, "Zelda: Links Awakening" on the Gameboy in Thailand.

OMG! He was the cutest little brown furry thing I ever did see, and I was desperate for him to have a bond with me like Zelda's and K's. I was more jealous of their relationship than K having one with another woman! I banned K from sleeping with Link for two weeks. He would be sleeping in my bedroom because we still lived in separate bedrooms, two years after being married. I sprayed catnip on myself, head to toe every night before we both went to sleep, desperately trying to create a bond.

Now that we had Link as well, we weren't that worried about Zelda being on her own. It was a mighty relief that she had a brother to play with during the day, and while we were in the office, they could now create their adventures together.

Link was so aloof. He was the total opposite of Zelda. Zelda was all about snuggles, cuddles, and love. Link was all about eating and being as far away from me as possible. I had always heard about those special bonds people have with animals and how sometimes they regard them as actual members of the family, even children. Zelda and K had this love. It was unbelievable how close they had become. But Link, he just sat in a corner on his own, in his own little furry world, and I loved him more for that. I was falling in love with Link, and I really wanted him to love me back.

I couldn't even bond with a cat.

Feeling this alone was so depressing. I was so close to choosing a date for my suicide. I had totally fallen head over heels for Link, and he wanted nothing to do with me at all.

***

I received an email from Dr. Jekyll out of the blue, with an offer of $50k, $250k short of the split valuation for our house, with no questions regarding rental income.

Dr. Jekyll had used my misery and desperation to try to buy my share of the house for absolutely nothing, saying that was her final offer. I even tried to negotiate an extra $10k, but it was a take it or leave it offer. My back was against the wall, so I emailed her and texted her to ask if we could talk about this. The only thing I got back was a letter from her solicitors saying, "Stop harassing my client."

I was harassing her client? I wanted answers, and I needed money badly. I rejected Dr Jekyll's offer and we decided to place the house on the market.

The IRD was going to make an example out of me for tax fraud and if I couldn't pay it all back, the IRD was looking for a maximum prison sentence of four years.

I was looking at four years in prison for something I'd never done. My accountants finally had worked out that all the money had gone into my former accountant's trust account, little by little, so I wouldn't notice it was gone, along with false IRD signed documentation. My accountant had even left the country and let me take the fall.

I sat down with the IRD in a formal meeting, trying to explain what had happened, present them with my findings but they were not even interested. I was facing four years in prison, and my only chance of avoiding this was to sell my house and pay them back. I also worked out why existing clients or consultants never wanted to work with me; the investigating officer from the IRD had phoned all my clients and told them they were investigating me for fraud, *fucking fraud.*

How the fuck was I supposed to pay it back when he'd phoned all my clients, including Auckland Council? I was left with absolutely nothing; he had completely ruined my professional career in New Zealand. How much more could I take?

With a prison sentence on the horizon, I had no other choice than to accept Dr. Jekyll's offer, a well-executed fourteen-year-long game plan.

I just needed anything, and I mean anything. I had to hire my own IRD lawyers to negotiate a payment structure on my behalf, but IRD refused all offers. They wanted $300k lump sum, or I was serving four years in prison.

K and I both knew I wouldn't last one night; I would have taken my life within twenty-four hours. There was no way I would survive. I even mentioned to my IRD lawyers my suicidal thoughts, depression, and mental health. I got nothing back apart from a substantial fucking invoice. How do you pay for something with nothing? I was so desperate that suicide seemed like the only option out.

The voices in my head were telling me that this was the only option I had; I was going to be raped again and again in prison. If I ended my life, I would finally be with my mum. This was on repeat, and it seemed like a good idea. There was no way I could carry on. It had been nearly two and a half years and I couldn't shed one tear for my mum. I just wanted to grieve. I wanted the pain to go away. I just wanted everything to stop and yet it was getting louder and louder and louder, *You're worthless, and you deserved everything you got. This world is better off without you; no one loves you, no one cares if you're alive or dead, and your brother and sister already think you're dead. Just let go and die. Listen to what your brother said. Die, die die!*

I was having a complete mental breakdown; I had no way out and nowhere to turn. I had no help. There was one person who could have helped me. After everything she did to me, she still didn't give a fuck about me, as long as she got what she wanted. I was dog shit. I had become a mentally weak individual. The number of antidepressants and sleeping pills I was now taking was getting ridiculous; nothing was stopping death knocking at my door.

K said, "Can we please ask my mum for help, please sweetheart? Please, she will help you, she loves you so much, and she would do anything to help you please."

"No, I don't want to ask. I'm a proud man and I don't want to break down in front of your mum. I promised I would look after you, and if I am seen as a weak man who can't support his wife, I am nothing."

I think K knew I was thinking of taking my own life, and there wasn't any point trying to change my mind. Then she said this: "Love me from here, not there. Love me from here not there," pointing towards the sky.

"I don't know what that means; love me from here, not there."

"For fuck sake, love me on this planet, not from there!"

I had to find $300k in thirty-five days, or the IRD was going to recommend prison. I had still not heard from Dr. Jekyll's lawyers regarding buying me out, or if our house was still on the market. I still had the chance we could sell the house, and I could clear this for the last time. Then I received an email from the estate agents who had been managing our property for over fourteen years, and they wanted me to sign the tenancy agreement. I looked at K and said, "I think we have tenants moving into my house, but that can't be correct? I haven't signed any paperwork, nor have I agreed on anything with them in regards to taking the house off the market."

Yet we had potential tenants moving in in two days. I quickly phoned the estate agents and asked to speak to the manager. He told me that my house had been taken off the market and now I had to sign new paperwork. He asked what was taking me so long. The manager was having a go at me, and I didn't even know my house was off the market.

"Who gave you permission to take it off the market, no one has phoned me? I have received no emails. I own half the house, and yet I wasn't even considered."

"Your wife phoned, asking us not to sell the property and to get tenants in."

"You are fucking kidding me, my wife. What wife?"

"Your wife, Dr. Jekyll."

"And you took her word, and never once did you question or follow up with the other property owner? Do you know I own half the house? I mean, surely you just don't take someone's word, and that's gospel for the truth. I mean, you could have just phoned me. My house is off the market, and you never contacted me until now that I need to sign permission for new tenants."

You could hear the cogs ticking. They had totally fucked up and illegally took my house off the market based on Dr. Jekyll telling them she was my wife, and she gave them my permission. What fucking estate agents do these monkeys represent?

"We just need you to sign the paperwork," was his answer.

"I am not signing anything. You took my house off the market, and never once did you phone or ask me if I authorized this decision as the property owner."

"Your wife did," he replied.

"I am not married to Dr. Jekyll! What don't you understand?"

"She said she was," the manager replied.

I was fucking fuming; I felt so betrayed again. I slammed the phone down and cried into my hands. Dr. Jekyll had taken my one last chance to avoid prison. I texted Dr. Jekyll, 'I am going to get four years in prison for something I haven't done, and you took our house off the market. How could you do this?' I received another lawyer's letter asking again to stop contacting her client directly.

The only option I had was to speak to MJ and ask for help; this was the last option on the table. I broke down in front of her and told her what had happened. I was too ashamed to even look her in the eyes; I'd failed as a husband to her daughter.

She just said, in the calmest voice, "Whatever you need, it's yours," and went to make a cup of tea as though nothing had happened. I looked at K and said, "Does she know what she's doing? Because we need $300k."

K had another option: if MJ could get a reverse mortgage and we could borrow that money, this would give me time to sell my house again. Then I could fight her with a U.K. lawyer for all the rental income that I was owed and get half of the sale. This would clear nearly the entire reverse mortgage. I gave MJ the biggest hug and kisses, thanked her, and promised her that I would pay her back the moment I sold the house. I really didn't want to exercise this option, but we had no choice. We just needed her two sons to agree, especially her youngest son, who was still living in the house.

The relief that day was unbelievable; it looked like I wasn't going to prison after all, and I could fight Dr. Jekyll for what was mine. But MJ's youngest son wasn't going to sign. He had no shares in the house, he had no claim at all, and yet, he said no. All he had to do was sign, acknowledging his mum's decision; K's eldest brother had no issues. We were back to square one. He wouldn't even pick up the phone whenever K rang him, he didn't reply or call her back, she was practically begging for his consent.

We got nothing. His mum was also begging him to sign and still he wouldn't. It wasn't even his money or house, yet he wouldn't even have to pay anything and wasn't legally bound by any of the contracts his mum signed. She wanted to lend me the money and yet he refused to agree with her. K's brother wouldn't even help her. He turned his back on his sister, and for what? He was worried he would lose out on his share of the inheritance when MJ finally passed away. Even though I had a house in London he still refused to help his sister out.

I drove around and sat him down, and for the first time in my life, I begged for help. I begged for him to sign the agreement so that his mum could lend me the money. I even told him what happened to me when I was young, about being raped, and that his sister would be a widow the first night I went to prison. "This no threat," I told him. "I won't last a night, and I don't want to be raped again, nor do I ever want to be forced to suck another man's cock," which was my fear. His reply was, "Not my issue," stood up, and left.

I followed him, begging for my life. "Please, think of K."

"Not my issue," was his reply again. I followed him upstairs to the kitchen area, desperately pleading with him and trying to get him to understand, begging him with all my heart that I wouldn't make one night.

MJ said to her son, "It's my money and my house. If I want to lend Cornelius the money, I know he will pay it back."

I have never seen anyone more reluctant. He signed the paperwork and stormed off.

We now had twelve days before an agreement was in place; we were not out of the woods just yet. On December 5th, 4:32 pm I was driving on the motorway at about 105km. With the pressure mounting, the voice in my head told me, *Let go, just let go, just let go.*

I knew if I let go, I would feel this enormous amount of relief leave my body, and I would be at peace at last. But this wasn't the right way to go. K didn't deserve a knock on the door, but I needed that relief.

On December 18th, 2018, at 2:35 pm, I consciously decided that in June 2019, I would commit suicide. My inner voice had convinced me this was my only option for inner peace.

Up until then, I'd never told anyone—not even K, because I didn't want to worry her—about the suicide contract I'd made with myself and with Death himself. I knew exactly when and how my life would end. I had worked out how it would happen and had arranged all the life insurance details so that afterwards K would be OK financially. I was going to die in a car crash, because that was the most logical way of having an accident rather than pills. I told her, and I thanked her for letting me go. I was finally going to be with my mum.

Around this time, I had also confirmed I had prostate and testicular cancer. I still kept this a secret since I was going to die soon, anyway.

On December 20th, all the money came through from my amazing mum, and I was able to pay to have an agreement in place with the IRD. No words can ever describe the kindness and the love my mum showed me when everyone else had turned their backs on me. Again, no words.

Now I needed to fight for what was mine. Norman kindly invited K and me over to his place from Christmas Eve through to Boxing Day. He had a few people coming, and we felt incredible that we had gotten an invite.

Over those three days, I started to observe something very strange; the people who I thought were our new friends weren't!

They pretended to like us, yet they very rarely ever engaged in any conversation with K and me. They were more engaged in their phones than the people around them.

K and I have a great rule: when we are out with people, we don't use our phones; we always want to be present. However, these people showed they would rather have a text conversation than a real conversation. Obviously, it was Christmas, and we wanted to talk with people via our phone, but what I was witnessing I had never seen before. No one talked. Everyone was on their phones.

This was such a strange concept to us both. Even when I used to be in meetings, my phone was always in my bag. But everyone else in the meeting was either on his or her phones, or they just placed them on the table, waiting for something to come through. Just so they could pick it up. They were never engaged in the meeting in the first place, so no wonder nothing was sorted out.

I was observing the same behaviour, but in a social dynamic, during the holiday event at Norman's. This type of dynamic required enough friends who would ignore each other, and well, K and I didn't, hahaha!

We were always in their event photos, but we never once saw the photos unless we were all socially connected via Facebook or Instagram.

I observed everyone for the whole three days, and the only thing I played around with was my Rubik's cube. I wanted to beat a person's best time, someone that we hung out with on the cruise ship. Her time was 1.32 minutes; my fastest time was 2.34 minutes, so I was happy in my little world.

K had gone home to fetch our babies. Norman said they could stay with us overnight. Link still wasn't bonding with me, but I loved him all the same, if not more. I loved this little guy with everything I had. I couldn't wait to see K and our babies; anything was better than what I was witnessing, everyone glued to their phones, and anyone hardly looked up.

One person did glance up and asked where K was. "K went home four hours ago to fetch our little ones."

I texted K and said, 'Come now, I am losing my mind, no one is talking, not just to me but to anyone.' Then one of Normans friends asked if K and I sleep with other people and if so, would we consider her. What the fuck! Of all the questions to ask, you ask that! Simon?

"It's a no from me." I told her, "K is attracted to people, not gender."

"So K is bi?"

"No."

"Lesbian?"

"No, she's just attracted to people, gender has nothing to do with it."

"So she's poly"?

"Nope."

Was this alien to some people? She stood up and left, going straight back onto her phone. That was the extent of my conversation over three days, riveting.

The day after Boxing Day, we had to take Link to the vet. He was struggling to pee, and K thought he might have a urinary infection, which is quite common in male cats.

As we were driving back from Norman's house, more childhood memories started to flood back this time; I was sucking someone's penis. I couldn't make out who they were. I was always on my knees, and once one person came inside my mouth, I was quickly forced to take another penis in my mouth. Every time I tried to look up, I was slapped in the face for doing so.

I started crying. I couldn't stop. I couldn't shake the images from my head. I was going in a tailspin.

While K was driving on the motorway at one point, I leaned over and tried to undo my seat belt; I just need it all to stop. I didn't want these memories—I didn't want to remember anymore. The only way I could make all this to stop was to kill myself right here and right now. The voice in my head was telling me not to wait for the death contract; today was the day.

I gave in.

I wasn't even thinking, I just needed to die, but the fucking seatbelt wouldn't undo. It was stuck. It just wouldn't budge. I mean, of all the things to go wrong, this happens now, *ahhhhhhhhhh!*

I just sat there, banging my hands against my head, screaming and crying, *why, why, why, can't I die.*

I was in a right mess; I was barely able to hold myself together. K kept saying, "We're nearly home sweetheart, just hold on. Please hold on, I need you to hold on."

We reached the vet, but I didn't want to go in for some reason, I just wanted to stay in the car. But K insisted I come with her. I had no idea where this woman got her strength from when her husband was having a mental breakdown. More memories came flooding back, this time I was on all fours sucking a man's penis, both of his hands were on the back of my head, forcing me down. He was sitting in a green upholstered chair, and he was wearing brown corduroy trousers, black shoes, and a blue jumper.

I think I was eight or nine years old at the time.

The vet checked Link, and she decided to keep him overnight to get a urine sample, so they took my boy into another room. All of a sudden I had this thought that I would never see my boy again. I was devastated, we had no bond, and yet I loved him like a son.

"K, I have to go home; something isn't right. I have a pain in my chest, and I can't breathe. I need to get back. I need my inhaler."

The overwhelming fear of never seeing my son again was too much; today was too much. I clutched my chest. "Something is wrong K; something is really wrong."

We got home, and the moment I stepped out of the car. I started to feel dizzy. I clutched my chest; I couldn't breathe. I was gasping for air.

"K, I need my inhaler, I need it now." I could feel myself blacking out.

I have no idea how I made it into the living room. I was holding onto everything I could find, hands on the walls, one step at a time, constantly blinking to stay focused and trying to make it to the sofa.

I blacked out, and K caught me just before I hit the floor. I came around shortly after, blinking my eyes to focus. The room was spinning, and I blacked out again in K's arms.

By the time I came around again, I was on a sofa. I stood back up, having no idea where I was. All I knew was that I was struggling to breathe, and my chest felt like it was on fire. It was pounding. I thought it was going to stop.

I blacked out again, hitting the floor and just missing the edge of the table. By the time I was conscious, I was on all fours. I could hear someone shouting at me. "Sit the fuck down! Don't move, I will get your inhaler."

I was unable to focus on anything; the room was spinning so fast, all I wanted to do was make my way to the kitchen. The voice in my head was telling me to smash my head against the refrigerator door.

"Sit fucking down, for fuck sake; listen to your wife!"

"Please sweetheart, and please sit down."

I ignored K in favour of the voice in my head. I have no idea how I managed to get to the kitchen; I placed both my hands against the refrigerator door and took a deep breath in. K came running out of my bedroom with my inhaler.

"Saweets, saweets, your inhaler."

I tried to use my inhaler, but I was unable to take a good breath in, I was gasping. I nearly blacked out again, but I managed to hold onto the worktop, stopping myself from hitting the tiled floor with my head while my other hand was still clutching my chest. I was so cold that I was shivering. I needed to get warm quick; I was going into shock. I'd had this feeling before, when I had pneumonia for the first time. I just needed to get warm before I completely passed out altogether.

I can't recall how I got into the shower, but I do recall K trying to take my clothes off in the shower. I was on my hands and knees shivering, then everything went black. I wasn't in the shower anymore, I was underwater. I couldn't see anything at first, then something small and sharp hit me in the back, then again on my feet, then on my hands, and they were coming from below me.

I looked down, but I couldn't see anything. Something scraped along my spine…what was that? I turned around and I couldn't see anything. Then something shiny and gold caught my attention in the corner of my eye; I wasn't sure what it was at first. Then I noticed more shiny gold reflections appearing through the dark black water.

FUCK! NO! NO, NO, NO, NO, NO.

There were about fifty little black and gold puzzle boxes, slowly making their way to the surface of the ocean. They were all coming at once. These boxes were my Hellraiser puzzle boxes, which was where I stored all my painful childhood memories again.

I swam to the surface of the ocean to see how many where already floating, but instead of crashing waves and rain like last time, this time the ocean was purely calm. There was no breeze in the air, no current, no light, no stars, nothing but pure darkness.

I looked all around me, and thousands surrounded me. Thousands of Hellraiser puzzle boxes, slowly opening up. In the far distance like a silent whisper, I could hear K's voice, "Saweets, saweets, saweeeeeets, wake up. Saweets wake up, Cornelius, Cornelius, Cornelius, please wake up."

I slowly came around. I looked at K, and I wasn't sure who she was. I just sat up and pushed myself back into the corner of the shower, holding my legs, shaking and shivering, unable to control my breathing.

"Saweets, you ok? It's me, saweets it's K, your wife, can you hear me? Where were you then?"

I just sat in the corner, crying and holding my legs. Eventually, I said to K, "They are coming, they are coming, they are all opening up."

"What is coming saweets, what's opening up?"

"HELL! HELL IS COMING!"

I am not sure how long I was in the shower, but K said I was in a trance-like state for about twenty minutes. I have no idea how I got to bed or when I woke back up the following day, I wasn't even sure what had happened.

K thought I'd had a severe panic attack. The thought of never seeing my little fur baby son again had triggered it all; my mind had gone into meltdown, unable to cope with life.

Every day, I would get glimpses of a new memory, like a single jigsaw piece, unable to place it in my life and only lasting for a few seconds. Some days, I would get more than one jigsaw piece.

I have no idea when my memory puzzles will be complete, or how many are left, and I have no idea what sort of hell lies behind them either. But I now knew who raped me when I heard "White Lines".

15

THE YEAR I DIE

Summer was here. We were invited to lots of our friend Norman's parties and events, and we had a three-day music festival to look forward to called Splore. Splore 2019 was going to be my last festival with K, and I needed it to be amazing. One final memory for her to keep. I wasn't sure if it was going to be a happy memory or not.

I thought about my upcoming suicide. I had no idea how it would affect the ones I loved. I would never get to witness what happened afterwards. Maybe that was a good thing.

Before Splore, we got invited to Norman's birthday event. I was crippled with anxiety, not knowing when a new puzzle memory would be completed, but I was close to working one out. I had about ten pieces left.

It was August 7th, 1984, 1:20 pm. I was ten years old, and my brother was playing football on the street as I could hear his voice; he was playing with his mate Calvin. Mum was in the hospital. My baby sister was born a few weeks earlier, but prematurely, so they were still in the hospital. I was in my house, but I had no idea what this memory was about. Nothing made any sense to me. But I knew sometime during the day, I would know more.

Everyone at the event knew that I struggled with anxiety, especially talking to people I didn't know. I had no more masks to wear, and I was petrified of what this memory was about. Or whether I was going to have another breakdown.

K mentioned to me a few weeks earlier that she noticed we only got invited to Norman's events, but never for Sunday roast and never for a cuppa or a chat. Only events. But everyone else was invited for midweek dinners and Sunday roast. This was a guy who called us family and said he would be lonely if we weren't in his life. It's probably why we got invited to his upcoming fake wedding, a marriage of convenience to Belinda, his long-term ex-girlfriend who wanted to move to New Zealand, as she was fed up with living in the U.K.

They both thought if they got married in New Zealand, Belinda would be able to move here. Norman was only on a two-year working visa, so getting married in New Zealand made no sense. He didn't have residency, so it was two people getting married in New Zealand; that's all it was.

His closest friends were also going to play their part. We both felt uneasy about being part of this ridiculous charade. Norman had described his perfect wedding during the New Year's AUM music festival. We'd invited him along as he'd had no plans for New Year's.

I sat in the back of Norman's garden with my legs trembling, sitting opposite someone I hadn't been introduced to. I didn't know his name or anything about this guy; I just knew that Norman had met him on Grindr. I have never been good at small talk, so I sat there in complete silence and complete panic. I didn't know what to say, or how to start a conversation.

I just sat trying to signal to K with my eyes that something wasn't right. I was struggling, but she was talking to someone else. I tried to get up and sit next to her on the lawn, but I couldn't. I didn't want to be seen as being rude, and it was just the two us at the table. In fact, no one knew who he was, and no one even made an effort to find out, either. But he was seated in front of me.

We both just sat there, in the most uncomfortable silence ever.

I didn't have my phone, but if I did, this also would have looked rude and disrespectful, as he was also in an uncomfortable space. I think he was waiting for everyone to leave so he could have sex with Norman.

So I sat observing everyone, including the people we had known for nearly a year. They kept asking the same questions. "So, what's been happening in your life? How has work been? How are you and K?" etc., etc. This felt like Déjà vu; I was asked the same questions by the same person only months ago, with the same boring 'can't give a shit' tone. He tried to come across interested in my life, but I knew he wasn't. He had no idea about me at all, yet I knew so much about him. I'd been genuinely interested in getting to know him, and I think I even tried to organise maybe ten times to try to get together, but it never happened.

Eventually, Norman sat next to me. I had been at his birthday event for over five hours. This was the first time I had a chance to engage with him, and this event had only ten people. I tried to ask him about his wedding preparations, about his work, his mum, because I was hoping to engage in a conversation with him. But he was so disconnected from reality; he never once turned towards me. In fact, he didn't even lift his head up from his phone.

I tried to have a conversation about what he was doing regarding his Instagram account, seeing that was my only way in.

Again, without even acknowledging me, he just said he had found a new algorithm on how he could get his birthday photos up to the top of the line, so to speak. He already had over 3,000 followers, but he needed more.

I found this confusing. I looked around the table, and everyone was glued to their phone, applying the same algorithm. I looked at K with such confusion; I could not comprehend what was happening right in front of me. I turned to Norman again, "Why do you need more followers? You have over 3000."

"This algorithm will get me to 5,000 followers in less than 24 hours."

I was perplexed. I was so confused as to what was unfolding in front of me. *What the fuck is happening?* K and I had given up our time once again to be here, and I hadn't spoken to anyone all day. He'd taken many photos of his birthday and now he was posting them in order to attract more followers. I was sitting right next to him, and yet he was more concerned that a random gay guy called Pablo from Brazil gave him a fucking like!

Then he started to have a text conversation right in front of me. *I'm sat right here, right next to you, and we haven't had one conversation all day.* I honestly thought this was so fucking strange. Was I so out of touch with social media, or were Norman and his friends so out of touch with reality? Norman even asked K and me to stay overnight in the spare room like usual, so we didn't drink and drive. Which we were always grateful for, but he was going to fuck this random Grindr guy, and it was only 8 pm. I was confused; was Norman gay, straight or bi.

Not to mention, Norman was getting married to Belinda in a few months, yet he's fucking a random guy, and no one has said anything? I said to K, "Are we just going to stay in the lounge and watch something on Netflix while he fucks? I thought we were here to celebrate his birthday."

He didn't even want to cut the cake. He just wanted everyone to leave. He had his own agenda, and we were not even considered; how fucking selfish was his behaviour.

We both couldn't drive home now, so we had to get a $65 Uber home. We both were fucking fuming; it now meant we had to drive all the way back to Norman's the following day to pick up my car.

He didn't even give a fuck about that, and we were family?

The following day, K and I sat up in bed chatting, totally pissed off about what had happened yesterday. Then K hit the nail on the head, she called us 'filler-friends.' A filler-friend is someone who gets invited to another person's social event, birthday, wedding, etc. to fill up empty background space in their photos, so it looks like they have more friends than they really do when they post online.

This made so much sense; it's why we only got invited to social media events and why we were always excluded from non-social media events, like having a Sunday roast, catching up over coffee, or even coming round to our place for midweek dinner. Norman seemed more addicted to social validation, rather than building a true, genuine friendship. He didn't want the world to know that he was lonely and unhappy, so we became filler-friends.

"Fuck," we both said at the exact same time.

***

Norman was coming to Splore with us, and we were going to his wedding. K and I were torn on what to do. We didn't want to pretend, and we didn't want to enable his behaviour.

Splore takes place on the ancestral land of the mana whenua, Ngāti Whanaunga, and Ngāti Paoa. It's a three-day music and arts festival staged annually on the shores of Tapapakanga Regional Park – perhaps the most beautiful festival setting in the world. I had always wanted to experience a camping music festival but never had. I had always struggled with crowds of people, so I avoided them.

Splore was the place I proposed to K; this is why it's so special. And we had now invited someone who we knew was using us as his filler friends.

The first day of Splore was fucking awful. Norman only brought another random Grindr guy and his obnoxious, foul, loud-mouthed,

29-year-old friend. This friend was the same person who, on Christmas Eve, sat down next to me and said in earshot of K, "You're either bisexual or gay, and you are just waiting for the right time to come out."

Forty-five years old, married, and I am still labelled bi or gay. She judged me based on a five-minute earlier conversation. I was fucking fuming, *Who the fuck does this person think she is?* But everyone excused her behaviour because she was twenty-nine years old. And now she was camping opposite our tent. We couldn't wait for George and his wife Lynn to arrive: some breathing space, a happy distraction.

Only a week before Splore, I had walked into my office and had a complete mental meltdown in front of George.

I had needed to download everything that was going off in my mind; I was so scared to be on my own with these negative thoughts. K wasn't working with me anymore, we had no money left, and the vultures were circling. I still had not heard from Dr. Jekyll's solicitors. My solicitors had given Dr. Jekyll a three-month deadline for her to hand over fourteen years of bank statements regarding our property. I had now issued a court order, but she was not responding back, and I was unable to place my house back on the market to clear this massive reverse mortgage loan.

K had found a well-paying job that just covered the $3k a month interest loan and all living expenses. She stepped up and became the sole earner, enabling me to take over a year off to recover from my mental breakdown. Therefore, George became my sound wall. I just needed to unload; he never said a word, he just sat there, watching his mate have a mental breakdown. To be honest, I'm not sure what I would have said, either.

Over the three days, Splore became a dark, negative, selfish, foul-mouthed, exhibitionist gay sex-, drug-, and alcohol-filled miserable, cold, wet music festival.

There was no love, no happiness, no joy. The energy in our camping section was so bad that I didn't even want to engage in any more conversations about gay sex. It was constant, and it was always on repeat, I didn't want to be there anymore.

Everyone became so fucking selfish at Splore that they ruined what this place had meant to K and me. This was supposed to have been my last music festival with K, and they even took that away from me. I needed to find another music festival quickly, and I didn't care what sort of festival it was. I just needed a music festival.

Earth Beat 2019, a co-creative, transformational spiritual and wellbeing festival of music and arts was held around the time of the autumn equinox in Aotearoa, New Zealand. This music festival kept popping up on my Instagram and Facebook accounts. I wasn't interested in any spiritual festivals, and I was definitely not going to hang around some smelly, vegan, tree-hugging, let's-save-the-dolphins, bang-on-drums-and-dance-to-the-moon people, that was for sure.

I had avoided these people all my life, and it wasn't going to change now.

I loved big classic dance hits, not bongos, pan pipes and flutes. Yet Earth Beat kept popping back up on my accounts, No matter how many times I reported this sponsor or ad, it consistently kept popping back up. K wasn't that keen on going either, but I convinced her to go. I had no other choice, I needed a festival, so I reluctantly booked the tickets, and when that weekend came around, I moaned all the way there.

It definitely wasn't Splore. Splore hosted over 9,000 people; Earth Beat seemed to have only about 1500 people, a mix of families and individuals walking around barefooted, wearing hippy tie-dye clothes, doing some stretches, which I later found out was called yoga, hula hooping and balancing other stuff useless objects and twirling some balls around.

And guess what? They only bloody sold vegan food, too! However, everyone seemed happy. Everyone seemed to belong. I just sat observing these tie-dye vegan tree huggers; they seemed to have no worries about how other people saw them. They kept hugging strangers with pure love and heart-based intention, and they also seemed to care about this planet.

I felt like I was watching the movie *The Village* directed by M. Night Shyamalan. It was so surreal. Eventually, we found some music we actually liked and laid down under some shade. I drifted off to sleep while K touched my feet.

Ever since K and I had been together, every night for about two hours, K always touched my feet; this was the only way I could control my anxiety. But for the first time in eight years, it felt like K wasn't rubbing my feet, and it woke me up. I watched her slowly stroking them, but K was also asleep. I laid there for about ten minutes, trying to work out where I knew this touch from.

It was completely different to how K touches me, and I kept thinking, *Where do I know this touch?* Was it part of my jigsaw puzzle memories, or was it something else? I didn't move a muscle for another five minutes, and I tried to recall.

Where do I know this touch?

I know this touch from somewhere; I have been touched like this before… where the fuck do I know this touch? It was doing my fucking head in. K was still asleep, yet she was still touching my foot. Then I realised where I recognised this touch from. It was my mum's touch. She'd woke me up from my sleep, so I woke K up.

"K, K, K, K wake up, K wake up, you just touched my feet like my mum used to, and it was a million times different from how you touch me. What does that mean?"

"You were asleep too?"

"Yeah, I was sound on, then I woke up when you started to touch my feet and I have been laying here trying to work out how I know this touch, and it was my mum's touch. What the fuck does that mean?"

"Wow, sweetheart, how nice is that? Your mum is with you."

"My mum, how can my mum be here? What does that mean? That makes no sense at all."

"That's all I know: your mum's spirit is reassuring you that you're loved."

"You don't believe in spirituality and shit like that, do you?"

"Well I asked the universe to send me someone, and they sent me you, so why not? I know you're not like that, so I never say anything."

"Why would my mum wake me up then, what's the point? It makes me feel sadder. I don't get it at all."

I shook my head in disbelief and then I noticed to my left and in the far distance, a guy wearing a white hemp T-shirt and white trousers, dancing, doing backflips, cartwheels, using his hands to create a love heart expression and expressing it everywhere and to everyone. As he danced and tumbled through the air, he was getting closer and closer to where we were lying down. His energy was something else. I had never seen anyone in my life who just loved life the way he did. Everyone was in awe of him. He didn't once stop dancing, giving everything he had, bouncing and flipping big hearts to everyone.

I turned to K and said, "Fuck me, we need those fucking drugs. Have you ever seen anything like that before? He doesn't care who's watching. He's in a totally different space to everyone. What the actual fuck! He just doesn't stop dancing, and he seems so happy."

I just started to cry. He was like that, and I was like this. K held my hand, trying to reassure me, trying to calm me down from all my pain and sadness.

I turned to K, tears streaming down my face, and said, "I want to be like him, K. I don't want to be me anymore. I want what he has, not what I have. I want to have his energy. I just want to feel like him.

"I don't want to be me anymore. I want to be like him, I want to be like him. I just want my sadness to go away. I don't want to be sad anymore. I don't want to be depressed or suicidal, and I don't want to die.

"I want to live, but I don't know how to do this; my memories and the voice in my head are just relentless. I just want to be like him. Why has this all happened to me? I didn't ask for any of this—I'm a good person, I'm a really good person. I don't want to die, saweets, I don't want to die.

"I didn't deserve any of this, why has this happened to me? I don't get it, why has all this happened to me, why, why, why?"

I just sank into my wife's arms and sobbed and sobbed until I had nothing left in me. "I don't get it at all, why me? I was a child, a fucking child and they took everything from me. All I have left are these memories—these awful memories of what I did and what happened to me. I am done."

Monday, March 25th, the day after Earth Beat, I tried to meditate for the first time in my life. I downloaded some apps to my phone and followed the guided meditation. I lasted no more than three minutes, the voice in my head was saying *Why are you wasting your time? You only have a few months to live.* Therefore, I stopped.

On Tuesday, the 26th, I tried to meditate again, and I lasted no more than four minutes until the voice in my head told me to stop again, so I stopped.

Wednesday the 27th, I tried to meditate once again, but this time I tried a breathing exercise as well, so I could try to stay focused. But the voice in my head yet again convinced me to stop, so I stopped.

Thursday the 28th, I realised that meditation wasn't for me. I honestly thought it would be a lot easier than it was, and the apps had convinced me meditation was easier than I thought it would be.

But there was absolutely no way—and I mean there was no way—I could stop my thoughts. I even tried a new breathing technique, seeing Wednesday's one didn't work, but the voice in my head again convinced me to stop, and so within minutes, I stopped.

K came in from work, and she asked me how my meditation was going and if it was helping. I just told her, "Nothing works; I am unable to stop any of my thoughts and I'm unable to focus on my breath. I did promise you I would give meditation a go, but I don't know what to focus or concentrate on long enough for me to get into a meditative state. The breathing exercise doesn't work for me, either.

"Also, tomorrow we have Norman's fake stag do to go to, a shitty show and meal in the city. Tomorrow night is going to be fucking shit, K. What shall we do? Shall we go? Or make an excuse not to go? I mean, we're just filler-friends after all; we will only be in the background photos anyway.

"Then we have to work out if we are going to his fake wedding. I am really not sure what to do; we don't want to be part of this charade or be part of his filler-friend's photos, either.

"What do you think, shall we go tomorrow night and then make the call next week?"

"Ok, well, I can drive us into the city; I am totally not in the mood to celebrate, especially now that we are his filler-friends. And I have a hair appointment tomorrow at 8am."

"Ok sweetheart, let's just see how we feel tomorrow, but I am not keen."

16

MARCH 29ᵀᴴ 2019. TODAY I RISE
PART TWO

In the moment of the Now, I was still lying on K's bed, fully conscious. I could hear the dog next door barking loudly and the owner shouting at it to be quiet, cars driving along the main road, birds outside chirping. I even adjusted my pillow slightly and wiped away more tears. Still, I was unable to open my eyes. All I could see was black nothingness. *Where the heck am I now? Is this another reality that I didn't know about?*

Then in the far-far distance, I saw a small blue light the size of a grain of sand. It looked very similar to how the universe began, with just one single light. I carried on staring at this blue speckle of light, wondering what I was seeing. I had no idea how long I was trapped in this place or when I would leave. I looked in every direction and there was nothing apart from this blue light.

In the Now, I felt a strange, faint electrical fire tingling sensation at the tip of my tail bone. This energic fire started to become more and more intense, and for some reason, it seemed to begin turning in a counter-clockwise circular motion at the base of my spine. Then it moved up my spine, one vertebra at a time before coming back down again. Eventually, it halted at a spot in my lower back, in line with my groin. There it continued to spin with the same circular motion as before. Every few seconds the energetic circular motion would speed up.

Then all of a sudden, I felt as if I was getting tasered, my back arching entirely off the bed. I gripped the bed with both hands, unable to let go. I was in a world of pain, unable to scream or shout for help and completely locked in this agonising position. I felt as if I was getting pulled into a vortex high above me. I gritted my teeth in pain. It was so fucking intense. Whatever this electrical fire, energy sensation was, it was getting even more and more intense. Tears were running down my face. I just wanted this to stop. This pain was like nothing that I had ever experienced before.

I didn't think the pain could get any worse, but I was wrong. This intense sensation moved into the middle of my chest, roughly where my heart is. My heart started to beat hard and fast. I clutched my heart with my right hand, thinking I was going to have a heart attack. Yet, I was still in this black nothingness, still fixated on this blue light which had now turned into a small blue sphere. I desperately tried asking Siri to phone my wife, but I was in too much pain to even say, 'Hey Siri.'

It felt as if I was in another vortex, but this time being sucked into the middle of the bed.

Instantly I knew I was in deep trouble; my heart was beating far too fast and I thought it was going to explode or pop out of my chest like in the movie *Alien*.

My entire body was now vibrating and twitching, moving from side to side. This intense electrical fire sensation was now running through my entire body. It became so severe that I was unable to breathe, as if my windpipe had suddenly collapsed; I started gasping for breath. My heart appeared to be beating over 500 beats per minute. I thought *This is it; this is my time.*

Still focusing on this blue light ahead of me, and observing the change in size as it seemed to be moving towards me, all of a sudden I noticed in my peripheral vision what seemed to be the edge of a large white circle moving towards the middle. The more I focused on the white circle, the more I was convinced that it was a tunnel compacting in size and heading towards the middle of the darkness.

The bright blue light was perfectly located in the centre of this white tunnel, and the electrical sensation was now running through every part of my body, a thousand volts of electricity. But with a difference, because all the circular motions that I was experiencing before had now started to turn clockwise, in perfect synchronisation and harmony with one another.

Then I experienced a new sensation at the top of my head, but it felt like it was more in my brain. This electrical sensation was moving all over the place. I had a tingling sensation similar to pins and needles, and I wanted to scratch my head so bad, but I was unable to move.

The top of my head began to throb like the worse migraine you could ever imagine. The pain was relentless. At the same time, it felt like my forehead was being split open. I thought I was going to have a stroke. I desperately tried to open my eyes, tried to get out of whatever I was experiencing, but still I couldn't.

Then the blue sphere began to slowly turn into a perfect sphere of white light, which was so intense against the backdrop of black nothingness.

I thought I saw millions of bits of information all around me, images, people, and I even heard voices, but I was unable to take in all of the information due to the pain I was experiencing.

Then the white tunnel slowly stopped rotating. When it had stopped entirely, the white sphere flew straight towards me, hitting me directly in the forehead. It was as if Thor had thrown his hammer at me with everything he had, creating a huge explosion of white light that shocked me out of whatever state I was locked into.

I bolted straight upright, leaning against K's headboard, breathing hard, clutching my chest. *What the actual fuck just happened to me?*

I had the most intense pounding headache immediately after Thor's hammer blow. The electrical sensations had gone and left me with this fucking headache.

Eventually, when I came around, I looked at the time. It was 2:24 pm. I had been locked in that state for over five hours.

I got up, walked to the kitchen to make myself a cuppa and looked for some pain relief, then sat down on the sofa to Google what had just happened.

I didn't stop Googling until K came home from work. I couldn't find any reference to what I had experienced earlier. To be honest, I had no idea where to start. K got home at 3 pm; we were both shattered, so we had a nap before getting ready for Norman's fake stag night.

I didn't think too much about what had happened earlier; I just needed the fucking headache to stop.

We arrived at the venue at 7:30 pm, and what a disappointment. It was not what we expected at all; we were placed at the far end of the table, which was a blessing in disguise. We started the evening off by ordering cocktails. We had the choice of three options. During the night, I tasted all three cocktails, and Option One tasted like piss poor cough medicine, Option Two tasted like a more expensive version of the first piss poor cough medicine, while Option Three tasted like the cheapest of all of the piss poor cough medicine cocktails.

We just knew tonight was going to be awful. Many of Norman's friends had decided to cancel at the last minute. *They were smart!* I said to myself, *We did say we would go, and we had already paid for tonight in advance, and we also wanted to be proven wrong regarding our filler-friends theory.* Don't even get me started on the piss-poor meal. But in comparison to the entertainment, the meal now seemed like a three-star Michelin restaurant dinner.

After leaving the stag venue, K had gone home because she had an early hairdressing appointment, and I decided to stay out with everyone else, seeing that it was only 11 pm. We all agreed to go to another bar, which was ok, wasn't brilliant, but it was better than where we had come from, that's for sure. We stayed here for a few more hours because they played some excellent music, and I got talking to this awesome couple at the bar.

Eventually I looked around and realised that out of the twelve people I walked into the bar with, I could see no one, and the bar was no bigger than 5m x 5m. So it wasn't that big!

I texted the group to find out where everyone was, and the response was that they had gone to another bar!

What the fuck! Are they kidding me? Out of twelve people, not one person let me know that they were leaving. They just fucked off and left me standing at the bar, fucking fuming.

I necked my drink and called an Uber to go home.

On my way home, I checked my Facebook; oh, fuck me! They had already uploaded the night's photos, and K was right: we were filler-friends. I sat in the back of the Uber on my way home. For the first time in my life I felt contempt, which was very strange; I had never felt this feeling before. It's why I can remember it so clearly. I also felt a great sadness at the same time.

The next day, still lying in bed, K kissed me on the forehead just before she left for her hair appointment and suggested that we go out for breakfast when she got back. Ten minutes later, I got up, fed the little ones and made myself a cuppa.

I picked up my phone to research yesterday's experience again, using a different search engine. But instead of typing something into my phone, I just gazed at it, as if I have never seen a phone before, trying to work out why my phone looked different. I knew it was my phone, but it looked like I had never seen this phone before.

I shook my head and laughed. *What the fuck!* So I decided to have my tea, picked up the cup, and just stared at that as well.

I looked over my shoulder behind me and then looked back towards the cup of tea. *Why does this cup look different as well? OMG! What the actual fuck is happening?* And I started laughing again. I thought I was going mad. I picked up the TV remote, and that also looked different. *Seriously, what the fuck! What the actual fuck? Why does this look strange? It's like I have never seen this remote control either.* I drank my tea and that also tasted different.

What the actual, actual fuck is going on? Why does everything look and taste so different?

I stood up and walked around our home. *Something is off, something is radically different.* Yet I couldn't put my finger on it. I picked up Zelda and immediately put her straight back down on the floor. *Why does she feel different?* I could feel every muscle in her body, and that also made no sense. *Zelda feels utterly different from how she felt yesterday.*

I picked up Link, and I held him up to the ceiling as if he was Simba from the movie *Lion King*, turning him from side to side. He looked like my boy, but it's like I had never seen him before either. I was noticing the smallest little details that I had never noticed before. I could see every strand of hair on his beautiful, shiny dark fur as a completely separate entity. I could even sense the space between each strand of hair, too.

I was not sure if I had ever seen a cat before; in fact, I wasn't even sure Link was a cat. *Obviously, he's a cat, right?* But then, I started to think, *Is Link a cat because someone told me he's a cat or is Link something else?*

I had never had a thought like that before. I know this sounds crazy, but this is the only way I can describe my boy.

I looked outside, and I noticed that all the trees had small separate green leaves growing from them, all blowing and moving in different directions. I could even sense the spaces between all the leaves as well. Even the trees seemed different; the colours looked so much more vibrant than I had ever noticed before, almost like they were in high definition (HD).

I looked at the family photo frames on our sideboard; they also seemed like there were in HD. I could even sense the entire space between each photo frame as well. I laughed, took my seat, and shook my head in disbelief. I couldn't stop laughing. Then I quickly realised that the air in the room seemed less dense than before, which also made no sense. *How can the air seem less dense, air is air, right? Density can't change overnight, can it?*

What a strange experience. I breathed in, but I struggled to feel any air in the back of my throat. I laughed again, *What the fuck?*

Then it dawned on me that I might be lucid dreaming. I had to be, right? I remembered reading somewhere that if you can't turn on a light switch, then you're dreaming! I walked around the house, turning on every light switched possible and anything that had a switch. Everything turned on.

I got dressed and walked to our local supermarket. As soon as I walked into the store, everything—and I mean *everything*—was so vibrant, all in HD. My depth of vision was so surreal, I had to wear my sunglasses immediately.

I ran back home, locked the door behind me, and sat on the sofa. *What the fuck is going on?* Then I realised I had just run back without stopping from the store, and I wasn't out of breath. *How's that even possible? I am so unfit.* I had piled on over eighteen kgs; even walking used to be tiring to me, which was why I usually drove the five-hundred meters to the supermarket. Yet I had just run home, and I'd felt nothing.

Thank fuck K came home, just at the point of me losing my shit.

"K, does everything look the same in the house to you compared with yesterday?" I asked, anticipating that she would say yes and noticed the difference.

"You ok, sweetheart?

"No, I am dead serious: does the house look different to you?"

"No sweetheart, everything is the same to me. Why?"

"Then how come everything looks so vastly different to me?"

"I have no idea. Maybe you're just tired?"

Later that day, K drove us to our local second-hand store located about a mile away. I sat in the passenger's seat looking out at the window with the biggest smile on my face. I felt like a child seeing the world for the first time; I was just in awe of the world.

It's so hard to explain in words the emotions that I was feeling. As if the drive to the second-hand store was out of this world, nothing could ever prepare me for the moment I walked into the store. If my house looked like HD, this store looked like it was in 100K HD, if there is such a thing. I just stood at the entrance, and I was unable to move. I didn't know where to look. *Was this really what I was seeing?*

I had been in this store so many times, and it had never looked like this before. I could isolate every single object; I could feel and sense the space in between each of the objects. The colours were so vibrant, and the red was the most brilliant red I had ever seen.

I walked over to an oil painting hanging on the wall. I could pick out every oil brushstroke, including the direction and the depth of the oil stroke compared to the adjacent strokes. I could have spent my entire life in this shop, never getting bored, with the amazement that I was seeing.

I have never tried LSD, but if I did, I think this is what it would look like, but stoned off my tits at the same time. I was so chilled, and I hadn't even taken anything, *Fuck me!* My mind was blown wide open.

I tried to explain this to K, but she wasn't getting it. To be honest, I wasn't really getting it, and it was happening to me.

This was how I spent the first six days after March 29th, walking around in 100K resolution and trying to find out what had happened to me. Though all of my research was pointing me towards a 'spiritual awakening.'

On the seventh day, I turned to my wife, who was sitting on the sofa next to me, and said "I need to tell you something, I really need you to trust and believe what I am going to tell you. I have never lied to you, and I am not lying now, either."

K sat up, waiting for me to talk. I composed myself and took a deep breath. But I just started to cry uncontrollably, "You won't believe this, but I don't feel depressed or anxious anymore. And for the first time in my life, I feel happy and content, with no more suicidal or negative thoughts.

"Even stranger than that, I don't seem to have an inner voice, or any more negative chatter, just pure silence. There is absolutely nothing in my head; I don't even have any thoughts. How is that possible? How can I have absolute silence?

"Whatever happened to me last Friday seemed to have cured my depression, and it feels like someone has forgotten to plug me back in. There is nothing, even now chatting with you sweetheart, nothing has popped into my mind. How is that possible, where has my inner voice gone?"

"What do you mean by you have no inner voice? Everyone has a voice in their head, that's who we are, aren't we?"

"I am not sure, to be honest. I know this doesn't make any sense, but I'm certain we are not who we think we are! I know it's so strange and I know what I am saying doesn't make much sense, but I am one billion percent convinced that the voice in your head is not actually you, and the voice that used to be in my head was never actually me."

17

WHAT THE ACTUAL FUCK IS GOING ON

April 7th, 2019, 1:32 am. I suddenly awoke and sat upright in bed. I thought I had heard a loud dog whistle outside my bedroom window. And then I remembered my dream, so I decided to wake K. It took a little time, but after calling her name several times and prodding her, she finally woke up.

I recall seeing two adult silhouettes, walking in a beautiful wildflower meadow towards a large tree. They seemed to be completely in love with one another and at total peace. Thousands upon thousands of red and blue fireflies danced all around them and in and out of all the flowers. Floating directly above the tree was a circular swirl. Situated in the middle of this swirl and transparently etched into the night sky was one word. That word was Oneo (pronounced "One-oh").

"Saweets, what does Oneo mean? I never heard of it before. Is it even a word?"

"I have no idea; I had never heard of it either until I just saw it in my dream."

"What do you think Oneo means?"

Then I heard the loud dog whistle again and said, "The swirl means enlightenment, and the acceptance of 'I' The tree means eternal life. Oneo means the 'Enlightenment of eternal life, the acceptance of I, and one with yourself.'

"Everything is Consciousness. We are Consciousness having a temporary human experience. We have a physical body like what we have now, and an astral body. The astral body wakes up to a higher dimension and a higher level of consciousness, depending on our vibrational state of being.

"Consciousness is all around us, guiding us to make the best choices for us and everyone else. But because we have so much inner chatter and distraction and we seem only to care for ourselves, it's hard for us to hear Consciousness or see the signs. We are now making so many poor decisions and ignoring our gut feeling and our intuition, in favour of making informed life decisions based on other people's actions and behaviour, only to regret shortly after. And everyone and everything is interconnected."

"Sweetheart, I thought you didn't know what Oneo means?"

"I didn't, but then all of a sudden I did?"

"Where is all of this coming from? What's a 'vibrational state of being' mean? How do you know all of this? And what do you mean by everyone and everything is interconnected?"

"I know this sounds mental, but I saw it in my dream; trillion and billions of individual faint stands or energetic waves all connected to one another. I have no idea what a vibrational state means"

In the early hours of the morning, K and I sat up in bed talking about what I had just seen in my dream and the knowledge I came back with. What was even stranger than that was I could easily remember my dream, when in the past I couldn't. We eventually fell back asleep at roughly 5 am, an hour before K had to wake up and get prepared for work.

***

It had been over three weeks since whatever had happened to me on the 29th, and I was convinced that it wasn't a spiritual awakening. I still hadn't come across any information regarding what I was experiencing.

I found it very difficult to get into any meditative state. I kept thinking, *I am already in a meditative state, I don't need to block out any thoughts.* But I tried anyway. I sat on my sofa, fully conscious with my eyes closed, in the most peaceful state you could ever imagine, observing the quietness in my head. I was trying to think about what it was like to have an inner voice, but I couldn't remember anything—nothing, absolutely zip. It was almost like it had never existed in the first place.

Then all of a sudden, out of nowhere, I was in a car. I wasn't sure if I was driving or not, but I was definitely in the driver's seat. It was a red and black rally car, and on the side of the doors was written 'F5' in bold black letters. I was speeding down a narrow four-meter road. I could see green hedges on either side of me, and in the distance, I saw an open field. I was heading towards a right-handed bend when all of a sudden, the car lost control and skidded to a full stop on a slight incline, with the front of the car pointing towards the road I had just driven down.

I had no frigging idea what had I just seen, but I knew it wasn't my memory either; this was something else.

I described what had happened to K and I made her promise me, no matter what, don't let me get into a car with the letters F5 on the side.

Five weeks later, I was having a cuppa, and I wasn't sure what to do, so I decided to watch *The Graham Norton Show,* Season 25, Episode 8 on May 24th. Michael Fassbender was one of Graham's guests, and they both got talking about Michael's passion when he's not working, which was driving rally cars. Graham showed a recent clip of Michael driving his rally car, and the clip was exactly what I had seen sitting on my sofa. *What the fuck, how could that be possible? How could I see something five weeks before it was even aired on TV?*

April 12th at 10:12 am, I was making a cup of tea for K when she gave me a massive hug from behind, telling me how much she loved me. I turned around and kissed her softly on her forehead, and in that split second when I kissed her, I saw three white lights in the far distance of the universe, evenly spaced out. Each white light had a vanishing point and its own perspective grid. These perspective grids were all interconnected with one another. Each grid had glowing red spheres of light attached to it. The most significant red spheres had two distinctive grooves that ran all the way around them. Some even looked like the Death Star from the *Star Wars* movie but mostly they reminded me of abacus balls.

I saw five major red spheres and hundreds of medium-sized red spheres, followed by thousands and thousands of smaller red spheres, all connected along these grids.

I sat down with a cuppa and immediately started sketching what I saw. I had never seen anything like this before, but I felt like this was all about K.

On April 19th, Good Friday, at 11:30 am, I was still no closer to finding out what had happened to me. Everything still pointed to a spiritual awakening, except for the 'no inner voice' part.

It was also the weekend of Norman's fake wedding. His mum had even flown in from Scotland for the event. We still had doubts regarding attending Norman's wedding. K and I talked about bailing since he'd left me in the bar on his stag night. But the way Norman had described all the little details and the effort he had put into his wedding, we just thought it was too late to bail, and we didn't want to let him down. After all, we were family!

K was lying down on the sofa in some discomfort; the pain in her vulva was too much that day. She had been feeling this pain for the last eleven years, a condition called vulvodynia. Vulvodynia is a chronic burning or raw pain around the opening of the vagina, for which there is no identifiable cause or cure. And due to this crippling condition, we struggled to have any type of sex. Even touching her in that area was too painful for her. K had no sex drive and was a shadow of the woman she was before she started suffering from vulvodynia. She also had fibroids (abnormal growths that develop in or on a woman's uterus), so having children was always off the table—something I knew from the moment we started dating. She understood my love for children, and how I wished we could have one. She had even suggested that we should end our relationship due to her condition. But that was never going to happen.

Over the last eleven years, K had seen over twelve different types of specialists, and the only advice she got was to start taking steroids, tricyclic antidepressants, or nerve pain cream. All they did was mask the symptoms rather than treating what caused it in the first place, and the side effects were shocking. For the past seven years, I had also been researching a way to heal her, "my obsession," so to speak, and I recently made a significant breakthrough. I used a combination of essential oils and homemade organic cannabis-infused lube. And we managed to reduce the pain by at least twenty-five percent. This allowed K to experience some sexual pleasure, not penetration, but enough to receive oral sex from another woman.

The slightest bit of hair on my face was like sandpaper on her vagina; this was why we talked about opening up our marriage, and even considered a poly-monogamous or three-way-monogamous relationship for over three years.

I placed my left hand on her vagina and closed my eyes, hoping that the pressure and heat from my hand would work similarly to placing a hot water bottle on her tummy when K had menstrual cramps. After about thirty minutes, I took my hand off K's groin and started to cry uncontrollably again. K asked me worryingly what was wrong. I smiled and said, "I know how to heal you."

"What do you mean, you know how to heal me? Heal what?"

"I know how to heal your condition; I saw it in the vision I just had. I need to learn energy healing from the person I trust the most."

"What do you mean you need to learn energy healing?"

"Actually, I was told to call it coherence healing."

"What's coherence healing?"

"Coherence healing uses the principles of quantum physics, the subconscious mind, and Consciousness to go beyond the boundaries of our perceived limitations, to make what seems to be impossible, possible.

"Coherence healing is about removing all negative emotional trapped energy and resetting your body to a harmonious vibration and frequency. Many people walk around completely unaware that we live in an energy-responsive world, and that each of us has an energy body and energetic field. So they don't know the importance of energy maintenance and routine cleansing.

"When our bodies are at a coherent frequency, we are in a state of balance, order, harmony vitality and good health. But when we are at a lower, slower and more incoherent frequency, we become susceptible to illness, disease and chronic, unexplained pain.

"Stress is one of the main reasons we create an incoherent frequency, which then fires incoherent messages to our associated organs, tissues, and systems like our autonomic nervous, digestive, immune and the reproductive system.

"Also, toxic people, painful past relationships, trauma or on-going life challenges can create an incoherent frequency, leaving negative energetic debris and imprints in our energy body and energetic field, and affecting our vibrational and emotional state of being."

"What the fuck, seriously what the actual fuck, how, how, how do you know all of this?"

"I told you I saw it in the vision I just had. Wait, there's more. I was also shown a glimpse of our future."

"What the fuck."

"I haven't finished yet, and this is the best part: I even saw you in my vision. I am not yet sure what it means, but you become 'the voice for those who don't have one.' I saw us both on a top-rated day time talk show and in *Ted Talks*. And I am pretty sure we live in California; I saw the Hollywood sign and the skyline. We finally have some real friends— actual, proper friends, sweetheart; friends who like us. I saw them sitting around our dining room table, and I even saw you having brunch with a group of girlfriends in Vancouver and San Francisco. We're going to have friends. What the fuck is happening to me? How can I see all of this? It's impossible? I don't get it."

Tears ran down both our faces thinking of that happy alternative reality. The one thing I have craved all my life is to be loved and to make some actual genuine friends, people who won't sexually, physically and verbally abuse me. Then reality kicked in: *We have zero money in our bank account, we're living off thin air, and I haven't heard anything from Dr. Jekyll regarding my house and my share of the rental income. She's just left me high and dry, thrown me to the lions without a stick.*

But for some strange reason, my body was vibrating, and I had an unbelievable amount of energy running through it, similar to the energetic sensation I had felt on the 29th. I knew what I'd seen, as clear as daylight; I knew what I needed to do. I immediately started to Google if anyone with vulvodynia had been healed using energy healing or coherence healing. And no one had.

***

It was the day of Norman's fake wedding and Derek's birthday. We drove over to Derek's house first thing in the morning to give him his birthday present. Today was the first time I would be seeing Derek since I had stopped feeling depressed and suicidal, and I was so excited to tell him about my experience.

"Mate, you won't believe it, but I don't feel depressed anymore, and I have no more inner voice telling me to hurt or kill myself." I shared my experience with him and his wife Lynn. "How amazing is that? I am not suicidal anymore."

They looked at one another and smirked as if they didn't believe me. I didn't get it. "I don't have depression or anxiety anymore, and seriously,

I don't have a voice in my head telling me to kill myself. Amazing, hey? Something happened to me a few weeks ago; I have no idea what, but something healed my depression and left me with no inner voice."

Again, they looked at one another. "That must be nice not to have an inner voice," Lynn said sarcastically.

Sharing my experience should have been a joyous occasion, but I left their place confused. I didn't get it. I kept thinking that they didn't seem happy that I wasn't suicidal anymore. Derek and Lynn were our closest friends, yet they were not happy for me. They didn't seem to believe me.

Eventually we got to Norman's home ten minutes before the start of his ceremony. We were the last to arrive. We gave him a big hug and told him he looked good in his suit and shirt. Then we headed towards the garden and took our places, waiting for the bride and groom to walk down the deck.

This was my first time being at a gathering since the 29th, and it was so fucking surreal. Everyone just looked and acted so differently compared to how they used to act before. I seemed to be observing everyone from a different perspective. As if I wasn't there and they had no idea I was watching them.

I just kept observing everyone. Then I watched Norman read his vows to Belinda. However, Belinda looked everywhere else but at Norman. I then nudged K, "What the fuck, they are not even looking at each other. Is this a fucking joke? I don't get it. And why are the guests crying? Everyone knows it's fake, and Norman told us all that it's all for show. So why are they crying? Are we missing something?"

I was watching a car crash wedding play out in slow motion, and there was nothing I could do, apart from taking it all in. Belinda then read out her vows and Norman looked everywhere else apart from in Belinda's direction. I was getting upset; they considered themselves part of the gay community, yet they were showing such disrespect for a ceremony that many had fought hard for. Couldn't they at least take their wedding seriously?

Then more people started to cry. *What is going on, are we missing something, or have we not been told some crucial information?*

After the ceremony, K and I sat down for our reception dinner. It wasn't what we were expecting. The way Norman had described his perfect wedding, all the small personal details he wanted to include, the beautiful finishing touches, and the way Norman described his reception food, I thought Gordan Ramsay would be cooking for us. But what we got was a Sunday kiwi roast served straight from the back of a van parked on his driveway.

Belinda thanked us all for turning up and presented us with a bag of five peanut M&M's, with the wrong wedding date printed on them. This was definitely not the wedding Norman described when he was at AUM, or a few weeks earlier when we met for dinner.

I was so conflicted about how I was feeling. On the one hand, I felt sorry for Norman. On the other hand, I felt so embarrassed for him, especially since his mum had flown all this way. We had been lied to again, In the last two weeks, ten people had cancelled on attending his wedding. Now it made sense why he kept reassuring us that we were family and that he would be devastated if we didn't turn up. *We had been at his wedding for over six hours and he hadn't even introduced us to his new wife or his mum, yet he calls us family?* We were filler-friends, all for social fucking media and validation.

An hour later, Norman was adamant about finding out what we had done when we arrived at his wedding. I had no idea what he was going on about, but he kept saying that as soon as K and I had arrived, the energy in the house and everyone's mood instantly changed.

"I was in such a happy mood this morning and so excited to get married. But then you guys turned up and I felt sad and depressed. It was like a massive energy shift took place. I had eight people come up to me saying they also started feeling down the moment you arrived. What did you do or say to people? I need to know. This is my wedding day and I have a right to know what you did."

Norman was relentless; he wasn't letting this drop. But I wasn't in the mood to talk or explain this apparent 'energy shift', whatever he called it. I had wanted to have an honest conversation with him two weeks earlier over dinner, to tell him that we didn't want to take part in his fake wedding and that we felt like filler-friends. But he wasn't even prepared to listen. He was so engrossed in chatting with someone random person on Tinder or Grindr and trying to get more followers on Instagram. Whatever it was, he didn't care enough about what we had to say.

He kept pushing and pushing me to explain this 'energy shift'. So I gave in and headed downstairs for a one-on-one. I had no idea what he was talking about, so I directed the conversation towards how he had been treating K and me. How we only got invited to his signature events and nothing intimate, not like everyone else in his tight-knit group of friends. We were there for him when he was depressed, we were there for him when no one else was, and we never bitched about any of his so-called friends, as they all did behind each other's backs. We even invited him to AUM when everyone else only looked after themselves. Still, we were always in the background of his photos as filler-friends.

He'd never once made a genuine effort to get to know us. So this 'energy shift', whatever he called it, was probably more of a true reflection of himself. "Mate, I have no idea what you're talking about, what energy shift? I can't shift energy, and I did not bring anybody's energy down."

I just sat there listening to him moan, blaming us for ruining his wedding day. K and I had only spoken to about four people all day and yet we were to blame. *Fuck this,* I thought. *I'm going home. K knew this was a bad idea coming, I should have listened to my wife. Will have to get that sentence tattooed on my arm, lesson learnt.*

The following day, I got a text message from Norman. "How dare you come to my place, bring everyone's energy down and call me out for being a filler-friend? I have treated you both as if you were family. You ruined my wedding day and marriage, and I don't want anything to do with you guys anymore. You're both dead to me. And that $650 I borrowed from you? You're not getting that back either."

What the fuck! Was he kidding me? We were the filler-friends, not him. I couldn't believe that we were being blamed for ruining his wedding day and marriage. *That's totally fucked up. I always knew I was never going to see that money again.* Another man of his word.

I told K, and she went ballistic. "How can we ruin a fake marriage? I mean, it's fake. Norman fucked a woman a week ago and another a few weeks before that, and that guy from Splore. And we ruined his marriage? Why is he blaming us?"

"He needs to blame someone for his unhappiness; I bet his fake wife asked him this morning why he looked so miserable. Instead of telling her the truth—that this wasn't the wedding he'd wanted or dreamed about—and that he feels no different than before, he is now committed to a marriage of convenience. He needs to blame someone for his unhappiness, and that someone is us.

"We were never really part of his family, truth be told. We never gossiped, never created drama, never moaned about the people we worked with or bitched about our exes. We never once needed social validation, and we never reinforced each other's stories, like he and his friends did. We were always on the outside looking in. We never got invited for breakfast, lunch, dinner or a night out by anyone. And we have known all of these people for over a year.

"Regardless of all the shit we have had to endure, you and I are closer than ever before. We have an unbreakable love for one another, and the fact is that they all crave what we have. We were always going to be blamed for his unhappiness. Especially now that his big event is over, Norman has nothing else to look forward to, so he's miserable. He thought that getting married would satisfy the craving he desires so badly. So we are the villains in his story."

"And what's that he craves?"

"The same thing we all crave: intimacy. But we think intimacy is about sex and companionship. The fact is, intimacy is about the truth. When you realise you can show someone your true self and your truest reflection without being judged, when you are accepted for who you are, that's intimacy. Sex is just an enhancer, which we sometimes get confused for intimacy."

"Where is all this coming from, sweetheart? That's pretty deep."

"I have no idea. I did have the weirdest experience yesterday at Norman's wedding though. During dinner, I was observing how everyone else acted and behaved, but unlike in the past, I was no longer interested in criticizing others or comparing myself to them. It was as if I was at home watching something on Netflix, and when I got bored with the TV show, I watched someone else. It was so surreal. I can't quite put my finger on it. It was like I was witnessing reality in its purest form; everyone seemed to be isolated or as if they were individual objects. Sounds crazy, right? And are you sure you can't hear any dog whistles of high-pitched frequencies? They are driving me crazy."

"Have you come across anything on the internet that explains what you're going through yet? There has to be more people like you out there."

"No, not yet. Everything is still pointing to a spiritual or a kundalini awakening."

"What's a kundalini awakening?"

"A kundalini awakening is the activation of a feminine energy that is said to lie dormant at the base of your spine located in our first chakra. Kundalini energy rises from your first chakra at the base of your spine, travelling up and along the spine or the central channel, activating and opening each chakra until it reaches the seventh one."

"What the fuck is a chakra?"

"A chakra is part of our chakra system, an ancient way of understanding the body's internal energy centres. Chakra means 'swirling wheel of energy'."

"How do you know all of this, I don't understand where this information is coming from. You're doing it again!"

"Saweets, I have no idea how I know this information, but I do. Some people talk about the same sort of energetic sensation that I experienced on the 29th. But there is no mention of feeling like you're being electrocuted for hours; nothing even comes close to what I experienced and what I am experiencing every day.

"All my research on the internet seems to be based on information either from a story that someone has read or from their own opinion. I am not saying that they haven't had a kundalini awakening, I just haven't found anyone that describes an experience like mine is all.

"Plus, a lot of people say it's very dangerous to awaken your kundalini and that it can lead to depression, anxiety and suicidal thoughts if you're not fully prepared. Well, I had all three, and now they have spontaneously disappeared along with the voice in my head.

"It's the only plausible explanation for what I experienced on the 29th. I just don't have any of the symptoms that they suggest I should have. And no one has ever experienced having no inner voice from a kundalini awakening.

"So I am not sure what to think. They do say that to become a master takes over forty years meditating in a cave, eating nothing but rice."

"Really, you have to meditate in a cave for forty years and only eat rice to become a master? Really?!"

"Hahaha no, that bit I made up, hahaha."

"Dickhead."

***

After Norman's wedding, I realised I had experienced different versions of the same person. Norman wasn't the same Norman from AUM or the Norman at Splore or the one at Christmas. Each Norman had a notable change in his personality, as if I were watching all four Normans at the same time in the same space—similar to my experience on the 29th.

I had seen four different types of Normans in the space of four months, but they all seemed to be at the wedding.

The first Norman was a flamboyant, sex-orientated, eccentric, over the top influencer and personality enhancer. He was demanding, always wanting, always needing.

The second Norman was resentful, angry, blaming, bitter, hateful, offensive, argumentative, unsympathetic, belligerent, and judging. He thrived on gossip and was always a victim in his stories.

The third Norman was apathetic, indifferent, distant, cold, emotionless, passive, laidback, uninterested, and blind to his consequence because he failed to process his actions; this Norman saw no reason to.

The fourth Norman was caring, helpful, attentive, beautiful, funny and loving.

I had no idea which Norman was authentic and which Norman was fake. Or was there ever an authentic Norman? I was so confused.

Why does Norman always need to be right and never wrong?

Why does Norman need to feel satisfied with materialistic objects?

Why does Norman need social validation?

Why can't Norman be content with what he already has?

Why does Norman create suffering and pain for himself and others?

Why does Norman create drama?

Does sexual orientation define who Norman is?

Our Norman was a combination of all four, depending on what he wanted to experience at that time.

I sat there, trying to work this out. *Have we stopped creating shared experiences in favour of creating individual experiences in a shared reality?*

And how many of us are in competition with one another all of the time? Is this the main reason why compromise is so hard to achieve?

And is this why those who believe in competition will try to demean your intelligence, skills, and abilities, in favour of their superior skills and experiences so they can move up the corporate ladder, earn more income to experience a new alternate reality? That explains why workplace harmony rarely exists and why so many relationships fail.

If we are always in competition, then surely there is a high probability that most people will get used, hurt, and thrown into the street like garbage, left with nothing but pain before they have even realised it's happened.

But, on an even deeper level, this means our identification of "who we are"—and "who we are not"— is based entirely on past experiences or the experiences we want.

Does that mean our environment, stories and beliefs create our identity, the fundamental base point of who we think we are and what we experience?

Wow! What an insight I had. No longer having an inner voice had given me a unique perspective and understanding of life situations. It was almost like 'mirror, mirror on the wall, who's the fairest of them all? Your truest reflection.'

Where was all this information and insight coming from? And when would these high-pitched frequencies stop?

***

Two weeks later, I found an energy healing course buried twenty pages deep in Google, and with a stroke of luck, the course was less than two miles away. I emailed the website and asked if they could fit me in ASAP.

I received a reply a few days later, saying they could fit me in the coming Saturday. Someone had dropped out. Never in a million years did I think I was going to learn about energy healing. I had never even heard of it before that vision, and now I was going to learn it. *Incredible,* I thought.

The morning of the course, I was super excited but also very apprehensive. In my research, I had read that many people had dismissed this alternative healing method, saying that it was fake, and people were getting ripped off. But my vision was crystal clear: 'learn energy healing from the person you trust the most.' That bit I still didn't quite understand.

I turned up on time, nervously knocked on the door, and a woman greeted me. "Morning, my name is Cornelius. I emailed last week regarding understanding the principles of energy healing. Is this the right place?"

"Yes, this is the right place. Hi, I'm Kodi." My head just exploded into a million pieces, and then all those pieces exploded into smaller pieces, and so on and so on. I have always called my wife K, but her real name is Kodi.

What the actual fuck is going on?

18

SURVIVOR. OUTWIT, OUTPLAY, OUTLAST

I had started to notice that every now and then, I could hear ultrasonic high-pitched frequencies. They seemed to be surrounding me even in the shower I heard these tones. I felt as if I was hungover, which was impossible. I hadn't had a drink since the 30th of March. I had never noticed this before, but come to think of it, I also didn't notice that during the day I only ate pears. K mentioned this some time ago, but I never gave it a second thought. But I had been eating nearly a dozen pears a day, I just craved pears. I thought I must be pregnant and cracked up laughing.

1:23 pm, the day after my energy healing course, K was lying down on the sofa. I said, "Let's do this, Bradley," a saying from one of our favourite TV shows called *The Chase*, with Bradley Walsh. Since the 29th, I had been starting to question and let go of everything I had learned about what I already knew. I was beginning to become limitless to the possibilities of the unknown and that we know nothing, John Snow.

What I thought, knew and believed all came from my ego. I realised that my ego had always wanted to be right, all the time. My ego would do anything and everything to be right, to never be wrong. Before the 29th, never in a million years would I *think* I would be able to heal my wife based on a vision.

But here I was, the biggest skeptic of them all, embracing the unknown. I used the word *think* instead of *believe* because I could see that belief had formed the notion of "I am already closed off and I don't need to learn anymore." This had closed down the option of further exploration, and kept me limited in how I could help her.

I saw that we look at life through half-closed eyes, constantly being reinforced that this is 'who we are.' We believe that what we told is the truth. And then we try to identify with our beliefs, giving these stories prominence. In order to come to terms with this 'known' reality, which is actually an illusion, we enter into a world of forgetfulness. This creates resistance in our lives and a feeling of emptiness, because at a deeper level, we sense there must be more. From there we live in fear, unable to love and accept ourselves and others as we truly are.

The same thoughts always lead to the same choices, actions, and behaviours. In turn, those will create the exact same experiences—a continuing comparable experience, over and over again. This will influence the very same thoughts we started off with and will continue to perpetuate, even subconsciously. Our day-to-day experiences are almost one hundred percent run by our subconscious mind, which means that we are on autopilot most of the time, versus being fully conscious and using our conscious mind, which only accounts for about five percent.

So, when we keep thinking the same thoughts, the future isn't going to change that much from what it is now. Similar things will continue to manifest in our lives. But if we want to change how our future looks, first we must change the stories that we are continuously telling ourselves, and change our reflection.

Some people might not be ready to let go of their stories and beliefs, which then creates another level of resistance to the possibility of being limitless. This is because when their frequency is low, the ego provides people with rewards for being ill or helpless, as crazy as that sounds. But they get a reward from all the attention they get from their drama or of being sick. They are afraid to let go subconsciously, because they need identity attention. They might not even be aware that they are like this because they believe that this is who they are.

Why was I thinking like this? Where did all this come from? I had never thought like this before.

I shrugged what I was thinking to one side and I placed my left hand on K's vulva, closed my eyes and waited to see what would happen. We were both one hundred percent convinced this was going to work. Why else did I have this vision? It made absolutely no sense otherwise.

My body began vibrating and pulsating like nothing I had ever experienced and my left hand felt as if it was part of Iron Man's suit. It seemed that I had massive amounts of energy coming from it. With my eyes closed, I waited patiently for something to happen. I had no idea what to expect.

Then something visually came into my mind, resembling a large grey shadow on the right-hand side of K's labia majora. Very similar to how you would detect cancer on an x-ray. I also saw something that looked like pulsating nerve endings on either side of this shadow.

The grey shadow was roughly thirty-five millimetres in diameter and about fifteen millimetres in depth, including a long thin dark line. I thought, *how am I going to heal K?* This shadow was massive. I waited patiently for something to happen, and then I nearly jumped out of my skin. Standing directly in front of me was the Night King from the TV show *Game of Thrones,* staring directly at me. He didn't move; he just stared at me. It was weird, but I instantly understood what this vision meant. If I could locate the Night King, the one abnormal cell that started K's vulvodynia, and heal that one first, then all the other cells would follow suit. Through the large dark shadow, I saw a smaller, darker shadow about the size of a split pea. The same time I saw this darker shadow, I heard a new higher-pitched frequency, a mantra, and the number 107.

Without the distraction of my inner voice, I was able to concentrate and repeat this mantra over and over in my head along with the number 107. I was fully committed to healing my wife.

About two hours later, the pea-sized darker shadow, which I sensed was like static energy, began to turn grey and less prominent. Then the larger shadow started changing to a light grey. I began experiencing a new oscillating energetic sensation, one that went from the centre of my chest to the top of my crown, almost like a cambelt in a car. This cambelt sensation was oscillating so fast it felt like I was projecting or radiating ripples of energy out of my body. This was utterly different from the energetic circular motion I experienced on the 29th.

In time the large shadow was almost gone and the smaller, darker shadow was barely detectable. Even the black line was starting to disappear, and the nerve endings on either side of the shadow were starting to reconnect.

Then *bang!* A bright flash of light suddenly appeared, similar to the one I had experienced on the 29th. Thor had again thrown his hammer at me, but this time not at my forehead. This time, his hammer hit me above the crown of my head. Then, another *bang!* I saw another flash of light, but this one was even higher than the first flash of light. I had two new, fully immersive visions.

In the first vision, I was viewing Earth from the perspective of Consciousness. The first thing I noticed was how clear and blue the skies were, followed by the stunning, transparent oceans, lakes, rivers and streams. I could see down to the bottom of every ocean, a kaleidoscope of colour and sea life. Stunning, breath-taking landscapes stretched for miles and miles. Everything was bright and vivid. All animals were coexisting with one another, and with humanity. Everyone was happy and everyone respected one another; we lived in perfect harmony. There was no more violence, murders, rapes, depression, anxiety, illness, disease, cancers, power, judgement, apathy or famine. All of those emotions and conditions had been replaced with love, joy, peace and happiness. Wealth was spread equally; we had the perfect distribution system. It wasn't about individual wealth anymore; it was about shared wealth.

It was as if Earth had been reborn and humanity said: "enough is enough." I didn't want to leave this place; this place was the vision of Collective Consciousness.

Then slowly from left to right and right to left, mile by mile, city by city, country by country, continent by continent, everything started to turn grey. As I looked on, the most apparent thing I noticed was that there was no more respect for this planet. There were no more blue skies, transparent oceans, or stunning landscapes. All the trees had been felled. All animals had become extinct.

I was overcome by an overwhelming sense of sadness.

We had done this to ourselves. We had drained everything that was beautiful from it, including one another. My heart was shattered. Apathy had taken over the world.

I then heard, *"To heal this world, one person at a time, starts within and then family. Humanity needs to change; will you help heal this world?"*

Without even thinking, I said *yes*. Instantly I saw the grey slowly start to lift all over the world. "But how? I have no friends, no job, no money, and K and I are in so much debt, we are living from week to week, and you're asking me to help heal the world?" I started to laugh. "How?" I asked in a dry, sarcastic tone.

Everything went black yet again, void of all colour. Then all of a sudden, K was standing right in front of me. She was wearing a funky red dress and looked stunning. I then gave her a beautiful, close, loving, passionate kiss, as if I had just returned back from war and it was the first time I had seen her in years. Standing to K's left was another woman, who I also kissed. She was holding K's hand; I think she was our girlfriend. "Where am I? Why are you both all dressed up?"

"This is your night. Look, everyone is waiting for you, go and enjoy yourself go. We will both be fine." I looked over my shoulder, and about a *hundred* people were clapping and gesturing for me to come over. Once I started walking towards everyone, the crowd parted and I saw a poster of a dusty grey man with white light appearing from his body and I saw my name above the word Oneo: *"Enlightenment of Eternal Life, the Acceptance of I, and One with Yourself. A self-reflective autobiography."* Underneath the poster and stacked on top of a table were hundreds of books, all with the same image.

I immediately pulled my hand away from K, as if I had gotten an electric shock, tears flowing out of me for no reason. There was another crazy high-pitched ultrasonic noise, which was ringing so loud it was piercing. *What the fuck was that?*

"K, I think I have to write a self-reflective autobiography regarding how our behaviour and actions can affect other people, enough for someone to consider taking their own life, someone like me. We live our lives in constant fear, lacking self-love, self-acceptance, and respect for one another. We are always compromising against ourselves.

"We continually stay in shitty, non-loving relationships due to the fear of being alone, or fear of the unknown. We don't give a flying fuck about treating someone like dog shit, even if they are our loved ones, family, friends, co-workers, or someone that we have never met before. We always need to look good, and we don't care about the consequences or the people we hurt.

"Consciously or subconsciously, we create misery, sadness, agony, despair, sorrow, suffering, torment, and torture. We have to take responsibility and be accountable for adding to someone else's misery. It might have only been a passing comment, followed by 'I am only kidding,' or we might have meant it.

"It could even be as small as a mean thought, or as big as we can create, but when we add to someone else's misery we are also contributing to our own unhappiness.

"We are Consciousness, naturally high-vibrational beings, capable of generating free and unlimited inner energy that runs through the entirety of our bodies. Nothing rests, everything moves, and everything vibrates at the most fundamental level.

"1921, Albert Einstein was awarded a Nobel peace prize for his contribution to Theoretical Physics by discovering the law of photoelectric effect, which aided the invention of quantum physics. Also referred to as quantum theory or quantum mechanics, it is the part of physics that explains the nature and behaviour of matter and energy at atomic and subatomic levels.

"According to the quantum model of reality, both particles and waves are also matter and energy. In short, everything that we know to exist, including us, has an energy field called a torus. Even the thoughts that we think, or our intentions, have separate tori as well.

"When you meet someone for the very first time, and you get the sense that they have a good or bad vibe? That's our torus energy field at work.

"The torus energy field is made of its surroundings but is distinct within it. Most torus energy fields contain two tori. Energy flows through one end, circulates at the centre, and exits from the other side. One torus is spiralling and expanding upwards, and the other is contracting and spiralling downwards, like a tornado or a whirlpool. It is completely balanced, self-regulating, and always whole, continually refreshing and influencing itself. It is a perfect self-organising system and the primary pattern for life at every level.

"There are about 8 billion people on this planet, and all our energy fields are interconnected. Our thoughts and intentions radiate throughout our energy fields and affect our reality. The reality we experience is influenced by our attitude and intentions. Our thoughts begin an intention, our emotions amplify it, and our actions give it energy-momentum.

This makes it possible for our thoughts and intentions to create quantum shifts in the structure of the universe and on this planet. Which would give us an infinite number of new parallel realities."

Whooooooooooo, where the fuck did all that come from? What the heck was that all about?

K said nothing for a couple of minutes then responded with, "What the fuck does 'nothing rests, everything moves, and everything vibrates' mean? I have never in my life heard you talk like this before; it was similar to how you talked after your dream and the vision to heal me. But that wasn't even you talking then; it was as if you were someone else. I mean it sounded like you, but sweetheart, seriously, it wasn't you."

"But I do know what vibrational state of being means now. It's our different levels of vibrational consciousness. If we are feeling alone or depressed; if we have anxiety; if we're holding on to some form of guilt; or have a fear of losing our job, home or partner; if we only care for ourselves rather than other people; these are all negative, lower vibrational states of being.

"What's even more interesting is that we only attract people into our lives who have similar vibrations to us. We repel people who have higher vibrations, like how a magnet works.

"That makes sense, right? When I was depressed and suicidal, why would anyone with higher vibrations want to hang out with someone whose energy levels were so low, hovering above suicide, bringing them down?

"Fuck me, no wonder I struggled to make friends throughout my life; since I was a child, my vibrational base point was set so low it made it nearly impossible for me to move up the scale. I only attracted the wrong people. Even though I had a loving, kind heart, I was always going to be used."

I started to sob, realising what these people had done to me; they'd taken almost everything from me, drained me of all my energy. No wonder I had wanted to die, I had almost nothing left inside of me. The only thing they didn't take was my heart, and if the 29th hadn't happened, they would have taken that, too.

But then I began to have another realisation. "So, if someone has been holding onto a grudge for some time, feeling like a victim, they are, in fact, holding onto that lower vibrational state of anger: 'they did this to me!' As long as they continue holding onto that pattern, maybe even unconsciously, they will continue to experience that lower vibrational level of consciousness and, like me, find themselves in situations that resonate with that lower emotional level. With that victim level of consciousness sitting in their energy field, as I had, they will continue to attract similar vibrations—other victims, villains and heroes you expect to rescue you.

"Also, we can affect others with our own energy fields. My energy was so dense, I was so negative most of the time without realising it. No wonder I pulled everyone else down when I was at work. Who would want to work with me? And then all those women I had one-night stands with. I wasn't very nice. And I had no fucking idea how I was affecting them. I was probably actually the villain in other people's eyes. What a bloody fucking cycle."

"Knowing this makes sense—what Norman said regarding that 'energy shift' on his wedding. Firstly, like attracts like; we all used to be part of his low vibrational filler-family. But if I did have a sudden and abrupt kundalini awakening, it could have somehow reversed my energy field and all my mental health issues, rather than bringing them on as many other people have experienced. I must have gone from a vibrational state of just above zero to a million in those five torturous hours on the 29th.

"Theoretically, that means Norman and everyone else at the wedding physically felt my higher torus energy field and vibrational state of being. My lower vibrations had jumped so much, it caused a physical shift in their reality. No wonder everyone felt it; it must have been so overwhelming that they all became sensitive to their own lower vibrations, possibly bringing up some suppressed, past emotions, feelings and memories, making them feel sad and depressed. Like magnets, they were repulsed by my higher frequency.

"We were that guy from Earth Beat, the one I said I wanted to be, the one who only had joy and love in his heart." I had tried everything possible to find that guy from Earth Beat. I posted on Facebook, Instagram but just like Keyser Söze, he didn't seem to exist.

"But that still doesn't explain why he blamed us?"

"Sadly, some people are so accustomed to drama and pain, they may subconsciously choose that form of unhappiness for self-validation of their ego and to convince themselves that it is who they are.

"Drama identification will only serve them so much until they realise that their reality is actually a reflection of how they feel inside.

Their reflection will eventually tell them the truth: they created their own unhappiness through their self-identification with drama and pain. In response, they might crave even more drama to mask their original emotions and thinking, until their reflection becomes unbearable. But if we try to blame a reflection, the reflection will only blame us back. Instead, we need to learn to accept and love our reflection. We need to let go of the stories that we'd been telling ourselves and see who we truly are.

"The self-reflective title of the book I saw in that vision is about the stories we often tell about how we see ourselves—as the villain, the victim, the hero, or all three. But more than that, it's about confronting our truest reflection. Like I did on the 29th.

"We have to be the change, and change from within. To heal this world, one person at a time, starts within, and then family. Or that vision of grey Earth will come true."

I still had no idea where all this information was coming from. I was surprised I could hear myself think with these high-pitched frequencies that were all around me. K just sat there in pure disbelief. I never saw K drink a cup of tea without looking before; she just reached out for her cup, took a big gulp and placed it back down on the arm of the sofa, at the same time fixated on me. She didn't blink once or move her head.

"But that doesn't explain why we get on so well with Derek and Lynn for over five years, if like attracts like. There must be a flaw in your theory; they have a very happy marriage."

"Ok, let's forget Derek and Lynn for a second, maybe they are the exception. But if I did write a book about my life, would that not resonate with everyone? Maybe change how we treat one another? Give people an insight into why they feel the way they do and how they could change their vibrational base point? You know me best; I know it all sounds crazy. I mean seriously, how can I write a book, being severely dyslexic? But what if I did, even if it took me ten years? What do you think?"

K was in tears.

"You ok? What's wrong? What's happening? Tell me that you're ok?"

K could barely speak, and her emotions were all over the place. "I think, I think, I think...I am healed? I don't feel any pain, even now touching myself, but something else is happening to my uterus and ovaries. I can't describe it, apart from the fact that I have a substantial electrical tingling sensation all over my reproductive system. I'm vibrating too. And it feels like someone is vacuuming all the years of dust that I have been collecting from inside of me."

I placed my left hand back on her groin and checked to see if I could detect the black shadow. All of a sudden, K started having body spasms and tremors. I thought she was having an epileptic fit. I grabbed my phone and started to dial 111. But she reassured me that she was ok. "Something is happening down there; let's just see what happens," she was so calm, with happy tears streaming down her face.

My own body was vibrating with such intensity, very similar to a ripple sensation. Something was radiating out from my body; this was a completely new sensation. We both just sat in silence for the rest of the day. We kept looking at each other and shaking our heads, smiling and trying to get our heads around what the actual fuck was going on.

Then I noticed something very strange: K's universal abacus had changed. One of her large red spheres had moved from the middle perspective grid and vanishing point to the last one. I triple checked with my original drawing, and I was right, it had moved! But not just that K had more medium red spheres as well on the last perspective grid and vanishing point, she had an additional twenty more than before. I had been checking K's universal abacus every day, trying to work out what I was seeing. And today was the first time it had changed.

It was also the first time K had pain-free sex in eleven years. I went into the office on Monday morning with such a bounce in my step, I felt like I was eighteen years old again. I was so fucking high on life, I just needed to tell someone, anyone, shout it out to the world. "I HAD SEX WITH MY WIFE."

K being healed was ignored by Derek and Lynn; they did not care in the slightest and dismissed everything I said. I was starting to get pissed off with them both. I had never lied to them, and I wasn't lying now, but they dismissed what I was saying so quickly. They'd seen me at my worst, and now I was happy. And K had pain-free sex for the first time that weekend, when they knew we had no sex life due to her condition. They couldn't comprehend the dramatic change that had happened to me; all I wanted to do was talk about what happened over the weekend. (You have just read this section of the book and it's insane, right?)

I had no understanding of what was happening to me, I just needed reassurance that I wasn't going fucking crazy. I went home shortly after arriving, completely deflated; I wasn't expecting that reaction from them at all. I couldn't get over the fact that they didn't even care. I didn't get it; I was no longer depressed, K had no pain, and they weren't happy?! I had no one to talk to about what was happening to me.

***

Six weeks later, K and I went round to Derek's house so we could celebrate K's birthday. It was the first time I had seen Derek since that Monday morning. I hardly left the house. The world to me looked so different now, nothing made any sense to me anymore. I could see waves of energy or consciousness all around me; trees, rocks, plants, objects, sideboards and even people were all vibrating and shimmering as if there was a hidden world within a world. All I did was Google, Google and Google. I needed answers to what I was experiencing, so I could present to them both evidence that I wasn't going crazy. I had a feeling that we were drifting away from one another. This was one of the symptoms of a spiritual awakening, but I was desperate to keep them as my friends.

One of K's presents was a beautiful purple dreamcatcher. Lynn said that their children had made it for her, and K was over the moon; she loved dreamcatchers. The moment Lynn said her children made it, a strange sensation came over me, almost like Spiderman's spider-sense, and I knew straight away that Lynn had just lied to us both; I also sensed an energy shift in the room.

I looked at Derek, as he oddly looked towards his wife after the "children made it" comment. He knew she had just lied; I could also sense Derek's energy shift. Derek agreed with Lynn that his children had made the dreamcatcher. What the fuck! Our closest friends had just lied to us. They made out that their children were creative and talented so that they could make themselves feel better. Wow, where did that come from?

Throughout the entire night, I kept trying to explain what had happened to me and my positive change towards life. Derek didn't utter a word; he just kept on looking towards Lynn. "We don't believe you. There's no such thing as a spiritual awakening, and there is no way you can cure depression. Everyone has a voice in their head. What drugs have you been taking?" and they both laughed.

"I am not sure why you're laughing. I don't really get it. I'm not depressed, and I have no more suicidal thoughts. It's all gone, along with the voice in my head." Again, Derek looked towards Lynn.

"We don't believe you, so there's no point in talking about this anymore. It's all in your head. I think you're delusional and deranged, and you sound like a crazy person. You can't go from being depressed and suicidal, and then all of a sudden, you're healed, with no voice in your head. We don't want to talk about this anymore and we would appreciate if you didn't talk about this in the office either. Derek has a lot going on."

"No seriously, I am not depressed anymore and what happened to me was real. It actually happened." I looked towards K.

"Cornelius is telling you the truth. You have known him for five years, and he's never lied to you, and he's not lying now."

"We don't believe you, it's all in your head. There is no such thing as having no inner voice. How can you not have an inner voice? You're making it all up. The mind is so powerful; it's tricked you into being happy, and you now believe that you have no inner voice anymore." Lynn kept making me feel that I was an idiot, as if I was talking bollocks and that she knew more than me. Yet it was something I was experiencing right at this moment in time: I was going to ask them if they could hear the frequencies, but I knew they would say that am losing my shit.

"You have to stop saying you have healed your depression. No one can heal depression; you're going to look stupid if you keep going along with all of this. Look, we are happy that you're happy, but we don't believe you. We don't believe in spiritual awakenings, and we don't want to talk about this anymore. This is your journey, not ours; we can't get on board with what you're going through, but we support you," Lynn said.

I stood there in disbelief, thinking *what a strange sentence. We don't want to talk about it. We can't get on board. But we support you? Well, how is this going to work then? That makes no sense whatsoever.*

Derek looked conflicted. Only five minutes ago, he had agreed to let me try and heal him of his urinary tract infection. He was already laying down on the floor. But Lynn kept insisting that there was no way I could heal him.

"It's true," K explained, "Cornelius has no more depression or suicidal thoughts, and he healed my vulvodynia; I can have pain-free sex, and we can have children."

Lynn said one word, in the driest tone possible: "Amazing."

No hug, no reaction, no nothing. Our closest friends have always known that we couldn't have sex, never mind children, and now that we could, all we got was one word, 'amazing.'

I was fucking done; this friendship was a joke. I grabbed our stuff and drove home; we were mortified. Who were these people? Did we misjudge these two as well? Was my theory correct after all? We only just looked after their children, surely that meant something? Or was it just that they needed someone to look after their children while they went on holiday? I was so upset; they turned out to be no better than our friendship with Norman.

I even used my contacts in the building industry to build them a brand-new guest bedroom, all at my personal expense. I wanted to show them how much they meant to me and that I was lucky to have friends like them. I even told Derek and Lynn what Norman said regarding the $650 I lent him and his text message. And can you believe this? The following day, they all became Facebook friends. They had only just met him at Splore. Piss-fucking poor, these guys were supposed to have our backs, but in reality, they only looked after themselves. I just wanted all my stuff out of the office; I wanted nothing more to do with these guys. What do you have to do to make genuine friends in this world?

They both took me back to my childhood, when if I had told anyone what had happened to me, no one would believe me. And they just did the same fucking thing to me at the age of forty-five.

The following morning, I woke up hearing more high-pitched frequencies. I kept replaying the events of last night. I couldn't get my head around the fact that they didn't believe me. Derek had witnessed me having a mental and physical breakdown, to the point that he was so disturbed at what he saw that he had to leave the room. Poor K had frantically tried to calm me down on her own to stop me from smashing my head against my desk or putting it through a computer. At the same time, I had been hitting the side of my head with my hands, begging for the voice to stop talking to me. I had been in full self-destruct mode.

Lynn reminded me of Agent Smith from *The Matrix* movies, where he had the ability to enter anybody at any time when the matrix was threatened by Neo. It felt like Agent Smith popped up and replaced the person I thought was a close friend, every time we threatened her reality and beliefs.

The more I thought about this scenario, the more I was starting to realise that most people only want to believe what they already know. Lynn didn't once consider the possibility that I was telling the truth. In her reality, she had already convinced herself that there was no such thing as a spiritual awakening (or whatever you call what happened to me) and that I still had depression and an inner voice.

Lynn also labelled me as a liar, crazy, stupid, deranged and full of shit when it came down to me healing K. This was Agent Lynn, reinforcing her way of thinking, keeping me locked into her beliefs. Which meant my theory was correct.

Also, I could sense their energy and knew that Derek and Lynn had lower vibrations. I had always thought they were both so happy. *Wow, no wonder Agent Lynn showed up last night. No wonder she was so negative and dismissive about my state of being; it's all in the stories we tell ourselves. Fuck me; they were both happy when we were struggling in our marriage.* It gave them a way of justifying and comparing their marriage to ours: 'See honey bear, our marriage in comparison with K's and Cornelius's isn't that bad after all. We don't have any mental health issues, we are not $300k in debt, we both have jobs with regular income, we have three beautiful, smart, creative children, we can have sex whenever we want, blah, blah fucking blah.'

My newly expanded awareness and Spidey-sense was an incredible way of observing reality. I realised why Derek had desperately wanted me to sign up for his CrossFit. His ego created identity labels so he could fit in, belong and be part of a community and tribe, and he wanted me to join to reinforce the label.

Every day, Derek mentioned how amazing everyone was at CrossFit and how much fun I would have. I lost count of how many times I had told him that I hated going to the gym. He always responded with, "You will love it, it's why I go ten times a week." Derek was trying to justify his self-created CrossFit label and the need to be part of something bigger.

In fact, I didn't need to go to CrossFit or the gym. Everything about my health and the way I felt was improving every day at an astonishing rate. I no longer felt my body was rotten inside. I wasn't bleeding from my rectum anymore and my lump in my testicles had completely disappeared. I felt that something I'd been carrying all my life had been lifted. My bones no longer felt heavy; in fact I wasn't even sure I had bones. I felt that light, my aches and pains were all gone. My eyes were vibrant, bright and sparkling. I even noticed a dark blue circle around my iris known as the limbal ring, which wasn't there before. The most noticeable change was my semen. Instead of a lumpy wallpaper paste consistency, I had silky smooth, healthier semen and lots of it, with a powerful ejaculation.

And perhaps even more important than my physical health was that I was noticing new and steady feelings of calm, bliss, peace, and contentment for the first time. I didn't know the names of what I was feeling at first. It took me a while to understand what they were, because I had never really felt them before. Until my awakening, I could never have imagined I could ever feel this happy.

Later that evening, K broke down in my arms. She admitted to me that from the time I'd first told her of my intended suicide until the 29th, every day of her life had been filled with fear and dread. Each morning she'd hated kissing me on the forehead before she left for work or to volunteer at the cat sanctuary, not knowing whether it would be the last time she'd see me alive. And each time I didn't respond right away to her texts, she wasn't sure if it was because I was already dead. And the worst was her 30-minute drive home on the motorway and the five minutes when she would sit in her car on the driveway, building the courage to open the garage door, not knowing what she would find. I never knew she was going through this; I had been so depressed I was totally unaware of the amount of suffering she was going through in her life. My depression had been like a virus, an invisible illness that grew to not only overwhelm me but my wife as well.

Now that I no longer had suicidal thoughts, we both had a real chance for a life of happiness together.

***

On the 11th of September at 3:33 am, I had an epiphany: I realised that I had been playing the largest interactive, real-time, fully submerged virtual reality role-playing game in the world. Seven continents, one hundred and ninety-five countries, four-thousand-four-hundred and sixteen cities. Eight billion players and one planet.

For nearly forty-five years, no one had told me I had been playing in a game called Survivor-Planet Earth: Outlast, Outwit, and Outplay. But I had. As far as I knew it was compulsory.

Since Level Seven, I didn't know I was in the game but was lost in it anyway, trying to understand how things worked, while at the same time navigating around the gaming environment, trying to find my tribe and build my alliances; collecting hidden immunity idols and competing in individual challenges for rewards. Hoping I wouldn't be voted out during tribal councils, and that I would make it to the merge and avoid being blindsided. I only realised it was a game after I had reached Level Forty-five.

This is my view of my experience playing the first forty-five levels of Survivor-Planet Earth, where most people play in the drama triangle of victim, villain, hero, or all three. During my forty-five levels of playing Survivor, I belonged to hundreds of tribes, built over a thousand alliances, dropped more buffs than I can remember, collected idols, rewards and enjoyed many experiences, some good and some not so good. I was used as a goat, always the first to be voted out and never once saw a blindside coming until it was too late. I am still trying to figure out how this game works in an ever-changing, open-world gaming environment. But I think if we all played by these four simple rules, we would all be winners:

1. In a world where you can be anything, be nice.
2. You can ask for help at any time during the game.
3. Enjoy your gaming experience and the open-world environment.
4. Don't get lost in your own game.

- h and you only have one life to play with.

Levels One through Seven. Welcome to Survivor-Planet Earth.
These first levels of the game are all about learning the essential tools, skills, and becoming familiarised with our open-world environment before moving onto the next fourteen levels of the game.

In these levels, it's about understanding the rules in play and developing our social game, including collecting idols and rewards.

While I tried to play by the six rules I mentioned, I later realised that a lot of players had created their own rules, depending on the type of gaming experience that they wanted to have. So be wary of whatever rules and gaming experience you create; they always reflect back on you.

Collecting advantages, idols and rewards and enjoying your gaming experiences is what keeps you wanting to carry on playing this game.

There are three main types of strategies:

Outwit. You master the rules to strategically to get the rewards.

Outlast. You earn special rewards given to you by others.

Outplay. You earn rewards by completing specific challenges, side games and inner quests. This might also be the most time consuming of all the strategies.

You interact with other players during your entire game. Many people believe they can only choose from the roles of Victim, Villain, or Hero and switch between them as they play. How you play your game affects other players; it can make the difference between some players hating or loving their own gaming experience.

These fourteen levels are some of the most creative, challenging, interactive and imaginative levels of Survivor-Planet Earth. They are all about developing personality, social identity, behaviour, communication, observation, discovery, and choosing the right tribes to win tribal immunity, while at the same time trying to forge alliances.

During these levels, you might have to go to tribal council more than once to fight and argue your case, so you can carry on in your gaming experience and avoid being sent to Exile Island. However, these levels do not need to define how you play your entire game, and you can change your strategy any time you want.

Levels Twenty-one through Thirty-five. Island of the idols. Congratulations, you have made it to the merge.

This is where the game really started to get interesting.

These levels are all about learning to play your individual game. Do you win individual immunities? Or do you carry on playing the social game and hope you're not being used as a goat along the way?

Winning individual immunities has its advantages and disadvantages during these levels. On the one hand, you're potentially saving yourself from being voted out of your tribe during tribal councils, thus keeping you in the game long enough for you to carry on enjoying that particular part of the game. But sooner or later, you will have to give up the immunity idol, and then you could get voted off.

Or you can play the social game. I noticed that the social game players would do anything and everything to carry on enjoying their gaming experiences. They had no issues with flip-flopping from one alliance to another, contradicting and bitching about tribe members. If they saw an opportunity to stay in their game longer, they would take it, even if it meant breaking promises of alliances to go all the way to the end.

I realised, after the fact, that during these levels my alliances had formed other alliances without me, and that they were also playing their own individual games. I played many levels believing in alliances that were never real.

While you're playing these fourteen levels, you're also playing for fundamental rewards to customise your appearance. The ability to unlock multiple characteristics and access additional hidden knowledge about your tribe members and alliances, to use later in your game if needed. Not to mention hidden immunity idols. Finding hidden immunity idols can let you back into particular parts of your game. A second chance, so to speak. Some players can also find idol nullifiers and use them during tribal council to render your immunity idol powerless, resulting in you still being voted off by your tribe. Be wary of finding fake idols; whoever made them are also playing the game.

Or you can drop your buffs and completely switch tribes, a big, ballsy move that could eventually pay off. It's also a precarious move, due to inner tribal alliances, bonds and strongholds. It might take many years to form trust, so you may want to offer some of the players of your new tribe your immunity idols or even share some of your experiences. This is one sure-fire way to build trust, enabling you to be part of their gaming experience, even as an initiate.

Levels Thirty-five through Forty-five. Applying your social game.

This is when the game really took a turn towards the unexpected. During these levels, for better or worse, I relied heavily on my previous level experiences.

At this point everyone has fully grasped and understood how their game works, and most know what it takes to play a strong social game with a prize collection of idols, rewards and experiences in our locker.

I learned that just because you make it to the merge and have formed what you feel are strong alliances, the last thing you want is to be blindsided when you least expect it. Don't get complacent; observation and awareness are key to these difficult levels. Notice if other players continually reassure you but at the same time, you're feel unsure where you stand in your alliances. This creates uncertainties, friction and isolation. Notice how these players used to play and how they play now.

Realise that there's no real safety in the herd. Some players' social games are so well defined and developed that they can influence your tribe, alliances, and even members of other tribes to play their game for them. These game players have built alliances all over their open-world environments, using every game advantage possible to find out who's voting for who. Manipulating everyone for their own gain. These players will do anything to carry on with the gaming experience with no consequences, remorse, shame, guilt or regret. They can sit back and reap more rewards, enjoying their game experience without even lifting a finger, knowing that they have so many idols, nullifiers and game advantages, including the super immunity idol.

The super immunity idol is one of the most powerful hidden immunity idols in Survivor-Planet Earth. A player can use this idol to nullify being voted out by their tribe, so that the player with the next highest number of votes will get cast out instead. This is often the player worked behind their backs to get them voted out in the first place, wanting to be the tribe leader. Now all the tribe members who followed the backstabbing scheme have been exposed.

This is also the middle portion of Survivor; these levels are some of the most thought-provoking in our game, where we often reflect back on our past levels, gaming experiences, other players, alliances, tribes, and so-called false merges. This part is about fine-tuning our individual game, understanding the lessons we have learned, trusting our ability to make the right decision during the game. Or realise that we should have pushed ourselves a little harder during the individual challengers and puzzles. Alternatively, some players who thrive at Survivor-Planet Earth look at how they can improve their gaming experience and look at controlling more tribal council outcomes, collecting more rewards to maximize their gaming experiences.

In Survivor-Planet Earth, there is a boss at the end of every level. I found the ultimate in-game reward: by having my awakening and seeing how things actually are, I was able to blindside The Ego Boss on level forty-five, one of the hardest bosses of them all.

THE GAME CHANGER ADVANTAGE

Depending upon the experience you want, you can keep this information, or you can share it with your tribes and alliances.

Villains, Victims, and Heroes

Most of the players in the game so far—and possibly yourself included—haven't worked out who they really are. And when you don't know who you really are, you don't have an internal compass to guide you, so you land up following what others are doing. Sadly, most of the other players will be attached to their ego role and their perspectives, believing in their own story as a Victim, Villain, or Hero. Realise that every player you encounter is reflecting something back to you; every victim needs a villain, and every hero needs a victim. Villains like to team up with other villains, while heroes often believe they are the only one who able to save the victim.

If you encounter a person playing a villain, they will try to do something to you, because every villain needs a victim. And if you remain in that perspective, as I did with Dr. Jekyll, of "I can't believe they did this to me," then not only are you playing the victim role with this player, it's possible that you've been playing that same victim role with others all along. To let go of that role, you must wake up to who you really are, and let go of any player who tries to keep up that false narrative of you; it's a small price to pay to get rid of a player who is toxic and full of negativity.

Let them say what they want. If you know the truth, your life will flourish. To feel free is to let go of all that doesn't serve you. Stop replaying your stories and corrupted scenarios in your head. Remember that victims are always looking at others to blame or to rescue them, but never look within themselves. Look at your reflection and tell yourself that the answers come from within, not from the outside.

Villains enjoy alliances with other villains, so eventually they land up becoming victims as well. When this happens, they look for heroes to rescue them, just as Dr. Jekyll did with me as I tried to save her and change her multiple times. So, do not identify or feed on any other player's victim stories, else you will become someone else's story. And you will only attract other players who will also associate with your story.

Finally, if you encounter someone playing the game as a hero, pay attention and notice when they become the villain or victim. When I was playing the hero, Dr. Jekyll blamed me for her sleeping with other men, making me the villain. And when she blamed me for that and not being able to hold onto a job, I became the victim. In the drama triangle, heroes always take the blame whenever things go wrong. They never hold the villains accountable for their actions, and so enable them to continue hurting others.

Alliances

Learn to choose your alliances wisely. Look for authentic relationships, not situational alliances, and let go of the players who bring you down.

Be prepared. When a toxic game player can no longer control you, they will try to pull you back into their game. That player will try to manipulate you and how other players see you, but your real alliances will see past it, as will you.

All of a sudden, another player can just wake up one morning and decide never to talk to you again, for no reason. With no explanation, they will leave you hanging, like you never meant anything to them, and they made it look so effortless. These are players in alliances that don't serve you, so let them go. Remember, they are also playing a game. As much as it may hurt at first, trust your intuition and stick with it.

Comparison and Competition

Observe yourself in game-playing situations in which you found another player attractive or you admired them, and you told yourself, *I need this person to like me. I need this person to pick me,* or even, *I'm not good enough for them/they are too good for me. I wish I were like that or like this, and I wish I had the life they have.*

When you need someone else to like you or validate you, you create a story between the two of you, with them as the hero and you as the victim. And, if they reject you, they become a villain while you remain the victim. When you put another player on a pedestal, you have built a narrative that puts them above you and of your reach, so you're unable to connect and build an alliance together. Try taking them off the pedestal and see them as another player, just like you.

The Game Loop

Do not ignore the first sign that you're not enjoying your gaming experience; this could be a glitch in your mental state. You need to take note of it.

If you want to change your gaming experience, you are going to have to change your stories and change the conditions in your open-world environment. If you're not creating anything new in your game, you will be continually brought back to your base point, which is another way to describe your loop or pattern.

If you see yourself at the same subconscious base point that you have always seen yourself, you will get the same results and be reaffirmed by your thoughts and feelings. This will keep you locked into your familiar past and your predictable future gaming experience without realising that your behaviour is on a loop and you're on autopilot.

The Social Media Mini game

Do you ever wonder why you're tired all the time? Social media is also an exchange of energy. Stop observing other players, ex-players and alliances in the game after you have been voted out at tribal councils.

Keep clearing your timeline of players who bring you negative situations and drama. Unfollow, delete, erase texts, block their numbers, and stop reconnecting with toxic players from your past just because you're lonely. One of the best gaming experiences in Survivor-Planet Earth is when you finally lose all your feelings and attachment to another player who wasn't there for you. It will be tough to accept at first, but deep down, you'll know it was the right thing to do.

Game Power-ups

Love yourself, because that's who you'll be spending the entirety of your time playing Survivor-Planet Earth with. Everything starts with how you feel about yourself, and then those feelings are reflected in your gaming environment. Remember, don't judge yourself, forgive yourself, and let go of what doesn't serve you.

Permit yourself right now: don't wait to give yourself validation or for someone else to give it to you; start giving yourself in-game validation right now. Imagine the best version of you and allow yourself permission to be just that. When you love yourself, you glow from within.

To replenish your health status, you must change your state of mind, which is connected to how you feel and play the game. Become self-aware; you can alter your emotions because you control your own thoughts. One of the quickest and most positive ways to maximise your gaming experience is to learn to let go of your thoughts and be in the present moment. This will help you catch yourself as soon as you realise you're thinking negatively and switch it to something you appreciate. Also, notice what might be draining you in your environment and in the food you eat. You can't heal in the exact same environment that you got sick in. Make choices that replenish you.

At least once a day, sit down for about ten minutes and focus on what you're grateful for in your life and focus on your strengths. The more you buy into yourself, the more you will resonate with other players, and then they will buy into you as well, creating a better gaming experience.

During Survivor-Planet Earth, if you want to experience love, give love back. If you want to experience happiness, be happy for others. If you want to experience kindness, be kind. If you wish to be treated with respect during your gaming experience, be respectful. If you want peace, encourage peace. If you don't want to be judged, don't judge back.

HIDDEN BONUS ADVANTAGE

As well as having found The Game Changer Advantage, you will also receive many individual hidden rewards and advantages throughout the next part of your game, which you can also share with your tribes and alliances.

Level forty-five onwards will now be played as Cornelius 2.0

19

YOU NEVER WALK ALONE

One of the most noticeable and distinctive changes that happened to me after the 29th was hearing these piercing high-pitched frequencies, either one at a time or many together. Just to be on the safe side, I had made an appointment to visit my local audiologist to be sure I hadn't developed tinnitus.

When I mentioned this to K, I was astounded by her response. She said that she could also hear these frequencies, but only when she was in the same room as me.

Another thing I noticed when I heard the frequencies was that when I closed my eyes, I could see a geometric pattern or a fractal similar to viewing a kaleidoscope. The lower the tone, the less complicated the patterns were. The higher the tone, the more complex they became, but I could also see them more clearly, never lasting for more than a second or two.

I am only just starting to understand the important role these frequencies play in my life and how they work. It's like Universal Consciousness is telling me to take note. So far, when I hear them, I've learned to pay close attention to my environment: to what someone is saying, or of a specific location, or to look for a particular sign or message. So far, each time I have downloaded information, performed healing, seen visions or created something beyond my known abilities.

For example, over the last fifteen years, I have wanted to quit my profession and design jewellery. I always said to myself: *Someday I'm going to quit my profession. Someday I'm going to become a jewellery designer.* But someday doesn't exist in a typical week, does it? Being depressed, I had no belief in myself, no desire, no enthusiasm, no designs and no starting point. Everything seemed to be firmly planted in the "too hard" basket; to be honest, I just couldn't be fucking arsed.

On the 26th of July, 2019 I was sitting on the beach, observing the world from this unique perspective and in total awe of the beauty that I was seeing. From out of nowhere, I started hearing multiple high-pitched frequencies all around me. They were so loud I started to wince. Then all of a sudden, I started sketching in my notebook; I was unable to stop. I had no idea what was happening or what I was sketching.

Within an hour, I had designed five pieces of jewellery. I knew my style, materials, and I even knew how to make them. What was more astonishing was I didn't have to think about any of the designs; I just saw them in my head, as if I had already made them.

Every time I hear that same frequency, I automatically start sketching another piece of jewellery. At present, I have a collection of ten so far. I never go anywhere now without my dinosaur pencil case and my notebooks.

A few months later, on the 24th of September at 1:30 am, I was sitting in the living room having a cuppa. I was unable to sleep. My body clock was so out of sync; or perhaps it was syncing up?

I thought to myself, *I wonder what Mum would say about what is happening to me?* Then all of a sudden, I started hearing multiple frequencies, as if someone was trying to tune into a radio station, until it finally became one single frequency. Then I heard something that I hadn't heard in nearly three years. I heard my mum's northern Muttly laugh.

I started laughing at myself. *Fuck me Cornelius, you're going crazy*, and I shook my head in disbelief. I glanced over at Mum's shrine of dead flowers located on top of the bookcase. Every year on her birthday, Mother's Day, the day she passed away, and the day she was laid to rest, I had bought her flowers. I had been unable to throw any of them out; they just sat in dusty vases. An unhealthy, depressing reminder that I was alone in this world and without the love of my mum.

Then I heard my mum's laugh once again. *What the fuck is going on?* I could only hear Mum laughing in my left ear, so naturally, I turned to the left, and I saw my mum. Not like in the movie *The Sixth Sense* with Bruce Willis, 'I see dead people,' nothing like that. If I had, I would have completely flipped the fuck out and run to K, screaming like a little girl, jumping into bed and pulling the duvet over me.

It's tough to describe, but I saw a faint transparent image of my mum in my mind. She had her left hand on the wall and her right hand on her tummy, and she was bent over in fits of laughter. It was as if she was right there.

During this entire experience, I felt a profound connection with her. I kept asking her questions, and I thought she was answering me back, which couldn't be right. Could it?

This lasted for about an hour. The middle of my forehead was buzzing, pulsating, and I felt an energetic circular clockwise motion, similar to what I had experienced on the 29th. This frequency that I was hearing was consistent and clear.

I mentioned to K the following morning what I had seen and that I had heard my mum laughing. K didn't seem surprised at all. Which I found strange because if she'd told me something similar, I would have dismissed it hands down as impossible and fake; no one can hear people who have passed away.

With a smile on my face, I jokingly and sarcastically said, "Morning, Mum."

Then I heard the same frequency as last night. My left ear was buzzing, and I had a swirling sensation going around the outside of my ear, followed by "Morning son, you ok? I didn't scare you last night, did I?"

I looked at K like a deer in headlights, the hairs on my arms standing straight up. "I think my mum is talking to me again; she just asked if I was ok. But that can't be right, how is that possible? How can I hear my mum?" I started to freak out, unable to keep still, continually walking around the sofa and saying that I must be going mad. There was no way I could hear my Mum.

"Yes son, you can definitely hear me."

What the fuck. "K, Mum just said 'yes son, you can definitely hear me.' What is happening to me? How can I hear my mum? How is that possible? You don't believe in all this mumbo jumbo shit, do you? You can't hear or see dead people, it's impossible. Absolutely impossible."

"Yeah I do, I have always had a strong connection with my brother."

"Brother? What brother?"

"I had another brother, his name was Christopher, but he sadly passed away at only three days old. This happened before I was born. But yeah, I have always had a connection with him. I always thought if he were alive today, we would be best friends, like the brother I have always wanted." I didn't know this about K; I was a little taken aback by her answer. I asked her why she never mentioned this to me before, and her response was: "You don't believe in this sort of stuff, so again what's the point in talking about it?"

Then I heard Mum say "Cornelius, text your brother and ask about your sister; she isn't well. Your sister won't text back, so you need to text him and ask. You can help her, as you did with K." *What the fuck! It's been nearly three years since Mum passed away and the first thing she mentions is to text my brother regarding my sister? That can't be right, where are our lotto numbers?* For the next week, I couldn't get my head around how I could hear and see my mum. I started to Google and watch documentaries and TV shows regarding clairvoyance and clairaudience.

From all my research, what I found interesting was how loose, flexible and inconsistent the clairvoyance process was for others. For example: "I am picking up a son who has passed over, or the friend of a son who has passed over. Maybe your neighbour's cousin's best friend's brother, who went to school with a Mary? Who then bought a coffee from a man called Karl, whose son has just passed over. I am getting a Simon? Sean? Stefan? Steve? Scott? Bulla? Bulla, anyone? Bulla, anyone? Someone who went to school or teachers at a school, maybe even volunteers at a school? He has short brown, blonde, black, long, curly, straight hair. Anymore Bulla?" as the clairvoyant addresses the audience.

The wider you throw your net out, the greater your chance of catching a Ferris Bulla. I am not saying this is all bullshit, but from my experience, I never did any of that. I just asked a direct question and I got a straightforward answer back. So K and I decided to try connecting with K's brother Christopher using the same direct method.

On the 1ˢᵗ of October, K and I tentatively sat on the sofa, waiting to see what would happen. I was thinking, *This is nuts.* Then I heard multiple high-pitched frequencies, again as if someone were tuning into a radio station. I then heard a voice, but this time from my right ear, with the exact same energy sensation as when I heard Mum.

"Hi Cornelius, I'm K's brother, Christopher. Just to let you know, I am standing behind my beautiful sister." Again, I was a deer in headlights.

I mouthed to K, 'your brother is here'.

"How can you connect with my brother if he passed away at three days old? Don't they stay that same age?"

"I don't know why you're asking me; this is fucking bonkers. Anyway, he's standing right behind you. I will describe him to you." I paused. I looked at K then back towards her brother.

"What's wrong, you look confused. You ok, sweetheart?" K was shifting from side to side. She kept looking over her shoulder and then back towards me.

"I am not sure how to say this, but your brother looks both male and female? He's six-foot-one with a slender toned figure, long straight brown hair down to his shoulders, amazing dark eyes, and a stunning smile." K's eyes lit up; she had the biggest smile on her face.

"Finally, I know now why I am attracted to androgynous people. It's because my brother is one. OMG that makes total sense."

"A what now? What's an androgynous person?" I had never heard of this term before.

"An androgynous person is partly male and partly female in appearance, having the physical characteristics of both sexes."

"Wait, what do you mean you're attracted to androgynous people? You have never said this to me before. Who have I married?" We both cracked up laughing.

K said, "Even though his name is Christopher, can you ask him if it's ok for me to call him Bro-bro?"

All of a sudden, I started to cry. For some reason, I could feel Christopher's emotions and I could see him crying with happiness as he nodded in agreement to being called Bro-bro. *How is that possible how can I feel what he feels? This is insane.*

"Bro-bro wants you to know that he never left your side since the moment you were born. And he was holding your hand for the first three months when you were born prematurely, lying in an incubator in Fiji. He was giving you all his love and energy.

"When you were fifteen, he was the one who called for help, and he directed you to a specific book while you were living in Sydney. When you wrote down your ten attributes and asked the universe to find someone, he was the one who showed you me." *Fuck, I just had a Stan moment.* I immediately stood up and freaked the fuck out. But K just sat there, tears running down her face. "Sweetheart, you ok? Does any of that make sense to you?"

"Everything you have just said is true."

"He also wants you to know that you're right regarding being best friends and that he is very happy where he is, so please don't be sad. He also says you asked for an adventure, and you're going to get one, and that he loves you very much. K, are you ok? Have I upset you in any way? I am so sorry, I'm not sure if I am doing this right, I'm only relaying what Bro-bro is saying. Regarding the question about his age, Bro-bro is showing me the best version of himself, and he wants you to know that he's twenty-nine years old and he's so excited to finally connect and meet you. He is also clapping his hands with the biggest smile on his face. This is how he wants you to remember him by, not as a three-day-old baby."

K gave me a massive hug. "OMG, I am connected with my brother and he's always been with me? He's always had my back?" K completely broke down; she didn't realise that she had been holding onto so much grief, sadness, pain and guilt for her brother and the moment they reconnected, it all left. Something profoundly changed in my wife in a matter of seconds. I felt a phenomenal energy shift in our living room.

I quickly checked her astral abacus, and another large red sphere had moved.

"Christopher, what just happened? Why did K's red spheres move again?"

"The perspective grids represent K's past, present and future. The red spheres represent life events, and their size reflects the level of significance. When new red spheres appear, they represent brand new opportunities. When they move from one perspective grid to another, or they disappear entirely, this represents significant life changes.

"You have been given a gift to change people's subconscious beliefs that are self-limiting and self-sabotaging, and for them to let go of their egoic-reality way of thinking and living. It returns a person to their natural, higher vibrational state of being. The process is called 'Unshackling, completing your past and letting go.'

"At higher vibrations, you no longer judge or criticize yourself or others, and your behaviours are not driven by the desire for other's approval or validation.

"At low vibrations you are slaves to your egos and use them in ways that are harmful to yourself and others. You spend your thoughts in judgement, criticism, guilt, and blame. You have a desperate need to be always right and never wrong. These needs are driven by your subconscious beliefs about who you have been told you are, and how you have been told to live. Unshackling helps people raise their frequency so that they have self-acceptance, acceptance of others, true intimacy, the ability to sooth and encourage oneself, and, ultimately, unconditional love."

Fuck me. Ego creates reality based on who we think we are, and who we think we're not. We don't create reality. When we believe in the illusion of who we've been told we are, and who we've been told we are not, the ego goes, 'you need to get this job, you need to get this money, you need to treat these people like this and those people like that, so you can get what you want, regardless of who you hurt in that process, I desire this car, I need that house, and I want that person' These are all used to create an egoic identity based on the overall belief that happiness comes from things outside of us. Your ego is what can keep you locked away in an endless cycle of chatter or external distractions, separating you from the present moment. You can then start to believe that if you surround yourself with materialistic objects and get social validation, then those things define who you are.

When we identify with our egoic-reality, we then start to give these stories prominence and end up actually resisting the truth; we slowly begin to activate our lower vibrational state compared with our natural vibrational state. This is the cause of disease, illness and mental health issues.

When we are constantly being reinforced that our egoic-reality is 'who you are', at some point we enter into a world of low vibration forgetfulness in order to come to terms with reality. And when this happens, if you begin to question your egoic identity, you can activate the process of remembering *who you really are*, and raise your vibration. Some people call this a spiritual awakening.

The truth of who we are is that we are eternal divine spiritual beings having a temporary human experience. Our bodies may die, but *who we really are* is eternal Consciousness.

It took me another month to let everything sink in, but I was now talking to Mum and Christopher daily. They were advising me on how to write this book, the style, which relatable life stories to include and their associated messages. I kept hearing so many different frequencies that I had started noticing a pattern. And based on the advice of my mum and Christopher, I placed a post on my local community group Facebook page looking for anyone open-minded and willing to try alternative healing.

I had gotten over thirty enquires, so I started to book two people per day, one person in the morning and one person in the afternoon. I wanted to know if healing K was a one-off miracle or if I could do this for other people as Mum mentioned. I made a makeshift healing table in the spare room. I didn't know how much to charge, so I never did; I wasn't sure I could even do this, so taking money off people just didn't feel right.

I would always start off a healing session by running my left hand about twelve inches over the person's body, from head to toe a few times, stopping every time I felt an energy shift or what I now call energy disturbances or incoherent frequencies. I would stop and ask them about that part of their body.

I was always taken aback when they confirmed what I was saying. Once I placed both hands on that body part, I would then hear multiple high-pitched frequencies and either a two- or three-digit number. My body would begin to vibrate, which somehow generated an x-ray type image in my mind. This allowed me to locate more precisely the direct source of that energy disturbance, enabling me to start the process of energy transference.

All thirty people were healed of what they came and saw me for.

***

I was still confused about what Christopher said to me regarding unshackling; I wasn't sure how it worked or what I need to do. Until one morning, when I saw a young man who didn't want healing. Instead, he wanted to understand why he couldn't voice his opinions in his working environment, why he was always overlooked during promotions, and why he struggled to keep a girlfriend for more than a few months. I heard new frequencies, which I had never heard before, three in my left ear, and six in my right hear.

Instantly I was watching a transparent movie in my mind, and I relayed what I saw. "The reason you don't think anyone listens to you at work and why you're struggling in relationships is that when you were seven years old, you came home from school one day all happy and excited; you had just received a certificate for a drawing you did. You were so eager to show off your achievements to your parents, but they didn't want to know at the time. They kept saying 'Be quiet, your dad and I are talking, this is an adult conversation.'

"You kept saying, 'Mum, Mum, please have a look at what I got from school.' Your dad also said to you, 'Be quiet, adults are talking. Go out and play and stop bothering us, we will call you in when dinner is ready. At the age of seven, you slowly started to convince yourself that no one wanted to hear what you had to say anymore; it's why you never voice your opinions at work, and why everyone takes all your credit. You thought that if your parents didn't want to hear about your day, then no one would. This is the story you have been telling yourself throughout your entire life, validating that this is who you are, a shy and introverted person who struggles to make friends. But in reality, this is what happened:

"The day you came home from school, your parents were talking about getting divorced. Your dad was having an affair, and their marriage was on the rocks. They were so preoccupied with trying to save their marriage, they didn't realise that they had been pushing you to one side and ignoring you. When you were eight years old, your parents were arguing more than ever. Your dad was hardly home, and when he was, all you wanted was his attention. You didn't care what type of attention you got, good or bad, you just needed his attention. So you started leaving all your shit all over the place, trying to get his attention, which drove your mum up the wall. Do you remember any of this at all?"

"Now that you mention it, I do. Why couldn't I remember it before?" He looked shocked.

"I don't know, to be honest. This is one of the reasons you have been single for four years, and why your last long-term girlfriend left you, because you were so untidy that it drove her crazy. But in fact, all you were looking for was her attention after coming home from work. But you struggled to express it any other way. Unfortunately, your girlfriend was unable to see it from your perspective. She also wanted you to take control of the relationship and start being more decisive regarding which restaurants and bars you wanted to go to, including holiday destinations. It's why you stayed in most nights; you were too indecisive, which you were unaware of doing. Correct?"

"That's exactly what happened."

"This is because you dislike arguments so much; you didn't want to repeat your home environment. So you went with the non-argumentative approach. 'You decide, sweetheart, I'm easy.' But in reality, this is what happened:

"At the age of twelve, your girlfriend was looking after her mum and her younger brothers, who were six and nine at the time. Her mum was undergoing chemotherapy for Stage 3 lung cancer. Her dad left her to be responsible for everyone and everything. She had to make all the adult decisions. All she wanted was for you to be the decision-maker, and to be acknowledged for all the hard work and effort, making sure your home was running smoothly and that dinner was always on the table, while you chose to stay behind working late at nights on your marketing strategies." He looked so dumbfounded.

"That's so accurate, it's exactly what I've been doing. I've been replaying the same patterns without even realising I'm doing it. I had no idea that my girlfriend was feeling like that. I knew she had to look after her mum during her cancer treatment after her dad left them. But it never occurred to me the responsibilities that were forced on her at such a young age and how much she had to cope with. I feel terrible now; I should have made more of an effort in my relationship, and I shouldn't have taken her for granted. To be honest, I only put sixty percent into our relationship; the other forty percent I just couldn't be arsed, because she couldn't be arsed either. So we became stagnant." I could see him fighting back the tears.

"Firstly, we need to forgive ourselves. Forgiveness is about letting go of the hold our stories have over us; we judge ourselves the hardest. We continually beat ourselves up for something that happened in our past, replaying the same scenario in our heads over and over again, thinking that we could have done something different." I told him the story of when I got beaten up on the train, and that no one helped me. I often wonder if those people replay the same scenario or if something similar has happened to them?

"Forgive as much as possible. Forgiveness is such a powerful practice. Forgiveness is understanding that everybody will always make decisions based upon their level of rationalisation. When you forgive, you will let go of all lower vibrational emotions. You need to let go of any victimisation and thinking of 'this always happens to me.'

"From an individual perspective, you could say that if somebody did something awful to you, then this terrible thing that they did came from their own thought process. It means that you may not understand their rationale from your perspective, but that person has rationalised it from their perspective.

"For example: one night, someone out of their own powerlessness and in a lower vibrational state decided to rob you while you were out walking your dog. One perspective is that they did something to you that was horrifying and scary. And if you attach the label of victimisation and 'that they did this to me', you will always identify yourself with being the victim and the need to hold onto it. Similar to why you always get overlooked for promotions at work, you're acting like you're the victim, blaming everyone else, taking it all out on your co-workers and your girlfriend.

"In return, those people will also take it out on their co-workers and respected partners and families, creating a vicious cycle. When in reality, this is what happened: you have wanted to leave your job for nearly a year, and you became bored, uninspired, and cynical. This is why you come home late from work, which is actually the bar below your office, but you never told your girlfriend that. Your mind was always elsewhere, detached from the present moment and from your relationship. Correct?"

"Yes, again you're bang-on. I've been lying to myself for so long, I created a new me. And if I am honest, I don't even like that version of me."

"So the emotions and feelings which you hold onto can create a new 'this is who I am' program unless you forgive. Otherwise, you will continue developing the new victimisation program.

"Whatever you are feeling, you will be attracting more of it; vibrationally, like attracts like. So you will always be fearful of walking your dog at night again. Please don't drive yourself crazy trying to understand why something like this happened to you. You will never understand, so don't try to rationalise it. Forgive and accept that it happened, but don't condone it and don't reframe it into positivity. Does this make any sense?"

He leaned forward in my direction and gave me a massive hug, and he started to sob. I also started to cry; I could feel all of his suppressed feelings, emotions, and that he felt trapped in life. *How can I feel what he's feeling?*

I was witnessing someone unshackling and completing their past right before my eyes. He left my house feeling a lot lighter than when he arrived and in a higher vibrational state of being.

Six weeks later, I caught back up with him. He had learned to forgive himself foremost, followed by other people. He had left his job for a rival consultancy and for the first time in a long time, he understood that he was the one holding himself back.

He'd also realised that driving to work was causing him stress and putting him in a lower vibrational state, even before he got to work. So he changed his living environment and he now walks to work instead. He had also disconnected from all social media and dating apps. He no longer needed social validation to make him happy; he was creating inner happiness with a direct change in his life. His energy and outlook had completely changed from the first time I met him. I was privileged to be part of this inner transformation.

20

ENERGY, VIBRATIONS AND FREQUENCY

About eight months since my awakening, I was even better at recognising the significance of what the frequencies mean. I could even detect if someone near me needed my help. I just had to locate them first. During my birthday movie marathon, my first movie started at 10:30 am, *Charlie's Angels*. I know, I know, I can hear you all moaning, *Cornelius why?* Two words: Miley Cyrus. Even though she wasn't in, I still liked the "Don't Call Me Angel" song, and I have a soft spot for her.

I was the only person in the cinema as the trailers started when I heard multiple frequencies. I looked all around me, but I couldn't see anyone. The frequency got even louder. Again, I looked around and still, no one was in the cinema. Just as the movie was about to start, I heard two people sit down about five rows behind me; then the movie began, *Ford vs Ferrari*.

What the fuck, where was Charlie's Angels? Ford vs Ferrari was my fourth birthday movie; how had I gotten this so wrong?

All the way through the movie I was thinking, *Did I get this wrong or was I always meant to be in this cinema helping the two people behind me?* But no one wants stranger danger, although for some reason, I believed this was no mistake. After the movie, I waited patiently outside for them. I thought to myself, *OMG Cornelius, what the fuck are you doing? You know this is crazy, right?* And I cracked up laughing about how idiotic this all seemed, but nothing since the 29th had made any sense. So I thought I would carry on waiting.

Eventually, the doors opened. A woman was struggling to walk while her friend supported her. I plucked up the courage and said, "This sounds crazy, but I believe we were supposed to meet. I have a feeling I can help you with your arthritis in your left knee?"

"How do you know I have arthritis in my left knee?"

"If you can spare about fifteen minutes, I will tell you a story while I look at your knee."

"You're so kind, but I have had arthritis in my knee for over fourteen years. I have seen so many people, and no one can do anything about it. I just have to live with the pain. Thank you for your kind offer, but I don't want to waste your time."

"You're not wasting my time at all. As crazy as this sounds, I think I can help you. Are you going to retire from working at the nursing home because of your knee?"

"How did you know I work at a nursing home? And that I was going to retire?" *Stranger danger, stranger danger, stranger danger*, is what she should have said. I smiled and placed both hands on either side of her knee, and then I started the process of energy transference. Instantly, she felt her body vibrating while I told her what had happened to me on the 29th.

Fifteen minutes later, I asked her to stand up to see if there was any improvement or difference. She started to cry and began hugging me and shaking my hand.

"What did you do? I don't have pain in my knee anymore, it's all gone. How did you do that?" Then she started walking up and down the cinema foyer with the biggest smile on her face.

"Thank you, thank you, thank you," followed by more hugs.

"You're welcome," and I went to watch *Jojo Rabbit,* my second movie. My body was pulsating, and I had a massive smile on my face, trying to understand what had just happened.

As soon as K arrived at the cinema to join me for my third movie, *Terminator Dark Fate,* she was blown away that I dared to approach a stranger who needed my help. But this got me thinking, why did this woman let me try to heal her when Lynn didn't believe I could heal her husband? Then I realised that out of the thirty people I'd seen via Facebook, only two people recommended me to their family or friends. Even though I was accurate in my energy readings and they'd felt massive improvements in their state of being; regardless of how amazing, positive and surreal their experience was, they still weren't prepared to let go of their egoic-reality and the belief that what happened had really happened.

I used to be one of "those people", and I know how our negative inner voice does such a good job of convincing us it's all bullshit, mystical, potions and Hogwarts, regardless of what we experienced. We are only looking for the answers that we want to hear or resonate with, regardless of how amazing we feel afterwards.

Anna was the only person who was recommended to me from the thirty people I saw, and she was worried about her husband's present state of health. She wanted reassurance that he would be ok. Instantly, I said yes. "If you can give him a call, I can see him today."

"He won't come, he's very skeptical. Is there any other way you can reassure me regarding his health?"

"Not without me seeing him, sorry." Suddenly I could hear new multiple frequencies and see an outline of a person, similar to how I had seen my mum laughing. I wasn't sure who this person was, but it turned out that I was seeing Anna's husband. I was able to visualise his energy disturbances. Stranger than that, I could also vibrationally sense his energy disturbances in my body, like it was confirming to me what I was seeing.

How is that possible? How are these two experiences related to one another when he's not even in the same room as me? How can I sensationally feel his energy disturbances in my body? That makes no sense. I took a deep breath and said, "I can see your husband itching his groin, in the location where his boxer shorts waistband is situated, and it's very red and inflamed." At the same time, I felt an energetic sensation in my groin area as well. I heard another single frequency and the word 'psoriasis', followed by the number 224.

"Your husband has psoriasis and a cracked C4 vertebra about twelve millimetres long. It's why he sometimes gets a shooting nerve pain in his neck. This happened when was twenty years old after he fell awkwardly during a rugby game. He also needs to start wearing a face mask when he chainsaws the wood for winter. Otherwise, his cough is going to get worse. If you're wondering why his right ankle is swollen, it's because when he was in the garage, he got bit by a whitetail spider in the crease of his right heel. It's why the doctor couldn't find anything, even though you told him many times to wear something on his feet. But he's stubborn and he never listens to you."

Anna started to laugh.

"He needs to start eating more vegetables and fruit. His digestive system is slightly blocked and it's why he's always bloated and gassy; he's been overindulging on red meat and takeaways at work. He is stressed, and his sleep patterns are all over the place due to him causing himself anxiety about getting all the renovations in the house completed before summer. Again, you have told him many times that there's no need to rush. He needs to start taking his fishing boat out; this is one way to get his blood pressure down. Does any of that resonate with you?"

Anna didn't say a word. I thought I had offended her, so I kept apologising and saying that I had never done this sort of reading before.

"How do you know all of this? It's impossible," shaking her head in disbelief. "I have no idea how you knew any of that, but you have just described my husband's present state of health, even down to how he cracked his vertebra and his swollen ankle. Amazing, I am speechless."

No one was more amazed than me. *How can I detect energy disturbance in people when they are not in the same room as me?* Over the next few months, I was trying to understand how I could visualise and energetically sense energy disturbances in Anna's husband, who was thirty miles away. Only to be confirmed in the exact location in my body, even down to his trapped nerve. On top of this revelation, I was still confused about how I could communicate with Mum and Christopher so easily.

***

During May through November 2019 I sent emails to 321 people all over the world who were seen as leaders or researchers in the field of consciousness, brain and mind, psychology, brain research, quantum physics and alternative healing. I was desperate to know what had happened to me on the 29th. I was looking for reassurance that I wasn't going crazy and didn't have a rare brain condition. I got twenty-seven replies back. *These leaders all talk about my condition and what to expect, but no one actually wants to talk or do any research with someone who has this condition?*

Twenty-six of the emails that I received back told me there is no such thing as not having an inner voice or pure consciousness, and that I needed to see someone who is experienced in treating schizophrenia, mental illness, and people who are disconnected from reality. *Regarding that last one, aren't we all? And these people are leaders in their field, and they don't believe it's possible themselves?* What a fascinating egoic insight this gave me.

The one person who was curious about my condition lived in San Francisco, so I phoned him up. K always said that the best way to explain my gifts was to show them exactly what I can do. I also needed confirmation. 6,600 miles was a lot further away than my previous thirty miles for Anna's husband.

The conversation went as follows. "Morning Dennis, thank you for reaching out to me. Just a heads up, I haven't done this before, so I apologise in advance, but I will be completely honest during your present state of health reading. Is that ok? You're my test subject, so to speak."

"Cornelius, I am more than happy to be your test subject. I am just fascinated to see what you can pick up. But I am very skeptical, just putting that out there too."

"Your right forearm and elbow are both inflamed, you have pulled your left chest muscle, both your knees are inflamed, your right ankle is swollen, and very badly bruised. You have a very active mind, which is causing disruptive sleep patterns, and you have a massive amount of anxiety. You have two dark, dense shadows. The first shadow is located at the tip of your tail bone. The second one is located three and a half inches inside your rectum on your right-hand side."

"How did you know all of that? I got diagnosed with prostate cancer three weeks ago, in those exact locations. No one knows this apart from my wife. Regarding the other issues, you're right. A few weeks ago, while playing tennis, I rolled my right ankle and at the same time, I pulled my chest muscle. Wow, amazing." He sounded shocked. I was in shock myself.

After a long moment of silence, I thanked Dennis, hung up the phone and paced around the sofa, trying to comprehend what had just happened.

***

I became more aware that what people were talking about online was what I was experiencing daily. But they were speaking from a theoretical point of view, rather than from personal experience. I was never going to get the answers that I needed from the internet. So I asked Christopher for his advice and his advice was just ask and you will receive. After several attempts, I learned that I just needed to ask precisely the right question in the right way using the correct terminology to exactly the right person. If I worded the question slightly incorrectly, I never got the correct answer; it had to be that precise.

I now had an unlimited amount of free data downloading to me faster than any Wi-Fi connection. I had access to my own personal universal search engine at my finger tips and the best thing about this was I didn't even need to remember a frigging password to login.

I then asked to speak to someone who wasn't my mum or Christopher, someone who would know the answers to my questions. Then a voice emerged that explained what had happened to me and more. Thanks for your amazing insights, HS.

There is no death, and linear time is an illusion. The dimension of time doesn't exist because we don't live a linear life as we are led to believe. Linear time is a construct of our minds, and, especially when it comes to 'clock time', is often used as a fear-based application to control how we live and move through life.

Instead we live a multi-dimensional energetic layered life, where past, present and future all converge at the same time in the same space, where all possibilities exist; this is the Now. And there is no such thing as death as we were never born. Everything is Consciousness. We are all distinct variations of Consciousness, and when we physically die, we continue to exist as Consciousness.

On the 29th of March 2019, I experienced a phenomenon physicists call a quantum superposition. This occurs when two or more conflicted states exist at the exact same time and in the same space at the quantum level.

The easiest way to explain a quantum superposition is if you spin a coin on its side, you can see both perspectives of the coin heads and tales simultaneously. It's only when the coin lands face up on a solid surface that it becomes one perspective of reality. But if that surface is transparent, then the view from below provides another perspective of reality. To be able to see both realities simultaneously, you would need two versions of yourself (not including a mirror as that would be called a mirrored reality). In my case I observed multiple versions of myself on the 29th while I lay in K's bed. In a way I was like the spinning coin, where I observed committing suicide in June 2019 from the perspective of the past, present and future, from the reflection of my ego and Consciousness, all in the moment of Now.

During my awakening I was given several gifts. One of those gifts include the ability to communicate directly with Consciousness. The reason for this is that I no longer have an inner voice. I am without the distraction of 60,000 to 70,000 thoughts per day. No jibber-jabber, chatter, monkey mind, "I", "myself", and no ego. I have pure consciousness, expanded awareness, a mind without a mind and constant stillness. The ability to observe reality without evaluating I only live in the Now. I am in a state where my mind is unable to be distracted or occupied by any subconscious thought I have no negativity, and no self-doubt.

As I discovered, I can easily communicate with more than Mum and Christopher. I am now communicating with over a dozen specific people within Consciousness who are providing me with a rich deep source of information. I like to call them "HS".

Another one is my future-self, which happens to be when I am fifty-five years old with short grey hair, grey beard, wearing a blue shirt, waistcoat, trilby hat and glasses. Cornelius 3.0, or "C3PO," as K likes to call him, is now showing Cornelius 2.0 (me) what I need to do in the present moment so I can catch up with that version of myself in the future, and that alternative reality. I had no idea it was even possible to communicate with Consciousness in this way. I even speak with K's future-self, and her name is Double D.

I was also given the gift of being able to see everyone and everything as energy, vibration and frequency, or as an object within Consciousness without any attachments. I can sense everyone's incoherent frequencies and energy and read the subconscious mind like you can read this book.

Because Consciousness is everything and everywhere, it doesn't matter how close or far away that person is from me. And although we have a different name for it, our subconscious is really just Consciousness, and it can tell me the optimal frequency and vibration needed to achieve coherence within that person.

And because I can access Consciousness, then I can access all its energy as well. This energy is available to me all time, confirming there is no such thing as linear time in Consciousness. My thoughts, intentions and visualisations come from a coherent frequency that brings the energy of mind, body, and soul into balance, harmony and a high vibrational state of being.

This gives me the ability to help others raise their frequency through energy transference with an unbreakable constant state of flow, focus, attention and heart-based intention.

I also experienced two additional awakenings which revealed the evolution for humanity. When Thor threw his hammer at me once again while I was healing K's vulvodynia, my second awakening opened a direct portal accessing space-time, past present and future. This was quickly followed by my third awakening which accessed the Blueprint for Consciousness, the process for the evolution of humanity. This process was explained to me, based on the following three principles.

Enlightenment of Eternal life

Consciousness is the primary function of everything. Without Consciousness the fundamental fabric of reality as we know it doesn't exist. Consciousness is what many people identify in religious terms as God. But they may have been led to believe that God is outside of them, that they are separate, and that we all are separate. The truth is that what they call God, Consciousness, is everything. You are not separate or disconnected from this world as you may have been led to believe, but rather an essential component, fully connected to everything and everyone, past, present, future. Time-space "alive" or "dead," you are Consciousness; the dualistic and materialistic ways of thinking are an illusion. The truth is Consciousness has always been, and has always been present in everything. At the most fundamental level, we have always been; there is no birth and there is no death.

The acceptance of I

Quantum physicists have suggested that at the quantum level, even electrons and photons are a conscious form of awareness that recognises space-time and consciousness. Other quantum physicists use the concept of the hologram as way to describe Consciousness in more relatable terms. We know holograms as three-dimensional images created by laser light. If we took apart a hologram, we would find that every piece, even down to the smallest particle, contains the essence of the full image within it. Likewise, we (and everything else) are the particles that make up Consciousness, while also containing Consciousness within us.

Some might say the only form of consciousness that can be truly known is from your own personal perspective. You know that you're reading this book right now and that you know you're about to turn the page. You may even know today's date and time. You know exactly where you are in relationship to yourself in this present moment.

What I have learned is that we were all born with a heart-based connection with Consciousness, and it is through our heart's intuition that we know its presence beyond our physical reality. It is from the heart, not the head, where we experience pure ecstasy, kindness, and unconditional love. You all have your very own personal version of collective Consciousness, like my HS.

I also learned that every one of us plays an integral part in how the universe works and operates. Thus it becomes critical that you have awareness of your true self, and how your thoughts, emotions and feelings have a vibrational impact on every single person living on this planet and throughout the entire universe.

Without this awareness, you will believe you are only a physical body and the ego that inhabits it. And as long as you are attached to your identity, you can never be free from the prison of your own mind. Instead, you will be a slave to your ego, unable to find fulfilment from the constant roller coaster of desires, wants and needs.

But if you have this simple awareness of reality, viewing yourself as holographic particle of a whole, or an object in universal space, then this way of thinking can help you learn to navigate through life with less resistance than ever before. The more we start to identify or experience this awareness of who we truly are, the freer we can become from the illusion and disillusion that we are separate from one another.

If you can master this simple state of conscious awareness and learn to make a deeper connection with yourself, then you can realise your potential for inner happiness, joy, peace, love and the highest form of contentment.

One with yourself

Consciousness is not limited to individual experiences. Each one of our thoughts, desires, behaviours and outcomes contributes to the continuous expansion of the universe. The future is made up of all the probabilities and outcomes based on each of our intentions. So it is our intentions that affect our future choices. We need a paradigm shift to align our intentions with Consciousness. Why is that important? Currently, much of our world of apathy has been created from our egoic intentions, influenced by our mistaken beliefs that we are separate. To align with Consciousness, we need to start moving forward with intentions made from the heart.

An unlimited amount of knowledge is accessible to us all through our heart-based connection with Consciousness. If we can accept this, if we aspire to it, we will experience it, not just individually but also through collective reality. Because through our intentions, each one of us has a vibrational impact on every other person living in our world.

By going within and returning to a state of coherence, we will naturally operate from heart-based intentions. In doing so, we then have a real chance for social coherence. A new way of working collectively, in harmony, within and across any group—family, work, colleges, company, friends, cities and even countries.

In this way, we can change the way we operate as a society and finally bring about a whole systemic way of thinking and interacting, radically reorganising into a society necessary for the wellbeing of our humanity. Rather than superficially shuffling chess pieces around for our individual outcomes and gains, we can achieve the 'Blueprint of Consciousness' and have a real chance for real change, Earth 2.0.

The only way we can change is to change within and be at "One with yourself."

Thank you, HS for another amazing insight.

***

C3PO recently showed me the following information on how to quantum manifest and create alternative realities.

Whatever we want to create, or whatever we imagine in our life—good or bad—already exists in some form because all alternative realities that we imagine already exist in a multiverse. So we have a myriad of choices to choose from when creating our reality. All our choices are based on our thoughts and intentions. So it is important to be conscious of our intentions and thoughts, as they affect our future choices and our reality.

Most people live within the reality based on their 'identification', created and reinforced by the stories they tell of themselves and others. These are built by their parents' beliefs, their friends, education, media, religion and labels; all shaped by their environment.

This way of thinking reminded me of something a man recently told me regarding his son. He'd said he wouldn't be surprised if his son ended up being addicted to drugs or in prison because 'he's a right annoying little shit.' His son is only seven years old at present. I couldn't get my head around what he had said. He'd already made his mind up regarding the outcome of his son's future. Subconsciously, he'd created an alternative reality based on his beliefs in the Now. Surely, he could change that outcome or reality in the present moment. But first, he would have to change the way he views his son and himself, for that reality to change.

If we think about this in more detail, there is a version of you that is doing exactly what you are doing in your life right now. This version reflects your current vibrational state. Then there's a version of you that is even more refined, in the perfect relationship and in the ideal job. This version reflects you at your highest vibrational state, where your inner voice will always be loving. And another version of you that is less refined, at a low vibrational state, who could be addicted to drugs or end up in prison. This low vibrational version of yourself may be constantly plagued by a negative inner voice, as I was. And, due to the negative chatter, it will be hard to see the good in others, or things in their lives to appreciate. I did not fully recognise all the times Colin and others had treated me with trust and kindness until after my awakening.

In addition to your own thoughts, the thoughts of others create additional realities as well. There is a version of you that exists in the mind of every person you have met. Those versions live in the multiverse.

So if the seven-year-old son grows up to believe in his father's current version, he will end up subconsciously choosing the reality created by his father's opinions. I lived in the alternative realities created by my father and others throughout most of my life, until I shifted to my current reality.

There are still versions of reality where I chose my heaven over K's hell and continued with my suicide. I also realised that I have lived 60 different lives, or aspects of consciousness, and in my last 46 reincarnations I committed suicide every single time until I realised I had a choice. What I have learned from Consciousness is that when you commit suicide, you come straight back to Earth at your same low frequency. There's no choosing your parents, there's no choosing where you live. And you have to relive the same pain and are faced with exactly the same decisions again and again and again, until you learn to love yourself and others. During each lifetime of low vibrational states, you not only hurt yourself, but also the other people in your life with your intentions, actions and behaviours.

Basically, your vibrational state at the end of your life determines your choice of the conditions in your next life. So even if you don't commit suicide but leave Earth in a low vibrational state, when you come back as Consciousness 'reincarnated' you will return at the same low vibration. You will have very limited choices in the conditions. You might be able to pick your parents but not your location, your career but not your relationships and vice-versa. In each lifetime you are given the same opportunities to learn to love yourself and others.

If your outgoing vibration from your prior life was high, you would have had the choice of your parents, location, career, and relationships in your current life. If you can think of those people who seem to have a high vibrational life, this is could be the reason why: they entered the world in a high vibration and have been able to maintain or even raise their vibrational levels. But it also could be that they entered their lives in a low vibration and, after learning to manage their thoughts and intentions, made their way up to a higher vibrational state.

I learned that some people may have left in a high vibrational state but chose to return to Earth in low vibrational environments, families, relationships, or careers. These souls are often referred to as 'light workers' and have come with the intention to learn about suffering first-hand, in order to better help humanity. During their lifetime they experience cruelty, selfishness and fear, and must learn forgiveness, compassion and unconditional love.

What this means is that in every lifetime, regardless of where we start, we are continuously given opportunities to learn to be kind to ourselves and others. Our actions and behaviours in today's reality determine how we experience the future as well as how others live and experience their future.

***

You are continually shifting through different alternative realities based on your beliefs, thoughts, emotions, and actions you take based on those perceptions. Your reality fundamentally has no meaning other than the meaning you give it. Attention Deficit Hyperactivity Disorder (ADHD) is an excellent example. For instance, you might be concerned that you're unable to concentrate at work or school. You have an excess amount of energy, unable to sit still for more than five minutes, struggling to focus on the task at hand. Then, after doing some initial research on the internet, you find other people with similar experiences and begin to believe you have ADHD.

Some of us believe in the system and structure so much that we give our own power away by placing a high level of credibility on our doctors when we visit them. Especially if they confirm what you already suspect, based on what you're telling them. Subconsciously, you have just created and agreed to a new reality based on an identity label about 'this is who I am,' continually being affirmed every time you tell the story, "I have ADHD." This is now how you will see yourself, and how others will see you, your mirrored reflection.

If you want to change your external reality, you need to change how you perceive it. Rather than 'this is who I am' based on what other people say, make a conscious choice to define the terms for 'this is what I want'. Every human wants to feel whole, complete, and happy, and this is our natural state. So you can disagree with your initial research and your doctor's analysis and opinion. You can change your perspective and realise that your inability to concentrate is simply due to having an excess of energy with no outlet. After all, we are energy. You simply need to rebalance that excess energy with something else, something meaningful in your life, something that comes from within that allows you to be connected to the present moment. This creates a brand-new reality for yourself, one that is whole and complete, living happily in that alternative reality and in turn, this is how others see you.

If you want to heal or change anything in your life, you have to change from within, then the outside external reality will shift; it is just a reflection of you. Every second we create a brand-new future with each choice we make.

I didn't sleep for two days straight after being given this information. *Fuck me backwards, sideways and upside down; we have the ability to heal ourselves depending on our belief system and our vibrational state. No wonder K was healed: in her alternative reality she never had vulvodynia. She believed I could help her heal. My energy raised her vibrations so much, it kick-started the healing process and shifted to her alternative reality. Our body and mind don't know the difference. We know absolutely fuck all apart from our egoic-reality way of viewing and living life.*

I was so excited to discover that we can heal one another and ourselves. Just by changing the way we think. I just needed confirmation from published research that I was on the right track and on December 27th 2019, I found two.

The first was an excellent example of the power of intention by Dr. Masaru Emoto's water crystal experiment, in which he discovered the difference between negative and positive intentions over water. Saying 'I love you' or even thinking 'I hate you' changed the crystallisation composition of the water molecules.

I was blown away with what I was learning. If intention can change water molecules and our bodies are over 70 percent water, think about the power of intention when you judge yourself or someone else. If positive thoughts, intentions, beliefs, and love can heal, then what do you think negative thoughts and intentions can do?

I then found another: Hawaiian therapist Dr. Ihaleakala Hew Len cured an entire ward of insane patients without ever meeting or visiting them. He studied and reviewed all the patients' files, and then he healed them using a powerful Hawaiian prayer called Ho'oponopono and quantum physics. Through Ho'oponopono, he meditated with the positive intention of healing himself and reflecting this to his patients.

Instead of trying to change all of his patients, Dr. Len changed the perception he had of them through meditative prayer. He knew that everything in our reality is a reflection of our own thoughts. If we believe or judge someone based on our perception, then we have just created a label, thereby creating the matching experience in our reality. Dr. Len saw them as sane, and consequently, they shifted to an alternative reality in the multiverse where they were.

Along with shifting his perception, he used one of the principles of quantum physics called quantum entanglement, sending healing energy across time-space to the patients. In a very basic sense, quantum entanglement is a way that two or more particles are linked and can send information between each other, even if separated by billions of miles. Distance has no impact on their connection.

Quantum physicists like to use this funny example: if you tickle one particle in America, another particle in New Zealand laughs at the same time. This example is known as 'Einstein's Nightmare.' He used to call it "spooky action at a distance" because, by its very nature, it defied scientific logic, reason and conventional reality. But scientists have shown that quantum particles can have properties that take on more than one value simultaneously and communicate with each other faster than the speed of light.

Quantum entanglement allowed him to heal the patients' energy levels from afar, similar to the way I use energy transference.

So, if we change our perception of people, we shift to a new alternative reality where they're not crazy or ill; in fact, they are already healed. If you consider all these things together, you have to admit, reality is truly unknowable and changeable at the same time based on our choices, and quantum healing and communicating with Consciousness is possible.

Similar to Dr. Hew, I don't have to be physically present to help others heal themselves; I can raise people's vibrations and energy remotely, as if we were face to face.

21

CONNECTING WITH CONSCIOUSNESS

The other day someone asked me how exactly I tap into Consciousness. And I'm still figuring out how all this works. I don't tap in. All I have to do is just ask, and I get it. At any moment in time, my inner voice is silent. There's nothing there. There's nobody there. There hasn't been anyone there since the 29th. But, when I need advice or an answer, or when someone asks me a question, I ask my universal search engine, HS, and it will speak to me and give me the answer to relay back to them. It's instantaneous. It doesn't feel like a man or a woman. I know it's actually collective Consciousness, which is always available. That's my Google, my go to.

But when I do want to speak to individual people, I ask that individual person a question.

So, for a good example, about three weeks ago K and I were watching a program on Gaia TV about free energy. K, as always, paused the show, turned to me and said, "Can you ask someone what is free energy?" So I asked HS for advice and HS said, *"You need to speak to a man called Tesla."*

When I asked Consciousness for Tesla, he responded, *"You can call me Nikola."*

So I said, "Hey, Nikola, how does free energy work?"

"Free energy isn't what you think it means."

"In that case, based on what I just watched, what is free energy then?"

"Free energy isn't run by any power grid. Free energy is the energy that we have inside of us to heal ourselves. That's free energy." Nikola went on to explain to me in more depth. Free energy was actually this amazing frequency of energy inside us. Everybody else thought free energy was like power, like the electricity or general power we get off power grids. People had misinterpreted free energy to mean externally harnessing energy from

this planet, rather than our inner free energy. So that's how it works. It's always there we just need to tap into it.

K, immediately asked, "When you talk to Bro-bro, Nikola, or HS why is it so easy for you and what do you hear back? Is it a voice outside of you like as in how you can hear me right now or is it something else?"

"Well, Consciousness can talk to every single one us at any time even showing us messages or guiding us to make the right choice. The issue is our brains are so scrambled it's hard to hear Consciousness. Our subconscious has the capacity to send over 20 million bits of information per second to the brain for processing, yet the conscious mind can only process about 60 bits per second.

Add that to the 60, 000 – 70,000 thoughts per day, you can imagine how hard it is to hear Consciousness. But, if like me you don't have an inner voice, then I can hear Tesla and the subconscious as clear as you're talking to me right now, but more as an inner whisper, a continual communication of thoughts that turn into sentences.

"Or as you witness every other day a term called channelling when Consciousness talks through me; this is when I hardly stop to pause for breath—it depends on how Consciousness best wants to work—can you imagine how you would separate your inner voice from Consciousness? It's very difficult."

"Yeah, it would all feel like it was coming from my own thoughts."

"Exactly. So you have that challenge. And then you also have self-doubt: 'Did I really hear that? Nah, nah, I didn't really hear that.' Self-doubt kicks in and makes you dismiss any messages coming from Consciousness.

"But because I have complete faith in my connection with Consciousness, I don't have any self-doubt. And I have zero self-doubt regarding healing, clearing and removing negative energy; increasing people's vibrations and frequencies; or accessing their past, present and future. Because I was unable to do this before the 29th, I know what I can do and couldn't do. And I can do it anywhere in the world."

"Because of your connection to Consciousness?"

"That's it. Because we're all connected. Like when I wrote about how quantum entanglement works, I didn't know anything about quantum physics before the 29th. I'd never even heard of it. But when I was downloading all this information, I was asking myself, 'What is actually happening? This doesn't make any sense...how can I be writing about aspects of quantum physics and see mathematical equations?' Or when I write universal language on my IPad, for some reason I can actually understand what I'm writing."

"But, if we all have this connection, there must be a way for the average person to learn to connect with Consciousness. Can you ask HS?"

"Hey, HS. K wants to know what are the ways people can access their own connection with Consciousness."

"You know, we can hear K. You don't have to repeat her questions out loud to us."

Everyone's a comedian.

"HS says there are several ways to connect with Consciousness: through intuition, meditation, heart-based intention, and identification of the separation of me, myself and I.

"Consciousness is always sending you messages and guidance to help you to live your best life. Essential to learning to connect with Consciousness is learning how to receive those messages. Following your intuition and your gut instincts, which come from your connection, is one of the easiest ways.

"Practicing meditation is a powerful way to quiet the mind so you are able to receive messages from Consciousness. You don't need to go into a cave and sit in a lotus position for ten hours to do meditation. It can really be any activity in which your mind is quiet, and you are focusing on, but not evaluating, something outside of yourself. With practice, meditation helps you learn the difference between your inner chatter and thoughts coming from Consciousness, which will often not be related to a subject you are thinking about and seem to come out of the blue.

"The practice of gratitude is an action of heart-based intention because it involves the vibration of the emotions of love, appreciation, compassion, and kindness. It is very similar to meditation in that it is another method for quieting your inner chatter, and a way to come into a coherent state. During the practice of gratitude, your thoughts are singularly focused and so your mind is relatively quiet. When done with pure emotion, this activity will immediately bring you into a state of coherence. Being in a relaxed state, out in nature or with loving pets are common ways to experience gratitude for things outside of yourself.

"The Blueprint for Consciousness provides the foundation for understanding the difference between me, myself, and I and learning to communicate with Consciousness. Practicing meditation or mindfulness are ways that help you develop the ability to recognise in your daily life whether a thought comes from a self-protective ego (me), myself (the you without the ego mask, your true reflection), or the universal I (Consciousness). By knowing that Consciousness is pure love, you can easily identify thoughts coming from the ego because they will have the negative vibrations of fear, anxiety, anger, shame, greed or hatred."

I realised that before the 29th I was so internally blocked off from my connection with Consciousness that if anyone had tried to say to me, 'Consciousness is within you and you're Consciousness' or 'Consciousness is always sending you signs,' I would have told them to fuck off, I am not interested in your hippy dippy cosmic bullshit, similar to my attitude at Earth Beat, if not worse.

And yet, despite how I was so completely disconnected, I could also see that Consciousness was always sending me messages throughout my entire life. Had I taken a moment to connect the dots, I would have stopped and wondered about all the times I should have died, and all the things that had to happen in order for me to meet K.

It dawned on me that I was like that paper bag that tumbled down the roadway and landed at my feet. I felt like I was that bag, moving through the world, being swept along by Consciousness this way and that, in order to ultimately land at K's feet. Everything I had to experience got me to New Zealand to meet K in order for her to show me what kindness is.

***

One of the funniest things about having access to my own universal search engine and the ability to connect with Consciousness is that my wife wakes me up in the middle of the night to get me to ask HS questions.

We would sit up in bed for hours at a time, having the most in-depth surreal conversations, I always start off with the same joke 'Saweets, can you imagine if we did this as a YouTube channel? 'Join us in bed for a live Q and A session with HS!' We just crack up every time. We never get bored of the same joke; my wife says we are simple.

So I thought I would share one of these Q and A sessions that took place on March 17th at 2:25am.

"Saweets, the other day I was talking to Steve, a work colleague, about why we are booking in so many patients who need treatment for either breast cancer or heart operations. Steve was saying those conditions are hereditary, while one of the nurses said they're caused by other things, like diet or stress. Can you ask HS what's causing all this illness and disease? I am really concerned."

I connected with HS with my usual respectful acknowledgment, "HS, how are you?" And HS responded as usual, *"I am good thank you very much for asking. How are you Cornelius?"*

"I am good, thank you."

"Cancer, or any form of pain, illness or disease is a manifestation of an incoherent frequency in the body. Many people are unaware they have an energy field which needs to be maintained. If they experience negative emotions and don't address them, the negative energetic debris remains in their energy field, adversely affecting their vibrational and emotional state of being, and in time affects their physical body."

"But some of the women I know who have breast cancer seem like lovely, caring, giving people. I can't imagine them having lots of negative emotions."

"An incoherent frequency is the result of negative emotions directed at others, the self, or both. Any time anyone experiences this emotional trauma but suppresses it, the energy gets trapped in the body. In time this can accumulate, and their frequency will become more incoherent. There are different types of trauma—stress being one of the primary ones, but also toxic people, painful past relationships, or on-going life challenges."

"Wait, stress is a trauma? I thought trauma was a major event."

"Trauma is anything that stops you from moving forward in a happy, joyful way, keeping you in a low vibration. While it can be caused by what we might normally call a traumatic event like the death of a loved one, it is anything that leads to self-sabotage or being anything less than who we really are. Overhearing someone making an offhand comment about you can create trauma. Misinterpreting someone else's innocent behaviour as negative towards you can create trauma. Not wearing the latest fashion, putting on weight, not having the latest gadgets, not looking the way mainstream media says you should look, all these can create trauma. Even thinking about another person's suffering can create trauma. A trauma is any experience that leads to judgement, criticism, guilt, or blame of self or others. Each person caught in a villain, victim, or hero drama triangle is caught in a continuous cycle of trauma. There is no scale to trauma; trauma is personal to everyone. Just because you don't understand someone's trauma doesn't mean it's not trauma. It is to them."

"But this happens all the time."

"Yes, and because people usually only associate trauma with very bad experiences, they tend to overlook the smaller, day to day events. If those smaller events go unprocessed and unresolved, they accumulate and create incoherence that then manifests in various forms, within the body or through unhealthy behaviours, depending upon which energy centre is incoherent"

"Energy centre? What the fuck is an energy centre?"

"Remember when I experienced those circular energetic sensations during my kundalini awakening, those ancient 'swirling wheels of energy' called chakras? I have been told to call them energy centres. An energy centre is the central point of an energy system located in a specific area of the body.

"Universal energy cannot be created or destroyed, only transferred. All matter is nothing but vibrating energy ($E=mc2$). The speed at which something vibrates is referred to as its frequency, which is the number of vibrations per second. You are composed of matter and matter is made of molecules; molecules come from atoms, and atoms in turn consist of protons, neutrons and electrons, particles of energy. You and everything around you is a form of energy.

"When atoms come together and bond, they begin to exchange energy. When you have enough atoms, they form a molecule; if you have enough molecules, they will form a chemical. If you take enough chemicals and assemble them in order, they will create a cell.

"If you group enough cells together, they begin to form tissues. If you have enough tissue, they will form an organ. Our bodies are comprised of multiple organs. Each organ has its own energy, vibration, frequency and information. Our organs also make up our reproductive, immune, digestive, muscular and nervous systems. Each of these systems also has its own energy, vibration, frequency and information.

"The body's energy runs through a network of one-hundred fourteen internal, interconnected energy systems. Each of these systems has an energy centre which corresponds to different ways Consciousness is expressed through our physicality. If you could see them they would look like spinning discs. Also, each energy centre has its own frequency, which, like a radio signal, carries its own intent and message because all frequencies carry information.

"We have seven main energy centres which run parallel to the spine. Each energy centre is connected to specific nervous systems and organs, and also serves as the location where we can experience the vibrations of certain emotions.

"Breast cancer, for example, is caused by energy blockage in the fourth energy centre. Located in the middle of the chest, the fourth energy centre includes the heart, lungs, breasts, and other organs in this part of the body. When a person has incoherence in this energy centre, they can experience one or more health problems in addition to breast cancer, like pneumonia, asthma, or a nervous breakdown."

"Wow, you have experienced those last three several times throughout your life."

"Yes, beginning with asthma when I was fourteen; I must have gotten it after the shadow man. My heart was shattered, but my memories were blocked so I was unable to grieve."

"Is this why some people can die of a broken heart?"

"Incoherence in the fourth centre is created by trauma which, if not dealt with, causes us to withhold or withdraw from love. In the case of a broken heart, one is unable to process grief, unable to move forward and give or receive love. That's where I was, until I met you."

"Oh, saweet."

"Now, with my gifts, I can immediately see whether someone's energy centre is coherent or not. When we are in coherence, each of the energy centres are running at their optimal frequency, fully open and clear, aligned along the spine, and spinning smoothly in a clockwise direction.

"Because energy should always be flowing, blockage in one energy centre will cause imbalance in a person's entire energy field. I can see right away which energy centre is causing the incoherence. It will be rotating counter-clockwise, spinning too fast, motionless, blocked, off centre or gyroscopic."

"Well, we don't all have your gifts, do we? But, with our energy centres being invisible, is there a way an average person can tell whether they have a blocked system?"

"You can tell by how you feel. Early on, you may start to feel stressed, anxious, or depressed. You may also have unexplained pain in the area of the energy centre, because when you're out of balance, energy that normally supplies the organs or nervous systems in a particular energy centre will instead be drawn away.

"In the case of the fourth energy centre, when energy flows freely, a person feels healthy in their body and in their relationships, loving and loved, compassionate and grounded. But when it's blocked, they will tend to have emotions of loneliness, resentment, jealousy, or other negative vibrations that arise from co-dependency, lack of healthy boundaries, or when we give ourselves away and lose our centre. Situations in which we are no longer giving out of love, but out of obligation, having an attachment to ego and expecting something in exchange."

"This is so fascinating. To think that every illness, pain, or challenging area in life is directly associated with an imbalance in one of our energy centres."

"Yes. Emotions are vibrations, and negative emotions are negative energy that causes incoherence and lower our vibrational state. But if we notice and address our negative emotions by responding with kindness to ourselves, we can keep ourselves in good health.

HS then gave me more in-depth information we can use to learn to heal ourselves and each other. The following is a download of the most common illnesses, diseases, and emotions associated with energetic blockage or imbalance for each of the seven major energy centres.

THE SEVEN ENERGY CENTRES

Our first energy centre is located at the base of our spine in the perineum and represents our sense of security and stability in the world. Through this energy centre we can experience vibrations related to sexual trauma, molestation, the fight-or-flight reflex, confidence, trust in life, and self-esteem.

When the first energy centre is coherent, we feel safe and secure with a sense of belonging; we feel we have what is needed, we have willpower, abundance; we are trusting, independent, and feel alive.

When this energy centre is out of balance, energy is drawn away from the adrenal glands and the major associated organs such as the spleen, kidneys, bladder, and the large intestine.

Adrenal glands are small, triangular-shaped glands located on top of both kidneys which are actually two separate glands in one, the medulla and the cortex. The medulla is responsible for our ability to respond instantaneously to stress. This part of the gland releases adrenaline. The cortex secretes the steroid hormones like cortisol, also called hydrocortisone, aldosterone, and dehydroepiandrosterone (DHEA.) These hormones balance and harmonise our long-term response to stress by managing our blood sugar levels, among other things. The adrenal cortex produces small amounts of testosterone, estrogen, and progesterone in both men and women. It makes very little difference whether the stress is caused by an actual or anticipated threat; either situation will trigger the adrenals glands to respond accordingly.

Symptoms of imbalance in this energy centre include hemorrhoids, constipation, irritable bowel syndrome, disorders of the bowel, sciatica, fibromyalgia, chronic fatigue, knee and feet trouble, immune system issues and lower back problems.

Until this energy centre is balanced, and you have recognised and dealt with the traumas that are held there, you will find it hard to focus your attention elsewhere. You will be plagued by a negative inner voice, and your emotions will be dominated by loneliness, insecurity, doubt, panic, anxiety, depression, and the fear of change or abandonment.

*

Our second energy centre is located below our navel and represents our sexuality and inner intimacy or full acceptance of our bodies. It is the source of our passionate emotions and embodies our innate inner pleasure and sensations.

Through this energy centre we can experience vibrations related to sexual desires, physical intimacy, attraction, procreation, shame, unworthiness, victimisation, shyness, guilt, and excessive concerns about what others think.

When this energy centre is coherent, you will have healthy boundaries, feel "comfortable in your own skin," and be friendly, passionate, sexually fulfilled, good-natured, playful, emotional intelligent, and sensitive to the body's subtle messages of incoherence.

When this energy centre is out of balance, energy is drawn away from the major associated organs and systems like the sacrum, pelvis, lower abdomen, genitals, prostate, the reproductive system, kidneys, bladder, hamstrings, anterior and posterior tibialis of the leg muscles.

The endocrine glands that relate to this energy centre are responsible for producing androgens, estrogens and progesterone in the testicles and the ovaries. A monthly menstrual cycle and menopause make the hormone-related problems experienced by women much more obvious than those experienced by men. The equivalent of menopause in men is called andropause, resulting in declining levels of testosterone.

Imbalance can manifest as an overall feeling of disconnection from the body, or as prostate and testicular cancers, urinary tract infections, impotence, ovarian and bladder problems, uterine fibroids, lumbar pain, arthritis, and menstrual issues.

Your emotions can be dominated by envy, lust, jealousy, promiscuity, lack of desire, shame of one's physical appearance, excessive boundaries, poor communication or excessive emotional sensitivity.

Until this energy centre is balanced and you have recognised and dealt with the traumas that are held and have been suppressed, you will often seek pleasure in addictive behaviours and in the control or manipulation of others.

*

Our third energy centre is located above our navel and just below the sternum represents our sense of personal power. This energy centre is receptive to the impulses that inform our gut instinct, that way of knowing without knowing why.

Through this energy centre we can experience vibrations related to ego, competition, control, impatience, rage, violence, determination, self-acceptance, willpower, and intuition.

When this energy centre is balanced, you will have integrity; respect for self and others; be confident, self-disciplined, outgoing, problem-solving, calm, and well-integrated. It is through the third energy centre that we develop our courage, determination, independence and sense of our own free will.

The endocrine gland influenced by the third energy centre is the pancreas, which produces the hormones insulin and glucagon. Insulin is produced in response to elevated blood sugar or glucose levels. It stimulates the removal from the bloodstream of glucose, fats, and amino acids in order to store them within the cells. When this gland functions properly, it helps regulate blood sugar levels and maintain lean body mass.

Although our society claims to support free will, most institutions and mainstream media outlets seem to stifle the development of observation, questioning or freedom of choice. Obedience, silence and conformity are stressed throughout our education, workplace environment, most religions, and governments, creating a herd mentality.

We're bombarded with the message that it's irrational or even dangerous to attempt to question, change or disobey. This is because we see that those who try are ostracized, ridiculed and punished. Our response then is to distance ourselves from those who don't follow the herd and conform to a standardized identity. We become disconnected from our own unique needs, wants and desires. This creates incoherence, and once disconnected, we're easily manipulated.

If someone asks you how you're feeling and you reply by saying either, 'I'm not sure' or 'I think I feel such and such', then you're disconnected. We don't think with our feelings, we feel them.

If someone asks you what you want and you frequently reply by saying, 'I'm not sure' or constantly defer your decisions to others, then you're disconnected.

When this energy centre is unbalanced or blocked, energy is drawn away from major associated organs like the liver, gall bladder, stomach, spleen, duodenum, pancreas, digestive system, small intestine and abdominal quadriceps. When the pancreas is affected, its ability to produce the hormones insulin and glucagon is impaired, removing the ability to regular blood sugar levels.

The imbalance can manifest physically as anorexia, binging, bulimia, inflammation, mental confusion, hypoglycemia, diabetes, gout, pancreatitis, abdominal pain, hepatitis, stomach ulcers, digestive disturbances, including indigestion, heartburn, gas, bloating, nausea, vomiting, diarrhea, excessive fat formation, and cancer of the liver and stomach.

Your emotions can be dominated by depression, claustrophobia, low energy, low self-esteem, rigid thoughts and beliefs, stubbornness, arrogance or intimidation.

*

Our fourth energy centre is located in the centre of our chest and serves as the bridge between the lower energy centres related to the physical and the upper centres related to the soul.

It is only through the fourth energy centre that we can fully manifest health, wellness, and the reality we desire. The heart, not the head, is where we experience pure ecstasy.

Through this energy centre we can experience vibrations related to love, compassion, emotional security, forgiveness, kindness, self-acceptance and the ability to feel unconditional love.

When this energy centre is coherent, we feel harmonious, loved, loving, empathetic and sympathetic, compassionate, and romantic. This centre, in conjunction with the sixth and seventh energy centres, are responsible for the autonomic nervous system outside of conscious control that regulates the body, heart rate, breathing and promotes digestion.

The autonomic system is made up of the sympathetic nervous system and the parasympathetic nervous system. When our autoimmune systems are functioning properly, we are resilient to viruses and infections.

The endocrine gland associated with this energy centre is the thymus gland. The thymus gland is a specialised primary lymphoid organ of the immune system located behind the breastbone and between your lungs. It plays an important function in the immune and endocrine systems, which produce the hormones thymosin and thymopoiesis. These hormones stimulate certain white blood cells—our internal immune system's defence network—where they mature and develop the ability to protect against and resolve infections and cancers.

The energy of this centre is one of the easiest to feel. Unfortunately, many people build defensive or offensive reactions to protect their hearts in response to trauma. The trauma may be associated with pain from never having received unconditional love or the intense feelings of what we describe as a broken heart. This can happen after experiencing the breakup of a desired relationship, the loss of a loved one, or the failure to realise one's dreams, all resulting in pain felt in the centre of the chest.

It is our false belief that love generates these feelings.

When the heart centre is fully open to receive, these feelings and behaviours disappear because we realise that pursuing love, joy and happiness is irrational. The vibration of love is our natural state of being; the more we give away, the more we get back and the more we want to give. While the heart is only interested in what it can give, the ego is only interested in what it can get; this is the key to knowing when we act with heart-based intention.

When this energy centre is out of balance or weak, energy is drawn away from major associated organs like the heart, blood vessels, lungs, diaphragm, thoracic spine, ribs, breasts, circulation, vagus nerve, arms and hands.

An imbalance can manifest physically as asthma, pneumonia, bronchitis, emphysema, lung cancer, breast cancer, hypertension, heart attacks, nervous breakdowns, palpitations and immune dysfunction including allergies, susceptibility to colds and infections, immune deficiencies and autoimmune diseases.

Your emotions will be dominated by isolation, loneliness, low self-esteem, resentment, jealousy, anxiety. You will likely be involved in co-dependent or other relationships lacking healthy boundaries, where you give yourself away and lose your centre, always expecting something in exchange for your giving.

*

Our fifth energy centre is located in our throat and represents communication, truth, self-expression, individuality, and creative expression.

Through the fourth energy centre, we can feel love. Through the fifth centre, we experience the vibrations of sound; therefore it is here that we have the ability to express love.

When this energy centre is coherent, we have the ability to process, release, and express emotions; to express our thoughts and feelings with authenticity, confidence, and clarity; and to speak and listen with compassion.

The endocrine glands associated with this energy centre are the thyroid and parathyroid glands located in the base of the neck and in front of the trachea. The thyroid gland is a butterfly-shaped gland which captures iodine from food to make two thyroid hormones that regulate the way the body uses energy. It functions as an internal thermostat controlling our body's temperature and the metabolic rate of every cell in the body. The parathyroid glands are responsible for maintaining healthy minerals, calcium and phosphorus in the blood.

When the fifth energy centre is out of balance, energy is drawn away from their major associated organs and systems like the cervical spine, lungs, bronchus, larynx, large intestine, vagus nerve, trachea, vocal cords, throat, mouth, gums, teeth, tongue, ears, jaw and shoulders.

Imbalance can manifest physically as chronic sore throats, strep throat, neck and shoulder pain, earaches and infections, laryngitis, swollen glands in the neck, hearing loss, respiratory issues, TMJ, and cancers in the associated areas.

Your emotions will be dominated by indifference, paranoia, extreme introversion, fear of speaking in public, or insecurity with expressing emotions. To compensate for these fears, you may have a habit of constant chatter, or of loud and boisterous behaviour.

*

Our sixth energy centre is located between our eyes, and this represents the truth about the universe, ourselves and other people.

Through the sixth centre we experience the vibrations of light and insight. Many mystic and esoteric spiritual traditions suggest it serves as a metaphysical connection between the physical and spiritual worlds. Through meditation, visions, dreams, the power of Consciousness, we can move from physical reality and journey to other dimensions and realms.

When this energy centre is coherent, we feel intuitive, charismatic; we know our purpose; we are able to see into the past, present and future; we are adaptable, maintaining clarity and vision in times of stress and uncertainty; we are innovative, bringing new ideas to reality; we are capable of complex thoughts and decisions.

The endocrine glands associated with the sixth energy centre is the hypothalamus, pituitary and the pineal glands. The pineal gland is roughly the size of a small pea and is located in the centre of the head in a cavity known as the third ventricle of the brain.

In some animals, the pineal gland is still located very near the surface of the forehead and is directly influenced by light radiation. In humans, the influence of light is mediated through the retina of the eyes and propagated along a complex nervous pathway to the pineal gland.

The pineal secretes the hormone melatonin, which is responsible for synchronising our internal rhythms with those of the natural world.

When this energy centre is out of balance, energy is drawn away from major associated organs and systems like the skeletal system, the left and right hemisphere, central cortex, ears, nose and the left eye.

This can manifest physically as sinusitis, allergic rhinitis, frontal headaches or migraines in the left eye, mood disorders, sleep disturbances, insomnia, blindness and eye diseases, dyslexia, retinopathy, hallucinations, schizophrenia and manic behaviour.

Your emotions will be dominated by hopelessness, despair, lack of vision and insight, anger, rage, chronic stress, indecisiveness, irrationality, indifference, or anxiety. You will lack moral courage, and be easily influenced by others.

*

Our seventh energy centre is located at the top of our head or the crown and represents Consciousness and understanding.

Through this centre we experience compassion, connection to universal Consciousness, unity of Source and mind, oneness, silence, and spirituality.

When this energy centre is coherent, you feel at one with yourself. You have a greater connection with your mind, body and soul. While the first energy centre anchors the roots of our being to the Earth, the seventh energy centre expands our consciousness and enables us to become superconscious. Here we have a level of awareness that sees beyond the material world and comprehends the link between the atoms of the quantum world and of stars that shine bright in the night sky. We see we are the atoms that form the molecules of life. We are also the single-celled organisms that interconnect to become the organs, systems and structures we call our bodies. We see the body of every organism on this planet as an individual object within the body of Consciousness and reality.

The endocrine glands associated with the seventh energy centre are the pituitary and the hypothalamus glands. These two glands, together with the pineal, orchestrate the hormonal symphony of the human body. The hypothalamus is the composer, the pituitary the conductor and the pineal the metronome.

The hypothalamus acts as the central command centre between the brain and the body, coordinating, receiving, transmitting, translating and understanding all our thoughts and emotions with our digestive, cardiovascular, and immune systems. It influences our appetite, thirst, sexual behaviour and emotional responses.

When this energy centre is out of balance, energy is drawn away from major associated organs and systems like the central nervous system including the cerebrum, cerebellum, brain stem spinal cord the skull, right eye and facial muscles.

Imbalance of the seventh energy centre can manifest physically as headaches in the right eye, memory loss, personality changes, cognitive impairment, confusion, alienation and a loss of meaning of life and purpose. Alzheimer's, Parkinson's, ADHD, multiple sclerosis, seizures, dementia, depression and learning disabilities are diseases associated with incoherence in this energy centre.

Your emotions will be dominated by sexual and nonsexual obsessing, melancholy, delusions, phobias, illusions, arrogance, pride, indifference, or apathy. You will be driven by the need for attention, validation, approval, and to always be right. You will be unable to grieve, and will be frequently misunderstood.

*

This detailed information from Consciousness gave me new insights into my own illnesses prior to the 29th. Looking back, I could tell where I'd struggled all throughout my life. For each energy centre, I was in constant suffering from at least one of the associated emotions or symptoms. From the first energy centre where I suffered from an unrelenting negative inner voice as early as I could remember, all the way up to the seventh energy centre with my dyslexia and constant obsessing and replaying what if scenarios, over and over again.

If anyone has all their energy centres blocked and incoherent, I'm pretty certain they are in the same position as I was, wanting to commit suicide. And suicide isn't always physical. Although the usual definition of suicide is the physical act of giving up on yourself, we can also mentally and emotionally give up on life. So you can actually have a suicide of life and still exist in this reality. This manifestation is usually what we describe as depression.

ENERGY TRANSFERENCE AND UNSHACKLING

This information also gave me a more in depth understanding of how I can do what I can do. Because of my gifts, I can hear the frequency of a person's entire energy field, energy centre, or specific body part and know precisely what its associated number means. All frequencies carry information which I then use like tuning into a radio station.

The higher the number, the more coherent the frequency, the more we generate homeostasis, energy, order, balance and health; and the healthier the person. The more coherent we are we are less likely to decline over time due to illness and disease.

The lower the number, the more incoherent the frequency and the more the person may be susceptible to illness and disease. We are pure energy, and if our energy is weak, then our physical body is weak. A weakened body fires incoherent messages to its systems and organs, creating disorder. This places the immune system into survival mode, drawing energy from our energy system.

Every energy centre, system, organ or body part has an optimal frequency that is unique to the person and their present vibrational state. This number is communicated to me through the person's subconscious.

So healing involves rising from a lower, negative vibrational state to a higher, positive vibrational state. When I perform energy transference, I am helping the person raise their frequency to a higher, coherent frequency number specified by their subconscious. And every time they vibrationally shift upwards, they create a new moment in the Now, and a new reality.

Looking at emotions and the types of physical or emotional incoherence,

I could see that one person might only need energy transference while another might need unshackling.

Energy transference and a coherent frequency cures a physical ailment. This may be temporary or permanent, depending upon whether the trauma that caused the incoherence is dealt with. This could happen in the moment when the person recognises the original trauma and sees how they have been holding themselves back. However, if they don't recognise or deal with the trauma, the cure will only be temporary; the incoherence will return to the energy centre along with the same or new illness.

Unshackling resolves deeply ingrained trauma. It is helpful in situations where the person is unable to recognise the trauma that is causing the incoherence and has allowed the negative energy to build over the years. This is where their subconscious can help pinpoint the origin. Your subconscious doesn't mince words. Within one unshackling session your subconscious can tell you what the original trauma was, how you're holding yourself back due to the various limiting beliefs and behaviours you've developed. It gets straight to the point; there is no need for weeks of therapy.

22

COHERENCE HEALING

Each morning before I get out of bed I say, 'I am grateful for everything that I have in my life. I'm thankful for my beautiful wife, for providing food on the table and having enough money in the bank to pay out weekly rent and bills. Thank you K for loving and supporting me on this journey of transformation. I'm thankful to be alive and able to enjoy all the wonderful things in my life. I am blessed to have our 2 little chickens aka Zelda and Link who keep me on my toes and provide me with their unconditional love.' And then I set my intentions for the day, excited to get started and to learn something new, something that I can use in the future. When I think back on my entire life before the 29th, I can't recall one single morning beginning this way. Now, since my awakening, I'm already grateful before I even step out of bed.

And as for K, coming home is now one of the best parts of her day. She no longer sits in the driveway crying and building up the courage to open the garage door. Now she bounces out of the car with a renowned joy in her heart, eager to hear what new things I have learnt regarding my gifts. She is also so thankful for the connection she has with her brother Christopher, and the newfound knowledge that there is no such thing as death. We are both fully present with each other in the Now, and grateful to be able to spend each day and our lives together.

I have lost over 14kgs without doing any exercises. My entire diet has changed without me even realising. I learned that what we feed our bodies directly affects our state of mind and our vibrations. It affects how we think and feel, including the feeling of abundance in our lives, and our ability to be grateful.

I now prepare plant-based dinners every day for K and me, using K's secret ingredient, 'love and intention.' I also thank a beautiful man called John for his fresh, clean, fluoride-free natural spring water for hydrating my family every day. Each month we travel almost four hours to fill up our five 20 litre containers. I also place intentions on the food that feeds our little chickens to keep them healthy and energised.

I have gone from having a diet that consisted of meat, shitty take outs and bags of lollies to eating high vibrational vegetables and fruit. Today I am not far off from being completely "vegan". This is another over-used label that I might have identified with in the past.

But since my awakening, I realised that identifying with labels just limits the expression of who we are. Before the 29th I'd placed so much importance on my Diesel watches, chatting on Tinder, and getting friended on Facebook. We limit ourselves when we define ourselves by our materialistic objects or social validation. The truth is, apart from our egos, no one gives a flying fuck about our clothes, how many likes, subscribers, friends or filler-friends we have. We are so much more than any label or definition, so we need to be curious, bold, and open-minded.

This reminded me when K asked me about Norman and why many people place so much importance on Facebook, Instagram, and social validation. No matter how many YouTube subscribers, Facebook friends, and Instagram followers we collect, there will never be enough for us to truly feel fulfilled and happy. This type of energy exchange will never bring you true inner happiness or joy. It is an addiction that serves as an escape from the Now.

How many of us have fallen captive to the constant need to scroll upwards on our phone, eyes fixed and dilated in place, mouths agape as if hoping to win a cash prize on a scratch card, only to feel disappointed when we don't win? So we play the same game over, and over and over again.

This game is called 'The checking of the phone and replacing it back in to your pocket before your partner or friends return back from leaving the room that you were in, all in less than 30 seconds without them noticing your addiction.' Or 'since finishing my starter and waiting for the main course to arrive' Or, sometimes even 'walking less than 5 seconds from the bar with your drink to your table.' We even check while driving on a motorway or waiting at the traffic lights.

Until we finally scratch away to reveal that instant win prize we have been hoping for: *Off go the party poppers, the cork from the bottle of champagne flies high and across the room, thousands of golden buzzer ticker tape stream down from the sky above, the marching band paying in the background. Like Mega Ryan in the iconic 80's movie 'When Harry Met Sally'. YES, YESS, YESSS, YESSSS, YESSSSS, YESSSSSSS, YESSSSSSSSSSS, YESSSSSSSSSSSSSSSSSSS, OMG YESSSSSSSSSSSSSSSSSSSSSSSS YES, YES, YES.*

All your hard work has finally paid off. What a dopamine climax rush we just had when someone new likes, comments, or subscribes; or when someone sends you a friend request even though you have no fucking idea who this person is! But we don't care! It's instant gratification, so we start the game all over again there is nothing like it on this planet; like a crack addict we need more and more.

But in reality we're crave something more meaningful. Something that the outside can't provide. Just like Norman, they long for intimacy, unconditional love and an inner connection between mind, body and soul. But they haven't learned that intimacy is about truth, when you can show someone your true self and your truest reflection without being judged. And when two people are intimate, their actions are unguarded and authentic, not just because they love each other, but because of the unconditional love they have for themselves.

Que another 'In Bed with HS' session. "Saweets, can you tap into someone and ask them what they think unconditional love is?"

"Ok. Most people use the word 'love' to describe what they experience through the perspective of ego. This is a lower vibration influenced by the ego's barriers of fear, attachments, wants, needs, and desires. With this type of egoic love, a person's happiness is conditional; the love they feel makes them either happy or sad, based on the other person's actions, emotions, and perspectives. This is the perfect setting for the drama identification triangle of the victim, villain and hero.

"Unconditional love is the highest form of vibration we can experience; there is no higher. Absent of all egoic barriers, the vibration of unconditional love flows fully through you, regardless of the other person's actions, emotions, and perspectives. This is because when you feel unconditional love for another, you experience it through the perspective of collective

Consciousness. And when you feel unconditional love for yourself, you experience through Consciousness of self."

"'What the fuck! 'Experience through Consciousness of self?' I love you, but honestly, what the fuck does that mean? I'm not tapped into Consciousness like you are. You sound like this guy I watched on YouTube yesterday. Eckhart somebody, Tolla? Tole? Could even be Toley, to be honest I was so lost I stopped watching; I had no idea what he was saying. But you seem to have a similar perspective to him, when it comes to understanding the ego, Consciousness, and unconditional love."

"It is sometimes referred to as 'seeing yourself through the eyes of the observer,' or imagining how pure soul loves you. The nearest thing to describe it is the love a parent may feel for a child, or even how one may feel for a beloved pet. It's the full acceptance of the other, exactly as they are, without the need for change. There are no conditions to be met in order to be loved. When people understand this, they can begin to learn to love others and themselves unconditionally."

"That's how I feel about you and our little chickens. But it's easier to feel that for someone else. How are we supposed to learn to love ourselves unconditionally?"

"First you have to realise that all of us are divine spiritual beings experiencing reality through our five senses as well as Consciousness. You are Consciousness, and Consciousness is pure love. When you understand this, you will realise you don't need others to validate you. You can never be a victim, villain or hero. All those notions come from the ego, and, unfortunately, although we all want to be loved unconditionally, it is the ego that blocks it."

"How exactly do our egos block intimacy?"

"Much of the ego comes from wants, needs, desires, and the fear of getting hurt emotionally or physically. To have true intimacy, each person first needs to have acceptance of self, rather than striving for the illusion of perfection. Acceptance comes from the fine balance between who you are and who you are not, between what you want, and what you don't."

"In what way do they relate to each other, can you explain in layman terms? I can't just ask anyone's Consciousness or their subconscious mind for the answers like you can. I mean did you hear yourself last week? Your ability to communicate with Consciousness is just nuts."

"I know right, what a turn-around I have had; actually, no wait, what *we* have had since the 29ᵗʰ. You can't make this shit up. On the morning of the 29ᵗʰ I wanted to commit suicide and now I can communicate with Consciousness, the subconscious mind, and I can heal people on the other side of the world. Absolutely fucking nuts.

"But in all honesty, regardless of the gifts I was given on the 29ᵗʰ, no one needs a gift from the universe to make a direct change in this world. Humanity just needs more people like you, who have heart-based intensions, acting with harmony and with coherence, in regards to living, working, caring for animals and Earth.

"And getting back to your question regarding who you are and who you are not, what you want, and what you don't: you see, we've been led to believe all our choices are limited to the options that have been approved and mandated by our society, government, family, tribe. From generation to generation, many untruths have been passed down, often unknowingly. But the biggest, most devastating deception of what we are taught is the illusion that we don't have any choice. So when we want something different, something that is unconventional or not wholly acceptable by society, we then believe we're somehow flawed. It's why we feel threatened when others disagree with our point of view. It's why we constantly seek approval and validation from others.

"It's why we try to manufacture new identity labels like Gay, Bi, Lesbian, Queer, Transgender, Transsexual, Agender, Bigender, Cis, Cisgender, Gender Fluid, Genderqueer, Third Gender, Gender Nonconforming, Gender Questioning, Gender Variant, Intersex, Androgyne, Androgynous, Non-binary, Pangender, Autistic, ADHD, Black, Coloured, etc. We create 'Pride' and 'Straight' parades rather than the 'I Am Who I Am' parade.

"All these examples are attempts to add more options to the limited range of predetermined choices. Because we believe in the illusion that we can't choose for ourselves.

"Nature is constantly expanding and diversifying while also seeking balance. Each of us is unique and has individual needs for achieving our own personal balance of internal energy. This is why people want to define so many variations of gender as they seek to balance their own energy. So the illusion of no choice goes against the natural evolution of abundance, variety, and unlimitedness, in order to force everyone into a narrow band of conformity.

"As a result, many of us strive to meet this illusion of perfection, defined by others or even our own assumptions of how we need to be to fit in. This will always be a compromise, because there's no 'one size fits all' life or Standard Model human. Conformity requires you to want only what society has deemed acceptable to want, and to not want things that have been deemed inappropriate. Eventually we believe our choices are limited: Who You Are equals Who Others Want You to Be. But when we remove the boundaries imposed by society or our own limited thinking, Who I Am equals Who I Want to Be."

"I think I understand. But even when I think of what I want, I'm not everything I want to be."

"That is the fine balance that leads to acceptance of self, the understanding of our natural evolution. When we can see ourselves as continuously evolving beings, we're able to realise we're already whole and complete. We're able to feel unconditional love for ourselves and others."

"That makes so much sense. It's so simple. But, if it's so simple, why are we so fucked up?"

"It all leads back to the ego, the part that is continually influenced by mainstream institutions, consumerism and the media. In almost every place you look, there are endless messages that reinforce the wants, needs, desires, labels, identity, and fears of the ego. As a result, we end up feeling less than complete or perfect in our eyes. All the while, those nonstop messages condition us to ignore our connection with Consciousness and instead look outside of ourselves for who we are, how we are supposed to live, and how we are supposed to love. Each time we ignore how we feel and what we want, we create incoherence. And, like the shadow man, there are people who use the illusion of perfection to hold those they abuse in silent bondage, just as there are people who enable the abuse, like those on the train who just sat and watched me and Mum get mugged. No one wants to question the illusion because they've based their lives on pretending it is perfect.

"In the very initial stages, incoherence is a negative vibration based on fear. If we can learn to recognise the incoherence and deal with it in the present, then we can return to a coherent healthy state of being and wellness. But if the incoherence is allowed to persist, it eventually manifests as a mental or physical illness, pain, or disease.

"Unfortunately, most of mainstream society is unaware of their connection to Consciousness, as well as the incoherence created when they ignore it. Believing in the illusion of no choice, they spend most of their lives blocking, ignoring and suppressing their emotions and feelings about what they truly want or how they feel. When they are unable to recognise and deal with the early stages of incoherence, many come to suffer from the damaging effects of prolonged incoherence in the body, mind, and soul. So it is often a devastating crisis that causes some people to question, for the first time, the illusion of no choice."

"That's so sad. That breaks my heart. So, except for the few people I know of in the world who have experienced life without an ego, until they let go of their egoic-reality way of living and thinking humanity will likely live out their lives as slaves to their egos"

"Actually, we are not born with egos. Egos are created as we are repeatedly exposed to assignments of identity, labels, and conformity. This is how we are taught to ignore our connection with Consciousness and only look externally to our physical world for who we are and what we want. Much of this is fear-based conditioning which happens during our childhood and early teens. Whether the dangers are real or perceived, we learn to develop identities that help us cope with our environment when we're young and dependent upon others for our survival.

"But as we get older, we take these egos with us, along with the survival techniques we developed, and our beliefs about the world. And because our ego creates our reality, our vibrations attract people and experiences that resonate with us."

"So, if our vibration is high, then we attract positive, happy people and experiences?"

"That's right. But if our vibration is low, like mine was all my life until the 29th, then life is a continuous world of pain and sadness. Because we are also part of Consciousness, we always feel the dissonance of our incoherent frequencies, even when we can't pinpoint the source. The vibration of love, of Consciousness, is indescribably high, so the more incoherence we have, the more it hurts. We may feel this deep inexplicable sense of longing, restlessness, the feeling that there is more to life than this. That's the constant pull of Consciousness toward who you truly are and the life you truly want.

"It's only when we realise the sense of longing is the result of our disconnection from Consciousness—a gap that can't be filled by any person, place, or thing outside of us—we can free ourselves from the limits of our egos."

"Wow, egos seem more like a virus than anything else."

"Actually, we have egos so we can identify when we are seeing only from the perspective of the mind. This gives us the ability to then choose from the heart.

"Some people call it, 'transcending' the ego. But that message is old, contradictory and confusing. It often leads people to despise this part of themselves, reinforcing feelings of self-hatred and low self-worth. We can never learn to forgive or truly love ourselves if we believe a part of us is fundamentally negative, including the ego. Life is about learning, growth and discovery, which means there will always be the need and desire to evolve. When this is misunderstood, one cannot feel unconditional love, and cannot see or feel the joy in life. Instead, the key is in understanding that, because you are part of Consciousness, you already have the tools to transcend the ego."

"What tools?"

"Initially they come in the form of your knowing, intuition, your gut instincts, your fundamental sense of who you are. So when you experience a negative emotion or trauma, you can use those tools to identify when and how your ego is holding you back.

"We created our egos when we were children dependent upon the adults in our lives; when we move into adulthood, we then must become the parents of our egos.

"When our egos create incoherence, we can view them as opportunities to observe, learn, love and forgive ourselves. In essence, we would treat our ego as we would a small child. If a child is fussing or acting out because it's tired, we don't punish it or even try to reason with it; we lovingly forgive and tell it to take a nap. If the child is frightened, we soothe it with reassurance that they are safe. If the child is feeling unworthy, we teach it forgiveness and self-acceptance. And if the child is unhappy, we help the child identify what it needs and help choose the healthiest solution.

"It is this last process, of asking what I want vs what I don't want, that has the power to break free from the restrictions we place upon ourselves through our ego. And when we remove the barriers of the ego, we remove the barriers to unconditional love.

"Because this is something we don't know we need to do or practice, our egos are unevolved, often at the same level they were from childhood, but affected by the perspective of an adult living in today's reality."

"What the actual fuck, are you telling me we can evolve our egos. How would that work?"

"The mobile phone is a good analogy for ourselves and our relation to ego. The phone is a device with many complicated components for sending, receiving and processing data. Consciousness is always communicating with us, just as radio signals are always being transmitted. You know how every phone has an Operating System (OS)?"

"Yes, like the Android or iOS?"

"Exactly. Each OS is the foundation for the innate capabilities of the phone as well as the applications (apps) we install. Due to the ever-changing reality that we live in, communication companies frequently improve the phone's ability to send, receive or process information. This requires regular updates to the OS. If a phone isn't updated, its capabilities will become increasingly limited and, in time, may stop working entirely.

"Our egos are like the OS on our phones, and our beliefs are like the apps we install onto them. As we move through life, we encounter new and sometimes challenging situations which require us to learn, evolve and adapt. This requires regular updates to our OS that enable us to install newer, more useful apps.

"However, many of us are running on old OS that desperately needs an update. In fact, some of us are running on outdated, crippling OS that block all incoming messages, making the phones useful only for comparing against each other and repeatedly processing old information.

"In these cases although Consciousness is always sending us radio signals, unless our OS is updated, our ability to receive and process information from Consciousness will be severely limited or even impossible.

"Without undoing the back cover and voiding the warranty, the phone may look good from the outside with possibly just a few scratches and bangs here or there. You might have even purchased a fancy protective cover. However, inside the phone, the internal components are actually quite faulty, desperately in need of repair.

"From laziness or the fear of change, many won't update their OS because they think the process takes too long, or they're afraid of unexpected changes that force them to learn a new way of doing things. So they hang onto their old OS until their phone stops working. Then they buy the latest singing, dancing, flagship phone and immediately reinstall their old software and apps. Old stories, beliefs, relationships, material objects, attachments, work, wants, needs and desires. Their familiar past creates a predictable future."

"Installing an outdated OS onto a brand-new phone? That's fucked up, who does that?"

"Yes, it's totally fucked up. But that's essentially what we do."

"So, we spend our time and energy on how things look from the outside, never addressing how we feel on the inside. Because we don't know our egos need to evolve."

"This is the state of the world we have created, an apathy society in an over-competitive modern reality, an outward reflection of the speed of change and the high demands we put on ourselves and others. With a never-ending list of errands, demands and self-imposed expectations, so many—my old self included—become apathetic, depressed, anxious, suicidal, overwhelmed, unable to move forward, and entirely out of balance."

"Oh saweets, that's so sad."

"Even sadder is that most of the world lives in this incoherent state, struggling through life with outdated OS of the first three energy centres related to the material world. Caught in an endless drama triangle as a victim, villain, or hero, the incoherence eventually manifests in the body. Countless dollars may be spent on medical bills, trying to cure physical or mental illness. But unless the OS is also upgraded, the incoherence remains."

"Fuck that's so depressing, no wonder so many people are suffering from illness and disease."

"However, there's an important difference between us and mobile phones. Unlike mobile phones, when we change from within, the physical world outside of us naturally changes, because our world is always a reflection our internal self. So, each time we update our OS we remove an egoic barrier, rise to a higher vibrational state, and create a better life."

"So, creating a better life is all about evolving our egos and learning how to achieve and maintain a high vibrational state?"

"This is the way to the happiness, intimacy and unconditional love we seek."

"How do we keep our vibrations high?"

"Well, the first thing to understand is that our vibrations fluctuate throughout the day based upon how we choose to think and feel. However, we will have a tendency towards either a high or low vibrational state."

"What do you mean, a tendency for high or low vibrations?"

"It all depends on how we've been treated, how we've treated others, and how we treat ourselves throughout our entire life. So, for example, I was born into a low vibrational environment and lived life with one low vibrational moment after another, being mistreated by others and mistreating myself. Although I did experience some moments of joy, for the most part I stayed in a low vibrational state. So people with an average low vibration can still feel positive emotions, but their overall tendency will be to spend the lion's share of the time in low vibratory feelings. Those who feel they are suffering will spend most of their time on thoughts and emotions associated with shame, guilt, apathy, grief, and fear. Those who are just getting by will spend most of their time on thoughts and emotions associated with desire, anger, and pride.

"Conversely, people with an average high vibration may still experience negative emotions like anger, pride, or guilt, but will spend most of their time focusing on the positive things in life. If they spend often in a flow state, then most of their thoughts and emotions are associated with contentment, willingness, acceptance, and reason. And if they've found their true path in life, most of their thoughts and emotions are associated with love, joy, and peace."

"So how do we move from a lower vibrational state to a higher one?"

"It's a matter of awareness and practice. The primary difference between people with low or high vibrations is in their awareness of choice and their practice for dealing with incoherence. When people with high vibrations experience negative emotions, they quickly recognise it as incoherence, and make a conscious choice to move to a higher, coherent vibration through forgiveness, self-soothing, and any action of being a good parent to the ego. Forgiveness in particular is incredibly powerful, because when you forgive yourself or others, you let go of all lower vibrational emotions. Ultimately, developing and maintaining this practice of choosing a higher vibrational state is the way we learn to love ourselves unconditionally.

"We are love, and our ability to move into coherence or recognise incoherence comes from listening to the intuitive guidance system of the heart. The heart is the command centre for coherence, where mind, emotions, feelings and intimacy are brought into alignment. Practicing this coherent state, always following the heart, creates neural and physiological events that benefit the entire body. It can also affect the mental and emotional states of others around us."

"Wait a second, are you saying our vibrational coherence affects those around us?"

"When you love someone unconditionally, you're able to maintain your own vibration and coherence, even when their vibration is low. And if the other person is not closed off, your coherence can actually help raise their low vibration to a higher level of consciousness. Using this process with non-egoic, heart-based intention with no attachments, you can help someone you love heal, mentally, emotionally and physically."

"Is this how you helped me heal my vulvodynia?"

"Yes. Also, when two people are loving each other unconditionally, they are in an ecstatic state of true intimacy within a quantum reality and an energetic bubble of coherence. There's no resistance in that moment, so Consciousness flows freely."

"That's so beautiful."

"Sweetheart, with what I have learned through my connection with Consciousness, and all the gifts I received from my awakening, I want to help people learn how to raise their vibrational state. Everyone can have a better life when they know how to remove their egoic barriers to unconditional love, intimacy, wholeness, and wellbeing."

"One question: how?"

"Well, it's funny you said that. I had a new vision last week and I know exactly what I need to do and how to do it."

***

As you are reading this you might disagree or agree, but fundamentally, you are part of reality and your reality is an outward reflection of how you see yourself.

If you see yourself as whole and complete, or in a high vibrational state on your way to wholeness, the world will reflect that back to you.

But if you instead feel broken, incomplete, or disconnected, that will be the world that you experience. You need to realise that, like a particle within a hologram, what you see outside you is a projection of what is inside you.

But there is hope. You just need to realise that you have a choice for your life and the world in which you live. Every second you create a brand-new future with each choice you make.

In order to have a better life, you need to take responsibility for your intentions and your thoughts, your actions and behaviours, to update your OS and raise your vibrational state. And then recognise that every instance of incoherence, every negative emotion, every form of physical pain or illness, is an opportunity for you to learn and evolve.

And whenever you choose to suppress, deny, or ignore those opportunities, you're not evolving, you're not really living life. This is a life of suffering, or just getting by.

The next time you feel a negative emotion, an incoherence, ask yourself, am I striving for the illusion of perfection in order to gain approval or validation from others? And do I believe my choices are limited?

Is this the life you want, or do you want to be accepted and loved for yourself? Do you want filler-friendships, or true intimacy, mutual acceptance and love? These are your choices, moment to moment.

Also ask yourself, when you experience incoherence, am I acting from a place of insecurity to reinforce my ego identity, rather than from pure, heart-based intention that has no attachments to outcome? These are often the moments when you are being unkind to yourself or others.

If you want hope and change, they can only come from you. Otherwise, everyone assumes someone else (a hero) will either save them or deal with the problem, and someone else (a villain) is to blame.

Choosing to be kind to yourself and others might seem like a waste of time. You might believe your kindness won't make a difference. While it's true that, more often than not, being kind won't result in immediate gratification, it will still result in a profound difference. Oftentimes we may not even see the long-term positive effects on hundreds or even thousands of people that was started from one simple act of kindness. Yet, my story is a perfect example, where an act of kindness from K over ten years ago led me to choose life, and to also dedicate the rest of my life to helping others heal.

The more we change the way we operate individually, the more we can operate as a society, finally bringing about the Blueprint of Consciousness, the plan for the evolution of our humanity into a state of social coherence.

Every second we have a choice, whether we like it or not, and whether we recognise it or not, to be kind or unkind. If you make that choice from the best version of yourself, it will always be from the heart, not the mind.

But, if you don't want to change, it's not going to work.

You deserve to be happy, to have joy and to have love in your heart.

And if you haven't experienced what those vibrations are like, then isn't it worth it, regardless of your age, your past, your present conditions, to experience what that is?

Because it is the most beautiful way to experience life.

You deserve to be happy, and you have the ability to change, but you've got to want to change.

A new way of thinking brings new possibilities.

CONCLUSION

It's been eleven months and I feel I'm only just beginning to understand why I had a Consciousness awakening. The period since my awakening have been nothing short of crazy, nuts, and a constant what the fuck is going on? I even wrote this book in less than 60 hours; that's how crazy this has all been. It's not perfect, but not bad for someone with severe dyslexia. Correction: someone who **HAD** severe dyslexia, my new reality.

But even without fully understanding the reason for my Consciousness Awakening, I know that if I hadn't had the visions of my suicide and of a future world of apathy, I would never have had the energy, strength, courage and bravery to open up my Hellraiser puzzle boxes once again, to heal my life and share it with the world.

According to World Health Organisation 2020 data, there are more than 264 million reported cases of people of all ages suffering from depression. Depression is a leading cause of disability worldwide and is a major contributor to the overall global burden of disease. Depression is no joke. Look all around you, at yourself, your family and your friends. How many loved ones will it take for you to change your attitude towards yourself or someone else—or even consider taking your own life? I'm not sure how many of you will ever get the chance to witness your own death as I did. I saw the devastation that I would have left behind had I gone through with my suicide. I am one of the lucky ones. Unfortunately, some people aren't so lucky.

Not too far from debilitating state of depression is the devastating condition of apathy. Apathy comes when we believe we don't have free will, when we think our choices in life are limited to those controlled by others. It is in its own way a form of emotional, mental, and spiritual suicide, an incoherence that is unfortunately spreading as rapidly as the speed of change throughout our society.

For the millions of people around the world struggling with depression, apathy, anxiety, or mental illness, they're usually told, "Here's a pill. Here's a pill." But Consciousness showed me there's a way you don't need a pill. You can do this yourself; you just have to believe you are more than what we have been told. We are more than our bodies, and there's no such thing as death.

There is still hope, and I know Consciousness is on our side. I've written this book to inspire our humanity to change our attitudes towards one another, consciously and subconsciously, before it's too late. Be the change now, by changing how you see and treat yourself and others, and this will shift your reality to a better life.

The underlying principle is simple: if, from the start, we just treated each other and ourselves with kindness, no one would get depressed or give up on life. Because when we act with kindness, we raise our vibrations into perfect health, joy, and love.

So depression and mental illness can be eradicated—not by pharmaceuticals, but by just being nice. It sounds really basic, but it's the truth.

In fact, the only reason you're able to read my story today is because of how my life began to change—and ultimately was saved—from a single act of kindness. When K offered to cook me a curry with no expectations and no hidden agenda, that simple gesture kickstarted a chain of events that not only saved my life, but led me to a Consciousness awakening that today enables me to help so many others. It's only now that K has realised for the very first time the incredible power of heart-based intention; that being kind is the key to changing our world for the better. By giving without expecting anything back, you really never know what the butterfly effect can have on another person, even after 10 years. Or what effect that person can then have on helping humanity.

In writing this book, sharing my story, and helping others, it is my way of being K for the whole world. With an amazing amount of love for the world and an amazing amount of love for helping others, and no inner voice or ego to get in the way, I am on a mission with K to realise the vision of Earth 2.0. With the help of our extended family we are so grateful to have launched our first online interactive wellness centre, Coherence Healing. Through Coherence Healing, we are helping people upgrade their

OS and address their incoherence using the principles of quantum physics, Consciousness and their own subconscious. All services are donation-based, encouraging everyone to act from heart-based intentions and help create a world where wellness is available to all, regardless of whether they can afford it or not.

Our mission is to help heal the world by changing the way we treat ourselves and each other. Within each of you is the power to heal yourself. True, lasting healing only happens when you make a conscious choice to treat yourself with love, respect, and kindness.

Thanks to K, every day I am filled with wonder as I learn something new from this expanded awareness about how Consciousness and reality are interconnected. As I continue to gain new insights and discover more ways my gifts can be used to help others heal themselves, I am beginning to think my awakening has only just begun.

"To heal this world, one person at a time, starts within and then family. Humanity needs to change; will you help heal this world?"
— Collective Consciousness

To be continued...

Cornelius Christopher
www.coherencehealing.love

Lightning Source UK Ltd.
Milton Keynes UK
UKHW041356171120
373493UK00015B/509

9 781504 3208